BLOW

BLOW

How a Small-Town Boy Made
$100 Million with the Medellín
Cocaine Cartel and Lost It All

Bruce Porter

ST. MARTIN'S GRIFFIN NEW YORK

www.stmartins.com

Library of Congress Cataloging-in-Publication Data

Porter, Bruce.
    Blow : how a small-town boy made $100 million with the Medellín cocaine cartel and lost it all / Bruce Porter.
        cm.
    ISBN 0-312-26712-6
    1. Cocaine industry—United States. 2. Organized crime—United States. 3. Medellín Cartel. 4. Cocaine industry—Colombia. 5. Organized crime—Colombia. 6. Lehder Rivas, Carlos Enrique. 7. Jung, George Jacob, 1942–. I. Title.
HV5825.P625   1993
363.4'5'09861—dc20   92-54756

First published in the United States by HarperCollins Publishers, Inc.

First St. Martin's Griffin Edition: March 2001

10 9 8 7 6 5 4 3 2 1

Contents

Photographs follow page 120.

It's not at all so easy as you fellers think it might be. . . . You'd be satisfied with five grand. But I tell you, if you find something then, you couldn't be dragged away; not even the threat of miserable death could stop you getting just ten thousand more. And if you reach fifty, you want to make it a hundred, to be safe for the rest of your life. When you finally have a hundred and fifty, you want two hundred, to make sure, absolutely sure, that you'll be really on the safe side, come what may.
—B. TRAVEN, *THE TREASURE OF THE SIERRA MADRE*

A Note on Sources

This story is true. I've reconstructed the events and conversations in it from interviews with witnesses and participants whose names appear in the acknowledgments at the end of the book. I also drew on the extensive evidence available from legal sources, including the police investigations, indictments, plea agreements, and/or trials of George Jung, Carlos Lehder, Barry Kane, and Richard Barile.

In several instances, I changed the names of incidental characters whose involvement in one aspect or another of the drug trade has escaped the attention of the authorities and the media. In such cases, I refer to the characters solely by first name.

Prologue

1974

If you are a new inmate only recently sentenced by the courts, this will probably be an entirely new experience for you.
—FROM THE INMATE INFORMATION HANDBOOK AT THE
FEDERAL CORRECTIONAL INSTITUTION, DANBURY, CONNECTICUT

THE QUARTER-MILE-LONG ROAD INTO THE PRISON at Danbury seems more like a driveway into some fancy retreat for big thinkers than the entrance to a federal facility for convicted felons. Lofty spruce and elm trees throw shadows across the road as it winds up from the highway. Off in the distance a man on a tractor is mowing the meadow, bringing into relief the contours of the gently sloping hillside. Even when the water tower and the white concrete buildings loom into view, there's little about the place that appears ominous. Designed in the Art Deco style of the late 1930s, with rounded corners and strong vertical lines in the center, the prison has no guard towers or search lights up on spires, no fences or razor wire surrounding the perimeter. Inside, the men don't live in the steel cages piled high in cell blocks that you see in prison movies but in their own seven-by-nine-foot rooms, each situated off a dayroom or set back from a balcony on the second floor. They've got real doors instead of bars, and real privacy. Each room has a desk built in underneath the window so an inmate can write his letters while gaz-

ing out over the rolling Connecticut countryside. As a place to
spend several years, the quarters might seem a bit confining, but
not to a degree that would strike any freshman at a New England
boarding school as particularly Spartan.

George Jung was bused up to Danbury from New York City by
the Federal Bureau of Prisons in April of 1974, together with a
dozen other inmates from throughout the Northeast. Among other
events that spring, Saigon lay under siege by the Viet Cong. Patty
Hearst had joined forces with her kidnappers, members the Sym-
bionese Liberation Army, and helped them hold up a bank. President Richard Nixon was refusing demands that he resign from
office, because "that would lead to weak and unstable presidencies
in the future." When George arrived at Danbury, he was thirty-one
years old. He had shaggy, honey-blond hair and was five feet ten
inches tall, with broad, muscular shoulders and a massive chest.
He'd been doing work on that physique ever since junior high,
when he started lifting weights in his bedroom to get himself in
shape for the football team by the time he got to high school. The
"Jung" came not from any Chinese ancestors, as most people
assumed before they saw him in person. It was Dutch, pronounced
with a hard "J". And, indeed, the way his hair was cut, about two
inches longer than the style popularized by the Beatles, he looked a
lot like the famous Dutch boy on the can of paint. His grandfather,
Frederick Jung, a cigar maker, had migrated from Amsterdam in
1903 and worked as a cigar-roller for the J. A. Cigar Company in
Boston. His father, also named Frederick, but called "Fritz" by his
multitude of friends, ran an independent fuel-oil business for many
years with contracts to serve apartment buildings in Boston.
George had grown up in the coastal town of Weymouth, Massachusetts, about twenty miles south of Boston, in a house situated
just around the corner and up a hill from the Abigail Adams Homestead, birthplace of the woman who became wife to the second
president of the United States and mother to the sixth.

The event propelling George toward Danbury had taken place
a year and a half earlier, in late September of 1972, at the bar of the
Playboy Club of Chicago. At the fateful moment, George was being
mesmerized by a vibrantly blond Swedish hooker, a dead ringer, he
thought, for the movie actress Britt Ekland. As he was applying the
finishing touches to an arrangement that would get this luscious
piece up to his room, two men in suits approached and asked if he'd

mind stepping outside for a minute. They turned out to be agents for the U.S. Bureau of Narcotics and Dangerous Drugs.

What they wanted to talk about was the fact that three days earlier George had arrived at Union Station from Los Angeles with two steamer trunks, each of them packed with 150 kilos of marijuana, a total of 660 pounds' worth. George was delivering the goods to a well-to-do young man in Chicago eager to involve himself in something profitable other than his father's extensive scrap-metal business. The man had agreed to pay George $150 a kilo for it, or a total of $45,000, not a small amount in those days, when a brand new Porsche, now costing as much as $100,000, was going for $8–10,000. From the baggage room in the train station George had arranged for the trunks to be transferred by two limousines to the basement of the Playboy Club, where the manager had been given to understand that they contained a large amount of camera equipment and that George was an important figure in the world of fashion photography. Two days later the intended customer had showed up with a van and a guy to help him, and the two of them had carted the pot away. George was now waiting in the bar to get his money.

The thrust of George's drug business involved purchasing three to four hundred kilos of grass every month or so from small farmers in the Sierra Madre in Mexico, flying it in to dry lake beds in the desert country of Southern California, then trucking the load east in a rented Winnebago, where he would sell it to wholesalers in Amherst, Massachusetts, the locus of four private colleges and a large state university, with an aggregate enrollment of some thirty thousand pot-hungry students. Since 1968 George had made a good living doing this, and he had become familiar with a large part of America in the process. He was now hoping to add Chicago's hot spots to his market.

The deal would have gone off fine, if only George's prospective customer had not, three weeks earlier, tried to sell some heroin to an undercover policeman. Having unpleasant visions of himself behind bars, he had agreed to keep the authorities apprised of his pot transaction with George, in exchange for consideration on his sentence. Thus the appearance of these two federal agents interrupting George on this, his night of nights. Actually, they apologized for arresting him. It was really heroin guys they wanted, not pot smugglers. Marijuana at the time was coming into such

widespread use as to approach alcohol and tobacco as drugs of preference in the United States; and at least some people in the federal
government were urging the authorities to be a little less hysterical
about stamping it out. A report to the president from the Domestic
Council's Drug Abuse Task Force estimated that between 25 and 30
million Americans over the age of eleven—about 20 percent of the
population—had smoked pot. And when it came to how law-
enforcement agencies should be allocating their time, the drug was
relegated to very low priority—fifth, below heroin, amphetamines,
barbiturates, and cocaine. For that matter, cocaine wasn't causing
much of a ripple, either. Where the first three drugs were deemed
high on their ability to induce physical or psychological depen-
dence and in the "severity-of-adverse-consequences" category, pot
and coke scored a low on both counts.

The debate, of course, had little effect on George's predica-
ment; but one thing he had come to realize in his mere four years as
a professional drug outlaw was that in the criminal justice system
one's situation rarely stays bleak for very long if one applies some of
the basic rules of the game. Rule one: Be very skeptical in general
toward any advice of your lawyer to the effect that you should fight
the case and present yourself before the men and women of the
jury. Lawyers earn fees that way, and you earn time, especially if
you've been caught as red-handed as George was now. Not only
will the jury, without a doubt or a qualm, saw off your nuts with a
rusty blade and hand them up to you on a platter, but the exercise is
bound to cost a lot of money fruitlessly spent. Rule two: Plead not
guilty at the arraignment and get bailed out of jail. If necessary, you
can change your plea later if your lawyer works out something with
the prosecutor. The DA's a busy person and will cut a deal that's
better than anything you'd get from a trial. But you won't have to
worry about any of that, because according to Rule three, promptly
after the arraignment, you take off.

Thus, two days after pleading not guilty to a charge of possession of 660 pounds of marijuana with intent to distribute, George
got himself bonded out of the Cook County Jail, said good-bye forever to Chicago, boarded a flight to Los Angeles, and went back to
work bringing more loads across the border. Temporarily, at least,
he decided to forgo his dream of midwestern expansion in favor of
sticking with old customers who were trustworthy and dependable.

As a federal bond jumper, however, he now had the FBI on his trail, which meant that more effort would be exerted toward his capture than would be had he skipped out on a state charge, since states have little wherewithal to track people cross-country. But even the FBI had to follow budget priorities. Since bond defaulters were rated less of a threat than, say, escapees from federal prisons or people who were armed and dangerous, the effort to nab George was limited to sending his file to the FBI office nearest his hometown and a local agent advised to keep an eye out in case he showed up.

"Usually with a fugitive you look for the girlfriend, what is it, *'Cherchez la femme?'*" says James J. Trout, then a young FBI agent working in the Fugitive Squad in Boston. Trout had been with the Bureau for only a year at the time and had a caseload of forty other fugitives to track down. "Find the girlfriend and most of the time she'll lead you right to him." George didn't have a girlfriend; he did have a sister, Marie, four years older, but she had married a Ph.D. in chemistry named Otis Godfrey and moved away to Indiana, where Otis was a rising star in the research division of Eli Lilly & Co. The couple lived in the suburb of Greenwood, outside Indianapolis, in a neat little house with trees and a yard. It's safe to say the last thing they wanted was a visit from George the jailbird; they'd be sure to invite the neighbors over for that one. This left Trout to forage for information from George's parents, Ermine and Fred, who still lived on "the Circle," as the area around Abigail Adams's birthplace was known in Weymouth. So he'd stop by once in a while to see what they had to say, which usually wasn't much. Whereas Marie liked to phone her mother nearly every day, George wasn't too good in the keeping-in-touch department. Indeed, his parents hadn't seen him face-to-face in nearly two years, since before his arrest in Chicago. So when Trout visited to chat on the topic of their son's whereabouts, Fred and Ermine treated him pleasantly enough, talked with him and all, but said they couldn't help much.

"I felt sorry for them, which is almost always the case," Trout recalls. "They were nice people. The parents are always the ones who pay for it in the long run. It's in the newspapers, the neighbors all know, a terrible embarrassment."

Actually, as Trout thinks back, it was George's mother who was the gabby one. Fred didn't have much to say, at least to Trout. In truth, the visits rankled Fred, and he even called a lawyer at one point to see about preventing the agent from coming around, but

then dropped the matter. Arguing about their son was an old routine for Mr. and Mrs. Jung. The question of exactly how much they
should be helping the police to catch him had opened up another
unpleasant chapter. Fred also grumbled to George about the FBI
visits during one of the rare phone calls his son made from the West
Coast. That's how George learned that Trout had been upstairs
looking around his old room at the front of the house, where he
used to lift weights and tend his fish tank, and where clippings from
the Quincy *Patriot Ledger* about his feats as a halfback for the Weymouth High School Maroons hung on the wall. Also there for
Trout to inspect was a photograph of George down in Mexico, with
a wide-brimmed cowboy hat pulled down to shade his eyes, a long
cigar clenched in his mouth, cartridge belts criss-crossed over his
chest, a large revolver stuck in his belt, and a bottle of tequila in his
fist. He looked like one bad *hombre*, for sure.

As it happened, in November of 1973, a little over a year after
the Playboy Club bust, George flew to Boston to meet with a contact he'd developed in Amherst to firm up a deal that would effect a
major increase in the volume of his business. The man had
approached him the previous summer and said he knew people with
two twin-engine Cessnas who wanted someone to hook them up
with a connection in Mexico, to guarantee them an uninterrupted
supply of marijuana. They would handle the details of transporting
the stuff into the United States and distributing it thereafter. All
George would have to do is take care of the Mexican end and load
up the flights, a proposition that seemed almost too good to be
true. And with the volume this guy was talking about, it looked like
the operation could net him something on the order of a million a
year, ten times what he was doing at the time. Euphoric over the
new possibilities, and realizing it meant he'd be out of the country
for a long time, George had decided to drive down to Weymouth
and pay a short visit to his parents.

He knew what risk the venture entailed, which was why he'd
told no one where he was going. He hadn't even told his parents
that he was coming by. It was dark on a Saturday night right after
Thanksgiving, about eight o'clock, when he pulled his rented car
into the wooded area by the Weymouth Community Church, down
the hill from his parents' house. He cut up through a thick stand of
spruce that Mr. Stennes, the local clock maker, had planted in the
late 1950s as a way to earn extra money by selling Christmas trees.

(The scheme died abruptly a few years after George graduated from high school when old man Stennes shot and killed his wife after mistaking her for an intruder.)

Aided by the dim light of a new moon, George made his way through the trees, approaching the house via the backyard, and knocked on the kitchen door that opened onto a breezeway leading to the garage. It was cold. The door was opened by his father, a short, balding man, dressed in the khakis and plaid shirt he always wore—typical "dad clothes," as George called them. Ever since his stroke fifteen years earlier Fred cried easily over the things that disappointed him in life—mainly George. The tears came now when he saw his son standing there. Then Ermine showed up at the door, more shocked to see him than glad, it seemed to George, acting nervous through the whole visit. His father brought him into the living room, and the two began making headway into a bottle of Scotch. Fred asked him how things were going. George talked about California, how easy it was living out there. Ermine kept getting up and disappearing into the couple's downstairs bedroom.

Special Agent Trout remembers the call coming in just before ten o'clock. A voice said: "He's in the house right now in Weymouth." Hurriedly corralling two other agents to help out, Trout drove the half hour it took to get there and pulled up across the street. One agent went around to watch the back door. Trout and his partner went up the front walk and looked through the window into the living room. They spotted George sitting on the couch. Trout began banging on the glass-paned storm door, announcing loudly that he was with the FBI and demanding that they open the door. He saw George bolt off the couch and disappear from view. He yelled louder and banged harder, so hard the glass shattered just as Fred was opening up the inner door. "I ended up cutting myself fairly badly on the hand," says Trout. "And when we got inside, before we even started searching the house, the mother insisted on stopping the bleeding and bandaging me up."

George knew what was up at the first banging and instinctively raced upstairs to his room, thinking that maybe he could do a Huckleberry Finn out the window to the garage roof, drop to the ground as he'd done as a kid, and take off. He thought fleetingly too of his old double-barreled 12-gauge still stuck in the rafters; he used to bang away with it at the ducks flying over the marsh down back of the house. The shells were probably still in his dresser drawer. Suddenly his father called up the stairs: "George, this is your mother's and my house, and if you're doing what I think you're doing, you'd better stop right now." In the end, George just crawled into the back of his clothes closet, worming through an opening in the eaves into a cubbyhole where he'd played as a little boy. Soon he heard footsteps coming up the stairs. Trout poked his head into the room and called for George to come out. There's no need for anyone to get hurt, he said.

Because no one knew of his plans that night, because he came into the house through the backyard where the neighbors couldn't have seen him, because of her edginess and her suspicious movements while he was there, George has always believed that it was his mother who turned him in. Either she phoned Trout directly or she gave a prearranged signal for someone else to make the call. If the latter were true, George suspected the someone else would have been his father's brother, Uncle George Jung of Melrose. A retired U.S. Navy commander and George's namesake, Uncle George was the family patriarch and benefactor; for a number of reasons he had little use for his nephew and had treated George from his late teenage years with an ill-masked dislike. George never wanted to confront his mother on the matter. Trout says the voice he heard that night was male. "It was not the mother," he says. "Not directly, no."

George had been processed through Receiving & Discharge and sitting alone in a holding cell for about an hour, chewing on a dried-up baloney sandwich, no mayo, when Wong, a trustee from New York's Chinatown who was doing several years on a heroin charge, ushered him into a shower stall, hosed him down, then poofed him all over with delousing powder. From the supply room he issued George a plastic razor, a toothbrush, and a towel, and a set of regulation prison duds, consisting of khaki hand-me-downs from the U.S. Navy. The shoes were two sizes too big—a far cry from the comfort and suppleness of his five-hundred-dollar Bruno Maglis, and at the first opportunity George replaced them at the commissary with a pair of tennis shoes.

The next day, carrying his bedroll and personal gear in a plastic bucket, George was taken down to Massachusetts House, a large open dormitory lined with double-decker bunks. Here new inmates spent two weeks getting filled in on what to expect from prison life.

George dumped his stuff on an available lower bunk and sat down to consider his surroundings. The room contained about a hundred men, some sleeping on their beds, others playing cards, reading, or talking in groups, or watching TV in a glassed-off television room. The Latinos were off by themselves, as usual, engaged in a game of dominoes. That pastime exceedingly irritated the Anglos in the room, for they kept it up nonstop all day and up to bedtime, slamming the pieces down with a great *whack*, accompanying the play with continuous shouts and whoops.

About an hour later another new inmate walked in. He had arrived the same day but on another bus and had spent the night in a holding cell on a different floor. He was short, about five feet six inches tall, and looked to be in his mid-twenties. A Latino of some kind, he was clean-shaven and very handsome in a sultry way. George was struck by two other things about him. First, when he came over to the cot next to George and asked if it was free, he spoke quite formally and politely, as if he were introducing himself at a dinner party. "How do you do?" he said in only slightly accented English. "My name is Carlos Lehder." He said he lived in New York City but that his real home was in Colombia. Carlos also seemed unusually open and talkative, exuding none of the wariness prisoners instinctively feel when encountering an unfamiliar environment. "Usually you're a little careful about who you talk to in the beginning," says George. "You don't know who's who or what's going on. In prison you want to hang back a little, take your time about what you say."

Carlos's friendly manner invited quick intimacy. Right away George found himself explaining why he'd been sent to Danbury, all about the farmers in the hills of Mexico, the California desert, Amherst and the college kids. Carlos responded that he also was in prison for possession of marijuana—nothing, to be sure, on the scale of George's operation. In addition, he'd been charged with trying to smuggle a stolen automobile over the border from Detroit into Windsor, Ontario, whence he'd planned to ship it back to Colombia.

The two spent the next hour, until the public-address system called them to line up for supper, talking animatedly about their experiences in the marijuana trade, even forming some vague plans for when they got out. George had arrived at Danbury with a single thought in mind—to return to the smuggling business just as bloody fast as he could get free. In his mind, the smuggling itself had begun to transcend the material rewards of his trade—the money and the drugs and the Porsches and the women. Confronting physical danger, often of a high order, confounding the system, defying the straight world, staring down the terror he felt well up each time he landed in the desert or risked getting caught—these were the accomplishments on which his self-esteem had come to be pegged. Smuggling itself was the drug now, the therapeutic activity that got him through the day. Lacking a load to run or routes or schedules to devise, he felt as down and desperate as an alcoholic separated from his booze. Drug smugglers, George liked to say, shouldn't be sent to prison, they should be carted off to debriefing centers, to get their brains altered, their obsessions modified. Using prison as a chance to pay his debt to society and going straight thereafter had never entered his mind. He was looking to Danbury to further in some way the criminal enterprise that had become his life. "I wanted very badly to make something out of being there, to bring something back," he says. "I was looking for an opportunity, and I didn't want to spend all that time and come away empty-handed."

It was then, standing in line early that evening, waiting to get into the cafeteria at Danbury, that Carlos looked up at him. "George," he said, "do you know anything about cocaine?"

In the middle of the 1970s there was no such thing as the Medellín cocaine cartel. At that time, it would have seemed a farfetched notion that a handful of small-time thieves and hustlers from a city few Americans had ever heard of high in the Andes could create an enterprise that would blossom into the most lucrative, ruthless, and deadly criminal empire in the world, responsible for the murder in Colombia alone of fifty judges, including eleven Supreme Court justices, twelve journalists, including the editor of Bogotá's *El Espectador*, the attorney general, the daughter of the country's president, the head of the national police drug squad, hundreds of police officers, and uncounted thousands of civilians. In the United States in the seventies the "drug war" was a political coinage for the effort to eradicate the use of heroin, whose ravages, while serious enough, confined themselves largely to ghetto neighborhoods of big cities rather than permeating the society. There was no such thing as crack. Where cocaine was concerned, the 1975

Report to the President from the U.S. Domestic Council's Drug Abuse Task Force rated the substance "low" for the "size of the core problem." It said further that "as it is currently used [cocaine] does not result in serious social consequences such as crime, hospital emergency room admissions, or death." The demand for the drug, dormant since its previous heyday back at the turn of the century and in the Roaring Twenties, emanated from a thin, rarefied slice of the population—rock-and-roll stars, the Pop Art crowd, Hollywood luminaries, members of Café Society on Manhattan's Upper East Side. It dribbled into the country in small quantities, often less than a kilo at a time, inserted into the anal cavity of a "mule" flying into Miami International Airport or secreted in a seaman's bag aboard a merchant ship bound from Barranquilla, Colombia, to New Orleans or Houston. In all of 1974, the U.S. Customs Service seized only 907 pounds of the drug, a little over 400 kilos.

No one was predicting that cocaine would begin arriving in quantities so large it would have to be lugged around in duffel bags and moved from one place to another in trucks: 125 tons of it a year by 1985, according to a calculation made by Manhattan district attorney Robert Morgenthau. Or that the money generated by street sales of the drug—all cash-and-carry, no layaway plans, checks, credit cards, charge accounts, or promissory notes—would make of the cocaine business one of the industrial colossuses of the world. Selling at $100 a gram, for instance—one twenty-eighth of an ounce, fifteen to twenty lines' worth, sufficient to induce a heightened sense of well-being for an evening in a party of four— that 125 tons, cut two, three, four times by successive dealers, would generate retail revenue somewhere in the amount of $40 to $50 *billion* a year. By 1985, close to the peak year for cocaine use in the U.S., these earnings would have ranked the cocaine business as the sixth-largest private enterprise in the *Fortune* 500. General Motors, Exxon, and IBM grossed more money than the cocaine dealers did, but not AT&T, General Electric, Chevron, Sears, Roebuck, Chrysler, Boeing, R. J. R. Reynolds, Procter & Gamble, Dow Chemical, U.S. Steel, or the E. I. Du Pont de Nemours Company.

Not quite twenty-five when he entered Danbury in 1974, Carlos Lehder was the son of an engineer named Wilhelm Lehder, who had left his native Germany in the late 1920s, set up a construction business, and married a Colombian named Helen Rivas. The youngest of three boys and a girl born to the Lehder family, Carlos was four years old when his parents divorced—his mother charging she'd been beaten by his father, his father that she'd committed adultery. Henceforth he was raised by his mother, helping her run a small rooming house in the 1950s in Armenia, about 125 miles south of Medellín, that catered in part to countrymen of her former husband. Conversations that little Carlos had with the guests not only helped preserve his fluency in German but also implanted in him an admiration for the Third Reich and the leadership style of Adolf Hitler, which he later in life synthesized into "Never give a sucker an even break."

Whatever he retained of the Nazi nostrums, Carlos couldn't help but have been exposed to certain other lessons by virtue of growing up in a part of the country dominated by Medellín. Settled in the early seventeenth century by Basques from northern Spain and also a number of Sephardic Jews driven from the country by Ferdinand and Isabella, the city sits a mile and a half above sea level in a saddle formation of rock among the Cordillera Central Mountains. The temperature averages 72 degrees Fahrenheit year round, earning Medellín its reputation as "the City of Eternal Spring." From an incoming airplane the place looks like any other modern metropolis; the same glass-sheathed office buildings and hotels loom up from wide avenues and tree-lined boulevards; suburbs sprawl out into the surrounding pine forests. As Colombia's center for textile manufacturing, the city reigns as its fashion capital, lending it a certain glitter and style. It is also noted for its male prostitutes, leather boys and drag queens who populate the district around Forty-fifth Street. "If you drop a peso in Medellín, don't bend over to pick it up," goes one piece of advice. Economically, many residents secure an abundant living from the chemical and steel industries on the city's outskirts, the gold mines in the hills, and the coffee plantations and cattle ranches in the outlying regions. Unemployement, however, lingers at about 35 percent. And for most of the *paisas* (the name applied to residents of the surrounding province of Antioquía), life more likely promises to be desperate and mean.

The two big shantytowns flanking the road to the airport, *Comuna Nororiental* and *Comuna Noroccidental*, are filled with drugs, street crime, and violence. Like the other depressed barrios in the city, they teem with *desechables*, or "throw-away" kids, left by their parents to scratch out what money they can by running *basuco*, a smokable form of cocaine, or doing just about any *trabajito*, or little job, for the drug lords or the death squads or the police. Many end up as *sicarios*, the notorious hired assassins of Medellín, whose now-famous specialty is the *asesino de la moto*, or motorcycle killing, wherein the driver sidles up to the victim's car, the kid on the back empties his machine pistol into the interior of the vehicle, and the two take off into the chaos of Medellín traffic. Indeed, the violence level in Medellín seems almost beyond belief, even by American standards. Much of it is generated by the city's gang wars, which make the counterpart activity in Los Angeles, Chicago, and New York look like some playground imitation. From 1980 to 1990, the number of violent deaths in Medellín rose more than sevenfold, from 730 a year to 5,300. The last figure is startling when one considers that it's about twice the number of homicide deaths in New York City, which has six times the population.

Medellín has always played the loutish, second-city cousin to the more refined Bogotá, a situation of deemed inferiority that has long put a chip on its shoulder. Linguistically, the *paisas* are thought to speak in a crude accent, jabbering in too fast and unmannerly a fashion. Medellín might have three universities and a botanical garden, but little in the category of high culture. The tastes there are less sophisticated than in the nation's capital, the family trees not so long, if discernible at all. The sons of Medellín, unlike those in middle-class Bogotá, learn early on that the good things in life are not bestowed by inheritance; they have to be wrenched from the world through ingenuity and pluck. Crime, too, if it comes to that. "If you succeed, send money," Medellín boys are told when they get kicked out of the house to seek their fortunes. "If you fail, don't come home."

The result is a city with a sizable number of hustlers, smugglers, con men, and wheeler-dealers, ranging from the more pathetic sort, such as the one-legged beggars who flag down pedestrians with grisly photographs depicting close-up views of their bodily insults, to the host of pickpockets, sneak thieves, and sharpies pushing smuggled TV sets, stereos, appliances, cigarettes, liquor, and especially emeralds, the national jewel. There is a proud local legend about the Medellín cartel kingpin, Pablo Escobar, the son of a small-time farmer and a schoolteacher, who by the mid-1980s was sufficiently wealthy to offer to personally pay off Colombia's national debt of $13 billion if the authorities would stop hounding him. As the story goes, he first made his way in the world by digging up gravestones, grinding off the inscriptions, and selling them cut-rate to people in the market for cheap funerals.

In the end, what many *paisas* want, by foul means or fair, is to make it across the Medellín River, the city's social dividing line, to live in *El Poblado*. Here the good life is lived, in a neighborhood of august boulevards, fine restaurants, expensive boutiques, and houses built on the Miami model, white stucco with lavish use of marble and glass. To appear in *El Poblado*, ensconced with your Mercedes and your house, dining out at Kevin's Restaurant on the heights, looking out over the lights of the city—that was the pinnacle of success. And to do it suddenly, to one day be on the streets and the next checking on the armed guards that patrolled your little palace behind a high fence, that was when the people would start talking about you as one of *los magicos*—the magicians—for the sleight of hand you'd pulled off.

Carlos hadn't become quite the magician by the time he landed in Danbury that spring of 1974, but he'd been working diligently in that general direction. When he was a teenager, his mother had taken him with her to New York City, where she set up a life in the borough of Queens. An older brother, Guillermo, stayed behind to run Autos Lehder, the family-owned car dealership in Medellín. From what Carlos told fellow inmates, it specialized in Chevrolets and other American makes, some of which were acquired and sold legitimately, but not all. Carlos also boasted that the dealership served as cover for one of Medellín's more lucrative enterprises, which involved smuggling American-made automobiles into the country without paying the 100 percent import tax on foreign cars. Colombian car dealers in general felt abused by the tax, since it meant they had to find customers able and willing to pay twice what a car sold for in the U.S., and then hand over the difference to the government. It was much better to skip the tax by bribing a customs official to phony up the import papers so the duty would appear to have already been settled. It was better still to steal the vehicle outright in America *and* bribe the Colombian official. That way the car could be sold for twice the price.

Stealing cars was the reason, or part of the reason, Carlos ended up in Danbury. The first time he got caught was at age twenty-two in Mineola, Long Island, where he was given probation on a knocked-down charge of unauthorized possession of a motor vehicle. The following year he was arrested again for stealing a car and trying to smuggle it into Windsor, Ontario. He beat that charge by skipping out on his bail, but was caught once more a year later in Miami, this time for possession of marijuana. In any case, he was now in federal prison, and scheduled to stay there for some twenty months, until early in the winter of 1976. This gave him plenty of time to share his ideas with George about embarking on another line of work.

Chewed in its natural form, like a plug of tobacco, the raw leaf of the coca plant is perfectly capable in its own right of imbuing one's life with a rosier hue, and in South America it's been quickening the spirits of the native population for at least four thousand years. That was the age of a Peruvian burial mound where archaeologists found a quid of cocaine that some Indian had given a going-over right before he died back in 2100 B.C. The practice was also memorialized in the stone figures from 600 B.C. in Colombia's Valley of the Statues in San Augustin; the statues' oddly distended cheeks put one in mind of an old-time baseball player getting his mouth around a large chaw of tobacco. Eliciting a commercial-quality high out of cocaine, however, is much more complicated, nothing like in the marijuana business, where you strip off a bud, roll it in paper, and you've got yourself a good smoke. To provide customers with the form of cocaine they can smoke or shoot or snort, the pure cocaine alkaloid has to be chemically extracted from the leaf. This involves putting the plant through an elaborate industrial process requiring logistical skills, technical expertise, buildings and equipment, and large financial backing.

While the plants will grow virtually anywhere in the moist tropical climate of the Andes—Peru, Ecuador, Chile, Bolivia, Colombia—the really good stuff, with the highest cocaine alkaloid content—*Erythroxylon coca*, or the Huánuco leaf—likes it not so high up, about one to three thousand feet above sea level. One such area is the heavily forested eastern lowlands of Bolivia around the city of Santa Cruz, a remote region with few access roads and a hundred inches of rainfall a year. In the mid-1970s, during an economic crisis in Bolivia caused by falling demand for tin, the area was designated by the government as cotton country, and banks were encouraged to lend money to landowners so they could cut down forests and put large tracts under cultivation. Unfortunately, at just about the time the first crops ripened for harvest in 1975, cotton prices on the world market also plummeted. The landowners scrambled frantically for some profitable substitute. They found one, and after the farmers held discussions with would-be processors in Medellín and Cali in Colombia, the fields that had so recently teemed with cotton boles began to sprout dark green with the high-octane plants of the Huánuco family.

Viewed as a problem in industrial engineering, the main challenge in cocaine manufacturing concerns transportation. Not only have few roads been put through to the growing regions in Bolivia and Peru, but those that do exist are regularly patrolled by the authorities and don't do you much good if your cargo's illegal. Under these conditions, pack animals and airplanes—llamas, burros, and Cessnas—are relied upon to transport material via mountain trails and jungle landing strips. In leaf form, however, cocaine is a bulky cargo. Depending on the concentration of the cocaine alkaloid in the leaves, it can take anywhere up to five hundred kilos of leaves, about what you can grow on an acre and a half of land, to make a single kilo of cocaine hydrochloride—the white powder that goes up your nose. For this reason, interim laboratories, some of them portable, are set up close to the growing fields to reduce the leaves down to a cocaine paste, which can be shipped more easily.

Brewing up a batch of paste involves a several-stage process wherein the leaves are treated with successive solutions, of lime or potash, kerosene, sulfuric acid, then more lime, to begin separating out the cocaine from the thirteen other alkaloids in the plant. The resulting paste consists of a grayish muck, resembling joint compound used in drywall construction, wherein the bulk of the product has been reduced by about one-hundredfold, 250 kilos of leaves boiling down to about 2.5 kilos of paste. The cocaine alkaloid content has also been jacked up considerably, from 1 to 2 percent in the coca leaves to 40 to 90 percent in the paste. Known in this form as *basuco*, the paste can be marketed as a nice little drug product in itself, much cheaper than refined cocaine, since it hasn't gone through the final works. This is why it appeals to native Colombians, who mix the concentrate with tobacco and smoke it like a joint, attaining a high part of the way toward euphoria.

The leaves have now been reduced enough so that the product can be easily flown from the growing fields to the finishing laboratories in the forests of western Colombia. Here the paste undergoes more baths in solutions of kerosene and sulfuric acid, of potassium permanganate and ammonium hydroxide, successive soakings and dryings, to produce an interim form of cocaine called "base." Although grayish and gluey like the paste, the base is now 100 percent pure cocaine alkaloid, and very potent. Indeed, the base is so powerful that before the discovery of crack, some people—most notably the comedian Richard Pryor—employed a volatile procedure involving the use of fire and ether to treat the cocaine powder imported into the U.S. so as to transform it back into its prior form, no pun intended, which they could place into a little pipe and smoke, or "freebase."

But while base can provide a memorable high, from a marketing standpoint it lacks versatility. It won't dissolve in water, so you can't shoot it. And it refuses to be absorbed through the mucous membranes, so it's no good to snort. To create the cocaine of song and legend requires one more operation, the grand finale. This involves dissolving the base in ether—seventeen liters to the kilo is the formula—then combining it with acetone and hydrochloric acid, and once more allowing it to sit out and dry into a white, crystalline substance. The end result is Colombia's *primo* export product, cocaine hydrochloride. When it's pressed into a rocklike form for traveling, the material glows with an ethereal opalescence, like some kind of gem. At the user end, chopped with a razor blade on the face of a mirror and marshaled into inch-long lines of the famous marching powder, the drug emerges as a substance that is light, fragile, and flaky, like new-fallen snow.

Listening to Carlos explain some of this, sitting on his bunk in Danbury, George retained about as much as he had of the chem-lab lectures back in high school, which wasn't a lot. But when Carlos got to the economic end of the business, George started paying more attention. Adding up the cost of the coca leaves, the chemicals, and the cheap labor involved, it cost the processors less than a thousand dollars to produce a kilo of 100 percent pure cocaine, which they were selling then for six thousand dollars in Colombia. If they transported it to Miami, it would go wholesale for between fifty and sixty thousand dollars a kilo. In 1974 tenured college professors earned twenty thousand dollars a year and houses in the Hamptons went for a hundred grand. With a few trips to Florida, one could become a rich man.

Moving from wholesaling to retailing, the numbers climbed

higher still as the quality of the product got worse. Cut a number of times by interim dealers, who would add inert substances to boost the weight and maintain their profit margin, the common street product in some cases would contain no more than 15 or 20 percent cocaine. Dealers found they often had to add Methedrine to give the mix a decent amount of drive. But for argument's sake, say it was cut only once or twice, keeping the product fairly high-grade. Selling for one hundred dollars a gram, a thousand grams to the kilo, with all the deals running smoothly, no glitches along the way, this meant the kilo purchased for six thousand in Colombia would generate street sales in America of between two and three hundred thousand dollars, and even more if you dealt in shoddier merchandise.

By now George's jaw was fairly sagging toward his navel at the prospect of the profits involved here. But what about the supply? he asked, applying a dose of skepticism to this otherwise heady scenario. He knew from his own early frustrations in the marijuana business, knocking around Puerto Vallarta in Mexico searching for a pot connection, that sales projections meant nothing unless you could lay your hands on the goods. Don't worry, my friend, Carlos told him; they could get all the cocaine they wanted. He had several important acquaintances. One of them, named Gustavo Gaviria, was, like Carlos, in the business of stealing and smuggling cars, but with a twist. Gustavo stole the cars and smuggled them into Ecuador and Peru, where he sold them to buy coca paste, which he brought back to Medellín and had refined into cocaine; it was a good business, with very low start-up costs. He was now also getting connections for paste in Bolivia, Carlos had heard, and making arrangements with a number of labs outside Medellín. This Gustavo was in partnership with his cousin, a former emerald smuggler whom people in Medellín were starting to talk about as a man on the rise. Carlos had met this guy himself. The name meant nothing to George, no more than it did to anyone else in the United States at the time. It was only later that George came to appreciate the value of Carlos's having even this tangential a connection to Pablo Escobar.

As for the demand side, cocaine seemed on the verge of really taking off in the United States. Although it was hardly a mass-market commodity, interest in it was building fast, particularly on the West Coast, where rock stars and movie actors were touting it like crazy, as if they owned stock in the company. Coded references cropped up in songs by Steppenwolf and the Jefferson Airplane. Record producer Phil Spector sent out Christmas cards that read: "A little snow at Xmas time never hurt anyone." Peter Fonda and Dennis Hopper were proselytizing on its behalf, using it openly at Hollywood parties. In L.A. it had to be an out-of-it shindig indeed where guests didn't disappear into the bathroom, emerging with pupils dilated and a lot of sudden pep. It wouldn't be until 1977 that there existed enough national savvy about the drug to generate one of the major guffaws in Woody Allen's *Annie Hall*, when the Woody Allen character makes a hundred dollars' worth of cocaine disappear with a badly aimed sneeze. But by 1974, bedrock polling evidence had already suggested the balloon was about to go up: The National Household Survey announced that 5.4 million Americans over the age of eighteen had admitted to snorting cocaine at least once.

Alone, however, the Colombians didn't seem quite able to exploit the potential of this burgeoning market. Not many of them spoke English. They didn't feel comfortable in America, where their speech and manner of dress made them stand out; they were wary of foreigners. Their only experience in the U.S. had been in Miami and New York, both of which had fairly large communities of compatriots to provide them cover. They knew nothing about the West Coast.

Clearly the need now was for an American connection the Colombians could trust—a facilitator who not only knew how to get the stuff into the country safely and in much larger amounts than had been done so far, but who also had access to a distribution network of reliable individuals through which the product could be supplied to all the seemingly eager customers. Here was where George took over the conversation from Carlos, detailing his experience in the marijuana business. He told Carlos he could get airplanes, one, two, ten of them, if they wanted. He ran through his lecture on the dry lake beds. You could reach them just as easily from Colombia, in one or two jumps, stopping off in Mexico to refuel. He knew all about doing that. As he saw it, getting cocaine into the country posed no problem. As far as the marketing went, at about the time George was going off to prison he had noticed that many of the dealers who'd been taking his pot had begun to deal in cocaine as a sideline. And the word he'd been hearing was that they couldn't get anywhere near as much as they could sell, and what they got was sadly diluted. Nevertheless, the dealers were building up customers, developing the necessary market knowledge—what kind of people wanted it, where they could be found. George told Carlos he knew a guy, a hairdresser—never mind his name—who was plugged in to the entertainment industry in Los Angeles, who knew rock stars and movie starlets. This guy was crying for it, too. No doubt about it, George said; he could get the connections.

Once they had this thing cranked up, the money pouring in would make what George had been taking out of the marijuana trade look like a kid's allowance. Say they flew in three hundred kilos of 100 percent pure cocaine—an astronomical amount at the time, but if he'd flown in three hundred keys of pot, why couldn't he just as fucking well fly in the same amount of coke? That would cost them $180,000 in Colombia, and it would wholesale in the States for, what, $15 million? Eighteen million? And if they did that once a month? What are we talking a year, here? Pick me up off the floor! he thought, woozy over the prospect. Maybe once a strong market was developed, he'd back off it a little, just do the transportation part—pick it up at Point A and deliver it to Point B, without having to worry about selling the stuff. He'd make less money that way, but it would be a lot less risky. Ninety-five percent of how you got your ass caught in the dope business was by selling to someone you didn't happen to know was working for the police. George didn't need a lecture on that one. So for doing just the transportation, they'd charge the Colombians $10,000 a kilo, get some planes, provide constant service, run a regular airline. Flying in three hundred kilos a month, even half that amount— let's not be pigs about it—would come to $18 million dollars a year.

"Suddenly I knew I had the world by the balls and I just needed a little patience and I was going to get so fucking rich it was beyond belief," George says. "Have you ever known something like that? I knew it and I didn't care what kind of hell I had to go through. It didn't matter anymore. It was mine, all of it, and I couldn't believe it myself. I couldn't believe it—that here I was, a kid from a fucking shithole town like Weymouth, smuggling some lousy marijuana— and I thought *that* was money!—and all of a sudden I knew I was going to have millions and millions of dollars. I didn't just get sent to jail. I got sent a gift! I was thankful they put me there. Really! 'Thank you, federal government. Thank you, fucking FBI. You don't know what you did for me.'"

ONE

Weymouth

1946–1965

Cohasset for its Beauty
Hingham for its Pride
If it weren't for the Herring,
Poor Weymouth would have died.
                              —OLD SAYING

IN 1622 A SPLINTER GROUP OF PILGRIMS from the Plymouth Colony in Massachusetts journeyed up the coast to Weymouth to try to set up a trading post, and if they'd only heard about the herring they might not have made such a mess of it. As it was, they turned out to be a pretty sorry crew, bickering among themselves and stealing corn and other foodstuffs from the local Wampanoag tribe. In return, the Indians found little reason to help out the following winter when the Pilgrims ran desperately short of food and ended up either dying of starvation or dragging themselves ignominiously back to Plymouth. A permanent settlement wasn't established in Weymouth until two years later, when people with farming skills, rather than traders, gave it a shot, and after no less a person than Miles Standish himself had come up to Weymouth to win over the hearts and minds of the Wampanoags, who had gotten pretty ornery by then. Standish accomplished the task in ready fashion by inviting two of the more influential sachems to be his guests for a nice sit-down lunch, and when the Indians began to feel a little under the weather—he'd taken the precaution of poisoning their food—his men dispatched them with knives and axes.

The famous herring that might have saved the settlers migrated in from the ocean early every summer and swam upstream to their traditional spawning ground in a body of fresh water known as Whitmans Pond. During the height of the trek, all but killed off in the early 1900s by industrial development, Whitmans Pond would virtually boil over with fish, providing townspeople a nearly effortless and bountiful harvest. As a little boy, George could see the pond from his bedroom window, and in winter he'd walk over from the house his parents had in a subdivision known as Lake Shore Park and go ice skating with his chums.

To the other blue-collar families in the neighborhood, the Jungs seemed to have it pretty good in those years right after World War II. Where most of the men and some of the women worked on the assembly line down at the Procter & Gamble plant or as welders and steamfitters at the Fore River Shipyard across the river in Quincy, George's father led a relatively independent life, servicing heating accounts throughout Boston from his own truck. The family certainly had money enough. Every other year Fred bought a brand new car, either a Ford or a Mercury, always the roomiest model; his wife wore the best of clothes, had a fur coat.

George was too young in those days to help his father on the truck, so a boy from the neighborhood, Russell Delorey, who was nine years older and would often baby-sit for the Jungs, went along with Fred on Saturdays and school holidays. "In the winter I'd walk over there at six in the morning in the dark," recalls Russell, who grew up to become a masonry contractor on Cape Cod. "He'd start that big oil truck and I'd climb up and sit in it while it warmed up. When he finished his breakfast, he'd come out and we'd leave, and we wouldn't come home until ten o'clock at night." Fred invariably drove the same route, from South Boston to the South End, from Beacon Hill to Washington Street, and for Russell the work often proved grueling. Hauling the heavy oil hose over back fences and sometimes a hundred feet up an alley covered with snow or ice or mud, the boy would often slip and fall. "Some of the settings were also a little frightening for a young person," Russell says today. "There'd be drunks sleeping in the alley, and black people around, but I never felt threatened because of Fred's ability to manage everything, be a friendly person with everybody, no matter who you were. It seemed to me that he knew everybody in the city of Boston. Driving home, he would talk about the merits of a wholesome life, about working hard all day long. We'd always stop in Quincy on the way and get a large loaf of Syrian bread to take home. We did that every night."

In 1948, when George was six, the Jungs moved up, both geographically and economically, to a house on Abigail Adams Circle. Laid out as a subdivision just before the attack on Pearl Harbor, the Circle featured larger, two-story colonial-style houses, some of which, like the Jungs', occupied the crown of a hill and looked down over the salt marsh to the Fore River as it flowed into the sea at Wessagussett Bay, site of the original settlement. In Weymouth terms, the Circle rated as one of the better parts of town. Here the women mostly stayed home all day, and the men wore ties and worked as managers at General Dynamics in Quincy, or commuted on the South Shore Railroad to office jobs in Boston. The father of George's best boyhood friend, Malcolm MacGregor, had a degree from MIT and a prominent job as a ship surveyor that took the family overseas for long stretches. Across the street and three doors down lived the Fieldses. Mr. Fields was the president of a button company in Boston; his son went off to Colby College. It was in the Fieldses' driveway that George saw his first Porsche.

Financially, the Jungs held their own well enough, but the new neighborhood was something of a challenge socially. Looking back, Malcolm MacGregor's mother, Gladys, cannot recall Mr. or Mrs. Jung ever taking part in the annual Christmas dances that would be held at the Community Hall, or showing up for the Fourth of July picnics in the neighborhood. "They never mixed much," she says. Her memory of George's mother, Ermine, was of a "nice and quiet woman" who worked in the Ann Taylor shop in nearby Braintree. She was exceptionally pretty. In her looks and her flowing dress she resembled the actress Loretta Young; not by accident, it seemed, "The Loretta Young Show" was a program she never missed. Mrs. MacGregor recalls George's father as a heavy-set man, with a ruddy complexion and always a cigar sticking out the side of his mouth. "He was an ordinary man, a beer drinker," she says. "He'd park his oil truck in the family's driveway." And according to Russell Delorey, Fred got just about as much respect inside the household. "I don't believe that Mrs. Jung or the other family members really knew what Fred's day was like," says Russell. "I saw it as full, rewarding, and successful. But I'm afraid that at home he was simply regarded as an oilman."

Ermine was an O'Neill from Boston, and judging from her first impression of Fred when the couple met in the 1930s, she had reason to expect more in the way of a future when she married him. For one thing, in the hard times that characterized the Depression, the heating-oil business seemed safe economic territory, considering that people would prefer to stint on fancy clothes and cuts of meat long before they'd freeze to death in the harsh New England winters. For another, Fred seemed to be a man on the move. He owned a total of three oil trucks then, large tractor-trailer jobs; he had employees working for him and a long list of customers. There's a snapshot of him taken around then showing a prosperous-looking man in a suit and a fancy white hat beside a big Packard touring car. Family legend has it that Ermine's mother, a stage entertainer named Ethel O'Neill who sang in music halls of Boston, urged her daughter into the marriage on the grounds that Mr. Jung was obviously going places.

Unfortunately for his family, one of the places he was going fairly regularly was the Suffolk Down Racetrack. He had a winning streak at first, but pretty soon he was losing consistently and in large enough amounts so that he had to mortgage his fleet of oil trucks to pay mounting debts. He lost the trucks eventually, and when the war came, he ended up working at a defense job in the naval shipyard in Portsmouth, New Hampshire. Fred recovered a little of his oil business after the war, when the family moved to Weymouth. He acquired a smaller oil truck and secured a contract with the Stetson Oil Company to take care of a list of customers in Boston. But it wasn't nearly the same. There was tension in the family. One day George remembers his father teaching him the art of poker and how to handle cards smartly, doing the one-handed shuffle, the reverse cut, fanning out the deck over the table surface. George's mother came into the room, grabbed up the deck, and threw it into the wastebasket, saying something sharply to the effect that there'd be no more of *that* in this household.

George's uncle, George Jacob Jung—now there was a man for Ermine to admire! Whereas Fred came out of high school at the start of the Depression and went right to work, his brother, George, nine years his senior, had gone off to the Massachusetts Maritime

Academy, enlisted in the navy, and come home after World War II a full commander. A man of sound financial resources—he held a good-paying job as an engineer for the state, and his wife, Myrna, worked as a restaurant manager for Filene's in Boston—Uncle George traveled widely and frequently about the world. The couple occupied a substantial gabled residence on Norman Avenue in Melrose, a middle-class suburb located north of Boston, and considerably up the social scale from Weymouth. George and Myrna remained childless, but it was to their house that the Jung family members repaired for Sunday dinners, Thanksgiving, and Christmas. Besides Fred and Ermine and their two children, there were the two Jung sisters—Auntie Gertrude, a divorcée who was also childless, and Aunt Jenny and her husband, Ray Silva, whose son, Bobby, was George's only cousin. Bobby Silva went into banking and eventually became the president of the Citizens National Bank in Putnam, Connecticut. Starting out, however, he'd worked at a bank in Danbury at the same time Cousin George happened to be in residence at the federal prison there, a piece of intelligence he was undoubtedly not too eager to share with the guys at the office.

In the house in Melrose, Uncle George's navy dress sword hung over the fireplace, along with a photo of him in his whites. There was a prominent picture of the battle cruiser he'd served on in the Pacific. Making a big deal out of mixing daiquiris for the ladies, Uncle George would regale the company with tales of his recent travel adventures—he journeyed abroad seventeen times during his lifetime. Or he might talk about the latest charity drive of the Shriners, of which he was a stalwart member, or a horticultural award he'd received for his roses, or the story in the local paper on the occasion of his attendance at the Fourth International Rose Conference in London, where Queen Elizabeth had put in an appearance. Indeed, in Fred's eyes, no less than in Ermine's, George had always occupied such a commanding position in the family that when his own son was born on August 6, 1942, after discovering Ermine had told the hospital the boy was to be named after his father, Fred marched down and had the name on little Frederick's birth certificate changed to match that of his brother. Although he certainly felt honored at the time, Uncle George had good reason later on, and on more than one occasion, to regret the gesture. One of them occurred at JFK International Airport in New York City, where, on the way back from Europe, he was detained for an hour or so by U.S. Customs officials while they investigated as to whether this sputtering, angry old man was the George Jacob Jung wanted by the FBI for jumping bail on a drug charge.

For all his wide-ranging interests and exposure to different cultures, Uncle George maintained a fairly stern and unbending outlook on life, a dour Dutchman to the core. "My brother was what you might call a straight-down-the-line kind of a guy," says Auntie Gertrude, who also worked at Filene's, as manager of its beauty shop. "You couldn't really say he had much of a sense of humor." On the occasion when an underling would come by his office to ask the boss for an approval on some matter, a request for a raise perhaps, rather than waste words giving a reply, Uncle George liked to direct the visitor's attention with a wave of his hand toward a sign he had printed up and sitting on the front of his desk. The sign said NO.

When it comes to divining the root causes of antisocial behavior, criminologists have produced murky speculation at best. With even less success have doctors and psychologists been able to predict with any certainty which little boy will grow up to become a public enemy. The most recent edition of the *Diagnostic and Statistical Manual of Mental Disorders*, the *DSM III-Revised*, has nothing to say, for instance, about what to watch out for if you're worried your kid is in danger of becoming a drug smuggler. The "incipient criminality factors" detailed in the *DSM* are given to such generality as to forecast that a rascal like Tom Sawyer would emerge perforce as a serious menace to society.

Whatever the litmus test, little Georgie Jung scored very low when it came to committing the standard predictive acts: He showed no outstanding propensity for lying in his early years, or for stealing, playing hooky, vandalizing property, getting into fights, lighting fires, running away from home, or torturing helpless animals. At about age five he did purloin a neighbor's pet hamster to provide it the benefits of living in his own room, a move his father countered by getting a policeman friend to show up in uniform at the front door and scare George into taking it back. And he certainly was devilish enough to keep his mother on the run, chasing him about the house and poking for him with a broomstick when he'd wriggle under a bed to avoid his comeuppance. There are no reports from family members about any capital transgression on George's part. He received an honorable discharge after three years with the Cub Scouts. He dependably served the Quincy *Patriot Ledger* on his route every day after school, winging the papers with his left-hand sidearm pitch up onto the porches. He went sailing on the Fore River with Malcolm MacGregor in a little boat they kept moored down in back of the Circle. He dug for clams at Wessagussett Beach to earn spending money. A photograph of him in grade school shows a little boy with a carefully combed shock of hair sticking upright over his forehead, and a wide, impish grin that to one relative, at least, proved memorably disarming. "As a little boy he was a perfect charmer," Auntie Gertrude remembers. "He was really—what can I say?—he could just steal your heart away."

Were he enrolled in elementary school today, his parents might have been counseled to look at the possibility of dyslexia as a factor in his having to repeat the first grade because of reading problems, or Attention-Deficit Hyperactivity Disorder as an explanation for his general behavior. Little Georgie certainly appears to have been full-blown hyperactive, at times difficult to control, even subject to fits and explosions of temper, to the point where his mother once felt the need to consult the family doctor. His advice was to stick the boy's head under a faucet the next time he had an outburst. George still remembers with some annoyance the series of duckings forced on him after that consultation.

By the time George was entering adolescence, his parents were having serious marital problems. These usually didn't evince themselves to George until they'd reached an extreme stage, when Ermine would pack up her suitcase and leave home. George remembers her walking down to the bottom of the hill to get the bus for Quincy, and from there the train into Boston. He would follow her down the hill and stand across from the bus stop by the minister's house shouting out to her to come back. "I didn't want her to leave, but I didn't know how to stop her, so I threw rocks at her," he says. "Not really rocks, they were stones. But I didn't know what else to do to make her stay." On these occasions Ermine would stay with her mother, who lived on Commonwealth Avenue in Boston, or go down to Baton Rouge, Louisiana, where her brother, Jack O'Neill, owned a string of music stores. During one of his mother's absences, George lived for several months at the house in Melrose with Uncle George and Aunt Myrna. That was where he finally learned his multiplication tables, when he was going into the fifth grade. As George recalls, "Aunt Myrna sat me down at the kitchen table and said, 'You're not stupid, Georgie. There's no rea-son why you're failing all the time; you just don't know what disci-pline is.' There were these two little girls next door that I really liked, and she said I was never going to get to know those girls unless I learned the times table all the way up to twelve. And I did. I learned it that summer."

George's academic troubles dogged him in one way or another all the way up through high school. By contrast, his older sister, Marie, not only had an absolutely unblemished scholastic record, with never less than an A in any course, but would in every school she attended win the unqualified adoration of her teachers, qualities of which her younger brother was never allowed to remain igno-rant. One of Marie's biggest fans, for instance, was Mary Toomey, her English teacher at Weymouth High School. At the mere men-tion of Marie's name Miss Toomey's face still lights up and exudes an almost beatific glow. "Marie Jung was just beautiful, not in the sense she was all decorated, but she had a naturally classic face, lovely long eyelashes, beautiful manners, you could send her any-where, totally trustworthy," Miss Toomey says. "She really had everything—talent, looks, charm, brains. She was just so good, such a good person."

Miss Toomey, now retired and living in a cottage near the sea in the village of Eastham on Cape Cod, had taught at the school since the 1940s, when she also coached some of the athletic teams while the males were off at war. Later on it seemed natural that she was the teacher coaches came to when one of their players required extra tutoring so as not to fall below the C average needed to stay on a team. This was especially true of the football coach, Harry Arlinson, a legend in eastern Massachusetts for his teams in the 1940s and 1950s, whose record of 135 wins, 17 losses, and 3 ties earned Weymouth High a large picture spread in *Look* magazine in 1953. She recalls that Arlinson would take her aside and say in a near-whisper, as if engaging in some conspiracy, "I have a boy who I can't play because he can't pass English, and they're going to give him one last test. . . ."

This meant the boy would become one of Miss Toomey's "spe-cial cases," to be given private lessons after school; she'd even search the newspaper to see if there wasn't a Shakespeare play to take him to in Boston. Miss Toomey also played a large part in choosing the questions that appeared on the subsequent test, which may or may not have been the reason every one of her special cases managed to pull through.

Harry Arlinson had left Weymouth to coach at Tufts University several years before young George entered high school in the fall of 1958, but the new head coach, Jack Fisher, picked up on Miss Toomey's services to keep his boys qualified for play. Miss Toomey already knew all about the Jung children, however, and the very first week of George's high school term, she took it upon herself to send a note down to have Marie's little brother brought to her office. "I don't remember what year that was exactly, but I do remember calling him in and exhorting him to do better now that he was in high school. I told him I would spend the time and give him all the help he wanted."

George remembers sitting in homeroom that day when the word came down that Miss Toomey wanted to see him. He was certainly familiar with the name. "Miss Toomey was everything in our house; everybody loved her, Marie, my mother especially. And here I was in high school, and now Miss Toomey, she was waiting for *me*.

"I remember going up to her office on the third floor, thinking to myself, 'All right, here comes the bullshit.' I walked into her classroom and she introduced herself—a round cherub face, a little overweight, wide in the hips, a flowered dress. 'Oh, you're Marie's brother! She was such a wonderful student. Such a wonderful person. And I've looked over your grades in junior high, and I think you can do a lot better. You're a football player, and Mr. Fisher is my good friend. We can work together and I'm going to help you. I'm going to devote all my free time to you,' and blah blah blah. I listened through it all, and when she was all finished, I just said to her, 'No you won't, Miss Toomey,' and 'Thank you anyway, Miss Toomey,' and 'Good-bye, Miss Toomey,' and I walked out."

Marie kept up with Miss Toomey after graduation and down through the years, sending word every Christmas about what her children were doing, detailing the milestones in Otis's career at Eli Lilly. "She wrote me that Otis made a big breakthrough in robotics that's going to benefit his company tremendously. And the children, you could easily see Marie in the children. A son graduated from West Point, another son is an attorney, and Karen, I think, is at Purdue Engineering School. You could see there was good stock there. The genes were good." Of George, Miss Toomey heard nothing after graduation, not a word for nearly twenty years, until she was talking one day with her handyman, Paul Deschamps, whose son was a member of the Eastham Police Department. "It was in 1980, I think. Paul was working at the house one day, and, 'Oh, by the way,' he said, 'there's been a very big thing happened in Eastham with drugs. There's this fellow, actually, the fellow came from Weymouth. Did you ever hear of a George Jung?'"

Luckily for George, the path toward becoming a big man at Weymouth High was paved most readily not by getting good grades but by playing football. During the team's nine-week schedule, players served as the focus of attention, not only in the classrooms and corridors of the school, but also among the townspeople at large. Shortly after twelve noon on an autumn Saturday, by the time the players had suited up in their maroon-and-gold uniforms and were leaving the locker room for the half-mile walk to Legion Field, the streets of Weymouth would be lined several deep with people ready to cheer and clap and wave their banners as the heroes marched by, their cleats clattering on the pavement like a company of horse guards. Seats were reserved and almost always sold out. You couldn't get a parking space within a mile of the field. The pulse of the town mounted feverishly as the day approached for the pinnacle event, which occurred at 10:00 A.M. on Thanksgiving Day as Weymouth went up against its arch foe, Brockton, in a contest that would draw a hysterical crowd of more than ten thousand people. "Football back then, it's hard to convey the feeling, but it was just everything in Weymouth," says Buzzy Knight, an alumnus who later became the school's principal. "On Saturdays, for a home game, in good weather, this town simply came to a standstill."

Weymouth's fervid interest in football stemmed partly from the fact that in the way of local pride it had nothing much else to greatly distinguish it. Despite its location on the water and a history that stretched back to the Pilgrims, Weymouth emerged in the mid-twentieth century as a drab blue-collar town, made up of a mish-mash of development-style houses, low-end shopping centers, and little of the charming colonial residue found elsewhere in New England. Like nearby Brockton, it relied for employment on deadening jobs in the shoe factories or work in the shipyard in Quincy, both of them industries that deteriorated after World War II and in recent years have become extinct. Populated in large part by the Irish, many of them first-generation suburbanites who'd fled the Dorchester section of Boston (for years Weymouth was known as the Irish

Riviera), the town had much less social cachet than its three WASPy neighbors, Hingham, Scituate, and Cohasset, whose high schools might have stood little chance against Weymouth in football but sent more than twice the percentage of their graduates to four-year colleges. In 1961, the year George graduated, only 108 of the 502 graduates in his class put themselves down in the yearbook as college-bound. More males from the class enlisted in the armed services than went on for further schooling.

The Weymouth teams were usually pretty spectacular. Harry Arlinson had coached his boys to seven undefeated seasons, and by the mid-1950s Weymouth had become "the terror of the Commonwealth," as it was put in *Look* magazine, a reputation that, despite some stumbles, went undiminished under his successor, Jack Fisher. In 1956, under Fisher, Weymouth became the first school in Massachusetts history to play an entire schedule of Class-A teams and still finish undefeated. As half the town still remembers, it creamed Brockton that Thanksgiving 48–6, and at graduation the following June Weymouth sent off players who eventually starred at Brown, Harvard, Princeton, and Columbia, among other colleges.

Although George, in standard younger-brother fashion, tortured the daylights out of his sister practically up until she left home, he and all his chums regarded her boyfriend, Otis—team captain who later played in the Orange and Cotton Bowls for Syracuse—with uncamouflaged adoration, and before they got to high school they hung on his every piece of advice as to how to prepare themselves to make the big team. In imitation of Otis, George quit playing Little League baseball at age thirteen—despite the fact that with his bewildering left-handed sidearm pitch he'd thrown the league's first no-hitter—and gave over all his spare time to lifting weights in order to build up his upper body for the backfield. His pals quickly followed suit, and pretty soon all day on Saturdays the guys—George, John Hollander, Barry Damon—could be found trying to pump up their muscles in a homemade gym set up in the garage of Mike Grable, who played quarterback with George at junior high. Finally getting some payback now for being Marie's brother, George, with his friends in tow, was allowed to go over and observe the great Otis himself during his private backyard practice sessions, where he got himself into shape for smashing through the opposing line. He would wrap his right arm in padding, lower his body into a crouch, and charge at full tilt into a telephone pole, striking with such force that the top of the pole could be seen to shiver, as if the thing had been rammed by a wrecker's ball.

In the end, thanks to Otis's inspiration, all the effort the boys put into building up their bodies did not go unrewarded. George and most of his garage set did indeed succeed in making the varsity team when they arrived as sophomores at Weymouth High School in 1958 (in Weymouth the junior high school went through the ninth grade). The fact that George's own performance on the football field never quite reached the total triumph he'd so achingly longed for had less to do with any lack of ability or preparation on his part than with an increasing tendency to behave, particularly where adults were concerned, in a manner that was becoming more noticeably and perversely defiant.

Head coach Jack Fisher had developed something of an attitude himself, having arrived at the school in the long and heavy shadow of his predecessor. He had been given to feel from the start that serious questions existed as to whether he could measure up to the great Arlinson. "Jack Fisher was very aware that he followed God," says Buzzy Knight, the principal. "He was never allowed to forget it; they never let him off the hook." Arlinson had rarely raised his voice, exercising control over the players by gentle manipulation, by using the force of his brilliant record to make them stretch themselves to their fullest. Fisher, on the other hand, was excitable and temperamental, and worst of all where George was concerned, a strict disciplinarian, who shouted at his players and demanded they abide by his rules or face warming the bench. And most of all, in no small part to prove that he stood equal to his predecessor, Fisher wanted desperately to win.

A wiry man with a shock of white hair and aquiline features, Fisher had been a notable star himself, as quarterback at Fordham University behind the original "Seven Blocks of Granite," which constituted one of the most impregnable lines in college-football history. The blocks won their name from the sportswriters during the 1930 season after executing three successive shutouts over Boston College, Holy Cross, and New York University, then football powerhouses, by scores 3–0, 6–0, and 7–0, respectively. Coach of the famous squad was Frank Cavanaugh, known as "the Iron Major" for the shrapnel wounds he carried in his head from World War I, and whose exploits—he went nearly blind from his wounds in his final coaching days and died in 1933—became the subject of a 1943 movie starring Pat O'Brien.

Comporting himself at Weymouth in the take-no-guff style of the major, Fisher succeeded in ruffling feathers his first season by kicking six seniors off the squad for believing, as he saw it, that having played under Arlinson earned them the right to dog it during drills. Whether its purpose was to enforce discipline or just expunge the team of Arlinson worship, the move didn't go down too well in Weymouth, considering that football was the town's major social event. Fathers not only came down at nights to hang around watching their sons practice under the lights but would also follow the players back to school and mingle with them in the locker room. "I got a lot of phone calls and letters over that one," says Fisher, who had to finish out the season with a team composed mostly of sophomores. "I remember we did knock off Brockton that year, though."

By the time George arrived at Weymouth High, Fisher had a state championship under his belt, thanks in no small part to Otis Godfrey, and felt assured that his rules were producing results. On Friday nights, for instance, he wanted the players to be in bed by 10:00 P.M., instead of staying up late and raising hell, as they had under Arlinson. He told them he didn't want to drive around town and see them hanging out. "I'd tell them, 'Go to a movie or a friend's house, but whatever you do, I want you to get home early and I want you to stay off the street corners.'" Practice sessions were tightly organized drills, and he demonstrated little shyness about singling out a player over some transgression and yelling at him in front of the squad. "I coached hard, but I coached fair," he says. "I used to say to them, 'The time for you to start worrying about whether you're playing is not when I'm yelling at you but when I stop yelling at you, because then I don't think you're worth it.'"

Needless to say, George didn't respond positively to getting yelled at or to Fisher's rules in general. One of these rules required sophomores on the varsity squad to play Saturday mornings on the junior varsity as well as show up in the afternoon for the main event. George saw little profit in doing the JV nonsense, since the games drew a tiny crowd and produced little in the way of glory. He thought himself especially abused after the second varsity game against Medford, when he was put in as a substitute halfback late in the contest and smashed across the goal line for a score, his only carry of the afternoon. The following Saturday he decided not to turn out for the JV game. Coach Fisher responded by benching him not only for that day's game but for the rest of the season and a good part of his junior year as well.

To compensate partially for his football failure, George won a place on the varsity track team as the discus thrower, the same event in which Otis Godfrey had set the school's record. Track didn't command anywhere near the attention everyone paid to football, but George did eventually beat Otis's toss by seven feet. By his senior year, George had also inched his way back into Fisher's good graces, enough to become the team's starting right halfback. But even that experience turned sour. He got to carry the ball less than half as often as the other backs, despite averaging a fairly impressive 5.7 yards a carry, the best on the team. And he ended up missing the big Thanksgiving game because of a knee injury during a scrimmage, when he got decked by his pal John Hollander—which was probably just as well, since Weymouth got killed by Brockton that year, 54–0.

Fisher is now eighty-eight years old, but his memory of that team remains sharp, unfortunately so, in his view, because it produced the worst Weymouth record since World War II. "That's a class I'd kind of like to forget," he says. Of George in particular, he recalls a boy with a lot of natural talent and potential who, for reasons that remain a mystery to him, never fulfilled his early promise. "George, well, yes, in junior high he was a standout. He had all the physical tools, more so than most young boys. But something was going on with him, I couldn't understand. His attitude, something, where he just wasn't with everybody else."

During George's high school years the headlines were beginning to reflect the worrisome kinds of events that would dominate the coming decade of the 1960s. The Russians were leap-frogging America in outer space with the launch of the *Sputnik* satellites. President Dwight D. Eisenhower was forced to send in federal troops to protect black students during desegregation of the public schools in Little Rock, Arkansas. Fidel Castro was coming down from the mountains to take over Cuba. That was also when Charlie van Doren of Columbia University was convicted on perjury charges for denying that agents of the NBC-TV quiz show "Twenty-one" had supplied him the answers. Elvis had arrived, of course, but rock and roll still had to share slots on the jukebox—five plays for a quarter—with the likes of "Tom Dooley," "Volare," and "Itsy Bitsy Teenie Weenie Yellow Polkadot Bikini." The grown-ups, meanwhile, were trying to figure out the cha-cha.

In Weymouth, the football guys all had their hair cut down at Dick's Barber Shop on Washington Street, known as "Dirty Dick's" for the *Playboy* magazines and the more raunchy stuff perusable on the premises. Most ordered up crew cuts, which needed constant laminations from the old wiffle stick so the hair stood up right. George opted for the cooler, more sophisticated Peter Gunn style, after the suave TV detective—the hair a little longer and lying flatter than a crew. The girls wore long pleated skirts, and round-collared shirts under their sweaters, and if they were lucky enough to be going with someone on the varsity, their boyfriends' maroon and gold letter jackets with his name embroidered on the right sleeve. Weymouth being basically a one-class town, social divisions among teenagers were fairly narrow and ran pretty much along the lines of what kind of car your father could afford. Kids in the vocational high school, which was located in the rear of the regular school, were looked down upon slightly, but if vocational-program guys like Barry Damon (carpentry) or Brian Dunbar (sheet-metal working), played football—Barry at center, Brian in the backfield—they could hang out with the other football guys and partake of all the attendant privileges.

Friday nights were party nights. One of the girls invariably offered up her house for a gathering. Armed with beer bought by one of the guys whose beard was thicker than most, the boys drove over into Johnny's Lane near the sandpit and drank until half of them threw up, which in most cases required four or five beers apiece. George could usually hold the most, and Barry Damon, whose snow-white hair earned him the nickname the Great White Rabbit, often barfed first, not necessarily missing his sneakers and the shoes of some of the other guys. George had a firm policy of never taking his father's car out on Friday nights.

Saturday night was date night; guys would grab a car, a girl, and head to the Weymouth Drive-in for *Psycho*, or *Tammy and the Bachelor*, or Troy Donahue in *A Summer Place*. After that it was a race to Weymouth Great Hill, a 153-foot-high glacial drumlin with room at the top for fifteen to twenty cars that provides a spectacular view over Wessagussett Bay to the lighted spires of Boston. The movie would end at about eleven, and the girls had to be home by midnight, which meant the guys inside the cars with the windows steaming up fast had less than one hour to devise a strategy that would culminate in the laying of a hand on top of a female breast. "Let me tell you, you weren't going too far in those days," says George. His regular date, Gerry Lee, rated high up in the "nice girl" category, which compelled George to take one or two other girls out during the course of a weekend to explore a wider set of possibilities. "Every girl had her standard code. Some of them, if you tried to do anything, they'd start to cry. I liked to try to take out older girls; they were a little more, you know, liberal." The sexual revolution, after all, was a good five years off, and while few teenagers in Weymouth at that time gave any thought to sexually transmitted diseases, there was certainly plenty of anxiety about other exigencies. In one notorious incident, a boy at school had gotten his girlfriend pregnant his senior year, and the two had to quit school and get married, and he joined the navy; their future, for all its former promise, was now regarded by their friends as a closed book.

While George failed to become the school's chief football star, he more than made up for that by his lordship over the social life. "George always managed to have the action rotating around himself; he was the hub, the manipulator of the social scene," says Jack McSheffrey, who grew up on the Circle. "He was the one you called to find out who was going to drink beer at the sand pit or who was going into Quincy or to the beach. If you weren't with him, you had the feeling of being left out." After George's mother changed her sales job from Ann Taylor's in Braintree to Remick's Department Store in Quincy, more or less the Neiman Marcus of the South Shore, George became one of the few kids to have his own charge card and a wardrobe that stayed center-front in the style of the day—herringbone jacket, khaki pants, button-down shirt, crewneck sweater, penny loafers, Jack Purcell tennis sneakers with the blue stripe across the toe. "I would kind of emulate the way George dressed," recalls Barry Damon. "He always bought whatever was happening, Harris-tweed coats, saddle shoes; everything always had to come from Remick's. He'd look at what I was wearing and say, 'What are you buying that shit for?'"

On the rare Saturday night when they had no dates, George and Barry would lead a foray up to Great Hill and try to disrupt whatever activities were going on by treating the other guys and their girlfriends to moonshots under the stars. In chemistry class his junior year, George not only tortured the nerdy kid with the thick glasses next to him, violating his experiment with alien chemicals while the boy had gone to the bathroom, but also went after the teacher himself, a little old man with a cheap set of false teeth, whose jacket George would burn with acid and whose examinations he'd get a girlfriend in the mimeograph office to run off for him and his friends. To be sure, the teacher sensed that something was amiss when the class screw-ups all scored A's on the test, so he arbitrarily issued them D's in the course.

For date purposes, George had access to his father's 1956 Mercury Phaeton. White on top with aqua-blue on the sides, it was one of the sharper cars in the group, and George washed it so often the paint almost came off. He also had sophisticated taste where music was concerned, which made him stand out in sharp relief from his contemporaries. He liked rock and roll okay, but his real penchant ran to Cole Porter, a taste he acquired from his mother. He also raved to his friends about Duke Ellington, Lionel Hampton, and Ella Fitzgerald, about Tommy Dorsey and other bands of the 1940s, along with Ahmad Jamal and the other progressive jazz artists. He went in to Boston to listen to Bob Dylan and Joan Baez in the late 1950s, before they'd even started producing records. "George was years ahead of everyone else in Weymouth," recalls one of his girlfriends. "I'll never forget it, we were juniors in high school, and he took me in to see Erroll Garner at Storyville in Boston—George loved him; he played his records all the time—and here we are having cocktails, seventeen years old, doing the things that people did when they were twenty-three or twenty-four."

Jack Kerouac's *On the Road* was published in 1957, to little fanfare in Weymouth, but George read it as soon as he heard about it, along with *The Dharma Bums*. He talked endlessly to his best friend, Malcolm MacGregor, about Dean Moriarty and the adventures he and his bunch had stumbling around the country, drinking wine out of jugs, always seeming to be passing through Denver. George and Malcolm and Jack Leahy read Ernest Hemingway and idolized Jack London, the oyster pirate, the gold rusher, the master of the *Snark*. They talked of riding freight trains, hitchhiking around America, going to Alaska and Spain. He and Malcolm sat up nights plotting about the trimaran they were going to build and sail around the world on. "George had this thing about him that made people just want to be around him; they liked to tell their friends they'd been with George," says Malcolm. "George was always bolder than anyone, always doing things that were out of the ordinary. He'd do just about anything if it would make him different from everybody else."

Ever since his early teenage years George had exhibited a preference for playing it close to the edge, sometimes literally. At age thirteen, he and his friends swam regularly in a quarry not far from his house, where a forty-foot cliff loomed above two jagged rocks sticking out of the water, one close to the cliff face, the other about ten feet out toward the middle of the quarry. To do the jump you had to land exactly between the rocks; a little too short or too far and you had a hard landing. Not many boys besides George tried that one very often.

When George got his driver's license at age sixteen, he began treating the town as his own personal raceway. In one of his more spectacular accidents, George was motoring along in his father's Mercury with Barry Damon during his senior year when a car pulled up close behind him on the twisting two-lane road that ran by the football stadium at Legion Field. "I could hear his engine revving, and he starts to make a move for the outside," says George. "We get up to seventy or eighty, and I'm straddling the white line and won't let him get by, and so he tries for the inside, and we're neck and neck going around a right-hand curve, and I'm trying to force my way back in our lane when suddenly this car comes around the corner right at me." George jerked the wheel to the right, just in time to avoid a head-on collision with an elderly couple staring pop-eyed at what they must have seen as certain death. As it was, he sheared off only the whole side of their car, doors and fenders included, and sent the other dragster smashing into a fire hydrant. His father's Mercury was now also a total wreck and the road a howling litter of car parts, skid marks, gasoline fumes, and the smell of freshly burnt rubber.

"I've done a lot of thinking about George in recent years, and especially since I saw him on TV recently," says his other best pal, Mike Grable, who as well as being the team quarterback was also president of the senior class. "And back when we were growing up, I can't think of anything that happened in that town you could point to now and say that's why he turned out the way he did. The only thing I can say is George just always had what I would call a casual attitude."

"I think 'risky' is kind of a good word for it," says another girl-friend of that period. "He was different from everyone else, and I think that's what appealed to me. It did to a lot of the girls. They were fascinated with him. He was good-looking and popular and strong. And he was someone on the outs, like a James Dean, but preppy. He'd have all these loony ideas—he wanted to go to Tahiti, and he never wanted to, I absolutely remember him saying to me, 'I am never going to work for a living.' I remember that as clear as a bell."

Whatever image of himself George was projecting to his friends, his own life at home, from junior high on up, became pro-gressively less happy as the wrangling between his parents grew more strident. Today his memories of that period flow like lava and appear as fresh as if it all had happened just the other day. "There were constant fights in that house. My sister would go into her bed-room and close the door and read books. At the time I was young and wasn't into reading, so I had to listen to it—the same argument, over and over, my mother saying, 'I could have done better. It was my mother who wanted me to marry you.' But then, what was the matter? I think. My father took care of the family, he never betrayed them or left them. The old man was doing the best he could. He bought a new car every two or three years, he paid the bills, there were plenty of groceries in the house, he never owed anybody. He gave you anything he had on the face of the earth. But he just wasn't what she wanted him to be. Because she loved the violin—we had a Stradivarius in the house—and she loved the theater and the opera. Do you know my grandmother knew Sophie Tucker? That she once had a date with Cy Young? My father, his big day was to come home and read the newspaper and have a couple of drinks, smoke a cigar and watch television. He didn't know anything about the theater or classical music."

For purposes of comparison, Ermine would bring up Uncle George, as well as her brother, Uncle Jack O'Neill, also fairly pros-perous, who owned the music stores down in Baton Rouge. George recalls, "It was, My brother has this, and Uncle George—it was, Uncle George was better, he had a better house, the sword over his mantel. We had to go up there every goddamn Sunday. He was the god to everyone. At Christmas when Marie was going to college, he'd give her a present of a little Christmas tree with hundred-dol-lar bills tied on in bows all over it, for her tuition that year. Then it would get dark and we'd drive home and the car would be filled with boxes and ribbons and presents from Uncle George and my mother going on about wasn't it all so wonderful and how generous he was. What he did was always more than my father gave us on Christmas morning. And how did that make him feel? He never said anything. There was nothing to say. I'd be sitting in the back seat and that's when I began to hate Uncle George, and I decided in my mind I was going to get that son of a bitch. And I was just a kid."

George's father was popular enough with his son's friends, could talk football and joke in a manner that didn't put them off, as adults can do sometimes when they try to be too chummy. He also struck his friends as fairly tolerant of his son when word came back that he'd gotten into another scrape. "His father was always very easygoing," remembers Grable. "We'd be out late drinking beer, fooling around, and the next day he'd say, 'You guys had a good time last night,' and give you a little wink, letting you know that he knew. But never any lecture. My father would have taken my head off, some of the things we did. I think George had a freer hand from his parents than the rest of us had."

In the fall of George's junior year in high school, Fred suffered a cerebral hemorrhage and fell down on the kitchen floor. For a year his speech was severely affected, and soon his oil business died. After that he was never really his old self, not kidding much anymore, prone to become easily emotional. He got part-time work as a superintendent in a cemetery, where he worked out of a little shack and could be seen trimming around the headstones with a lawn mower and now and then helping to set up a burial monument. He also worked occasionally sweeping out a laundromat. George's mother still had her job at Remick's, George remembers, but things got tight now. Uncle George had to begin helping the family out financially. Uncle George liked to help out members of the family. After his and Fred's father died in 1952, he'd send his mother on vacations to Boothbay Harbor in Maine. He'd helped his sister, Aunt Jenny, buy a house. When his nephew Bobby, George's cousin, came home from being in the army in Germany and started working in the banking business, Uncle George gave him the down payment for a house for his young family; young bankers, he felt, shouldn't have to live in an apartment. After Marie and Otis got married, and Otis started graduate school at Michigan State University, Marie came to Uncle George. She'd been supporting them with a teaching job, but now she was pregnant and had to quit; they needed help or Otis would have to leave school. "I remember him saying, 'Otis has too good a mind to let it go to waste,'" says Auntie Gertrude. "And so he sent the money for tuition."

By the end of his junior year George needed to confront the fact that he was in serious trouble as far as going to college was concerned. Athletic recruiters from both the University of Massachusetts and Springfield College, the sports school that he'd long dreamed of attending, had discussed offering him a scholarship on the basis of his discus prowess. But he still had to pass the admissions standards when it came to grades, and during his sophomore and junior years he'd accumulated a record of six D's and six C's. His only B was in mechanical drawing.

George wanted so desperately to go on to college that in his senior year he made a heroic effort to improve his academic standing. For one, he got himself into the "general" class in English, an all-boys unit that served as a refuge for students who had problems with Miss Toomey and other grammar hardballers. It was taught by Clem Horrigan, a retired naval commander like Uncle George, but there the similarity stopped short. Silver-haired, with the rosy nose of a hearty drinker, Horrigan was plain-spoken in ways not then common in public high schools. He was in the habit, for instance, of giving colleagues the finger when he wished to make a point during faculty meetings, and endearing himself to the guys in his class by referring to fellow teachers as "assholes" and "fairies." "Horrigan was not your traditional-type teacher, but he was very effective," says Buzzy Knight, who was on the faculty then. "He had a wonderful sense of humor, and in class he could butter up a story so you'd be living it rather than just reading about it."

Horrigan lived in a sea captain's house overlooking Weymouth Landing, and he encouraged George and Malcolm and Mike Grable and Frank Shea and the other guys to come by on Friday nights, when he would sip his Scotch, tell them navy stories, and talk about Jack London and Ernest Hemingway. "He was really a wonderful man," recalls George, who honors few of the adults he ever knew with a compliment. "He tried to give you knowledge without making you feel insecure about it." In school, his assignments ran more toward Nordhoff and Hall than Shakespeare, and "if you wrote a composition," says George, "he'd say you had great ideas here, but not much grammar. But that was okay, because when you grow up and become a writer, they had people to put the grammar in, secretaries, people like that."

Whether or not it was Horrigan's approach that lifted George's spirits, certainly something made a difference that year, because his scholastic record took a big jump upward. Besides the not-too-unrespectable C he managed to get in physics, he ended up with a B in English, another B in economics, and an A in Problems of Democracy. In fact, that final spring he made it to the dean's list, truly a flabbergasting event for any of the faculty who'd encountered George in the other years. "I remember, Jack Fisher called me in and said, 'What's this, George, a mistake?' Then he said, 'You know, George, have you ever heard the expression a day late and a dollar short?'"

Fisher's assessment, unfortunately, was all too correct, in that George's smashing finish did not quite obliterate the general dismalness of his high school record. His first SAT scores, from the tests he had taken in the spring of his junior year, were less than stellar—a total of just over 600, out of a possible 1,600, on the math and verbal combined. He did have one more chance the following fall to take the SATs again, which is when he thought of enlisting the help of his best pal, Malcolm MacGregor. Malcolm had scored a perfect 1,600 the previous spring, even without much sleep the night before, and thought that sufficient to get him into his first-choice college, which was Worcester Polytechnic Institute. So he had no reason to take the tests again. And he didn't—at least not under his own name. In a fit of ill-advised friendship, he agreed to go into the testing room that Saturday morning in the fall, take the SAT, and forge George's signature. And it could well have worked. Indeed, Malcolm finished fifteen minutes early, and there was no challenge when he left by the outside proctor hired to monitor the exam, who didn't know George or Malcolm from a Pygmy warrior. But Malcolm forgot to do one thing. For some reason, possibly a Freudian explanation, it never occurred to him to lard the test with any purposeful mistakes, at least enough so George's scores turning up this time at the Springfield College admissions office wouldn't add up to a perfect 1,600.

The unraveling of the scheme occurred swiftly enough. At Springfield, the admissions officer took one look at the thousand-point difference and called down to Mr. Wallace L. Whittle, then the principal of Weymouth High School. Whittle knew enough about George to become overwhelmed with doubt concerning the validity of the startling improvement, and called in George and his parents to wring out the truth. He also called in Malcolm and his parents and informed them that he was going to have to notify Worcester Tech about their son's lapse of judgment. In the end Malcolm's father had to perform fancy feats of influence to keep his son from getting deleted from the acceptance list. As for George, for all the effort he'd put into his courses that year, the principal allowed him to graduate on schedule in spite of everything. But college certainly was out, at least for the next year. And although he listed himself optimistically in the 1961 edition of *Campus*, the school yearbook, as heading off into a career of "business administration," George's immediate prospects did not appear too bright.

Uncle George, on hearing about the unfortunate situation, did step in and offer to help. For all his faults, his nephew was still family, after all. In a telephone call to Fred, he said that as an engineer for the state of Massachusetts he was not without influence in certain places, and it might just be possible to find George employment. He knew some people down at the Boston Edison power plant, the one located on the line between Weymouth and Quincy, and it might be arranged, just might, for George to get work at the plant as a floor sweeper. Informed of the offer, George replied to his father that he didn't feel of a mind to accept the job. Indeed, Uncle George could take the fucking sweeper job and ram it right up his ass, was what he could do with it. George would rather go out and see what he could pick up on his own.

TWO

Manhattan Beach

1967–1968

I'd be safe and warm,
If I was in L.A.
California Dreamin'
on such a winter's day.
—THE MAMAS & THE PAPAS, "CALIFORNIA DREAMIN'," 1966

FROM JUST ABOUT ANYWHERE IN MANHATTAN BEACH you can look out between the houses and see the Pacific Ocean washing up along the broad expanse of sand that runs from one end of town to the other. Some local historians say the town got its name from a land developer from New York in the first decade of the twentieth century who wished to memorialize his hometown; others believe that it came from a rich lady of Dutch ancestry in honor of the fact that her forebears had been in on the deal to buy Manhattan Island from the Indians. Whatever the case, Manhattan, the beach, twenty miles southwest of downtown Los Angeles, with a population of 32,500 souls, bears as little resemblance to its namesake back East as any other coastal city in Southern California. Its soft pastel frame-and-stucco houses line a series of terraced streets that work their way up to the top of a sand hill sitting 245 feet above sea level, allowing each resident a wide glimpse of the ocean over a neighboring rooftop. In the early days the dunes of Manhattan Beach supported so little vegetation that they'd shift about from the winds. To stabilize the place, ladies from the Neptunian Club took to planting the dunes with mossy green ice plants that now abound everywhere, thus earning them the name "moss ladies." During the summer the town is cooled by the prevailing westerlies that blow off the water and in the evening fill the air with the perfume of hibiscus and night-blooming jasmine. Most of the time the winds also manage to blow the looming pall of brownish-yellow smog from the freeways back into the inner recesses of Los Angeles proper, leaving the local atmosphere clear and dry. Considering its location and its weather, the local chamber of commerce needed little poetic license to promote the town in its tourist brochure as truly "a little bit of heaven on earth."

As with the neighboring beach towns—El Segundo, Hermosa, Redondo, Palos Verdes, Santa Monica, Venice, San Pedro—it was World War II that spurred the real growth in Manhattan Beach, which for the course of the conflict played host to a pair of eight-inch railroad guns operated a little to the east of town by the men of Shore Battery E from New Jersey. The guns created such an uproar during artillery practice that a warden had to warn housewives beforehand to take their heirloom china down from the display cabinets. Since the only local action came on Christmas Eve of 1941, when a Japanese submarine snuck up the 245-fathom deep Catalina ship channel and torpedoed a schooner carrying a load of lumber, the boys of Battery E had a pretty soft billet; and a goodly number, like many other soldiers who came through the state, decided after V-J Day that what awaited them back in New Jersey didn't stack up so well compared to what they'd seen of California.

Manhattan Beach also stood right next to the burgeoning Los Angeles International Airport, which meant you could get in and out of the place quickly. But more to the point, it meant the town served as home base for the people who worked out of the airport, notably some one thousand nubile young airline stewardesses, who in short order made it into the reigning party town of the southern coast. "You've got to remember that in the 1960s you didn't have the kind of labor laws you have now, where the stewardesses can be sixty years old and ugly and weigh three hundred pounds," says Frank Yamamoto, a Berkeley graduate who in those days ran a restaurant, three doors up from the beach. "The airlines were a glamorous business. Everyone who was flying had money, and if you wanted to work for the airlines, you had to be really good-looking, and you had to have good boobs."

So from cock's crow to evensong the beach teemed with gorgeous women stuffed into bikinis of every variety, lying out on the sand, bouncing up and down around the volleyball nets, eyeing the ranks of surfers shooting toward shore on the eight-foot curlers. Bars and restaurants lined the approach streets; at night people jammed into the Buccaneer or Pancho's or Cisco's, a large rock-and-roll emporium owned by the Smothers Brothers. After closing time the parties came to life in the apartments off the strand where the "stewies" lived three and four together, loaded up with pot and free booze from the airlines. On Sunday afternoons the golden hordes repaired to an open terrace at Mike's Restaurant at the end of Manhattan Beach Boulevard to drink beer and dance and watch the surfers slalom in and out of the pilings underneath the town pier, while Mike "the Greek" slathered coats of his special barbecue sauce over the 75-pound lamb turning slowly on a spit. "I tell you, it was a very hedonistic situation," says Yamamoto, who eventually parlayed his restaurant into a large set of real-estate holdings. "This town was just one big nonstop fucking party all day and all night."

George showed up in Manhattan Beach in the summer of 1967, an occasion he soon regarded as one of the uneclipsable events of his life. "Coming from Weymouth, I thought somebody had dropped me out of an airplane and I'd landed in paradise," he says. He was twenty-five years old then, and was distinguished in town by his broad Boston accent, his great-looking muscles, and his shaggy hair made blond in the California sun, enhancing his luminous hazel-green eyes. That was the year when, among other events, Dustin Hoffman appeared in *The Graduate*, when the Mamas and the Papas came out with "Monday, Monday," and the Rolling Stones were singing "Ruby Tuesday." It was the year the jails were beginning to fill up with young people protesting against the Vietnam War, and it was when Timothy Leary issued his famous call to a Gathering of the Tribes summoned to San Francisco by Allen Ginsberg and Jerry Rubin, which was to "Turn on to the scene. Tune in to what is happening, and drop out." It was also the year George Jung looked at the diminishing legitimate opportunities open to him in his yearning to acquire wealth and esteem and decided the best chance for someone of his talents and brashness lay somewhere in the upper echelons of the burgeoning marijuana business.

In the six years since he'd graduated high school George had achieved little in the way of personal success. Stuck in Weymouth, and needing to earn money and to find a college that would have him, he ended up going to work as a bricklayer's helper for his old baby-sitter, Russell Delorey. The work itself, carrying hods of bricks and mixing mortar, seemed made to order for George, who could pick up two 94-pound bags of Portland cement, raise them over his head, and if need be, walk around like that all afternoon. "George had such great strength and endurance for physical work," Russell wrote in a little memoir of the period, "that I began to refer to him as the Crane." George also proved a valuable asset in the area of customer relations. Once, when Russell found himself getting stiffed by a contractor after installing a Tennessee-marble fireplace in one of his houses, he simply told the contractor that if he didn't get paid for the fireplace, he would take it back. "Whereupon I told George to get the two 16-pound sledgehammers from my truck, and we proceeded to crash the entire marble fireplace onto the new hardwood floor. We ruined the living room floor, the walls, the ceiling, the baseboard heating system, and wood trim. The dispute was finally resolved, but the news of our confrontation traveled around the Cape, and people got the message: Don't attempt holding up payment on Delorey, especially when the Crane is available."

In the fall of 1962, after a not-very-taxing review by the admissions office, George began college life as a matriculated freshman at the University of Southern Mississippi, located in Hattiesburg, in the sultry southeastern part of the state. "The word got around," he recalls, "that this particular college was a shithole going nowhere, but it was an easy place to get into and that that's where you could go if you were a fuck-up." He started off with mixed results, but by the spring, having scored two B's, with an A in Introduction to Business, George found himself on the dean's list.

It was the environment at the school that caused George some discomfort. The dorms were always oppressively hot and sticky. And one of the Saturday-night social activities among the fraternity boys was to get blitzed on beer, take up broom handles and other kinds of clubs, and proceed down to the area of town that ran along the Bowie River where the black people lived and engage in the

sport known to the locals as "nigger knocking." Growing up in
Weymouth, where there wasn't a single black student in the high
school, George had little reason to give any thought, one way or the
other, to the general racial situation in the country. But on the one
occasion at Mississippi when he went along to watch the fun—swat-
ting black people from behind out of the car window—the spectacle
so repelled him that he began sounding off on the subject around
the campus. After all, Jack Kerouac would never have countenanced
anything like that. He noised off so loudly and often enough that
one night a friendly bartender in a student hangout warned George
and his date to beat it out the back way, because waiting in the front
parking lot was a crowd of white boys who intended to beat the shit
out of him.

He eventually left school, but not because of racial intolerance.
Seeking to augment his funds from bricklaying, he had gotten hold
of a corporate telephone credit card from a friend back in Weymouth and began touring the college dorms selling long-distance
phone calls for five dollars apiece to boys who wanted to talk, sometimes for hours, with their girlfriends back home, a scam that
earned him forty to fifty dollars a night. So the calls couldn't be easily traced, he warned customers to ring up their girls only at pay
phones. But not everyone followed the directions conscientiously,
and pretty soon George got caught. To keep the offended corporation from pressing charges, his father had to send down somewhere
around a thousand dollars in payback money, which, much to his
embarrassment, Fred had to get from Uncle George. The school
suspended George for six months, which was why, when the news
came that John F. Kennedy had been shot, George remembers he
was back on a scaffold, passing bricks up to Russell, who was finishing off an ornamental rim on the top of a chimney in North Weymouth.

George picked up his old ways and his old friends, including
MacGregor, who much to his parents' annoyance had gotten suspended from Worcester Tech after a drinking incident. Shortly
afterward he and George took a couple of girls out in a little cherry-
red Austin-Healey George had bought with extra money earned
from digging clams off Wessagussett Beach. With everyone drunk
as usual, Malcolm totaled the car by driving it four-square into the
rear end of a parked vehicle outside a house in downtown Worcester. One girl suffered a broken arm, and George had his ear nearly

torn off. As the boys were furiously getting rid of the evidence, throwing the beer cans and bottles over a hedge before the police could arrive, a middle-aged gentleman in a white shirt and tie suddenly appeared demanding to know just what the hell was going on. Who was he? George asked belligerently. "I live here," the man responded, "and that's my yard where you're throwing the liquor bottles and beer cans, and this is what's left of my car you just ran into. That's who I am."

Nothing George or Malcolm did, however, could compare to the high level of chaos that attended any appearance on the scene by a boy named Waino Tuominen, or "Tuna." A former classmate of theirs at Weymouth High, Tuna was of Finnish extraction, had a short, barrellike physique, and possessed a resilient set of teeth, which he regularly employed for everyone's amusement in removing the caps off beer bottles. On nearly every occasion George and his friends gathered, Tuna could be depended upon to end the evening with some notable flourish. When the police, following up on complaints from angry neighbors, would show up to dampen the noise level at one of these parties, Tuna would slide into the idling cruiser while the cops were in the house and drive it down the road apiece, then return to the party via backyards in the neighborhood, forcing the officers to seek help from headquarters in finding their lost vehicle. Tuna was rarely seen to have a date. This was the consequence, no doubt, of one of his less resistible impulses, which was to drop his pants after a sufficient number of drinks and as a grand finale to the evening jump out from somewhere—a curtain, a door—with a beer bottle dangling on a string tied to his penis.

Not long after yet another near-fatal accident—a five-car pileup on the Southeast Expressway—and with his family's full encouragement, George and Tuna, who by now had received his own suspension notice from the University of Colorado for taking off his clothes in a girls' dormitory, acquired a 1963 black TR-3 with red upholstery and a white top, jammed their belongings into the tiny trunk, and in the winter of 1965 set out to see if living in California would have a positive effect on their lives.

The trip across the country was remarkably free of any run-ins or incidents, and when they got to Long Beach, just outside of Los Angeles, George and Tuna were put up for a while by George's ex-boss, Russell Delorey. Russell had put aside his bricklaying business

the year before and with a friend from Weymouth had also journeyed to California, where he was attending Long Beach City College, taking some business courses with the hope, unfulfilled as it
would turn out, of getting into the advertising game.

George soon moved to nearby Belmont Shores, took history
and philosophy courses at Long Beach City College—more to look
like a student than to be one—and hung out on the beach, where he
ran rapidly through dozens of girlfriends. "The girls were driving
me crazy—they were all over the beaches, in the supermarket, on
the sidewalks, wearing these little string bikinis, everywhere you
looked there were asses and tits hanging out. I had this feeling that I
wanted to make it with every woman that walked the streets." Exercising the social leadership skills he was known for back home,
George soon became king of the beach. At one point he organized a
contest in which the person with the best tan by the end of the
semester would be crowned with suitable fanfare as King of the Sun
Gods. He concocted a mixture of iodine and baby oil to enhance his
own tan, and of course, he won. Weekends, he and Tuna would venture down to Mexico, often getting into one minor scrape or
another. On one occasion they were thrown out of a bullfight in
Mazatlán after George got sick drinking tequila in the hot sun and
threw up all over the two people sitting in front of him, who turned
out to be the mayor of the city and his wife.

George's first fling at legitimate entrepreneurship involved
going in with a friend to buy a load of huaraches, the rubber-soled
sandals with leather straps, down in Mexico, and setting up dealer-
ships at colleges all across the country. In exchange for peddling the
sandals the students could earn bonus points toward free vacations
in Tijuana. The scheme languished after they made the mistake of
seeking help from college administrators, who saw the business as
counterproductive to their academic mission. Eventually George
quit school and got a full-time job with a pile-driving crew for
twelve dollars an hour plus overtime—good pay in the mid-1960s;
the job required him to sit up in a little crow's nest holding on to the
top of a five-and-a-half-ton, one-hundred-foot-high I-beam to
steady it while a giant steam hammer beat it into the ground. A one-
inch miss on the part of the hammer driver, and George's hands,
arms, and maybe some other important parts would have been only
memories.

Just about everyone George knew was involved in some way in

the drug business, as consumers or retailers, and George himself filled a steady part of his leisure time smoking dope. As someone who had never even smoked cigarettes, he found the crude marijuana joints so harsh at first that he had to filter the pot through a water pipe filled with ice cubes and crème de menthe. He got the hang of it soon enough, however, and before long he was smoking it every day. Then, at a wedding reception in Long Beach, he ran into a dentist who brought him back to his houseboat—replete with stained-glass windows and psychedelic posters on the ceiling—and gave him a tab of LSD.

One hit of "orange sunshine" while sitting on the dentist's couch and George knew that the sensations he'd been eliciting from pot and alcohol were ragged and paltry compared to what he was now experiencing. "Suddenly," he says, "I could see with a pill what the Dalai Lama sits for ten years in a cave to find out." The LSD gave him X-ray vision into his physical surroundings, and he and Tuna, who took to LSD like a pussy to catnip, would do things like hang around the local Baskin-Robbins shop, staring fixedly into the tubs of different-colored ice cream. More significantly, George found that under the influence he could now chat with God, ask the Man what was in store for the universe. "What it did was to take away my ego. It made me realize the unimportance of the self. I knew what my place was in the universe and that life was eternal, that there was no such thing as death, and you would live forever." But for George, the true value of LSD had to do with sex. "When you had an orgasm on acid, it was like the whole universe exploding. It would take about forty-five minutes for the acid to come on, and then you were in for an eighteen-hour journey, where the orgasms were intensified ten times. Ha! You don't think that's a good time?"

Hot on the trail of love and visions, George began taking acid virtually every day and in all forms—little BB-size "barrels," triangle-shaped red and pink "wedges," the stuff known as "white lightning," which was laced with Methedrine and came on with the force of a freight train. The more acid you dropped, of course, the more risk you ran of embarking on a bad trip. This happened once to George in the fall of 1967, after he arrived in Manhattan Beach and was living with his new girlfriend, Julie, a pretty brunette who ran a dress boutique in town and whose father owned department stores in Albuquerque and El Paso. George and several others were sitting around watching the surfers out the window, listening to the new Beatles record, *Sgt. Pepper's Lonely Hearts Club Band*, and after four hits of white lightning the music started to blur and whine; George looked around and noticed that all the people in the room had turned into monkeys. Leaving the apartment to get a little air, shake it off, he went into the streets of Manhattan Beach to find that the whole town had been struck by bombs. It looked like Berlin at the end of World War II, its buildings with gaping windows and the roofs gone. Everything was frosted over, glazed with a thin layer of ice, all white. The telephone wires were also coated in ice and began to sing with an increasingly unbearable screech, which George described as the noise of a million telephone conversations going all at once. He lost himself in the back alleys of the town. A fog descended, and it seemed like days before he made it back to the apartment. When he got there, George ran into the bedroom and hid under the covers until the visions faded away.

Tuna, meanwhile, had developed a nice little business supplying LSD to a local chapter of the Hell's Angels and was living with a snake dancer who kept her boa constrictor in a box in their bedroom. But one day down in Tijuana Tuna disappeared altogether during an acid trip. George had last seen him walking out of town on the railroad tracks, staring down at the ties, doing a Dean Moriarty act from *On the Road*, heading north toward the border and never looking back. The next time George saw him was in 1970 back in Weymouth, where he'd gone for a quick visit. There was Tuna, working on the grounds crew at South Shore Hospital, riding a mower around the lawn. "Hello, George," he said, as if three years had not gone by. Tuna was vague about what he'd been doing, George recalls, other than to say he had only recently emerged from his bedroom where he'd locked himself in for a long time, afraid to go out on the street.

In Manhattan Beach, George rented a house with a front-yard pool, three blocks up the hill from the beach. On weekends the gang—the women in long, straight hair and bare feet, dressed in shifts, with flowers painted on their faces—would get a bag of dope, a jug of wine laced with acid, and head for the Shrine Auditorium in Los Angeles to hear Country Joe and the Fish, or up to the Fillmore in San Francisco for Jefferson Airplane concerts, featuring Grace Slick. Invariably, one of the band members would christen the show, throwing out handfuls of LSD, like stardust, into the crowd, creating a pandemonium. For sure, George told himself, not much of this stuff was going on back in Weymouth. This was the youth of America living out the true American Dream, getting all the spiritual guidance they needed from Bob Dylan and effecting an overnight transformation in their lives. Take Lawrence, a friend of George's who had arrived in Manhattan Beach from Baltimore. One day Lawrence had been slogging away at his job as a rag salesman in the garment business, and the next he'd traded in his suit and tie for a white robe, had pink flowers plaited into his hair, and walked the streets calling people brother, talking about God, feeding himself and his Irish Setter on rice balls and processed seaweed.

For a while George fancied putting his own life on the track toward becoming a famous Hollywood star and even began taking acting classes conducted by the character actor Ed Begley. George had been encouraged in this by a friend of Lawrence's, another guy out from Baltimore, who was trying to break into the screenwriting business. His name was Barry Levinson, which didn't impress anyone at the time, since he hadn't yet written or directed *Diner*, *Avalon*, or *Good Morning, Vietnam*. George rented him a room in his house, where in the daylight hours Barry sat in front of the TV watching sitcoms and soaps, tapping out notes on a portable typewriter. At night he and George would go to their acting class. The drill was to assume roles of different characters and improvise scenes illustrating their personalities. George did pretty well as long as he could act gangster parts or tough guys. One day the instructor, saying George was getting too narrow and needed to expand his repertoire, gave him a part to perform that put him a little beyond his range. He was to be a homosexual, going on this long-distance bus ride, and to show how it would look if he tried to come on to that cute guy in the next seat. Well, maybe not acting, George thought.

Like a lot of other dope smokers, George had already been dabbling in the selling game—buying two bags, smoking up one, selling the other for enough to get two more. Although in the late sixties possession of more than just one marijuana cigarette was classified as a felony-level crime in California, you had to be heavily stupid or pretty unlucky to get busted for dealing dope in Manhattan Beach. The police department consisted of fewer than forty men, only one of them assigned to narcotics. He was a thirty-one-year-old detective named Fred McKewen, who had no budget for launching undercover operations and whose face was known from two hundred yards away by every drug dealer in town. It was a lonely job, McKewen recalls. "I'd get calls from other police agencies working cases in the Manhattan Beach area asking to talk to our narcotics bureau, and I'd say, 'You are.'" Considering also that he had a load of thirty or forty other nondrug cases to follow, from gas station run-outs to murder, it was no wonder Detective McKewen never got a very big handle on what was going on in the Manhattan Beach drug scene.

Most of the busts he did manage to log came thanks to the luck he had playing a little ruse with parking tickets. When McKewen got the name of a suspected pot dealer, for instance, from a snitch or from the talk on the street, he would run it through the traffic bureau looking for unpaid tickets. "In Manhattan Beach the parking is so bad it's not unusual for people to have one or two warrants against them, and if you're a lazy-type guy, you don't pay them. So if I saw where you had an eleven-dollar warrant, which is what they were then, I'd take that and go to your house. I'd knock on your door and say, 'I'm from the police department, I've got a traffic warrant for your arrest, and I'm going to have to take you into custody.' Nine and a half times out of ten I'd be invited into the house while whoever it was went upstairs to get the money. Now that I'm in the house, there was so much marijuana around it was not unusual for some to be lying out on the coffee table. You didn't need a search warrant in those days, so literally, if I saw one marijuana cigarette on the coffee table, your whole house belonged to me." When suspects started confessing their sins, Detective McKewen, in this pre-Miranda era, wasn't obliged to interrupt and advise them that they had a right to get a lawyer before they spilled their guts like this. "If you were a smart drug dealer, you paid your parking tickets, because that's how I made a lot of cases."

By 1967 marijuana was fairly streaming across the Mexican border into California, secreted in hollowed-out surfboards, hidden in false bottoms of bulk gas tanks, stowed under the floorboards of VW campers, in the engine compartments of sailboats. One notable smuggler even paid people to bring it over a desert border crossing at night in a caravan of electric golf carts. But until George entered the picture, the pot runs usually involved a lot of little people bringing in small quantities, rather than large shipping operations. The biggest bust McKewen helped make during those days was a hugely complicated, multidepartment effort involving only fifty kilos of pot. It had been purchased by American smugglers in Tijuana and driven over the border at Chula Vista in the trunk of a car bristling with fishing poles, spear guns, and other vacation camouflage. McKewen and the fifty or so other state and local cops involved in the operation had planned to follow the car up to Manhattan Beach to find out how the dope was going to be distributed. U.S. Customs, in a departure from normal policy, agreed to allow the shipment to go through the border untouched, but only if the local police promised to arrest the smugglers before any of the dope hit the street. Driving up on Route 5, however, the smugglers broke a water hose just north of San Diego and had to pull over to the side of the road. Not wanting to spoil their surveillance plan, the whole cavalcade of about thirty unmarked police cars drove right by the stalled vehicle, pulled off at the next exit, and came back going the opposite way, circling their prey like Indians around a wagon train. "We drove around them for three hours before they finally got the damn hose fixed," says McKewen.

By late in 1967 George had given up the pile-driving business and gone into the pot trade in earnest. On the wholesale market in Manhattan Beach he'd pay sixty dollars for a kilo-size brick, or 2.2 pounds, break it into thirty-five 1-ounce bags, and move those on the street for ten dollars apiece. If he did 10 kilos a month, and performed all the chores himself, George could make a profit of nearly three thousand dollars, this in the days when fifteen to twenty thousand dollars a year could support a family of four without too much scrimping. Through the stewardesses he knew and all the other California friends he'd made during the previous two and a half years, George soon found he could sell pot as fast as he could wrap it up and move it out. To expand the business, however, he now had to tie in with bigger suppliers. "The way I saw it," he says, "being in the drug business was like being an executive in any business: If you wanted to climb the ladder, you sought out people and pursued those who were better and bigger than you were, and you tried to ingratiate yourself. Then you find they're not as big as you thought they were, and so you go beyond them, and before you know it they're working for you. Anyway, that's the way I wanted it to work."

The person George needed to get friendly with was an ex-marine-turned-hairdresser by the name of Richard Barile, another refugee from the East and the lynchpin of the local drug culture. Only five feet two inches tall, with a receding hairline, Richard had dark eyebrows and a dense black beard that put one in mind of the characters in *Planet of the Apes*. He talked rapidly in a clipped Connecticut accent and avoided eye contact, looking off a lot. Barile was the son of a contractor in Branford, outside New Haven. After leaving the Marine Corps, he'd gotten a job as a conductor on the old New York, New Haven & Hartford Railroad, which allowed him to take free train trips across the country during his vacations. On one such trip the train eventually stopped at Manhattan Beach, where Barile got off and began looking around for something to do that would keep him in California. Back home an aunt and a brother-in-law were in the beauty-parlor business, so he decided to use his benefits under the G.I. Bill and go to hairdressing school. After eighteen months of perming women's hair at a local shop, he opened up a place of his own two blocks up the hill from the beach, the first unisex hair salon in town. He called it the Tonsorial Parlor.

Trained in the art of layering and shaping women's hair, Barile became a huge hit with the guys in Manhattan Beach, since long hair was fast becoming the style and just about the only way the old-time barbers knew to attack it was to shear it off. He also provided special services to special customers. For the airline pilots he fashioned straight-arrow wigs and tie-up jobs so they could keep their long hair for the beach parties but tuck it under their hats to pass the company's grooming inspection. He did the same for guys in the marijuana trade, who needed to clean up their appearances before going on a business trip south of the border, where the sight of long hair and ponytails registered in the minds of the Federales the same as if they'd had a sign on them saying ARREST ME.

For Barile, then, drug smuggling turned out to be a naturally coterminous extension of the hair game—like the old-time coal dealers who in summer got into selling ice—and he designed his shop in a way that seemed to nod approvingly at the outlaw's way of life. Paneled in old barn wood and decorated in a western motif, the walls were hung with portraits of famous bandits—Butch Cassidy and the Sundance Kid, Jesse and Frank James, John Wesley Hardin. The two cutting rooms at the Tonsorial Parlor were closed off by swinging doors so people in the back could converse without being seen from the street. There was a pool table in the front waiting room and benches out on the sidewalk, both of which invited people to loiter, discuss ideas, make plans.

Pretty soon the activities at the Tonsorial Parlor moved from the talking stage to something more concrete. "At first I'd just be doing people a favor, let them use the telephone, give them a place to hang out, or I'd know someone who wanted to buy some pot and I'd introduce them," Barile recalls. "Soon friends would be dropping off a couple of kilos of pot, and I'd hold them for them, and they'd sell ounces out of the barbershop. Then if someone needed a pilot or a place to stash something, whatever anyone needed, I had the connections, because through the business I knew everyone and they trusted me. Before I knew it, I was putting all three things together. But I was just doing it to be a good Samaritan, I wasn't making any money. So one day I said, the hell with this, man, I should really get in on the bandwagon here. And I did, and I became very successful at it."

Hearing the talk on the street, of course, Sergeant McKewen got wind that something was going on with Barile and the Tonsorial Parlor that didn't have to do with hair. But never during that period, nor in the decade following, when Barile would routinely pull off cocaine sales in the millions of dollars, did McKewen get even close to making an arrest. "Everyone knew Richard was involved, but it was tough to make a case on him," he says. "He was a very brazen guy, but he was clever. He never got caught because he was always careful never to be around where the drugs were. They might have been his drugs, but he wasn't the guy standing next to them if there was ever a bust."

George first walked into the Tonsorial Parlor for a haircut in August of 1967, and Barile remembers the occasion well. "He was friendly, looked like a Robert Redford dude, hair over the collar but not to the shoulder. 'Hey, come on, let's take some acid and go down the beach.' That was George. He brought friends around, they'd sit on the bench outside, just hang out. He was very friendly because of course he knew I had the potential to help him out."

So it was that George started getting his pot supply directly from Barile—not directly, actually, because the way Barile set it up he did everything through other people. He had someone else rent different stash houses for him, and when he heard of a load coming in, twenty-five or fifty kilos, he would arrange to get it delivered to one of his houses. Then, if George wanted five or ten kilos out of

that, Richard had someone pick it up from the stash house and meet
with George to transfer the goods. With his supply assured, George
now wanted to expand his market. He didn't want to keep ouncing
the stuff on the street. Not only was it bothersome getting together
all those bags, but to maintain his profit level he needed to make a
lot of little sales and deal with a lot of potheads—not the most discreet, levelheaded population group. Word of his operation could
easily reach the ears of Sergeant McKewen. Wholesaling seemed to
be the way to go.

Early in the fall of 1967, fortune struck in the form of George's
old friend and classmate at Weymouth High School, Frank Shea.
Shea and his girlfriend were on their way back to the University of
Massachusetts from summer jobs waiting on tables. Visiting George
overnight, he noticed a kilo of grass sitting out in a punch bowl on a
sideboard in the living room. It was all broken up, with the junk
sifted out so that you could just reach in and make a joint. And the
quality struck Frank as better than anything he could get back East.
"'Jesus Christ,' he said, 'where'd you get this stuff?'" George told
him the price and described how easy it was to get good drugs out
here. Shea said that back in Amherst, where the market consisted of
students from the University of Massachusetts, Mount Holyoke,
Smith, Hampshire, and Amherst—a group of schools known as the
Five-College Consortium—pot was selling wholesale for more than
three hundred dollars a kilo, six times what Richard Barile charged
for it and nearly as much as George was turning it over for in retail.
"When I heard that," George says, "I told Frank, 'Okay, this is it!
We're going into business. Big-time!'"

Which was why it seemed an especially cruel turn that at this
juncture George should receive notification from Uncle Sam that
for all his country had done for him he now had to return the favor
by joining the United States Army. The notice came as a rather
abrupt shock, since George had heretofore been classified 4-F,
thanks to the injury done to his right knee in a scrimmage just
before the Brockton game, when he was creamed by John Hollander. Given the exigencies of the Vietnam War, however, the army
had since widened its parameters of acceptance; so George might
limp a little, but he was going to have to serve the nation in some
capacity. Making the best of a bad situation, he called around and
found out that Uncle Jack down in Baton Rouge knew a general in
the National Guard who could secure George one of the hard-to-

get slots in the California branch of the Guard. In George's eyes, the Guard was punishment enough. "One day I'm stoned on LSD, selling dope, going to the Fillmore, having the time of my life. Then suddenly I'm getting off a bus at Fort Ord, California, and these monkeys are yelling and screaming, 'Get your fucking ass in line.' And you go inside this building and the next thing, there was no hair."

George submitted to eight weeks of basic training, then eight more weeks of advanced infantry training, during which he became a squad leader, and was finally mustered out to report once a month to Guard meetings in Pasadena. That would have been the end of it, except that shortly afterward his unit got a call-up notice. Whether in the army or in the Guard, George was going to Vietnam. Clearly the situation now called for some drastic countermeasures. "When I heard we'd been called up, I knew I had to do something quick, so I went to see a friend of mine in San Francisco, a hippie lawyer. He said, 'All right. Get five pounds of pot. Go to the Holiday Inn and call and tell me what the room is. The police will come over and bust you. I'll make a phone call and get you probation, and they'll kick you out of the army.'" And it all transpired precisely according to plan. Several days after his arrest, George was ordered to come in and see his commanding officer.

"He was sitting there at his desk with a big frown on his face and said, 'I'm sorry to have to tell you this, but I'm getting rid of you. Here's your papers. It's a general discharge. You've been arrested for drugs, turn your shit in, we don't want anything to do with you, you're a disgrace to the unit.'

"I said, 'Gimme those papers. I don't have to turn my shit in. I already threw it all away. I'll see you later.' And I left."

Around this period George had a fortuitous change in girl-friends. At Cisco's one night he met a remarkably beautiful and well-endowed young woman named Annette, who looked like Ali McGraw. She wore loose-fitting chamois vests with no bra, display-ing nearly the whole story of her large-size breasts. Taking her to Mike the Greek's on Sunday afternoons, George had a time clearing a path through the gawking clientele to a table. "When I first saw George, he just mesmerized me," Annette says of her first encounter with the incipient drug entrepreneur. "His sad green eyes, his eyes were very beautiful, and he had blond hair, not tall, but he had really well-developed shoulders. He wore those little hippie glasses, round green granny glasses, like John Lennon had. He was like no one I'd ever met." George talked to her about Aldous Huxley and *Brave New World* (the drug part), and he gave her his Hermann Hesse and Bob Dylan lectures, and also her first acid trip. "And I eventually ended up an extension of him, lost my identity. And I think he screwed every girlfriend I had."

Annette worked as a stewardess for Trans-World Airlines and could carry on and off the plane any amount of luggage she wanted to, without anyone batting an eye. Within a month George had put her to work. The first load consisted of twenty kilos packed into a couple of Samsonite suitcases that Annette agreed to fly for him to Logan Airport in Boston, where Frank Shea met the plane and transported the pot across the state to Amherst in the trunk of a rental car. Business grew in steady fashion; indeed it skyrocketed, and soon smaller wholesalers were putting in orders for ten and fifteen kilos at a time, taking it from the drop point in Amherst up to Stowe, Vermont, back to Cambridge and Boston proper, and out to the Cape. Before winter was over, the meager transportation capacity of the commercial airlines was causing a bottleneck in the supply line. Where's the stuff? people were shouting to George. When can you get more?

So George jacked up the scale a peg and began renting out Winnebagos for between $250 and $300 a week, using them to move greater quantities, up to 125 kilos, or 275 pounds, at once, on marathon cross-country drives. With a helper to keep the vehicle on the road twenty-four hours a day, George could make the trip in about sixty hours going flat out—no motels, no showers, eating in the cab. To avoid detection in case he got caught for some traffic violation, George paid a carpenter in Manhattan Beach—"the magic carpenter," he dubbed him—to construct a removable plywood bulkhead across the bathtub section in the RV's bathroom compartment, making the space look as if it contained only a sink, shower stall, and toilet. George stored the pot in back of the bulkhead, which he faced with a full-length mirror. To find the pot, one would have to know it was there and take apart the Winnebago to prove it.

Depending on the quality of the marijuana and the prices he negotiated at both ends, George was taking in anywhere from $10,000 up to $30,000 or so each trip, which meant that, after paying Richard and his helpers and deducting expenses, he was netting on average $5,000 to $10,000 for himself. This was when a brand new Ford Thunderbird like the one George was soon squiring Annette around in cost only $4,600, when a year at an Ivy League college, including room, board, tuition, and books, cost under $5,000, and when for $50,000 you could pick up a five-story brownstone in Manhattan. In addition to raking in the money, George now was treated as some kind of visiting hero each time the Winnebago pulled up in Amherst. While they waited around for the shipment to get sold, George and Annette and sometimes a small retinue of friends would put up at the gracious Lord Jeffrey Inn, order a log fire lit in their room to take off the chill, and quaffed drinks down in the bar with the Amherst alumni. "There were movie stars, and there were rock stars, so now we were the pot stars," George says. "And we were whacking out the whole campus."

George kept up this routine for five or six months more, until May or so, the mud season in Amherst, when the spring grass gets thick and the ground spongy and the lilacs and apple blossoms appear. Then he started making more calculations concerning the future of his booming business. The main thing he was thinking now was, why spend money on the middlemen in Manhattan Beach—the wholesalers who bought the pot that was shipped over the border, the smugglers who did the shipping—when you could go down into Mexico yourself and buy the stuff directly, from the growers? He'd heard prices like twenty-five dollars, fifteen, even ten dollars a kilo down there; he could sell that for three hundred dollars in Amherst, net out the whole difference himself. "We were making a lot of money, but I knew we could make a hell of a lot more," he says. "So Frank and I started thinking, why can't we get our own fucking airplane and go down to Mexico and get it ourselves? Then we can make this into something *really* good."

It was sometime around then, in early summer 1968, that the people in Manhattan Beach began referring to George Jacob Jung by a title more befitting a character of his stature, success—and accent. They started calling him "Boston George."

THREE

Puerto Vallarta

1968–1970

I kept telling them, "If we stay together, we'll be like a fist and have power. Every man contributes to the fist, and the fist is forever, like a brotherhood."

—GEORGE JUNG

THERE WERE VARIOUS WAYS TO SMUGGLE MARIJUANA into the States from Mexico. The quickest, easiest way, but also the riskiest, was simply to drive the stuff across the border hidden somewhere in a VW camper or a pick-up truck. Boats were pretty good, as long as they stayed at sea; the difficulty lay in locating a part of the coastline to put ashore at that was deserted enough so a cargo could be discharged without attracting attention. The safest method was just to walk the load in—lugging duffel bags over a desert crossing point at night and stashing them on the U.S. side to pick up later with a camper or jeep. But although this technique served well when a few pounds were involved, it required a considerable amount of schlepping as the load approached a half ton or more, which was the scale George was thinking on. And it just didn't fit well with those visions of Hemingway running with the bulls in Pamplona or Jack London shooting down the Whitehorse rapids on the Yukon. (George had been three or four times up to the Valley of the Moon, north of San Francisco, to see the shell of London's burnt-out house that Mr. Horrigan used to talk about back in high school.) No, the way to go here was definitely the air route. George would fly the stuff in by plane, and he would do it himself.

The choice certainly recommended itself as the best way not to get caught. Charter companies weren't yet in the habit of asking many questions about what the plane might be used for or where it was going. There were no such things as AWACs monitoring the skies over the border, and it was easy to stay below radar range to avoid random detection. Flying was also fast and efficient: You could land at a deserted airstrip or in a field somewhere, transfer the load to a waiting truck, and be back in the air within minutes.

As George shortly found out, learning to fly was the easiest part of the scheme. Within a month, after thirty hours of instruction at the Santa Monica Airport, George had qualified to fly solo by "VFR," or visual flying rules. This meant no fancy aeronautics; he could fly only in the daylight, and could not do anything that required an instrument rating or knowledge of radar. He'd learned just enough to get a single-engine plane moving fast down the runway and into the air, navigate by dead reckoning, put the thing back on the ground in one piece, and turn off the engine. As for the airplane, he planned on chartering a single-engine Piper Cherokee Six. It was known as a coffin plane, not for the danger it posed but for its long fuselage and double garage-style doors that allowed you to load it with bulky cargo, coffins included, a feature that soon made it a favorite of marijuana smugglers.

The plan was to fly the pot across the border and land on one of the dozen or so dry lake beds that lay on the desert floor around Twentynine Palms, in the southwest part of California. The lakes measure anywhere from two to fifteen miles long, and except for the forty-mile-long Salton Sea, which is filled with twenty feet of water leaching in from the Colorado River, they haven't been very wet since the glacier receded ten thousand years ago. At most they get a little muddy during the rainy season in the winter months, when the runoff flows down from the surrounding mountains—albeit muddy enough so battle tanks from the U.S. Marine base at Twentynine Palms have been known to roll out on them and get hopelessly stuck. The rest of the year, when the salt from the runoff dries out and binds itself with the clay in the soil, the lakes provide a surface that is as smooth as concrete and hard enough to take the weight of a one-hundred-ton space shuttle. Dirt roads come and go in all directions, and except for sporadic salt-mining operations, the dry lake region has about as many people hanging around as does the face of the moon.

By now George had built up a tight collection of dependable friends and operators, a regular little band of beach characters, who furthered the enterprise in various capacities. There was his girl-friend, Annette, who lived with two other women, both named Wendy. All three worked as stewardesses for United Airlines or TWA and were known to the crowd as "Annette and the two Wendys." There was Earl "the Pearl," a computer programmer for a hospital in L.A. who would soon put his organizational skills to use in the wholesaling end of the business, and "Pogo," a graduate of USC who had left his job as a stockbroker as well as his wife and a house in Bel Air to embark on the pot trade. Pogo would drive the loads back from the dry lakes for George; he also served as the radio ground controller for the incoming flights. General chores were handled by other beach habitués: Junior, a roustabout who had got-ten George his job on the pile driver; Sam the bartender, with a bandito mustache, who was a friend of Frank Shea's from Mas-sachusetts; Orlando, the son of a wealthy curtain-rod family in the Midwest, who had been a door gunner on a helicopter in Vietnam; Randy, who worked in the oil refinery next door in El Segundo. Along with Frank Shea, who knew how to fly, the pilots included Greg from Arizona, who had flown for the airlines, and Cliff Gut-tersrud, stylish and handsome, the son of a well-off Chicago family who paraded around in blue blazers and white polo shirts and sported a license plate on his Porsche that read FLYBOY. Then there was a pilot known as Here-We-Go Bob, for the unnerving habit he had of gripping the yoke with feverish intensity as he brought his plane in for a landing, announcing in a voice quivering with appre-hension and self-doubt: *"Heeeeeeeere we go!"*

Located about halfway down the western coast of Mexico, the city of Puerto Vallarta sits at the head of the Bahía de Banderas, a parabola-shaped bay eighteen miles deep and twelve miles wide, which from an airplane looks as if God had taken a big bite out of the shoreline. Ramón Moreno grew up in Puerto Vallarta in the mid-1950s, when it was just another sleepy coastal town of cobble-stone streets and modest frame and white-stucco dwellings poking out from the jungled foothills of the Sierra Madre looming in the background. Ramón's great-grandfather, a Yaqui Indian, came to the town in the late 1800s and began growing bananas, corn, and tobacco, which were shipped out on coastal steamers and sailing vessels. He had been driven out of Sonora, in the north, when the government confiscated the Indians' land and turned it over to wealthy farmers, leaving them with nothing to tend but the meanest holdings. Ramón's grandfather become a well-to-do store owner in town, and his father a schoolmaster and a famous local soccer player. You couldn't get to Puerto Vallarta by automobile until after World War II, and even then, when Ramón was little, the roads stopped short at the rushing waters of the Cuale River, which split the town vertically down the center, spanned only by a pair of swinging bridges. A broad jetty, or *malecón*, ran along the ocean-front, where on Sunday evenings the young people joined the *paseo* by the sea, as their elders sat on the benches watching the ungainly pelicans dive for fish and the large orange sun disappear slowly into the Pacific.

Because of its charm, its deserted beaches, and its great marlin fishing, word started spreading slowly in the late 1950s that Puerto Vallarta was an undiscovered paradise. Americans and Canadians arrived, hotels started going up to the north and south, and Ramón joined the flock of young men who earned money furnishing services to the *turistas* on the beach—selling souvenir hats, sodas, and a coconut-oil suntan concoction he mixed up at home. Eventually his grandmother staked him to an inboard speedboat, which he used to take people skin diving and exploring along the coast. One day in 1963 he was hired to provide water-taxi service for an American actress with a sensuous mouth and a raucous laugh, to deliver her regularly to Mismaloya, a tiny beachfront village south of town, inaccessible by car, where they were filming Tennessee Williams's *The Night of the Iguana*. Ramón, of course, had never heard of Ava Gardner. "She would give me a list of the things she wanted on the boat. Always it was a lot of ice, and plenty of beer, and tequila, and gin—a lot of gin. Sometimes she would drink it with an olive, or mix the gin and the tequila and pour it into a coconut with ice and stick in a straw. Sometimes early in the morning I would take her to an empty beach. She could take her clothes off and swim and lie on the sand."

With publicity from the movie, the town quickly became over-run by tourists and actors from Hollywood. John Huston, the movie's director, built himself a house just below Mismaloya, still reachable only by boat. The Oceana Bar in the center of town, whose windows open out onto the ocean, became the boozy haunt of Richard Burton and his new wife, Elizabeth Taylor, as well as Robert Mitchum, Marlon Brando, and his pal John Barrymore, Jr. Peter Fonda and Dennis Hopper hung out there after making *Easy Rider*, along with Groucho Marx's son, Fred, whose motorcycle starred in the movie as Fonda's bike. A permanent population of North Americans, including Richard and Liz, settled into a section of expensive houses and condominiums overlooking the center of town and known as Gringo Gulch. The population of Puerto Vallarta jumped from 12,500 souls to 82,000, with 200,000 more descending on the place at the height of the tourist season.

Retired by now from being a beach boy and chauffeur, Ramón was looking to get into something substantial. On the beach he had run into a wealthy young man from Mexico City named Sanchez, the son of a Mexican army general, who owned several sportfishermen he chartered out for marlin fishing. As a sideline, Sanchez was also helping to fulfill the increasing demand by Americans for pot, and he needed someone to liaise with the farmers in the hills, who had been persuaded by the law of economics to take a portion of their ten-acre plantations of corn and beans and turn it into a more lucrative tillage. Ramón became his man. Then in his late teens, fluent in English, Ramón wore his hair long, straight down to the center of his back. Like other Indians, he possessed a pair of penetrating, heavy-lidded eyes that betrayed a distant ancestry somewhere in East Asia but gave away little else, a distinct advantage in the marijuana business. Sinewy, tough, and quick, Ramón had already earned the nickname Garavato. Strictly speaking, the word translates into "hook" or "sickle," but carries many subtler meanings, among them a darting movement, a piece of scribble, or an entwining action—a tree that wraps itself around another tree is called a *garavato*. It was Ramón's father's nickname, too, for the way in soccer he seemed to be all over the field at once.

Brought to the New World by the Spaniards in the sixteenth century—the word *marijuana* comes from the Spanish word for "intoxicant"—the cannabis plant particularly appreciates life in high mountain valleys because of its exposure to the sun and the protection from harsh weather afforded by the surrounding peaks. It likes warmth and humidity, which Puerto Vallarta, at 250 miles below the Tropic of Cancer, has in abundance the year round, and in the 1960s the growers liked the relative secrecy the foothills afforded. The weather there also enabled farmers to reap two crops a year: one harvested in October, at the end of the rainy season, and the second in March, which had to be irrigated in the dry winter months by a network of hoses feeding water to the fields from the springs and streams higher in the hills. The plantations were small, a half acre to an acre and a half, tucked away in ravines and at the back of canyons, difficult to find if you didn't know the way. The only access was over a maze of donkey trails that wound through the mountain villages, ensuring that snoopers and others who didn't belong there were quickly discovered and discouraged from venturing further.

At first the pot farmers of Mexico, faced with little of the competition that came later on from Jamaica, Colombia, and parts of Asia, carried on their job pretty crudely by current standards, leaving the plants to grow however they would, expending little effort to thinning them out or providing fertilizer. In addition, the growers sold the whole plant—flowers, leaves, seeds, and stems— chopped into bits, pressed into brick-size kilos, and shipped off to California. All in all it was a pretty raggedy product, providing only a weak buzz, and a harsh smoke in the bargain. Gradually, however, the pot culture improved. Although the plant will grow plentifully almost anywhere—hence the nickname weed—its quality can be boosted dramatically through the use of certain cultivation techniques. The most significant one, reportedly developed in the second millennium B.C. in India, involves culling all the male plants out of the field before they have a chance to release their pollen and fertilize the females; it's during this period, while they're waiting to be fertilized, that the female plants achieve the most potency. To snare the pollen wafting around in the air, they produce a sticky resin compound in their buds. Once pollination occurs—they get their guy, as it were—the girls shut down the factory. For pot smokers, that's bad, since it's the resin that contains the highest concentration of THC, or delta-9-tetrahydrocannabinol, the element you need to get good and blasted. In concentrated form, the resin and the buds become hashish. Boiled in solvent and extracted further, the mixture is turned into hash oil, the most powerful pot there is, with a THC content ten to one hundred times greater than what's found in ordinary marijuana. This is the stuff that calls forth visions.

Ramón saw it as part of his job to increase awareness among the farmers that those female plants had to be kept deprived; that way, he told them, they could charge more for their pot. "If you're a good farmer, you go out every morning and every male plant you spot in the field you rip that fucker up," says Ramón, whose English was refined in the 1960s and qualifies as landmark-status hippiespeak, littered with "chicks," "old ladies," and "bummed out, man." "Those fuckers sneak in and they hide, they seem to know when you're looking for them, but you see those little seed buds poking up, and you get that fucker right out of the ground and put him in a plastic bag, so they won't reseed, and you have more and more. You have to be on top of it to get good grass."

On his trips into the hills at harvest time, Ramón would travel up alongside the Cuale River, past its waterfalls and rapids, then branch off, following the trails leading into the farms. He'd bring along six men to help and a team of twelve donkeys, spend a day going in, a day assembling the load, and a day coming out. The animals carried fifty to eighty kilos each in burlap bags, a total of five or six hundred kilos a trip. The trail was narrow and in many places ran along deep ravines. More than once even one of the sure-footed burros would go over the edge, Ramón recalls; he would hear it crashing down through the forest, then silence, no time to stop and search. Ramón's personal record load on a single trip was five thousand kilos, eleven thousand pounds, which he brought out during a particularly good harvest in 1969. It took fifteen days and thirty donkeys to get the job done.

For premium-grade marijuana, Ramón paid the farmers a high of one hundred pesos, equivalent to about eight dollars back then, for each kilo. This added up to a lot of money, compared to the twelve hundred dollars a year that a family of six might otherwise earn off its small holding and a few animals. With three to four hundred marijuana plants to an acre, each plant producing up to a kilo of pot, and two harvests a year, the farmer could make with a single acre of marijuana three to five times what he could on all ten acres of corn and beans, and still have the corn and beans. For this reason, Ramón's appearance in the hills above Puerto Vallarta became for the *campesinos* an increasingly significant event. "We'd go to many fields and the farmers would say, 'Take my pot, take my pot,'" he recalls. "The farmers would have their kids and old ladies helping out. Sometimes the farmer that had the littlest field had the best shit, man, because he takes care of it more. Sometimes they go even into the higher places, where there is nobody's land, although sometimes a farmer would go on somebody else's place and there would be a little discussion over it, you know."

As the marijuana business became large-scale and serious, it was not advisable for a gringo, or a nonindigenous human of any persuasion, to wander about up in the hills around Puerto Vallarta. The farmers found it difficult to imagine what a stranger would be doing there were he not an informer or someone out to steal their money. And then there were the *banditos* to watch for, especially if you were an American. "The Americans," says Ramón, "sometimes they would be in town asking for someone to take them up into the hills, maybe they want to buy something. They would be taken this way and that way, and pretty soon they are way, way up there with all their money, away from everything, and all around are only the *banditos*. Or you buy something from a farmer in the hills and they put rocks in it, and you don't know until you get down here, and then it is too late. One year an Italian who was buying loads had come with a lot of money, and they took him to one of the fields and buried him in the field and took his money. His mother came down looking for him, but it took a long time. He had to be identified by a dentist."

Late in the summer of 1968, George arrived in Puerto Vallarta on a commercial flight with Sam the Bartender and Frank Shea, ready to put their grand scheme into play. The word had been out in Manhattan Beach about Puerto Vallarta being the place to get marijuana in large quantities, but for all their talk and planning, George and company had almost no idea of how to make a connection. None of them spoke more than pick-up Spanish. They knew nothing about the city or where to go. They had no names or contacts to start with. For days that stretched into weeks, they wandered about the beaches and the hotels and bars, chatting up strangers, leaving behind veiled queries about whom they might talk to regarding the possibility of scoring some dope. Sloshed on beer and Cocos Locos, they'd lie down under the palm trees at night and pass out on a deserted beach, deaf to the crash of the surf, to rise the next day in shaken condition and resume the quest. "There were Americans down there, and you could tell what they were doing," George says, "but everyone wanted to keep it to himself. No one wanted to involve us."

The center of the city still retained much of its old charm, particularly in the categories of recreation George liked to pursue. At four o'clock in the afternoon, across the street from the *malecón* in the Oceana Bar, where the old wooden ceiling fans pulled in the sea air through open windows, he'd meet up with Richard Burton and Liz Taylor. The three became friendly, putting away large quantities of Scotch and ruminating on the ironies of life as the waves flopped languorously along the beach. George had seen *The Night of the Iguana* several times, putting the defrocked minister, Shannon, on his list of icons. Liz would disappear on shopping trips with her retinue of thin-waisted males. "Here comes the queen with her six little sissies," Burton would taunt on her return. One night the three attended a traveling circus, during which one of the clowns nearly drowned when he lay underneath the elephant and was inundated with several gallons of steamy urine. To George's consternation, Liz stepped into the ring and let the Mexican knife-thrower hurl near-misses all around her body. Back at the Oceana, when Richard was off in the men's room, George leaned over and kissed Liz on the mouth. "'I've always wanted to do that,' I told her. 'I think you're the most beautiful woman in the world.' She said, 'You're cute, but you don't have what Richard has. And you don't have his money either.'"

They'd heard the scary stories of Americans rotting in Mexican jails, so George and his cohorts were somewhat chary of announcing their quest too openly, lest they fall into the hands of undercover policemen. "Finally, it was the fourth week," says George, "and everyone was getting really pissed. We couldn't find a connection, we were running out of money. They wanted to go back home. 'Fuck this, we can make more doing what we were doing, it's never gonna happen.' Then one afternoon we were coming out of the Oceana, and this little yellow VW bug pulls up in front and this girl with straight blond hair pokes her head out the window, a hippie type, and says, 'Get in the car, you guys. I know what you're up to.'"

She drove them up into the foothills, where the cobblestones turned into a rutty dirt track running past tin-roofed shanties, with naked children playing in the street and junk cars sitting under poinciana trees in the yards. Eventually she parked, and they walked up a hillside and through an archway that opened onto a large stucco villa with jutting balconies and a red-tiled roof. She left them for a minute and returned with a couple of pounds of pot. "It was beautiful stuff, I mean like nothing we'd ever seen before," says

George. "She said she worked for some people who'd been watching us in town for several days and wanted to see if they could do business." Inside the house, where it was dark and cool, she introduced them to a thin, wiry young man with long, jet-black hair, whose name was Ramón.

When Sanchez showed up soon thereafter, George told him they had a plane and asked if he could provide them with two or three hundred kilos to fly to California. "Sanchez said he could get us as much as we could carry away, a thousand kilos, whatever we could handle." The deal they worked out was that George would pay $25 dollars a kilo, which because of its high quality he knew he could turn over for as much as $150, maybe more, in Manhattan Beach, and twice that easily if he took it to Amherst. The expense of staying the month in Puerto Vallarta, however, had drained their finances, so Sanchez agreed to front them three hundred kilos, taking payment only after it was sold. In exchange for the favor, George agreed to sell an additional hundred kilos for Sanchez himself at the prevailing price in the United States. This deal meant not only that George got the pot for no money, but since it was Sanchez's load now mixed in with his, in effect he'd also acquired a Mexican partner, created a relationship. "If he was in a partnership with you, he wouldn't fuck you around with the quality or the delivery or the price."

Sanchez also saw it as a much better way to go. For his own pot, which George would sell on Sanchez's behalf, and for the pot he sold George, he would get a total of $37,500, as opposed to the $10,000 from selling the whole four hundred kilos to George straight out. Ramón would get $2,500 of this for the trip into the hills, and another $2,500 went to the farmers. Other expenses came up, too. But getting along in Mexico was so cheap—the weekly paycheck, for instance, of a government worker came out to just over $8—that Sanchez figured he could earn a small fortune here. George wouldn't do so badly either. Every four-hundred-kilo shipment he took to Amherst netted about $80,000, or nearly twice what his gang was doing buying it through Richard Barile in Manhattan Beach. If he could do this once a month, he thought, he could soon retire.

An elated George flew back to Manhattan Beach to get the airplane, while Sam and Frank stayed down to work out the mechanics with Sanchez and Ramón. Moving 880 pounds of anything is not an inconsequential task, and especially when it had to be done in secrecy. The city police in Puerto Vallarta, the *policianos*, prompted no worry in this regard, since all they did was direct traffic and enforce local ordinances. What you watched out for were the Federales, or Federal Judicial Police, a sort of Mexican FBI, which had outposts in all the important cities and acted as the country's main dope hunters (only later would the Mexican army get into the act). But in Mexico, as George soon learned, the authorities chose to do their duty or didn't, depending on how much they got paid, which meant that in the marijuana business you always gave some of your proceeds over to the Federales. In Puerto Vallarta this meant a deputy chief, who went by the name of Candy Man, for his readiness to take extracurricular pay. Sanchez gave Candy Man the equivalent of four hundred dollars every time one of Ramón's donkey trains came down from the hills; in return he would find police business for his men to attend to in some other part of town.

The pot was wrapped in one-kilo packages, twenty-five kilos to an army duffel bag, a total of sixteen bags. The Cherokee could take a lot more weight, but this was about the bulk limit that would fit into its cargo space. The load would be assembled in a shed at the back of Sanchez's house and be trucked down at night—the police were paid off, but there was no sense alerting the whole town—and transferred to one of Sanchez's sportfishermen at the marina. The boat would transport it over water to a lonely spit of land called Punta de Mita, on the northern tip of Banderas Bay, eighteen miles out from Puerto Vallarta. A desolate, wind-swept point of land, with breakers piling in over a long stretch of shallows, the point is visible from the city on a clear day, but when the low-lying fog rolls in, all you can make out are the vague peaks of its mountain range riding like ghost ships on top of the mist. The airstrip consisted of a flat piece of grassland just back from the beach, which offered plenty of landing room for a small plane, as long as Ramón and his men were given time to chase out the Brahman bulls that used it for grazing. The isolated landing strip at Punta de Mita was used also by the three other marijuana-smuggling operations in Puerto Vallarta, which meant that at times it took a little coordination to avoid congestion in the area.

The plan called for George to fly into the commercial airport at Puerto Vallarta, stay overnight, take off again the next day, land at

Punta de Mita to pick up the dope, then fly back. Once over the border in the United States, he would head for the dry lake beds, where Pogo would be waiting with a camper truck to unload the plane and drive the pot back to Manhattan Beach. There it would be repacked into the bathtub compartment of the Winnebago and trucked east to the students of the Five-College Consortium.

There was one complication. The Cherokee's cruising range was only about 600 miles, half the distance from Punta de Mita to the California desert. Down and back, George needed to refuel somewhere, and somewhere secluded, since on its return the plane would be stuffed to the ribs with marijuana. For this purpose they found a rarely used airstrip near the city of Guaymas, approximately halfway up the coast. It was built on a deserted marsh a little way out of town and used mainly for flying out loads of shrimp, Guaymas being the shrimp capital of Mexico. On his way down, George would take along Orlando, the helicopter gunner, and drop him off at Guaymas, together with twenty or so 5-gallon jerry cans filled with airplane fuel. Orlando would hide the fuel, sit tight for a day, and gas George up on the way back.

Considering the primitive nature of George's flying skills, the most remarkable feature of that first trip was that he made it alive. "Taking off was easy enough," he recalls of his thirty hours' worth of flying lessons. "You get it up to speed, pull back on the stick, and you're gone. And the flying-around part was no problem either. You just have to watch out where you're going so you don't run into anything. The landing, though—that was where I got a little insecure." Like many lefties, George had minor problems with hand-eye coordination under any circumstance, and more so now that he had to keep in mind the several operations needing to be performed simultaneously to bring the plane down successfully: adjusting the fuel mixture, setting the flaps properly, compensating for crosswinds, keeping the prop at full RPM in case he blew the thing and had to get airborne again. It had taken quite a few attempts, with the instructor aborting a number of landings, before George got anywhere near having the hang of it. On the flight down to Mexico, however, he figured he'd get in a little practice before having to land the thing on the floor of an ex-lake in the middle of the California desert.

The first part of the operation went smoothly enough. George landed okay in Guaymas, okay again at the airport and on the landing strip at the point, where he took on the four hundred kilos of marijuana. On the trip back, however, heavier by nearly half a ton and coming in to gas up at Guaymas, he suffered a little equilibrium problem, wherein the plane went into what is called a "tipping and touching" mode—hitting first on one wheel, then the other, careening down the landing strip like a drunk after closing time. He managed to straighten it out before one of the wings actually scraped the ground, loaded up with more fuel, and at 3:00 P.M. took off for the border on the final leg of his journey. After Guaymas, he planned to head up the middle of the Gulf of California, cross the border directly over the city of Mexicali, then change course slightly, heading a couple of points west of due north so as to graze the eastern edge of the Salton Sea, which would be easy to spot in the desert. About halfway up alongside the sea, he'd head northeast over the Chocolate Mountains, toward the pass between the Orocopia Mountains and the Chuckwallas, go right up the slot to the Colorado River aqueduct, follow that along as it wound to the northeast, then look for Granite Pass between the Granite and Iron mountain ranges, which opens right onto the bed of Danby Dry Lake. To spot the lakes, one looked for the whitest and brightest splashes on the desert floor. These marked the salt concentrations that made a hard surface for smooth landing. He'd been warned to stay clear of the darker brown areas at the edge of the lakes, possibly muddy ground that could grab the wheels and flip the plane into a somersault. Danby Dry Lake measured about ten miles long and two and a half miles wide and was identifiable by the slight bend to its shape, looking something like a boiled hot dog. Driving out there from Manhattan Beach, Pogo would figure out where the wind was blowing from and park his truck at a point upwind of a stretch long enough to give George at least three thousand feet of landing room. After the transfer, while Pogo headed back to Manhattan Beach, George would take off a final time and return the plane to the Santa Monica Airport. That was the plan.

George found Mexicali easily enough—only it turned out to be Tijuana. Or San Diego. Some damn place, but definitely not Mexicali, because that was the Pacific Ocean out there, and according to the chart Mexicali wasn't on any fucking ocean. This meant that through some bit of miscalculation or inattention he'd gotten off course, at least a hundred miles west and who knew how many miles north of where he was supposed to be.

Abruptly he banked to the right and headed due east, to the vicinity of the Salton Sea, to try to get himself oriented. After an hour's flying he found the sea, but then experienced more confusion looking for the right mountains to line up with and the pass he had to go through. One mountain seemed just like the next, all of them a mottled brown color with scrubby growth, like a three-day beard. Flying only at thirty-five hundred feet, he was running into a discouraging amount of turbulence, made worse by the wide wing configuration of the Cherokee. The plane bucked and heaved, buffeted by rising currents of hot air welling up off the desert floor, hitting a ridge line and tumbling down the other side. "I was bobbing up and down like a goddamn cork on the water up there, plus I really had no fucking idea where I was." He could see dry lake beds all over, gleaming white against the red rock of the hills. But which one was Danby? Where was the Colorado aqueduct, and the pass?

It was now getting late, the sun slipping fast toward the Sierra Nevada. Once it slid behind that mountain wall, it would be as if someone had pulled down a giant window shade. Sun would still be shining down on the beach bunnies back at Manhattan Beach, but east of the Sierra it would soon be as dark as a malefactor's heart. "I remember following the ridge of mountains, following it along, there'd be four or five passes, and I'd take one, and, Jesus Christ, I hoped this was the right one. I'd lost a lot of time getting off course. What scared me most was still being up there after the sun went down, because then it was all over. I was running low on gas. I'd end up crash-landing, or plowing into the side of some mountain I couldn't see. In that plane I discovered what it was like being in a state of total fear—all the things I didn't know how to do. I thought, 'George, you stupid son of a bitch, here's where you're finally going to get yourself killed.'"

Finally, coming down through a pass, jagged mountains on both sides, he saw another patch of white, another dry lake bed, this one long and narrow with a slow curve. It looked about right. There was a set of salt evaporators up at the north end—that seemed right— and, by fucking Christ, there was Pogo down there, his truck sitting up near the top of the lake, flashing his headlights on and off and on and off, a big piece of something white waving from the aerial to show which way the wind was blowing. George banked right, then left to get downwind, and lost most of the memory of what happened next, except that suddenly he felt one of the landing gears touch down, then the other, both of them now, and he was taxiing up toward the truck, with Pogo outside the vehicle punching both fists into the air in triumph. "I'll never forget what it was like finally getting on the ground, the whole trip—it was a dream I had had for all those years. I'd said, 'I'm going to do this.' And I actually did it. I'd never felt anything like that in my life." Simultaneously, George had another thought, one that moved him so strongly he uttered it out loud to himself: "I am never, ever going to do this shit again."

Early in 1969, after that first trip from Mexico to Massachusetts, the whole crew—Annette and the two Wendys, Frank and Sam and George, and also the pilot, Greg, who George determined would now handle the flights into the dry lake beds—decided to pick up and move the operation down to Puerto Vallarta, so they could run the business from the source. On the beach about a mile north of town they found a large white villa to rent, with rooms enough for everyone. It came with a cook and a gatekeeper to watch out for strangers. Hotel construction was going on to the north, but between the house and town was nothing but empty beach lined with coconut palms, and a view across the bay to the misty mountains of Punta de Mita. Every five or six weeks now Greg would land the plane there, then take off with another load for the happy students of Amherst.

Life for the inhabitants of the villa assumed the qualities of an endless holiday. Mexican boys came by every morning to bring them fresh oysters, which they laced with *salsa picante* and combined with whatever the cook was preparing for breakfast, which they ate out on a balcony, watching waves breaking along the sand. An endless procession of pelicans drifted by, gliding just an inch or two above the water, supported on a cushion of warm and humid air. Occasionally one would climb to about fifty feet, then do an acute right turn and crash into the ocean with a great splash and racket to grab a fish. Later in the morning, more Mexican boys would come along, leading horses for a ride up the beach, or they would land with catamarans to take George and his friends out for a sail.

The women grew especially fond of Pedro, the gatekeeper; they introduced the old man to smoking pot and provided him a pair of binoculars to look through after he got stoned. Another old guy, Wally the Human Fly, age seventy, lived a couple of villas down the beach. During his working days back in Chicago, Wally could attract quite a crowd when he'd dress up in his cape and tights and scamper up and down the sides of skyscrapers off Michigan Avenue. Now the women would fly a white towel off the balcony to signal that it was okay for Wally to sneak out on his wife and come over and drink tequila, while Pedro smoked dope and stared out at the ocean through 8 × 50 magnification, the pelicans winging by. Toward the end of the afternoon, George would leave the villa to put in an appearance at the Oceana Bar, where Liz and Richard and other movie people held forth. He befriended the screenwriter James Poe, whose film *They Shoot Horses, Don't They?* had just come out. Poe had recently been diagnosed with cirrhosis of the liver, and his doctor had given him six months to live if he didn't stop drinking. To take his mind off booze, George drove him out to the mahogany forests north of town, where they ate magic mushrooms George had gotten from the Indians, observing how the mahogany trees would entwine their branches around one another as if grappling in some arboreal orgy. When they came back to town, Poe told George he'd like to do that over again—it was more fun than Scotch and a lot better for his liver.

It was getting well into the summer of 1969, the summer Mary Jo Kopechne went off the bridge at Chappaquiddick, Charles Manson's followers went on a murder spree in Beverly Hills, and a huge rock concert was held in a farmer's field twelve miles northwest of Woodstock, New York. George was in the midst of a pot trip, but Sam the Bartender attended Woodstock in bandito mustache, Mexican sombrero, and a shawl. He took a load of their dope along, set up a pot stand in the mud and the rain, and sold out.

On one trip, George, Annette, and Orlando and his girlfriend took a detour off Route 90 and stopped in Greenwood, Indiana, just outside Indianapolis, to see George's sister and brother-in-law, Marie and Otis. The couple now had a little baby, Steven, destined for law school. They lived in a two-story white house in a new subdivision, Otis beginning his rise as a research chemist at Eli Lilly & Co. During supper, Otis and Marie seemed glad enough to see George, but Orlando struck them as a little weird, with his orange-rimmed sunglasses, Jimi Hendrix Afro, and Fu Manchu mustache. "What are you doing with that freak?" Otis asked, taking George aside. After dinner George asked if they'd like to try some marijuana; everyone's doing it, he said. They happened to have some out in the Winnebago. Marie had never smoked pot but said that some of their friends had tried it. She took a few puffs when they passed it around, only to be polite, it seemed to George. Otis also gave it a try, but it made him feel sick and he disappeared suddenly into the bathroom. That night the gang stayed in the Winnebago and the next day they went on their way.

When George got to Amherst, he left the camper there, and he and Annette rented a car and drove down to Weymouth to see his parents. It was his first visit in about two years. His father asked him how the pile-driving business was, and George said it was coming along pretty well. And the classes at Long Beach City College? Well, actually, he was putting off the college thing for a while, George said, to see if he could earn a little money. George took everyone out for steak and broiled lobster at the Red Coach Grill in Hingham, where his parents liked to go for Sunday dinners. His father seemed not a little taken with Annette, dressed demurely now in a shirt dress but still causing a few heads to turn at the Red Coach Grill. He called her Darlin' and Honey and made over her during dinner. Annette brought out snapshots of the villa on the beach in Puerto Vallarta, of George and the guys standing in their bathing suits under the palm trees, of their Mexican friend Ramón, his hair in a long braid. It was a great place to spend a vacation, she told the Jungs.

In the early 1970s the pot business changed dramatically, as marijuana started arriving in the United States from other countries besides Mexico. The increase in supply created more competition among the dealers. Quality and price began to count. People became much more knowledgeable, and the market changed from one where the seller controlled the action to where the buyer was now king; there was a lot more scrambling around for customers now.

One of the major causes of this change, according to Michael Armstrong, a drug historian who at the time headed an organization called LEMAR, for Legalize Marijuana, was President Richard Nixon's Operation Intercept. Put into effect during the summer and fall of 1969, the program was designed both to reduce pot smuggling out of Mexico and to goad the Mexican government into adopting a more aggressive stance against the trade, even to get the Mexican army involved. It was inaugurated with a total sealing-off of the U.S. border at San Ysidro, just north of Tijuana. Customs officials stopped and searched every single vehicle going through. This produced miles of jammed traffic and a great amount of disruption on the Mexican side. The U.S. Border Patrol also embedded military-style sensors in the ground all along the southwestern border to try to detect crossings at places other than official checkpoints. Operation Intercept didn't seize pot so much as it began discouraging land-based smuggling operations. People were now going by sea and taking to the air, as George had been doing all along. But for a while the crackdown resulted in a dearth of Mexican pot, which motivated wholesalers to seek loads from elsewhere. Thai stick came heavily on the market from Thailand, as did Colombian Gold and Santa Marta Red from Colombia, Panama Red from Panama, and the dark, powerful, resinous Ganja from Jamaica.

Earl the Pearl, who had moved into big-time wholesaling, with dozens of customers on one side and smugglers on the other, soon had his business perking along like a little supermarket. Methodical, well organized, and meticulous, he had moved his operation out of Manhattan Beach to a Victorian house overlooking Bodega Bay, north of San Francisco, where he provided buyers with samples of fifteen to twenty varieties, all labeled and graded according to quality and price. Customers came in, tried them out, then placed an order. The increase in competition meant that suppliers like George no longer called all the shots. They had to develop marketing skills. "Now sometimes, you'd come in with a load, but someone else might come in with a better load, better-quality stuff," says George. "Earl would say he'd still do your load, but the other stuff was going first, customers wanted that pot more than your pot. So you had to wait around. Or you might decide not to wait and take it East. The West Coast was becoming like a Kmart for drugs. There was so much of it that it had to be pretty special stuff to move fast. In the East they weren't that particular." Even there, George felt he had to give his customers something different to maintain his market share. In the tourist shops in Puerto Vallarta he bought strings of tiny blue beads and sprinkled them among his kilos, telling the wholesalers in Amherst to get out the word that this stuff came straight from the Indians, had the beads in it from their secret rituals and shit. Soon he was overhearing students at the bar in the Lord Jeff raving on about this special Yaqui Indian pot, the stuff with the beads. Dynamite grass.

By its very nature, drug smuggling is marked by movement rather than stasis. Getting the loads from one place to another is how smugglers earn their living. And moving around reduces the chance of discovery by the police. No one moved farther and faster than George's Yaqui Indian friend, Ramón, who almost overnight was jerked out of a landscape of burros and swinging bridges and set down in a world peopled by creatures with strange possessions and exotic habits. Although he had never traveled more than three miles out of town, it now became routine, if the Rolling Stones were playing in Albuquerque, for Ramón and the gang to charter a plane, fly up there for the concert, have a limo waiting at the airport. Or the guys would stop off in New York City on the way back from Amherst, take Ramón in to get a bite at the Four Seasons, where the fucking maître d' had an attitude problem about Hawaiian shirts. He didn't understand that in California you could get served dressed as a Camperdown Elm if you had fifty thousand dollars in your pocket; he still brought out jackets for them to put on and made them wear these stupid little bow ties.

Or Ramón would board the Winnebago in Manhattan Beach, where it was 80 degrees in the California shade, and when the door opened in Amherst, at the Lord Jeff—well, he'd heard about snow, but he'd never seen it. "I never knew it could be so fucking cold, man. And they have these snowmobiles. I thought to myself, 'What the fuck is this?' The guy there, one of George's friends, said, 'Hey, get in one of these babies, Ramón.' So I had mine cranked up as fast as that fucker would go, and you know how they clean the roads and they make the big piles of snow on the side? So I come up to one of these and I think it's just a little hill of snow, so I was flooring it, man, and suddenly, Bang! I'm in the middle of the fucking road, and the snowmobile, she's all wrecked. But the guy just said to get another one, Ramón. Watch where you're going."

By 1970 the group seemed to be close to cracking under the general strain. The first one to go was Sanchez, Ramón's boss, who went berserk one afternoon after Annette gave him some LSD. Inspired by visions, Sanchez barricaded himself with Annette and the other women inside his house on the hill, informed them he'd received a message that "God is coming to dinner," and began firing random shots out the window with a shotgun to keep the local police at bay. Someone finally summoned Sanchez's father, the general, who showed up and took his son off to a mental hospital, which meant that Ramón now had charge of the business.

For Sam the Bartender and Greg, all the money pouring in

allowed them to fulfill long-harbored fantasies on the Great White Hunter line. Thousands of dollars' worth of expensive gear began piling up in the beach house—Mannlicher Schoenauer hunting rifles from Austria, engraved Purdy shotguns from England, thermal jackets and boots you could do a moon walk in, the ultimate in tents, outdoor cooking gear mail-ordered from Abercrombie & Fitch, infra-red scopes for night sighting, longbows and crossbows for quiet hunting. They also ordered brochures on expeditions to the Northwest, to Alaska, where guides would take them up mountains and into the bush for brown bear, black bear, elk, mountain goat, Dahl sheep, moose, mule deer, antelope, and caribou. They asked Ramón if he wanted to come along on a trip to northern Montana to see what was worth shooting up there. Sure, he said. Montana, why not? Where was that? They have any armadillos up there? Ramón's grandmother knew just how to cook armadillo so you'd think you were eating roast pork.

"It was in the winter and we got warm clothes and our own plane and we fly up somewhere near Canada," Ramón recalls. "This kid is waiting for us, a guide, and he also does the cooking. I have a gun, very super-powerful rifle with a scope. We start walking, then on horses, then walking, then horses again, and finally we make camp, sitting up in the mountains and the snow, fucking freezing like a motherfucker, man, so whatever you cook it was freezing by the time you get it to your mouth. But the worst was going to the bathroom. That was bad. You have to take your pants off in the middle of the night, it was cold, man, your balls were like *pasas*, man, you know, prunes." The guys were going for moose, which meant two days more of trudging through waist-deep snow, uphill and down, until they spotted one on the side of a mountain and Sam brought it down with a couple of shots. "But then they couldn't carry it back, it was bigger than a cow. So they just took the horns and left the rest. They just leave it there. I think, you know, you kill something, you eat it, something like that. But they were measuring the horns with their rifles so they can nail it to the wall and put their rifles on it. They wanted it for that."

Sam and Greg were now thinking of themselves as apart from the group, which disheartened George considerably. He was the one who'd tried to mold them into a tight band of outlaws. After seeing *Butch Cassidy and the Sundance Kid*, he'd even christened their drug plane *The Hole in the Wall Gang*, in honor of Cassidy's outfit.

But despite his efforts, the organization was fraying at the margins. "I kept telling them, 'If we stay together, we'll be like a fist and have power. Every man contributes to the fist, and the fist is forever, like a brotherhood.' That's the way I felt, even afterward, with Carlos. But I got tired. Everybody was making money, and the money changed everything."

Then their paid-off police honcho, a deputy chief in Puerto Vallarta, got weird and demanded the guns off the wall. It happened when George and the other guys were off in Guadalajara on business, and the women were alone in the beach house. The deputy, a short Mexican with close-cropped black hair and a bushy mustache, had been receiving a handsome retainer from Sanchez and then from Ramón to make sure the flights went off without interference. Nevertheless, he showed up one day and made a great to-do with Annette and the two Wendys, threatening to arrest them all if they didn't give him the hunting rifles. Frightened, the girls handed over the guns. George returned from Guadalajara ahead of the others and invited the deputy to the villa for a talk. To encourage an open discussion, George broke out the Johnny Walker Black Label he'd had flown down from Manhattan Beach, and the two of them proceeded to put away about a bottle apiece. Based on body volume alone, the deputy stood little chance against George in this realm. He got himself so cross-eyed drunk that it came as a complete surprise when George suddenly picked him off the chair on the balcony, slammed him against the wall, and pinned him there by his neck for the time it took to inform the deputy that he was an insignificant piece of shit, that he was going to bring back those fucking rifles forthwith, and that if he wanted to keep doing business and making his money, he was to keep the fuck away from the house and stay the fuck away from the girls. He then carried the deputy over to the doorway and threw him down the flight of wooden stairs out into the cement courtyard.

But that wasn't how George came to be arrested.

FOUR

Mazatlán

1970–1973

*If you're going to make a start, keep on going—if you know what you're doing.
But if I were you, I'd think it over.*

—LOOSELY TRANSLATED FROM A SIGN POSTED ALONG
A TRAIL IN THE SIERRA MADRE

THE POLICE DEPUTY, FOR REASONS HE KEPT TO HIMSELF, chose not
to pursue the matter, and shortly afterward one of his men appeared
at the door with Sam and Greg's guns, and the household heard no
more of it. Nevertheless, George and Ramón questioned the wisdom of continuing to use the landing strip at Punta de Mita. Perhaps it was time to shift the landings to a different airfield, one far
away, in another state and jurisdiction. Given their run-in, it might
be even better to seek out another connection altogether, and eventually move the whole operation out of Puerto Vallarta. It was at
this juncture that Ramón introduced George to a colleague of his
named Cosme, who supplied marijuana out of Mazatlán. Located
270 miles up the coast from Puerto Vallarta and two states away in
Sinaloa, Mazatlán featured the same palm-lined beaches and strips
of hotels, but it was three times the size, a real port city. Most of its
290,000 people were packed into a dense urban section south of the
tourist hotels, a maze of red-dirt streets crowded with squalid one-
and two-story brick and cinder-block houses where gringos rarely

ventured. Spanish galleons had put in at Mazatlán four centuries ago and sailed away laden with gold bullion taken from the mines back in the hills.

Taller than Ramón, with a neatly trimmed mustache, Cosme had connections with farmers who grew pot in the Sierra Madre east of the city. But he was much more the city boy. Always sharply dressed in a white guayabera shirt and crisply pressed black slacks, he had light skin and a few more Spaniards than Indians in his ancestry. Cosme was crazy about hot American cars, particularly the Shelby-designed, four-on-the-floor, fast-backed Mark I Mustangs, powered by a 429-cubic-inch Cobra engine and dual quad carbure-tors. The Shelbys hit 60 miles an hour in 6.5 seconds and, laid down on the red line, could top out at about 140.

George saw here a chance to help Cosme out. He consulted an acquaintance of his back in Manhattan Beach named Alberto, who lived with his brother in an apartment directly overlooking the beach. The brothers had achieved fame for their weekend parties, where the women danced topless and guests ladled drinks out of a crystal punch bowl brimming with 200-proof grain alcohol laced with LSD. For George's purposes, the useful thing about Alberto was that he worked as a sales manager of a car lot owned by Ralph Williams, then one of the largest dealers in the state, whose bleating TV ads were regularly skewered by Johnny Carson. The lot covered eight acres, and the sales force ferried customers around in golf carts to look at all the cars, among which were a good number of Mark I Mustangs by Shelby. Furthermore, according to Alberto, the accountants for Williams did an inventory of the place only twice a year, which meant that during any particular six-month period no one had the slightest idea whether a certain Shelby was sitting on the lot waiting for someone to come around in a golf cart and buy it or was proceeding rapidly along the Avenida del Mar down in Mazatlán, its driver lowering his sunglasses and giving a wave to the girls as he thundered on by. Even when the accountants came around, Alberto said, the dealership did such a high-volume busi-ness that it was possible to fiddle the records in such a way as to cover the fact, at least for a while, that several cars had just upped and vanished.

Alberto was driven to larceny by his addiction to the dice tables and the need to keep himself flush for regular trips to Las Vegas. Thus he agreed once a month to sell one of the Shelbys for one-fifth the sticker price of six thousand dollars, and in the bargain he would hand-deliver it to George's place in Manhattan Beach, complete with California registration and ownership papers. In turn, George had Pogo, his wheel man, drive the vehicle down to Mazatlán, where it would be traded to Cosme for three hundred kilos of marijuana. In this fashion George managed to turn a twelve-hundred-dollar investment into ninety thousand dollars. Over time he became such a good customer that Alberto began urging bigger deals on him, using more and more cars. One morning George stepped out his front door to discover that his view of the houses across the street was being blocked by an eighty-foot-long, double-decker car carrier loaded up with eight brand new Shelbys driven by Alberto himself. "Get that fucking thing out of here, are you crazy?" George yelled at him. "We're doing this one at a time. That's it! One at a time."

In any event, that was how George's operation changed, in the fall of 1970. They now trucked the pot from Cosme's farmers near Mazatlán 200 miles up into the Sierra Madre, to a tiny paved landing strip just outside the mining city of Durango, 6,197 feet above sea level. This was high-desert country, filled with mesquite and cactus, land formations carved into mesas and buttes by centuries of weather action and erosion, arroyos running down into flowing riverbeds. For the way in which the terrain resembled parts of the American West, Durango had gained popularity among Hollywood movie companies, John Wayne's among them, as a location for shooting westerns on the cheap and avoiding certain U.S. corporate tax laws. As a result, a portion of George's marijuana-for-a-Mustang loads, the part he couldn't get into the airplane, often got trucked back across the border secreted inside movie trailers filled otherwise by camera equipment.

The drive from Mazatlán to the landing strip just outside of Durango involved negotiating one of the more singular engineering phenomena in the Western Hemisphere, the Mexican mountain road. Barren of guardrails, shoulders, streetlights, and any other safety features of modern highway construction, the road to Durango writhes through the mountains like a serpent in heat. Around its hairpin turns one can expect to confront anything from short-haul Mexican buses, whose drivers whip them into the curves in a manner defying the known laws of physics, to an assortment of free-ranging farm animals, including pigs, donkeys, cows, chickens, dogs, goats, and occasionally a dour-looking bull. Flower-strewn crosses dot the roadside to mark the spot where some unfortunate soul, perhaps a little slow to notice his side of the road had washed out in a deluge, had plunged to his death. The scenery almost anywhere in the mountains can be pretty distracting—lofty peaks all around, waterfalls cascading down the sides of cliffs, thousand-foot ravines—but the prudent driver allows it only stolen glances, eyes fixed for signs of danger ahead. One of the more familiar is PAVIMENTE RESBALOSO, announcing a stretch of very serious potholes, wide and deep enough to be easily mistaken for an excavation project. There are also little picture signs advising drivers that, depending on when God wants it to happen, at any minute they can be struck on the roof by a large boulder and other debris. Drivers resolve to take the warnings very seriously every now and then when they run into an unruly pile of splintered wood and rubble that shortly before had been a rock formation and a tree anchored somewhere on higher ground. Once having reached Durango, George and his men buried the pot near the landing strip in a deep hole roofed over by plywood planking and camouflaged with a covering of sod. There it awaited the arrival of the *The Hole-in-the-Wall Gang* airplane, which these days was being piloted in tenuous fashion by the knight of the white-knuckle landing, Here-We-Go Bob.

The big trouble came in the fall of 1970. It was the time when rock-and-roll fans had to adjust to the fact that the Beatles were breaking up; Jimi Hendrix and Janis Joplin were both dead of drug overdoses. The FBI finally nabbed Angela Davis in a motel room in Manhattan, and someone, a farmer most likely, spotted George's man Orlando burying a three-hundred-kilo stash of pot at the north end of the landing strip and phoned this piece of information in to the Durango office of the Federal Judicial Police. The call eventually was patched through to a boyish, clean-shaven officer of the Federales named Alfonso, who wore heavy, horn-rimmed glasses and combed his hair back in a D.A., in the manner of Buddy Holly. After listening to the farmer, and since no one in George's organization had thought to bribe the police up there, Alfonso had little choice but to perform his duty. Consequently, when George flew to the Durango airport on a commercial flight, rented a car and drove out to the airstrip to dig up the load and get it ready for when Bob came in, he found his car being converged upon by police cruisers staking out the field and himself suddenly very much under arrest.

At the time of George's apprehension, the federal police were, and to only a slightly lesser extent are still, an extremely powerful political entity, just about a law unto themselves. Regarding persons who came into their custody, they conducted themselves pretty much as they wanted to, despite the provision in Article 19 of the Mexican federal constitution, which was written to protect citizens against wantonly cruel treatment at the hands of the police. The article says, in part: "All mistreatment in apprehension or in prisons, every molestation inflicted without legal motive ... are abuses which ... shall be corrected by the laws and repressed by the authorities." As Alfonso saw it, he had no end of "legal motive" here where this smart-ass gringo with the big shoulders was concerned. When he was brought to the police station, George had not only refused to sign the proffered confession but did so in an insolent manner, telling the Federale that he could go fuck himself and suggesting the same for his piss-ant deputies as well. This was an ill-advised response to the situation, as George shortly found out. The next thing he knew, he was taken to a little room, his clothes were stripped off, and he was placed in a chair and doused with a bucket of water. One of the policemen approached him holding in his hand a black truncheonlike implement, eighteen inches long, that turned out to be an extra-high-voltage cattle prod, capable of making a two-thousand-pound bovine creature do an involuntary *tour jêté*. The deputy poked the thing in the direction of George's testicles, and when contact was made, an electric shock surged through his lower region that made George double over in agony and exhale a large amount of air.

After the cattle prod incident, George, still naked, was taken to another room and shoved inside a little wooden box, called a *joula*, which resembled a doghouse and was constructed so as to force a man inside it to sit in a severely bent-over position, his head pressed to his knees and his legs crossed Indian-style. The lid of the box was locked down tight, so the only light came in from two air holes about an inch in diameter. That's how George spent his first twenty-four hours in custody. Late the following day, stiff and fairly bursting with the desire to modify his behavior toward the police, he was brought once again into the presence of Alfonso. The Federale said there were two ways to go here. One was for George to exercise his right under the Mexican constitution, get a lawyer and challenge the arrest in the courts. Given the backlog in the system, it might take two or three years for the case to be heard, and since it was unlikely that bail would be granted to a foreigner, George would have to spend the intervening time in jail. The alternative was: How much money did he think he could raise to buy himself out of this mess?

"I did not have a difficult time choosing," George says. "We settled on a figure of fifty thousand American dollars, twenty-five for him and twenty-five for the federal circuit judge to sign the papers." George told the Federale it would take a little time, since he had to call Los Angeles to have Annette get the money—twenty thousand dollars as a down payment to show his good faith. She would have to make contact with a man named Esposito, a bail bondsman in L.A. whom George knew from the drug business and who would bring the money down to Durango. Esposito had a cousin who was high up in the Federales in Mexico City who could vouch for him to Alfonso. After Annette reached him, Esposito called down and he and Alfonso had a conversation. "When he hung up, he turned to me and smiled and said, 'Okay, Jorge. It's gonna be okay. You come and stay at my house, with me, until the money comes. I will make you comfortable. You will be my guest.' He also said he was sorry for all this, and the next time I wanted to use the airstrip I should notify him in advance. We could work something out."

Awaiting Esposito, George would go out on the town at night with Alfonso's deputies, hitting the *zona*, or red-light district, where the women did their business behind partitions of blankets strung up on clotheslines, and for free if you were a friend of the constabulary. In a few days Esposito showed up with the twenty thousand in cash, promising to return a week later with the balance, and George was coming to regard this business of being in Mexican police custody as not so terrible, when all was said and done.

But before the final payment was made and the release signed, a federal prosecutor from Mexico City unexpectedly showed up on the scene with his own idea as to how the case was going to be handled. It seemed that the federal authorities, who had been exceedingly irritated by Operation Intercept and the fuss the United States was creating over drug smuggling, wanted to use this big marijuana bust in Durango as a way to show that gringo president Nixon with the nose that looked like a mashed *tamale* that the Mexican government was doing more than it got credit for when it came to stamping out the international marijuana peril. Instructed to milk the case for all the publicity he could get, the prosecutor loaded the three hundred kilos George had been arrested with into a truck, notified the local newspapers and the TV people, and drove the pot and George and the arresting police officers out to the airfield. There he piled up the duffel bags in front of the big hole they'd been buried in, set George up in front of the bags, positioned the policemen off to the side pointing at him with their carbines, and told the press to fire away. A news photo of the scene ran the next day on the front page of the local paper under a blaring headline that read, NORTE AMERICANO NARCO TRAFICANTE CAPTURADO EN LA PISTA, *pista* meaning "airstrip." This interruption of their impending deal with George hugely pissed off Alfonso and the judge, as well as the deputies, who were to share in the pay-off and muttered to George as they drove him back from the press conference that they should shoot the son-of-a-bitch prosecutor and bury him in the hole that had been dug for the pot.

To everyone's relief, the prosecutor flew back to Mexico City the next day. Nevertheless, he'd kicked up such a fuss with the news story that the Federale determined reluctantly that for form's sake George would have to spend time in the state *penitenciaria* until the thing blew over. About three months should be sufficient, he thought. Then they could get on with the arrangement.

In its report on the Mexican penal system issued in 1991, Americas Watch, the organization that monitors human-rights violations in the Western Hemisphere, criticized the prisons for being dirty and overcrowded, for not providing inmates proper medical care or a well-balanced diet, and for tolerating a high level of corruption among the officials and guards. "Corruption is an endemic feature of life in Mexican prisons," the report said. "Prisoners in almost all the prisons we visited reported that drugs, alcohol, and heterosexual and homosexual prostitutes are available for a price. We heard many accounts of prisoners paying other prisoners for protection, and bribing guards for jobs, visiting privileges, food and other necessities. Corruption seems to be accepted by both officials and inmates as an inevitable part of the prison system."

This was all so much for the better, as far as George was concerned. In Mexico, as he found out, the prisons themselves aren't the problem, it's being there without money or friends or influence, so you can't glom on to the wide array of goods and services that can make your stay less arduous, not to say agreeable. Without resources, as noted by Americas Watch, you could be in for a bit of trouble, especially if you were an American.

Newly completed that year, the prison sits about a mile out of town, encompasses fourteen hectares, or thirty-four and a half acres, surrounded by a twenty-foot-high granite wall, and holds about twelve hundred men, along with a couple of dozen women housed in a separate unit. The men live in groups of cells in one of several unattached buildings, or "houses," located inside the wall. The first inmates George met in his house were two American schoolteachers from Arizona, Terry and Jerome, who had a harrowing story to tell. Two years before, they said, they and their wives had been touring the Sierra Madre in a brand new camper van when they were stopped by the police. They were beaten up, their wives were raped, marijuana was planted among their belongings, their van was stolen by the authorities, and they themselves were thrown in jail. Their families back home had only a small amount of money to send down for legal help, and in the two years their Mexican lawyers had achieved no discernible progress in moving the case toward resolution. Terry and Jerome now despaired of ever getting out.

George had every good reason to believe this was not the fate that awaited him. He'd already cut his deal with Alfonso, who wanted not only to get the rest of the money but also to explore further business arrangements that might be worked out regarding the landing strip. George had been delivered to the prison gates by his not-terribly-sober claque of Alfonso's deputies, who said they'd miss George's company and would try to make his prison stay endurable. It happened that they were members of the police baseball team, which came out to the prison each weekend to play the inmates. So they'd see him that very Saturday, bring plenty of tequila with them, and some pot, and some girls, too, how would that be, eh, Señor Jorge?

But even for inmates lacking his connections, life in the Durango prison was not as onerous or as rigidly monitored as it was in similar institutions in the United States. For one thing, inmates were allowed out of their cells from six in the morning until seven at night, when they were free to roam about the large prison grounds, read books, work for small pay in the prison shops if they wanted to. You couldn't get out, of course, but despite its wall, the Durango prison did not give inmates the feeling they were in a cage. For only a small bit of money they could supplement the prison fare with chicken and green peppers and onions, which they could cook up on hibachis scattered about the yard and sit and eat with their friends. There was a *bodega* on the grounds. Every weekend the inmates' wives and children were allowed in, and they would bring the makings of family picnics, which they ate at tables under umbrellas to keep off the sun. On Saturdays there were ball games—soccer, baseball, basketball—and also guitar playing for dancing. Every three weeks an inmate could spend all night with his wife in a private motellike unit on the prison grounds. Women inmates with newborns could keep their children with them until they are three years old. "I'll take a Mexican prison over an American one any day," says Ellen Lutz, chief of the Mexican desk of Americas Watch in Los Angeles and the principal author of its prison study. "They're loaded with corruption and violence, but there is a much higher level of human dignity allowed the inmates than in the United States. In Mexico, you're confined, yes, but you're not treated like an animal."

What George remembers most about the prison was Sunday afternoons, approaching five P.M., when the families would have to leave. As he wrote to Annette: "Sunday afternoons, good-byes are said between tears and kisses, children holding on to their fathers' pant legs. There are sisters and brothers-in-law, nieces and aunts and uncles. It's sad to see them go, but they'll be back. I think about this. Mexico, a primitive country, has a more humane penal system than the United States. Why? Monday the place returns to normal, back to tedium, but you remember the good time you had, and now we can wait for the next one."

George also got busy doing what he was good at, which was making friends with people who might do him some good. "When I first got there, I asked these guys Terry and Jerome who runs things around here, and they said, wait until tomorrow and you'll meet him. This guy ran the baseball team, and he had all the dope, he had liquor. In your cell you could build anything you wanted, and he had this little stove made out of a ten-gallon oil can; he'd cut out the bottom and you put charcoal in there. He had guys who were gofers, who would get him food and cook it. So I met him, he invited me over and asked me what I did. I said I was a marijuana smuggler, and I could get transportation into the United States.

That was it. Within twenty-four hours, I was the second *jefe* of the prison, the assistant gringo boss."

The man who had appointed George his number two was Manuel Perez, a native of Mazatlán. He had also been sent there for marijuana smuggling, along with his wife, Martha, who lived over in the women's unit. Manuel was getting out in six months, and after George described his operation, the two resolved to go into business together. "The bust had been all over the papers, the plane and landing strip and all, and Manuel said he had a bunch of people working for him, just like Sanchez and Ramón, and he could get whatever I wanted. Suddenly here I was all set up again. I often think about why people down there trusted me, how I got them to do things they'd never do for other Americans. Why? I think I had some kind of presence, the way I presented it all, and because I had no fear, and I treated people well. I loved most of them in Mexico, and I didn't hold it back. I grew to love Manuel. A lot of Americans came down there and treated them like they were shit, second-class people, people like Ramón, he was always getting screwed. But I really loved them. I think they saw that. Above everything else."

In mid-November, after George had been there about three months, Alfonso, faithful to his word, pulled up in a car at the prison gate with the bail bondsman, Esposito, and Esposito's cousin, the Federale from Mexico City, and told the warden to bring him out. They took him into Durango, to a small office up a set of rickety back stairs where a circuit judge, an older man with a suit and a gray mustache, was sitting at his desk. "Esposito handed him the briefcase," says George. "He opened it, counted the money, then took a piece of paper out of his briefcase and a little seal and he stamped it. 'Jorge, *suelto,*' he said. 'George is free.' Then he took out some more pieces of paper for the warden and stamped them. We took them back to the prison and Alfonso gave them to the warden, and that was it. I was gone. Alfonso seemed sorry to see me go. He wanted to talk about forming some kind of relationship. I told him that seemed like a good idea and I'd call, but that was just because I didn't want to offend him. I already knew where I was going."

Whereas Ramón was little more than a boy, Manuel was a man in his forties, and he was connected to the Mexican Mafia in Mazatlán. This meant for George that very serious consequences would now attend his failure to produce whatever he promised. The deal he worked out with Manuel was that the two would be straight partners. Manuel would furnish the pot, and George would transport it across the border, sell it in the United States, and return to Mazatlán to split the proceeds fifty-fifty, minus expenses. Manuel's farmers were guarded by heavily armed members of the Mafia, referred to simply by its initial, *Eme*, or "Ehmay," a vast criminal enterprise engaged in the same range of activities—drugs, gambling, extortion—as its Italian counterpart in the States. The Mafia ruled through fear and intimidation, and in the mountains, if you were caught where you shouldn't be, there would be trouble. As connected as he was, Manuel, for instance, never ventured north of the Rio Tomazula, which runs down from up in back of Culiacán, from the region of the Espinazo del Diablo, or Devil's Backbone. The marijuana grown in that territory was intended for someone else. There used to be a sign along one of the trails off the Durango road, near a place called Buenos Aires, that, loosely translated, said, "If you're going to make a start, keep on going—if you know what you're doing. But if I were you, I'd think it over." Right beyond the sign was where the charred bodies of Cosme and the Mazatlán police chief were found, a couple of years after George had left Mexico. For some transgression against the *Eme*, they'd been burned alive and left hanging from a tree.

Even by Mafia standards Manuel was a tough customer, someone George saw good reason to emulate. About George's height, tall for a Mexican, he was a classy dresser with a small, neatly clipped mustache. He could just about out-carouse George, a large piece of work for any healthy man, especially when it came to downing the Cocos Locos that Gordo, the bartender at the Shrimp Bucket, would whip up—two ounces each of tequila, vodka, gin, Grenadine, and 150-proof Mexican rum, poured into the hacked-off shell of a fresh coconut and filled with ice and coconut water. Manuel was also an exceptional baseball fanatic, and after a night in the bars and the whorehouses of Mazatlán he'd be up the next morning to field the semiprofessional baseball team he both owned and pitched for as a southpaw sidearmer—the same delivery as George, the Weymouth Little Leaguer. After the game he'd take off in his truck to arrange his business in the mountains. He had read Hermann Hesse and spoke French and English. His hand-tooled boots came from Durango; he wore a broad-brimmed white Stetson. Except when he pitched ball, he kept an automatic pistol tucked into his belt underneath his shirt, a small .32 caliber Beretta for in-town occasions, but when he went into the hills, where he didn't mind if people saw the bulge, he brought his bull-stopping 9-millimeter Llama. Like Manuel, George started sticking a big pistol in his own belt, a nickel-plated .357 Smith & Wesson. He smoked long cigars like Manuel and bought a big white hat. On one occasion he posed for a snapshot with *bandoleras* filled with cartridges criss-crossed over his chest—that was the big bad *bandito* that FBI agent Trout saw in the snapshot in George's bedroom while George was on the run. Nobody fooled with Manuel, and he lived long enough to die of cancer in 1982 in a hospital bed in San Diego, California.

Because of the need to pay Manuel his half of every deal, George now arrived in Mazatlán from Amherst with a considerable amount of cash on him, sometimes fifty to seventy-five thousand dollars. Carrying all that money made him more than a little nervous—he hid it in the battery compartments of large road-service flashlights—and it didn't ease his mind when Manuel invariably reserved a room for him at Rosa's, which was a combination whorehouse and hotel four blocks back from the beach. Manuel had a financial interest in the place, and it was a favorite haunt of many of the *banditos* when they came down from the mountains. George would often have to wait there a day or two for Manuel to show up, during which it didn't fail to strike him that he was literally sleeping in a den of thieves and cutthroats. The bandits would show up in the morning and hang around in the courtyard, George looking out at them from behind a curtain in his room. "There would be ten pick-ups out there, with all these guys with big mustaches, drinking beer and tequila, with pistols in their belts. These guys were very serious people. Killers. Some of them, just to look at them scared the shit out of me. They made me think of the old story about the swan and the scorpion. Where the scorpion asks the swan to take him across the river and the swan says, are you crazy, you'll sting me in the neck, and I'll be dead. I wouldn't do that, the scorpion replies, because then we'd drown and both be dead. So the swan finally agrees, and they start across. But in the middle of the river the scorpion stings him anyway. Why'd you do that? Now we're going to die, the swan says. And the scorpion answers: Because it's my nature."

Although flying in and out of the mountain landing strips meant there was less chance of getting caught, the runways themselves were shorter, three thousand feet rather than five thousand, and the jungle growth at the edges made landing and taking off a little more hairy, which was not appreciated by Here-We-Go Bob, who raised a constant lament over George's new style of operation. Some of the fields were so closed in by trees that the planes had to be "sling shot" into the air, a maneuver that required a half dozen guys to hold on to the tail while the pilot revved the engine. Then they released their hold of the plane abruptly so it would catapult forward with enough speed to achieve liftoff before exhausting the runway. Another problem was the general lumpiness of the landing sites, which were nothing but cornfields, after all. This created a dangerous condition for some of the planes George had been using that had tri-cycle landing gear, with one wheel under the nose and the other two attached to the wings. This sort of plane came in hard, nose down, and if it struck a rut or any kind of a hole, the impact could shear off the front landing gear. Much more suitable for the mountains were any of the "tail-dragger" models, which touched down on the rear wheel first, then settled gently onto the pair of wheels under the wings, like a duck landing on a pond.

Since Manuel had access to more growers than Ramón did, the new level of business demanded more frequent flights, and so George needed additional planes and pilots. Rather than cutting other people in on the operation, he began contracting with Cliff Guttersrud back in Manhattan Beach, the handsome blond pilot with the FLYBOY license plates, who supplied him fliers for a fee. Cliff had his own Lockheed Lodestar, the same twin-tailed model used to fly Ingrid Bergman away in the farewell scene in *Casablanca*, but Guttersrud didn't much fancy taking it into the mountains and setting down on one of George's cornfield-cum-runways. Indeed, he didn't like to get his hands too dirty in any regard, preferring to supervise the pilot operation from a distance. He'd fly down to the Mazatlán airport, dressed in his usual blazer and polo shirt, sometimes bringing along his girlfriend, even his mother and father on one trip, asking George to show them the sights of the city. Cliff leased the planes for the drug flights through a dummy corporation in Manhattan Beach, then changed the markings so their origin would be hard to trace. But as George needed more and more planes—and he now wanted strictly twin-engine jobs with a greater range, ones that could reach the dry lakes without all the rigmarole of stopping on the way for refueling—he was suddenly struck with an idea.

"You know what's the easiest thing to steal in the world?" he asked over lunch not long ago at a harborside restaurant in Plymouth, Massachusetts, looking around to see who was listening, his voice dropping to a whisper. "An airplane," he said. "I can take you around the country and show you hundreds of little airports, and you'd sit in the car all day and no one would show up. Millions of dollars' worth of aircraft just sitting there, and nobody around, not even a watchman. Sometimes these owners don't fly them for weeks, so they don't even know they're gone. So, suddenly it came to me: Why go through all this insanity of trying to buy and lease planes under phony names or corporations that they could trace eventually anyway, when we could just take one—get a nice hundred-thousand-dollar Beechcraft or Cessna, twin-engine, with tip tanks and a fourteen- or fifteen-hundred-mile radius? For free! We were breaking the law anyway. So why leave a trail?"

To try out his scheme, on the occasion of his next trip East in the summer of 1971 George brought along Here-We-Go Bob, rented a car in Amherst, and the two took a little driving trip out to Cape Cod. For two weeks on and off they monitored the traffic at the tiny airport in Chatham, a well-to-do town located at the elbow of the Cape, notable for its nineteenth-century shingled cottages trimmed in hazy blue. A few planes used the airport on the weekends, but on weekdays the place was usually deserted, and always so at night. Landing or taking off after dark, you turned on the runway lights yourself by calling in on the proper radio frequency; no airport personnel was needed. On the final evening of their vigil, George took along a bolt puller normally used to remove corroded fittings from engine blocks and yanked out the ignition system of a sleek twin-engine Cessna with blue striping. He screwed in a new ignition unit, one that had its own key, and reconnected the wires. Bob fired up the plane, set it loose down the runway, and they were off. It took a day and a half of leisurely flying to cross the country, stopping at a couple of local airports to gas up. Reaching the West Coast, they landed at a little field, Hawthorne Airport, near Manhattan Beach, where they stored the plane a few days before Bob made the run south. In what became a routine, after using the planes a few times, George would park them at the Santa Monica Airport, tie them down to the tarmac, and go off to get another one. In this fashion he secured the loan of about fifteen aircraft from airports at Plymouth and at Sandwich and Barnstable on the Cape, from one outside Santa Fe, New Mexico, and another near Mammoth Lakes in California.

The only drawback to this plan was that there was no way of knowing if the borrowed planes had any mechanical problems or how well they'd been serviced. "As long as the engine started up, we figured it was okay," says George. And it was, at least most of the time. George did experience a slight brake problem once with a twin-engine Cessna he'd procured from Santa Fe, which was being flown by one of Cliff's rent-a-pilots named Donny. Coming in to the dry lakes, both George, who was sitting in the copilot's seat, and Donny had to stand up heavily on the pedals to bring the plane to a halt before it got to the end of the salt flat. Donny argued for leaving it there and driving back with Pogo in the camper, but George had other uses for the plane and told him to fly them on to Santa Monica. It was a bad mistake. When they hit the runway at Santa Monica, Donny reversed the props to slow it down and applied pressure to the brake pedal, gradually at first, then with increasing desperation as he saw his effort producing no discernible effect. "'Georgie, they're gone,' he says, we're whizzing down the runway at about a hundred and ten miles an hour and there's nowhere to go—planes are all lined up to the left of us, incoming traffic on the right. Straight ahead I could see a big ditch they'd dug for a storm drain." Before they figured out what to do, the plane had run out of runway and plunged into the ditch, ramming its nose into the dirt and gravel, its tail jerking up into the air.

The first sound after the crunch was the keening of a siren, then men in silver suits were darting about spewing the area with foam. The police were reported to be on the way. Oh, great, George was thinking. "The pilot took off immediately, just ran away. I'm collecting the maps of Mexico and the lake beds, the guns, the pistols, into a bag and I'm trying to get the hell out of there also. One of the silver suits is asking, 'Who the hell are you? Where's the pilot?' 'I don't know, I hitched a ride from Santa Fe. Maybe the pilot's in shock, wandering around somewhere. Why don't you look for him? I don't feel too well myself, I gotta go and throw up.'" George hobbled over to the executive part of the airport, his football knee bothering him now. He saw a young woman coming out of the office and getting into a car. "'I got an emergency, sweetheart. Do you think you could take me to Manhattan Beach?' She said she was only driving as far as halfway. 'That's just where I'm going,' I said. 'Let's go.'"

Stealing airplanes wasn't the only innovation George brought to the smuggling business. He also pioneered the art of the road landing. This practice not only proved useful during the rainy season, June through October, when the fields turned into mudholes, but it also kept the flights clear of regular airports. He didn't have to worry about the police, who were thoroughly paid off. But pressure from the Nixon administration to stem the drug tide continued to mount in the early 1970s, so much that the Mexican government had gotten the army involved. Military authorities put out the word that money could be earned in exchange for information about anyone who was landing planes at night or buying gasoline for unclear purposes. In this connection, Mexican soldiers came uncomfortably close to nabbing George and Manuel on one occasion, when someone at the Mazatlán airport apparently leaked word that a large amount of airplane fuel and hand-operated pumps were being transported up into the mountains. They thanked their escape on the fact that Manuel always had scouts stationed along the lower trails to monitor the presence of hostile parties in the area. Thus, when the army actually sent up a troop of men to investigate the reports, word was rapidly passed on up to the airstrip, just in time for the plane to get in and out and for the farmers and *banditos* to fade into the jungle. With the soldiers firing away aimlessly into the trees, Manuel led George down a hidden series of trails back toward Mazatlán, spending a night on the way in the thatched hut of a friendly *campesino*.

The highway landings obviated the problem of spies, since George moved them around to various roads in the northwestern part of the country. Greg was brought in to fly these jobs, because landing an airplane on a strip of road pocked with potholes and barely wide enough for two cars to pass did not hold much appeal for Here-We-Go Bob. The last and the most memorable of the landings occurred right on Route 15, the main highway from Mazatlán to Culiacán in late August of 1972, about when President Nixon was making a campaign speech in Kentucky promising "peace with honor and not peace with surrender" in Vietnam. Greg had flown down to the Mazatlán airport, and George drove him out to inspect the highway. To keep cars away during landings, George customarily blocked off the road with vehicles at both ends of a few-thousand-foot length, while a couple of Manuel's *banditos* stood around holding guns and staring in an unfriendly manner at anyone who approached. About ten miles north of town they found a smooth-enough stretch, but Greg didn't like all those high-tension power lines strung along-side the northbound lane. Given the slightest miscalculation on his part, his wing tip could nick into a pole or hit a wire. Noting that the poles were wood, George told him not to worry about the power lines. They wouldn't be there when Greg came in for the landing.

It was a little misty that day, with a light rain falling, when George and the bandits pulled up at the landing site with a Win-nebago full of pot. The men blocked the southern access of the road, and George stood by the van at the north. Suddenly, down the highway came a station wagon. It bore Arizona plates, a middle-aged man and woman in front and a couple of boys, twelve or thir-teen years old, in the back, and suitcases strapped on top—an Amer-ican family on vacation. George, his cowboy hat lowered over one eye and a cigar in his mouth, stood in the road and put up his hand for them to stop. They did as he bade, probably because he was car-rying an M-16 semiautomatic rifle, as well as having a revolver tucked in his belt. "Excuse me, sir," he said, leaning over to see into the car. "We're just doing a little drug operation, and you'll have to wait here a minute. Just be patient and you can go on your way very shortly, after the plane leaves."

Just then, Greg called in on the radio to say he'd be touching down in a few minutes and remember the power lines, George. With the vacationers staring in wonder, George ran over to the camper and withdrew a McCulloch chainsaw he'd gotten in a Mazatlán hardware store, ripped at the starter cord, and one by one he lopped off a half-dozen or so of the poles. He made sure to cut them on a 45-degree angle, right to left, so they would topple over away from the road. Radioed the all-clear, Greg then brought down the plane. Quickly the *banditos* helped load it up, Greg spun the craft around in a 180-degree turn, gunned the motor, and took off whence he came, soon appearing as just a receding dot in the distant sky.

George waved the station wagon on through before climbing into the camper and heading back to town. It was dusk when he reached the city limits, and strangely dark. For some reason the streetlamps seemed to be out. Traffic signals weren't working either. When he got to the bar at the Shrimp Bucket, the place was illuminated with the eerie glow of candles, and Gordo, the bartender, was passing out free Cocos Locos. Gordo said he didn't know what it was, but something had happened a little while ago and the lights died suddenly, all over. It was only then that it dawned on George, and was confirmed by a page-one story the next day in the newspapers, that for the sake of providing Greg a safe place to land he'd succeeded in knocking out the power to the whole northern half of the city of Mazatlán.

FIVE

Danbury

1974–1975

Nothing was meant to be. You are the designer of your life. If you want some-thing, you can plan and work for it. Nothing is easy, but nothing is impossible either.

—FROM A PLAQUE OUTSIDE THE COUNSELING CENTER AT THE
FEDERAL CORRECTIONAL INSTITUTION, DANBURY, CONNECTICUT

ONLY TWO MONTHS ELAPSED BETWEEN GEORGE'S lights-out high-way landing in Mazatlán and his equally memorable encounter with the hooker who looked like Britt Ekland—and his arrest—in the Chicago Playboy Club later in the fall of 1972. It would be still another eighteen months, and after the collar by Agent Trout in his childhood bedroom, before the federal marshals would finally get George to a Chicago courtroom to face the music.

Technically, he could have been sentenced to up to five years for the bail jumping alone, plus another fifteen on the marijuana charge. But with his lawyer's nudging, the hugely overburdened U.S. attorney's office in Chicago proved amenable to going along with a term of three years. This meant George would actually do only twelve months in a federal prison if he behaved himself, and that in a low- or medium-security facility, where time passed more or less agreeably.

At 6:00 A.M. on March 14, 1974, federal marshals picked him up at the Cook County Jail and escorted him into the holding pen in the

U.S. District Court building, where his lawyer again went over the deal worked out with the U.S. attorney and coached George on the little speech he should make before Judge James Austin, who would be presiding. Tell him you're sorry, the lawyer said. Tell him you made a mistake and you're going to change your life. Describe your plans for the future. Whatever you tell him, be sure you do it in a way that convinces him you're contrite, repentant. The marshals who brought George over also tried to be helpful. This judge was a son of a bitch, but fair, they said. The best way to deal with him was not to give him any shit and not to talk too long.

At midafternoon George finally found himself standing before the bench. A man in his sixties with glasses and a gray, balding head was looking down at him in an impassive manner. The assistant U.S. attorney reviewed the case and said the bond-jumping charge would be dropped and that a term of three years on the marijuana sale was acceptable to the U.S. government. George's lawyer confirmed the arrangement and larded in some details about Mr. Jung's plans for going back to college after prison, taking some business courses, maybe getting into advertising. The judge then turned his gaze to George and asked him what he had to say for himself, which was when the whole thing slid off the track.

It was the old problem George had when it came to authority figures. George didn't tell his lawyer, but he had a feeling right when he entered the courtroom and saw the federal judge sitting up there that he wasn't going to do the speech they'd agreed on. "I had it all planned, what to say, but when I got in there, something came over me," he recalls. "Suddenly I got this feeling, I became very hostile, because I really didn't believe that what I did was wrong. I mean I was selling stuff that people wanted, it wasn't hurting anyone, people were calling it 'God's herb,' and it was all going to be legal anyway someday." What he actually told the judge was: "Your Honor, I realize I broke the law, but I want to tell you in all honesty that I don't feel it's a crime. I think it's foolishness to sentence a man to prison, for what? For crossing an imaginary line with a bunch of plants?" George found himself expressing other general thoughts as well. He mentioned the Vietnam War, and something about how none of the real criminals in the world ever end up behind bars, a little distillation from the oral philosophy of Bob Dylan. *You say that I'm an outlaw, you say that I'm a thief. Well, where's the Christmas dinner for the people on relief?*

There might have been more, but what he remembers next is his attorney giving him a stamp on the foot, which the judge couldn't see, and the eyes of the court officers lifting up to search the ceiling. George remembers Judge Austin smiling down at him in a way that made him think at first he might just have pulled it off, said things that had gotten through to the old man. "That's an interesting concept you have, Mr. Jung. Very interesting," he recalls the judge saying. "Unfortunately for you, the imaginary line you crossed is real, and the plants you brought with you are illegal, and what you did constitutes a crime." And after hearing the speech, he told George he just might also have a little attitude problem, in view of which the judge didn't think he was of a mind anymore to go along with the three-year deal. Mr. Jung was now going away for four.

As a Level 2 facility—federal prisons are rated on a scale of 1 to 6, 6 being the designation for an end-of-the-line joint, such as the one in Lewisburg, Pennsylvania, or Marion, Illinois—Danbury was designated as a "correctional institution" rather than a "penitentiary," which meant that its inmates had been given relatively low sentences for crimes that entailed no violence. From a quick look at the celebrity roster, they also promised to afford engaging company. George just missed the two Father Berrigans, Dan and Philip, who had been released after doing a year each for pouring bottles of blood plasma over Selective Service records in Baltimore as a protest against the war. But Clifford Irving was around, the author who had made the headlines for his hoax biography of Howard Hughes. From the world of sports came Johnny Sample, the defensive back for the New York Jets whose terrorizing of would-be pass receivers helped his team to victory in Super Bowl III back in 1969. He was now working off his sentence for cashing some fifteen thousand dollars in stolen U.S. Treasury checks as a prison recreation aide, laying down the lines for the ball field, making sure the weight racks were set up properly. Representing the Nixon administration was G. (for George) Gordon Liddy, the unrepentant Watergate defendant, who at the time George arrived was awaiting sentencing on two counts of burglary, two of intercepting oral communications, and one of conspiracy. From his first day, Liddy had made a big hit with the other inmates for the way he turned prison conditions on end and in general made life more difficult for the administration. In the crowded orientation dorm, for instance, where there were only three toilets for one hundred inmates, he succeeded in reserving one for his exclusive use by putting up a fake memo on the bulletin board informing inmates about the myriad of ways they could catch venereal disease, then posting an official-looking sign over one of toilets announcing V.D. ONLY. Using his knowledge of surveillance techniques, he actually managed to bug the administration's telephone lines and drove the guards crazy by spreading the word among prisoners about which guards were sneaking around having affairs with other guards' wives. He also won a lawsuit against the warden that forced guards to honor due-process rules before putting prisoners into solitary for disciplinary infractions. George would encounter Liddy at the weight rack now and then, where he could outpress Liddy by about twenty-five pounds. He determined against trying to make friends with him, however, after Liddy announced one day that in any country given over to him to run he'd put a quick end to drug smuggling by categorizing the offense as a capital crime and doing away with the bastards.

The prison also held an assortment of city and state officials doing time on corruption charges, among them a one-time mayor of Atlantic City and a former head of the New Jersey State Highway Department, as well as a large complement of doctors and business executives convicted for variations on the theme of stealing money. For the untruths he told the Internal Revenue Service, Old Man Grossinger from the famous Catskill hotel family was there working as a gardener, tending the rose beds outside the warden's office and complaining to George that he'd offered to pay the money back but that the government would rather see him die in prison.

During their first two weeks at Danbury inmates attended the prison's orientation program, which consisted of lectures by staff members for four hours every day. Among other objectives, the handbook said, the program was geared toward "helping inmates develop a positive and meaningful attitude toward institutional staff. . . . During this phase, the inmate is encouraged to take an active and realistic part in his program planning. He should express his needs as he sees them."

The quality of an inmate's life in prison depends not on whatever he gets from the staff but on the bounty of one's fellow prisoners, who really run the institution. They operate the laundry, so they're the ones you see to get pants that fit right and a razor-crisp shirt. They run the kitchen and the dining room, so you go to them if you want a tender cut of meat, some special piquancy added to your spaghetti sauce, or a table over in the corner for you and your buddies. They do the clerical chores in the health service, so they're the ones who can provide you a day off from the work detail, on account of the terrible cold you have, the back acting up again, whatever. Two realities prison shares with the free world, however, are that there's no such thing as a free lunch, and altruism exists in pitifully short supply. On the other hand, inmates can nearly always be relied upon to deliver on what they promise, as long as they get something in return.

One of the most lucrative of the prison jobs was clerking in the warden's office. This was where the files were kept containing interesting facts about fellow inmates that held high value as articles of trade. The most salable piece of information was the name of a snitch—someone who had sold out a former acquaintance in exchange for easy time, and maybe not so much of it, in one of the less onerous prison settings (Danbury being a prime example), while the buddy he'd done in was languishing less happily, for a longer period, in some other institution. The identity of the snitch, and the nature of his helpfulness to the authorities, went for a high price at Danbury—payable in cigarettes, money, friendship, or favors. For example, Inmate A in Danbury has a good friend, Inmate B, doing hard time somewhere else. The two of them had a relationship on the outside, and will again someday. Inmate A would give a lot to find out the name of the fucker who turned his friend in.

When George arrived at Danbury, it was his good fortune that the chief clerk in the warden's office was a thirty-three-year-old man named Arthur Davey. Just a year older than George, he turned out to be not only a fellow marijuana smuggler but also, coincidentally, a native of Weymouth, Massachusetts, whose family had moved him away when he was age twelve. In the course of becoming pals, Arthur and George arrived at various ways to make each other's life in the prison more pleasant, if not cushy. Raspy-voiced, with a machine-gun delivery and a mania for orderliness, Arthur had graduated, class of 1964, from Northeastern University with a degree in business administration. After school he had spent several years in the fuel-oil business before deciding abruptly to buy a boat on Cape Cod and become a fisherman. "Codfish don't talk back," he explained. He spent a year or so running after tuna before a cousin persuaded him in late 1970 to join him in another seafaring occupation that paid a lot better, which involved steering the boat down to Jamaica in the West Indies and running it back to the States with large loads of marijuana.

After about eighteen months of operations, Arthur was arrested in 1972 as part of a major bust by agents of the CIA, the U.S. Bureau of Narcotics, the FBI, the Jamaican navy, the Jamaican Coast Guard, the Jamaican military police, and the Jamaican Defense Force, while he was ferrying seven and a half tons of pot to an eighty-four-foot steel-hulled mother ship sitting six miles off the Jamaican coast. Before facing charges in the United States, he had to do his Jamaican time, eight months in a prison just outside of Kingston. Constructed around the time the Pilgrims were landing at Plymouth, it contained eight-by-ten-foot stone cells, each with a single barred window ten inches square. One of the units had been reproduced by a French movie director and set up a hundred feet away for the filming of *Papillon*, about Devil's Island, where it served as the Dustin Hoffman character's place of solitary confinement. In real life, eleven inmates plus Arthur were crammed into the same space, and with the prisoner-classification system being fairly primitive, Arthur found himself thrown together with an interesting array of characters. One cell mate was an eighteen-year-old sugarcane worker with a barrel chest and a normally equanimous disposition. While he was cutting cane in the field one day, something went awry in his wiring system, and before anyone could successfully interfere, he'd whacked off the heads of seven coworkers with his machete. In prison he was known as Time Bomb.

In Danbury George was trying to make friends with a certain inmate who lived three bunks away from him in the dormitory, an endeavor in which Arthur would prove of great help. About six feet tall and weighing three hundred pounds, the inmate was known as Fat Harry. Harry carried such bulk—the upper part of his legs contained as much mass as some people's whole bodies—that later, on the outside, George observed that he had difficulty inserting himself behind the wheel of even a commodious Cadillac Eldorado. Fat Harry was an important member of the Winter Hill Gang in Boston, a now-extinct organization of Irish-American mobsters headed by Howie Winter, which operated out of an auto-body shop in the town of Somerville. The gang split operations on a territorial basis with the Italians, including control over the distribution of every cigarette dispenser, jukebox, and pinball machine in the Northeast. Along with running the book on the South Shore from Boston to the Cape, Harry was also an associate in the Teamsters union. It was some trouble involving union matters, an accounting problem, Harry said, that had landed him in Danbury.

George wanted to get close to Harry, not so much for his connections, although they did come in handy later on, as for the fact that Harry worked in the prison kitchen, as a baker. This meant he and his friends had access to steaks, pastrami sandwiches, desserts, anything they wanted, and at almost any time of day or night. Given the tedium of prison life, what an inmate gets to eat looms as one of the major preoccupations of the day, and so George set out to get the inside track on this bonanza. "I'd keep going over to his bunk and talking to him, but he'd constantly ignore me, try to get rid of me. 'I'm reading now, can't you see?' Or he'd get up and talk to someone else to get away from me. This went on for three weeks. Then one day he looked at me and laughed. 'I checked you out,' he said. 'You were driving me fucking cuckoo, kid. I thought you were a cop they planted in here.'" So now, at least, Harry didn't cringe when George came over to chat. He even gave him some tips on how to be a successful hijacker. Think small, he said. "Razor blades. Did you ever imagine how many of those little boxes of razor blades fit into a semi? Easy to carry, everybody needs them. We hijack a truck and there's razor blades, we just take them, leave everything else." But Harry didn't grant him any food privileges, until one day when he asked George to do him a favor. George knew Arthur in the warden's office; would he mind asking him to look up this certain person in the records, see if there was anything to indicate whether he'd been sent to Danbury after cooperating with the government? Harry would greatly appreciate knowing this. Arthur told George this was easy. The jackets of all the snitches were starred with an asterisk—as seemed to be the case with this guy he was asking about.

Soon George's life improved considerably. First off, he and Arthur got preference getting into the dining hall, which normally involved waiting for a half hour in line because the room could only accommodate so many at a time. And once inside, they were treated with the same deference as Harry's pals. "If you worked in the kitchen, your wife might be getting a thousand dollars a week for you to take care of certain guys," George says. "So when you came along, they'd take your plate and bring it over to a different pot and put on the special stuff." Thursday night was spaghetti night, and whereas the regular inmates got the Franco-American treatment, the Italian mob guys, who had the kitchen jobs, would whip up some dishes from home just for their designated friends; they'd take all day working up the sauce, doing the sausages and meatballs just right, veal *piccata* or chicken Parmesan. At breakfast, the normal cooking style with eggs was to break the yolks and fry the thing up so it looked as if it had been run over by some vehicle. For George it could be eggs Benedict, poached just right with fresh-made hollandaise sauce. He, Arthur, and a British hash importer they liked who played classical music in his cell and told the guys all about the high life on the Spanish island of Ibiza, had a table specially reserved for themselves; they didn't have to scramble around for seats or sit with guys who chewed with their mouths open. On weekends, when everyone was out in the yard on a warm day, the mob guys had the trustee in charge of driving the prison garbage to the city dump stop in town and pick up some Smirnoff at fifty dollars a bottle; they would mix it with a little orange juice and sit out in beach chairs, sipping and catching some rays. The time could slide right by doing it this way.

One thing everyone had to do in prison was work from eight in the morning until four in the afternoon. The pay was twenty cents an hour, and the jobs ranged from swabbing floors to working in the prison factory on a subcontract Danbury had through the Defense Department to make wiring harnesses for intercontinental ballistic missiles, the inmates helping keep Uncle Sam out front in the cold war. Thanks to an Italian he'd befriended through the mob guys in the kitchen, George got recommended for one of the plum jobs, which was teaching high school classes for inmates preparing for the General Equivalency Diploma exam. Inmates lacking high school degrees didn't have to take the classes, but Danbury had a merit system whereby you could earn up to fifty points on your record as a way of showing the parole board you were using the time to enrich your life. The GED classes were worth six points. They were also a good deal for inmate teachers. The school was the only place besides the warden's office that had air-conditioning, and you also got to schmooze with outside teachers, most of them female, who would arrive in the morning with doughnuts and a cheery smile.

More important, the school happened to be run by George's caseworker, the one who would watch over his situation and make the
recommendations at his parole hearing. While others had to wait
weeks for a half-hour appointment with their caseworker, George
could chat with him anytime he wanted. "Mainly," he says, "I spent
the time giving him reason to like me a lot."

And much to his surprise, George found he actually took to the
teaching itself. His first class consisted of twenty-two black pimps
from the streets of New York City, who wound up at Danbury as the
result of an experimental tactic by the U.S. attorney's office, since
abandoned, of charging pimps with income-tax evasion as a way of
combating prostitution. On racial grounds, the hustlers were the
wrong color for Danbury, since its population of white-collar
offenders, mob guys, and upper-echelon drug dealers was mostly
white. Educationally they were also at a disadvantage, since a majority couldn't read. So before they could learn how to give the correct
answers on the test, George had to first teach them to read and
understand the questions.

From his initial confrontation with the group, this didn't look
like it was going to be easy. "The first day of school I stood up in
front of the class and told them who I was and what I wanted to
teach them and passing the GED was going to help them get jobs
on the outside. And they said, Fuck you, man, we're not listening to
any of your bullshit, whitey motherfucker." Now, normally
George's response would have been to not care whether they
learned anything or not. But their attitude posed a threat to his job
security, because if he couldn't get them to do the lessons and take
the GED, he'd be back in the prison, with no air-conditioning,
maybe pushing a broom. "I knew I had to get them in line, so I said,
'Okay. Okay. Any of you know how to smuggle dope into the
United States out of South America and Mexico?' I could tell I had
their attention. 'You can make a hell of a lot more money smuggling
than you can being pimps, I'll tell you. So I'll make a deal with you.
We're not going to tell anyone, but we'll teach a little class in that,
too. I'll teach you everything I know about it, but the deal is that
then you have to learn the other bullshit, okay? And get your
GED's. We'll have smuggling classes for a while, and then we'll
have regular classes.' So they started asking questions, and I began
about airplanes and Mexico, the price structure, how to take a
motor home across the border. There are no black smugglers, I told

them, but we might have twenty new ones right here! I didn't tell them that black people wouldn't get too far taking a motor home full of pot across the Mexican border. But that was okay. They didn't know where Mexico was."

With Professor Jung popping up the flash cards and sounding out the consonants and vowels phonetically, the class learned slowly and steadily how to read and write. And after that they learned English grammar, arithmetic, history, and geography—becoming especially knowledgeable about the California desert country. "It turned out that most of them, once they started studying, did pretty well. We got into areas I enjoyed, like the Civil War, and certain presidents I liked. I told them about Teddy Roosevelt and the Rough Riders, how his men were pinned down at the bottom of San Juan Hill and he charged up on his horse and got his glasses shot off. He put on another pair, and how this inspired his men to charge up after him. I told them how Harry Truman was a regular guy, and wasn't from a wealthy family, that he started out as a haberdasher. And John F. Kennedy, how he was killed by the oil people and the money brokers. They were interested in the slave issue, and I told them a great injustice had been done to them, and how they were still enslaved. I didn't have to say much on that, of course; they already knew it. But I told them I understood how they felt. I'd been to school in the South and almost got the shit kicked out of me for standing up against the injustice down there. A majority of them became very involved in the class and did fairly well. And when they got their GED's, there was a little ceremony. They tried to be cool about it, but you could see they were really proud of the diplomas. It gave you a good feeling."

Along with the celebrities and public officials doing time at Danbury because of momentary lapses in judgment, the prison contained people with a lot of expertise in criminality—the tenured faculty, if you will, of a school for scoundrels. They had a lot of good advice to impart when it came to making money doing something illegal, and when he wasn't busy scheming with George, no one took more advantage of this opportunity than did George's good friend from Colombia, Carlos Lehder. It helped that Carlos was friendly, attractive, and likable, with an ingratiating manner that was almost courtly, and which had he not possessed a foreign accent would have earned him a reputation as a weirdo. "He was very charming," says George. "He would act almost subordinate to you. It was always, 'You know so much. I respect you so much. I'd really appreciate it if you would share some of your knowledge with me.' He'd befriend people. Then he'd suck their brains out."

George's friend Arthur, for instance, was planning to get back into the fishing business after prison and had brought his charts of the waters off Cape Cod into Danbury with him, along with a set of parallel rules, a manual on the tide tables, and a small compass. Carlos soon had him explaining the arts of navigation, showing him the difference between true and magnetic north, showing him how to plot a course and set up a deviation card for the ship's compass. Arthur spent hours with him, demonstrating how to locate your position off the coast using buoy markers and other navigational aids, how to plot out and follow a course by dead reckoning, working out the time, rate, and distance calculations for, say, hitting somewhere along the Florida Keys from the Colombian coast.

Carlos also spent time with Dan Moore, the former president of the Surety Bank and Trust Company of Wakefield, Massachusetts, who had scarpered with $8.1 million of his institution's assets, and regaled inmates and guards alike with the travel brochures on places he planned to visit after getting out. Carlos taught him Spanish in return for lectures on how the banking system worked, what transactions had to be reported to the government, how to set up accounts in offshore institutions and move money around in ways no one could follow, which banks had the numbered accounts in the Cayman Islands, the Bahamas, the Netherlands Antilles. Banks with home offices in Canada were good ones, Carlos was told, especially ones with branches in Freeport and Panama City. "Carlos was mesmerized by people who knew about things, and Danbury was a regular mind factory," says George. "He never got past the seventh grade, but if he'd gone on to college, he was the kind who'd go right for his doctorate." Everything he was told he wrote down on pads of paper, which he filed away. What he learned about planes and boats and real estate and money laundering all went into separate pockets of one of those expandable cardboard files you can tie up in a string. "He was obsessive about details that I'd get bored with after a while. All I wanted to know was that a twin-engine Cessna had a fifteen-hundred-mile range and you could put tip tanks or saddle tanks on it and it could go so much farther, and you went from point A to point B. That was enough for me. Carlos wanted to know the kind of engine it had, the dimensions of the cargo space, the different radio frequencies, the climb ratios, everything."

Carlos talked a lot with a doctor who had owned a string of nursing homes in New York State and had been convicted of defrauding the government by charging Medicare for the treatment of patients who didn't exist except on his phony rosters. After being indicted, he fled the United States for Belize, formerly British Honduras, a tiny country in Central America just east of Guatemala in the Caribbean. He had spent a couple of years down there, but finally grew homesick for his family and agreed to a deal with the U.S. attorney involving a couple of years in Danbury. Belize was what Carlos wanted to hear about. The doctor told him the country had no army and no extradition treaties with the United States; government officials were easy to bribe, the police rode around on bicycles, for God's sake. One use for the place, Carlos thought, was as a way station to that California desert George was always talking about. "But soon, Carlos was having these ideas about not just using the place, but taking it over," George says, "doing it big-time, overthrowing the government. He wanted to set up gambling casinos, build condos, a yacht club, build an empire. He talked of making it a safe place for fugitives. It would be a haven for criminals to come to, where you couldn't get extradited to the country that was after you. 'You're on the run, you can stay here, you pay us $2 million.' Once he got on to that idea, it was all he talked about; he wouldn't stop."

Carlos modeled his dress and bearing after the tough ex-marine G. Gordon Liddy. Unlike Carlos, Liddy wasn't very solicitous toward fellow inmates; when he talked to people, it was to bark out opinions, not invite a lot of discussion on the matter. He also stood out at Danbury for the way he carried himself about the yard, with his shoulders erect, immaculately dressed, even in prison-issue. His khakis were pressed with a crease that could slice meat, his black shoes were spit-shined, his chest was always out. Carlos watched Liddy and began imitating him—keeping carefully groomed, his clothes crisp, strutting around the yard with his file of information under his arm. "Put Carlos and Liddy together, they looked like they were about to graduate from Annapolis," says George.

Carlos also pumped George for what he'd read and the things he knew. He was particularly interested in listening to what George had to say about the philosophy of existentialism and about Kierkegaard and Nietzsche. George had read them during a philosophy course at Long Beach City College and, with modifications here and there, had adopted existentialism as his own life view. "I didn't know about existentialism before Jack Leahy would come home from college and talk about it back in Weymouth, but then I studied it and found out it was simple. It's free will, I told Carlos. Nobody has the right to tell you what to do or how to do it, and you do what you want and you set your own moral standards, something within reason, and you take full responsibility for your acts." George had also studied Machiavelli's *The Prince*, and was impressed by what he had written about acquiring power and manipulating people to achieve your ends. The prison library didn't have a copy, so he ordered Carlos one from a bookstore in Danbury.

George and Carlos would talk as they walked around the yard after supper—they had to be back in their rooms for the evening count at nine—and increasingly, it seemed, as the months went by, Carlos would raise the topic of revolution. He spoke of starting with Belize and eventually taking over Colombia. His hero was Ché Guevara, who with a shave would be a pretty close look-alike for Carlos, with his longish locks and penetrating eyes. Cocaine would be the vehicle to fund this enterprise, Carlos said. It was the Achilles' heel of America. The gringos were too morally weak to resist it. They were going to go for it in a big way, especially now that the rock stars and entertainment people were into it. The Americans would do anything they heard the movie stars did. Carlos also had admiring words to say about Adolf Hitler, how he'd worked out a specific plan for achieving power, laid it all out in *Mein Kampf*, and possessed the strength of will to carry it through.

"I'd listen, but I wasn't very enthusiastic about his political aspirations and all," says George. "Plus what he was saying about Belize, it would only be a matter of time until the world became aware of the arrangement there and brought an end to it. We didn't need Belize, I told him; Mexico would be enough. I was only interested in moving a product people wanted for cash, not running a country. I wanted to make as much money as I could in a couple of years and then get out of it. Get the motor sailer, go to Ibiza or maybe Australia, the Great Barrier Reef. I told him that in my opinion there were already enough dictators fucking up the world. Ché had come to a bad end, dying in the mountains of Bolivia a broken man. I told Carlos he should read Ché's life story again. All revolutionaries come to a bad end in one form or another. I'd read history; revolutions never work out. One man's freedom fighter was always another man's dictator. I told him he should concentrate on our future smuggling enterprise. But it was like talking to a deaf person. He'd start going on about Hitler again. I decided it was best not to pursue the subject any further."

For all his tendency toward the grandiose, at 135 pounds Carlos was still a relative pipsqueak when it came to his general effect. "When you first met him, he looked like just a kid," says Arthur. "He may have been twenty-five, but he looked sixteen, like a teenager. He had protection in prison, because George stuck with him, and no one was going to screw around with George. Otherwise the black guys would have loved to make a little girl out of him." George tried to beef Carlos up by taking him out to the weight rack, to put some bulk into his upper body. George was pressing 240 pounds then, with ten repetitions. Carlos was struggling to get up to 150. And one day at the rack a dispute arose over one of the weights, and an inmate came up and struck Carlos hard in the face with his open hand. "And Carlos didn't do anything!" recalls George. "Now, in prison, you never do *nothing*, even if the guy's Mike Tyson and you know you're going to get the shit kicked out of you, you have to go after him. If anybody ever slapped me in the face, I don't care who it was, they'd know they'd have to kill me. Otherwise your life is down the toilet. So I told that fucking guy, 'I'm going to hit you in the fucking face with this fucking barbell, I'm going to fuck you up bad, you ever touch him again.' He backed off after that. Yet I couldn't believe that here was this big Mafioso Colombian guerrilla fighter, always talking about Ché Guevara and taking over countries—and didn't throw a punch!

"But then, I don't know, you look back at it, and in Danbury Carlos knew just what he was doing. He might have backed down from the fight, but he got exactly what he wanted out of every single person in that place. I mean, I thought I was slick, and here he was about to take me on the biggest roller-coaster ride I'd been on in my life."

It was February 1975, and according to the math of the criminal justice system, George's parole hearing was due up shortly; he hoped it would be the prelude to his release from prison. He'd entered Danbury the previous April, having been sentenced to four years. He was eligible for parole after serving a third of that, or sixteen months. He'd already done more than four months in jails in Boston and Chicago before arriving at Danbury. So with a favorable ruling by the parole board, early April was when he'd be set free. He'd performed exceptionally as a schoolteacher, getting all his classes through the GED exam successfully. And during coffee breaks he'd been assuring his caseworker, that he had a plan and the desire to go straight when he got out. He wanted to buy a boat, he said, and go into the fishing business on the Cape, like Arthur. There was a little money saved up, and his parents would help him. He'd already screwed his life up enough, and he wanted to start off new. He was only thirty-two. It wasn't too late, even to go back and finish up school, maybe at the community college on the Cape. A degree in business administration wouldn't hurt when it came to marketing his fish. Don't worry, his caseworker told him. "He said he was behind me one thousand percent."

On the appointed day, George shaved carefully, dressed himself in a new set of khakis, and walked down to the little hearing room near the warden's office, where he was ushered in by his caseworker. At the head of the table sat the two hearing officers. One was a kindly looking, middle-aged white man with glasses, dressed in a cheap-looking light-colored suit. The other one was a thin, balding black man, a sharp dresser who struck George as a lot more savvy than the white guy. During the thirty minutes or so that George was in there, the black guy never said a word, never smiled. He was the one George worried about.

"The white guy starts off, asking me all these questions. How I felt about my crime and the things I did, and I said I realized it was wrong and I had screwed up my life and I didn't want anything to do with drugs anymore. He asked me what I was planning to do now, and I told him about the fishing boat and the plans I had to get it. He liked that I was going to stay with my family, not just go off. They wanted to be sure you weren't going to fall into any bad company. And I told about the college classes. And on and on with all the bullshit, and still the black guy hadn't said a word. I was getting real uptight about him. He's just looking at me. I'm thinking to myself, He knows what I'm all about. He's going to get me, I know."

"Then the white guy said, 'Okay, George, go on outside and

we'll call you back in a little bit and let you know.' It was a little torment they do to you. I mean, why can't they just let you know, right away? So I sat on a bench outside the hearing room, while my caseworker was in there talking to them. And I sat there for twenty minutes or so, worrying about my case. Then they called me back in. And the white guy is smiling. 'Congratulations, George, you're going home! We hope you'll use this opportunity to get your life in order, and that we won't be seeing you back in a place like this.'

"'Oh, thank you, thank you, I won't let you down, believe me. Thank you for everything.' And I shook both their hands and turned around and started walking to the door when the black guy opens his mouth.

"'Hey George,' he said. I turn around and he gives me this big wink. 'Keep that fishing boat out of South American waters.'"

SIX

Cape Cod

1975–1976

Cocaine is for horses, not for men;
They say it'll kill you, but they don't say when.
— TRADITIONAL BLUES

ON THE DAY HE WAS TO BE RELEASED FROM DANBURY, George overslept. Fat Harry came banging on his door after breakfast shouting that they'd been calling his name over the loudspeaker and to get down to Receiving & Discharge; his father was there to take him home.

George could in fact have gotten out two months earlier if he'd gone to a halfway house in Boston where parolees worked regular jobs during the day and returned at night, thus acclimating themselves to the free world without dying of the shock. But after his parole hearing George's enthusiasm for leaving was somewhat diminished. In prison he was picking up a lot of useful information, gathering names and numbers, which he noted down in a black phone book packed away with his gear. Carlos wouldn't be getting out for another six months anyway, and then faced spending additional time in custody while the Immigration and Naturalization Service, convinced he was someone America could get on nicely without, arranged to deport him to Colombia.

But what most eroded George's enthusiasm for being released was that as a condition of his parole he had to live at home with his parents, at least for the next year. He'd be back at 30 Abigail Adams Circle, back in his old room upstairs with his Little League trophy still sitting on the dresser. No more the Big Bad Bandito, the neighbors would no doubt think; nothing like a taste of prison to take Mr. Smart-ass down a peg or two. He was also looking at thirty months on parole, during which any infraction could send him back to finish his sentence. A federal parole officer out of Boston would be stopping by the house every week or so for a talk with his mom about whether George was behaving himself. It was a teeth-grinding prospect.

After Fat Harry's wake-up call, George made his way down to where Wong, the Chinese heroin dealer who had dusted George with antilice powder on his admission, now stood ready to exchange the prison duds for a nice suit, compliments of the U.S. Bureau of Prisons. George glanced at the government threads, which looked like something off the rack at Wal-Mart; it was gabardine, with a funny weave to it, weird orange with a blue tinge. He cast a fond thought back to the soft Cabrera jacket he'd been wearing the day of his arrest, a luxuriant doeskin that had cost twelve hundred dollars at Neiman Marcus in Dallas, and that was back in 1973. He thought also of those five-hundred-dollar Bruno Magli loafers, of their wafer-thin leather that fairly caressed the feet. Thanks, but no, he told Wong. "I told him I wouldn't wear that thing to a shit fight. Wong also looked disgusted and told me that's what everyone said. 'I don't know why we keep this stuff. No one ever wants it.'" On the way out, his caseworker shook his hand and told him to behave himself. Hey, don't worry on that score, George said, throwing him one last promise on the fishing boat. He handed his papers through a glass partition to the guard, who pressed a button sending the electronic door sliding back into the wall with a low moan: *brooooooo*. And George walked out into the glaring spring sunlight, a free man—in a manner of speaking.

George greeted his father with an enthusiastic hug and asked him to stop at the first liquor store he saw so he could get a couple of bottles of champagne for a little celebration. The trip back proceeded pleasantly enough, Fred tooling up Route 84 toward Massachusetts, George draining the champagne while watching the Connecticut hills undulate on by, until they got to Middletown, when the Mercury threw a rod and they had to rent a car to get them home—not a good omen.

Back home things didn't go too badly for the first few weeks, mostly because George's friend the Sad-Eyed Lady often stopped by the house from her place down on the Cape. Her name was Beth, and George had met her three years before when he was back East with Annette doing business. She was forty-three at the time, ten years his senior, about four feet eight inches tall and plumpish, a diminutive Mama Cass character dressed in flowing white muumuus with Indian-style braids and lots of beads. George had nicknamed her from the Bob Dylan song "Sad-Eyed Lady of the Lowlands," with the line "Your eyes like smoke and your prayers like rhymes." She called him Kurt Kruger, because that's what she thought his name was. It was an alias George had picked up from a German movie actor and used when he had to be in Massachusetts, once the FBI was after him. He didn't tell her for two years who he really was.

Beth lived in a large, rambling house in Dennis, presiding over a ménage of children from her broken marriage that resembled the Munster clan, hippie division. When home from college, her oldest son, Nicky, stayed down in the basement mixing up batches of crystal methamphetamine and putting together explosive devices he used for blowing up mailboxes outside draft-board offices. The two younger children, aged eleven and nine, sat around smoking pot in the living room. Upstairs a fifteen-year-old anorexic-looking daughter named Dulcinea worked on her oil paintings—mournful landscapes mostly, along with portraits of stricken children. She took George up there one day to have a look at her artwork and suddenly was all over him, kissing and caressing him, working her way down his body, eventually unhooking his belt, pulling down his zipper, and honoring him with a very educated blow job. "After that," George recalls, "she started acting a little crazy, getting all excited and talking fast. 'I'm going to take you out to Provincetown and have some fags fuck you, and I'm going to watch.' I told her I didn't really think I could get into that."

Topics of conversation ranged from the passionately loathed Richard Nixon (Nicky doing his David Frye number complete with the scowls and eyebrows) to the Trilateral Commission's plot to seize control of the world's resources to Beth's theories on reincarnation, the collective unconscious, and time travel. After having a little smoke, she'd tell George he'd been a Greek warrior in a previous life. "She'd ask me to take off my shirt so she could see the battle scars from the Peloponnesian War. She said I was in the favor of the gods, but that there was an evil force that was totally destructive and I had to watch out for that one."

George would perk up, though, when talk turned to the subject of Nietzsche. "I'd talk for hours to him about Nietzsche," says Beth, who last saw George in 1976 and has since moved her family from the Cape to Los Angeles. "Nietzsche argued that a person is a whole thing, consisting of light and dark images. If you try eliminating the dark ones, how do you know that you might not also be eliminating something that's light, too? They're intertwined. George was very enchanted with that part of it, about the Damons and Angels. It seemed to provide a perfect rationale for the things he did. 'They're both in there, inside me,' he'd say. 'There's nothing I can do about it. And they're in you, too. I'll show you.' And he'd go right to where your devils were and command them to rise. If he said, 'Rise,' they lived. If you were the slightest bit greedy, he had you in the palm of his hand. That was George Jung. That was the secret of his success. I found that out very painfully."

As George had foreseen only too well back in Danbury, it didn't take long before life with his parents became unendurable. Over supper at night, his mother always maneuvered the talk to her favorite topic, how George had ruined his life, and theirs too, while he was at it. "You're thirty-three years old and you're a bum," was her main theme. "You're a common criminal. You've been in prison. You've disgraced us with the neighbors. We can't lift up our heads. You've thrown your life away. You've never been any good. You can't hold a decent job." George couldn't get away from it by moving out, because that would get him in trouble with the parole office. Malcolm MacGregor, Mike Grable, and Barry Damon were all married and most raising children—there was nothing in their lives he could identify with. He also gave a wide berth to the big colonial at the bottom of the hill, where his high school sweetheart, Gerry Lee, now lived with her husband, John Hollander, who'd played end on the football team. They had two kids now, and a big yard with nice woods in the back. George felt like an invisible man, thrust backward into a former life but lacking the ability to connect with anyone who lived there. He snuck around the town, not wanting to be seen. "Here I'd been up in the hills with Manuel and the

Mazatlán, 1970: George and a business colleague.

(*Above*) Twenty-five years later, a reunion with Ramón Moreno at the Oceana Bar in Puerto Vallarta.

Carlos Lehder Rivas, at the controls and on the rise. (*Lope Medina/Sygma*)

Barry Kane, a. k. a. the Silver Fox, after his arrest in Hyannisport in 1989. (*Steve Heaslip/Cape Cod Times*)

A stylish George, taking the air on his deck in Eastham, 1978.

George and Richard Barile, busted in Eastham in 1980.

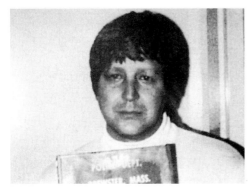

George Jung, age three, with his mother, Ermine.

The schoolboy with an impish grin.

Members of the Weymouth High School Varsity Football squad, 1959. *Left to right:* Brian Dunbar, Dick Murley, George Jung, Ron DiGravio, Mike Grable, Jack Fisher (coach), and Barry Damon. (*Courtesy of Barry Damon*)

Beneath his graduation picture, the yearbook listed George's credits as "Football 10, 11, 12; Spring track 10, 11, 12; Winter track 10," and his career plans as "Business Administration."

George and a friend dancing at the Weymouth Senior Prom, 1961.

In his country's service—briefly—in 1968.

Kristina Jung turning seven in 1985, just after George's arrest in Fort Lauderdale.

Mirtha and Kristina in California, 1991.

Carlos Lehder at his arrest, February 1987. (*AP/Wide World Photos*)

George Jung, private citizen, West Yarmouth, 1993. (*Sara Roszak*)

(*Left and below*) Trooper Billy McGreal, undercover, and at the award ceremony for "Trooper of the Year," 1980. (*Courtesy of Billy McGreal*)

Señor Pablo Escobar Gaviria, El Padrino. (*AP/Wide World Photos*)

Detective Greg Kridos, undercover in Fort Lauderdale with a wagonload of cocaine, 1985. (*Courtesy of Fort Lauderdale Police Department*)

The haul in the Fort Lauderdale bust. *Left to right:* Detective Tom Tiderington, Fort Lauderdale Police Department; Jack Toal, DEA group supervisor; Detective Greg Kridos, Fort Lauderdale P.D.; and Mike McManus, DEA special agent. (*Courtesy of Fort Lauderdale Police Department*)

Indians, running free for years, making more money than anyone I ever knew, leading my own life. Suddenly there I am with no car, living with my parents, going by their rules, sleeping in the bedroom where I was a little boy, and them yelling at me, even Fred started doing it. 'I don't want to catch you going down to the bottom of the hill and start making any trouble,' he said."

George busied himself reshingling his parents' house and duly broached the fishing idea to his parole officer in Boston, a young woman named Jo-Anne Carr, who'd visit the house regularly to check on his progress. "My mother and Jo-Anne got along real well. It was, 'Oh, Jo-Anne, darling, come on in and have some cake and coffee.' She was a little lame for a parole officer, naïve to the whole thing, and young. Kind of cute face, but heavy in the legs. I used to play with her—give her a hug. 'You're not bad-looking, you know. Maybe we could go out sometime.' I don't think she got asked out on many dates. 'Oh, George, we're not supposed to do that,' she'd say."

At Danbury, George had hoped to do his temporary fishing stint with his friend Arthur Davey. Arthur had a magic touch when it came to putting his boat right where the fish were. One time out on the Georges Bank he landed such a huge catch that he ran out of space in the hold and ordered the crew out of their bunks so he could fill them up with haddock and cod. Arthur wanted George to come out with him, but their parole officers nixed the arrangement on the grounds that two ex-convicts couldn't be going into business together.

George had more than enough money—$50,000 in hundreds stashed in a safe-deposit box in the Rockland Trust Company in Weymouth. It was all that remained of the quarter of a million or so from his smuggling days, most of which he'd blown in the last six months before the FBI caught him. He'd taken one of his girlfriends on a tour of first-class hotels in Santa Fe, Mammoth Lakes, and other parts of the West. What with the champagne-and-caviar breakfasts and the sprees at clothing stores, $200,000 of it disappeared with remarkable speed. He couldn't touch the remaining money unless he could show he'd earned it from some honest endeavor. Clam digging at Wessagussett Beach wouldn't quite fill the bill. As it was, his guilty plea left him owing the IRS $286,000 in special taxes the government imposed on large marijuana seizures. So as long as George continued in the pose of a law-abiding member of society, the fifty long ones wouldn't do him much good.

In regard to his problem with the IRS, George sought the help of Fat Harry, who on his release from Danbury went back to running the book on the South Shore and living with his wife and mother-in-law in their neatly kept house near a cemetery just outside of Boston. Harry advised him to go down to the Federal Building in Boston and see a certain lady named Mrs. O'Toole. "She brought me up as a kid," he said. "Get a dozen roses and I'll call and tell her you're coming down. She'll take care of it." George did, and Mrs. O'Toole proved to be an old fan of Harry's. "He's a bad boy sometimes, but I love him anyway," she said. "He told me all about you, and we can just eliminate this because if you sign a pauper's oath that you don't have any money, I can take care of it." So one minute George owed the federal government $286,000, and the next, with the stroke of a pen, he didn't owe it anything at all.

He turned now to establishing himself in the fishing business. The Sad-Eyed Lady put up ten thousand in cash from her divorce settlement and signed a bank note for thirty thousand more, which was enough to purchase a slightly leaky forest-green thirty-eight-foot dragger out of Plymouth Harbor, which George christened the *Hunter*. The vessel was too small to make the seventy-mile trip out to the rich fishing grounds of the Georges Banks, where the seas could get pretty rough in sudden bad weather. On the other hand, it was shorter than the sixty-foot length that would have required George to hire a captain with a master's license from the Coast Guard. To take out the *Hunter* he had only to know how to read a compass. But there were several catches. When Beth agreed to put up the money, it was with the understanding that George was going into the fishing business for real, to make money at it. To do that he had to work hard, meaning the boat had to put out to fish every day, weather permitting. He didn't tell Beth, but George didn't quite see the venture that way. He viewed the vessel as a sort of Potemkin village for Jo-Anne Carr to inspect. He was also silently hoping the boat would put her in mind to reduce the number of months he'd have to spend on parole.

To keep the boat going out every day, George hired a captain, a guy he knew named Gordon, whom George had found selling used cars on the Lincoln-Mercury lot in Quincy but who harbored great ambitions of making it in the fishing business. George took on another acquaintance, named Peter, as a deck hand. Peter was an airplane pilot who happened to be visiting from Los Angeles, having just jumped bond on a three-year sentence for marijuana smuggling in California. He knew all about the dry lake beds. George wanted him close at hand—not just for net hauling. Beth complained at first about why they needed to pay an extra hand—it meant less money all around, she said. But George's persuasive charm had not been diminished at Danbury. "I don't remember what reason he gave," she says, "but one of the things about George was he could get anybody to do anything he wanted. I never saw so much power in a person, so much charisma. He had such great charm, perfect manners. He'd talk to the waitress or someone in a bookstore, anyone, and he could transform them, bring joy into their lives. They were beaming when he left."

Whatever his talents might have won for George in some other field, they certainly availed him of very little in his fishing enterprise, where he was dogged by bad luck and inexperience. Not far into the venture, he and his crew snagged a sunken wreck of another fishing boat and tore their net all to hell, which cost them several days in port. They were hunting in largely depleted waters, netting only five hundred to a thousand pounds' worth a day, which added up to only three hundred dollars a week apiece, even going out all the time. That winter of 1975–76 it stormed constantly, and got so cold that Plymouth Harbor froze over for the first time in local memory. Fishing in the freezing weather was about the least amount of fun George had ever experienced. After taking in the net on a big reel, the catch would be dumped on the deck, to be gutted and sorted in the howling wind, with sleet or snow icing up the deck. They wore insulated boots and gloves, but water seeped in and soon numbed up their fingers and toes. The boat would be pitching 20 or 30 degrees. Fall over the side now, and someone had to do quick work to save you from a watery death. It got so miserable that Peter finally made the decision to return to California, do his prison time, and get on with his life; at least he'd be warm. This meant George had to go out on every trip or leave the boat idle, which would bring both Beth and Jo-Anne down on his neck.

Then one foggy day the engine failed as the boat was coming through the Cape Cod Canal, and the current took them in toward the rocks. George radioed for help, but the Coast Guard rescue ship passed right by without seeing them. George became so apoplectic shouting into the transmitter—We're over here, you fucking assholes!—that the commander in Hyannis later called him in to account for his breach of radio etiquette. Just before disaster struck, the engine somehow restarted, and they got the boat safely back to port. Subsequent breakdowns, however, so debilitated their fishing effort that, in the end, George let the repo people from the bank simply come and tow the *Hunter* away, to sell it for whatever they could recoup. Beth's ten thousand dollars went down the drain, along with what remained of her faith in George as a business partner. Shortly after that, word also leaked back to her about some of the things going on between George and her daughter, Dulcinea, the little session with the art critique not having been the last of it. George wasn't completely surprised, therefore, when one day in mid-February of 1976 the Sad-Eyed Lady ordered him to clear the hell out. When he arrived at her house, she was standing in the doorway. "She was shrieking, 'You son of a bitch. I've put a curse on you that's going to last the rest of your miserable life and destroy you.'"

All this sudden misfortune might have weighed heavier on George's mind had a telegram he'd been waiting for not arrived at his parents' house shortly after the rupture with Beth. It was from Colombia, the city of Medellín. WEATHER BEAUTIFUL. PLEASE COME DOWN, it read. There was a telephone number he was supposed to call. And it was signed: YOUR FRIEND, CARLOS.

For all his bravado back in Danbury, the bragging about his big contacts, George harbored some doubts as to how he was really going to move a load of coke. Who wanted it? Where were they? During a three-day furlough he'd taken toward the end of his prison term, George had called up Richard Barile at the Tonsorial Parlor in Manhattan Beach to discuss the potential of the cocaine market in Los Angeles. Richard said he'd like to hear more about what George had in mind but remained a little vague about the specifics. "He said it was going on big out there, but he couldn't quote any prices, just that if I came out, it could happen. I was just a lousy marijuana smuggler. I don't think he took me really seriously."

On the Cape there seemed to be hardly any demand at all. What cocaine you could get was of such poor quality, cut so often, that the preferred drug for people in the euphoria market seemed to be methamphetamine, or speed—especially in the form that Beth's son, Nick, was concocting in the basement. This was "crystal meth," later known as "ice," a smokable crystalline form of methamphetamine that produces a high of several hours' duration; it is also highly addictive. One day the previous fall Beth had asked George to deliver a batch of Nick's product to a guy who'd be waiting in a car down the street from the house in Dennis. The man turned out to be a gaunt, furtive-looking character in his late twenties, with deep-socketed, penetrating eyes, who seemed as jumpy as a blue jay. Obviously he was on the stuff himself, George thought. From the way he darted glances around the landscape, you could also spot him as a drug dealer from a few hundred yards off. George produced the crystal and the guy turned over a bag containing fifteen thousand dollars in cash. He went by the name of "Mr. T," and he was the son of a fairly prosperous Portuguese fisherman. George noted down his phone number, thinking Mr. T might prove useful later on.

During his furlough, George had also called Manuel down in Mazatlán to talk about cocaine, but his former colleague proved far from encouraging. He said, "You're getting into a dangerous game, Jorge, with some dangerous fucking people. Not like it is in the marijuana business, where we are all brothers. Why do we not continue the business we were doing? We'll always be safe, and have our friendship and enough money. The road you want to head down leads to self-destruction and evil." George dismissed the warning as exaggeration; Manuel always did tend to overdramatize things.

With limited phone lines available between the United States and Colombia, it took several frustrating hours for George to get through to Carlos. The number turned out to be that of Autos Lehder, the family car business located in downtown Medellín, and it was Guillermo, Carlos's brother, who finally answered. Carlos had gone out, he said. George should call back the next day. "When Carlos and I finally connected, we talked in a very general way, no specifics. He said he wanted me to come to Medellín to talk about how things should proceed, that everything down there was just as we had discussed. I said give me some time to make arrangements and I'd let him know when I was coming."

Only after hanging up did George think that it probably wouldn't be smart to go down himself, at least not on this trip. He was still on probation and supposed to be staying at home. Getting a false passport was no problem, but what if something happened down there, some kind of delay, and Jo-Anne—her visits always came on short notice—chose that moment to drop by? It seemed safer to send down an emissary, he thought, a go-between. The person who came to mind was Frank Shea, his old childhood friend and contact at Amherst. He'd also done some flying for George out of Mazatlán. Frank was back in Weymouth now, working at the Fore River Shipyard. He'd never been arrested, wasn't on any customs checklist. Frank seemed ideal for the mission. As a pilot, he had the knowledge to check out possible airfields and discuss arrangements for getting planes loaded up. "Frank was also the kind of guy who'd do something, but then go away from it," George says. "And I didn't want to involve any more people in this than I had to."

It turned out Frank had just been laid off from work at the shipyard and quickly agreed to go. George gave him money for tickets, and in mid-March he was in Colombia, meeting with Carlos at a ranch the family owned a little way out of town. He called George the next day. "Frank was basically ecstatic over the phone. He liked Carlos very much, and he was looking at the coke, saying something to the effect that we've really hit the jackpot this time. I'd really put it together."

Whereas George, however, had anticipated that the flights would start right away, the Colombians seemed to want to move a little more slowly. "I had sent Frank down there to start the airplane trips, only Carlos switched it all around. They had no concept of airplane flights or major drug loads." Over the telephone the conversation had to be circumspect, but it boiled down to the fact that the Colombians also didn't quite trust this gringo friend of Carlos's yet. To front out a load of kilos, send them up to someone they'd never heard of, had no control over, maybe couldn't even find if something went wrong, that was far too big a gamble. So the deal, Frank said, was to try a little bit at first, and see where that goes. Then maybe they'd talk about airplanes.

Frank told George to call Carlos back the next day and settle the details directly with him. This time George went to a pay phone. It cost eighty quarters to talk for three minutes to Carlos in Medellín. George was soon keeping a little Tupperware container under the seat of his car filled with $100 in coins—and the Drug Enforcement Administration, the successor to the U.S. Bureau of Narcotics and Dangerous Drugs, was soon pegging cocaine smugglers by how low their pants were riding, or the little pocketbooks or satchels they'd have sitting by the pay phone. Carlos said the plan was to smuggle in fifteen kilos. Although certainly not a planeload, fifteen kilos rated as a significant amount of cocaine back in 1976, $750,000 worth, if it could be moved for, say, $50,000 apiece. *If*, George was thinking.

Carlos told George to go out and buy fifteen hard-shell suitcases, Samsonites, seven blue and eight red, one for each kilo. Then find two people to act as couriers, to board a plane with half the suitcases and fly down to the island of Antigua in the Caribbean, one of the Leeward Islands in the Lesser Antilles, property of Great Britain. It was a popular resort, with flights going in and out all the time. The Colombians Carlos was dealing with had made several runs through Antigua and knew the lay of the land there. George was instructed to have the couriers check into the hotel, where Carlos and Frank and an associate of Carlos's named Cesar Toban would also be staying. After the couriers arrived, Carlos would come to their room and replace the suitcases taken on the flight down with ones he'd brought from Medellín. The new suitcases would also be blue and red Samsonites, identical in every respect, except that the metal stripping around the edge that held in the plastic inner linings on each side would have been removed and the linings lifted out. Underneath would be laid out a thin layer of cocaine, a half kilo on each side, one per suitcase. Carlos wanted to hide only a small amount of cocaine in each, so that with the plastic liner fitted back in place and the metal stripping refastened with rivets, it would be difficult, even taking out all the clothes, to see or feel that there was anything secreted between the two layers. Of course, the false-bottom trick was not exactly a startlingly new ploy; it was well known to customs agents. The trip required a certain amount of performance art to attract the inspector's attention *away* from the luggage. The couriers should be women, well-tanned, pretty, vacationing-schoolteacher types, with a lot of personality. Their luggage should be packed to reflect the great week they'd had, filled with resort clothes and souvenirs from the islands. Most important, the couriers should be people who in no way felt frightened or uneasy about what they were doing. Customs agents possessed deers' noses when it came to sniffing out a guilty conscience.

George had just the person in mind. Several weeks before, in the Riverside Bar in Weymouth, he'd taken up with a very lively, good-looking woman named Betsy. She was twenty-eight and had jet-black hair, electric-blue eyes, and a light complexion—unmistakably Irish. She was also free, not tied down to a job. Her parents had died the year before in a head-on collision at the rotary in Orleans. She'd collected on both insurance policies, coming out with $300,000, a lot of cash then, along with their house in Weymouth, which was located, as it happened, on Whitmans Pond, the old spawning ground for the famous Weymouth herring. And, more to the point, along with her all-American appearance, Betsy was a kleptomaniac, possessed of rock-steady nerves and a brazen self-confidence. "I've seen her walk into a jewelry store and just mesmerize them," George says. "She'd put on a ring or try on a necklace, looking right at the clerk, and then say, 'Well, I'll think it over,' and walk out."

George broached the subject of the Antigua trip with her the same day he talked to Carlos. Betsy was sitting on a blanket watching her ten-year-old daughter, Lisa, playing softball at school. With her was a friend of Betsy's named Winny Polly, who by coincidence was also Frank Shea's girlfriend. George said he had a surprise for them. How would they like to have an all-expenses-paid week's vacation in Antigua? They could go down, swim, eat, stay in a fancy hotel, have a blast—all on him. All they had to do was bring something back for him, a few suitcases. What was in the suitcases? Betsy wanted to know. "Don't worry about it, it's nothing," George said. "Just drugs."

As it worked out, things couldn't have gone more smoothly. George drove them to Logan Airport and helped them check the bags through, joking with the clerk about how women could possibly fill up so many suitcases for just a little vacation. Betsy and Winny flew down to Antigua, checked into the hotel, and met Frank and Carlos and his friend Cesar who came from a wealthy Colombian family in the coffee business. A couple of days later they called George to say Antigua was a tropical paradise and they were having a terrific time. They'd been renting catamarans, doing the samba every night. Betsy especially liked Carlos's friend, Cesar, who was slim, bronzed, so gracious, and a great dancer—Was something going on there? George wondered, but let it pass. Five days later he got a call telling him they were on their way home, and several hours later they showed up at Betsy's house having taken a bus down from Logan. What about the bags? George asked. Oh, don't worry, they're safe, Betsy said. They didn't want to bring eight pieces of luggage down on the bus, so they'd checked the suitcases into several lockers in the bus terminal in Boston.

The bus terminal in Boston? George nearly hit the roof. "I told them that was an insane fucking thing to do. One thing you never do in the drug business, you never, ever want to lose control. As long as you're in possession of it, you always know what's going on. But once you lose sight of it, you don't know what's happening. Three or four hundred thousand dollars' worth of cocaine that belongs to someone else, that I could get killed for if it's lost, and they've left it sitting in the fucking bus terminal?! People were always breaking into those things, stealing shit, the police making random checks."

George took a now-contrite Betsy with him and drove rapidly into Boston to pick up the bags, which were unmolested, it turned out, and brought them back to Betsy's bedroom. George took out their vacation clothes, and with a screwdriver pried off the rivets and lifted out the liners to see what they'd brought. The cocaine lay in the bottom underneath a layer of shelf paper and stuck down with aluminum duct tape to keep it from shifting position. It was glistening white and flaky, sprinkled with clusters of crystals, or rocks, which signaled a high level of purity. After opening up all the suitcases, George repacked the coke into one-pound packages, wrapped them with duct tape, then slipped them into heavy, waterproof Mylar bags. After dark he took them outside to a vacant lot belonging to the house next door and stashed them inside one of several drainage pipes that lay in the weeds, abandoned there after some construction work. One of the things he'd learned from the jailhouse lawyers at Danbury was to never stash drugs on your own property. That way, if the load is seized, the police will have a hard time proving the stuff belongs to you. The following day, the women flew down to Antigua to pick up the rest.

For his part in arranging the transportation, George was to keep five kilos for himself, to sell for whatever he could get. He would deliver the remaining ten kilos in Boston to Cesar Toban, who would fly up from Colombia, picking up Carlos's girlfriend on the way, a young Cuban-American from New York City named Jemel Nacel, a student at the College of the City of New York. They would call George to arrange the meeting.

While the girls were still down in Antigua, George put a quarter of an ounce of the cocaine into a plastic bag and drove it to where

The Sad-Eyed Lady's speed dealer, Mr. T, lived in Hyannis. No one was home, so he slipped the bag under the rubber mat by the back door and drove back to Betsy's house, a place he was now beginning to call home, at last out from under the collective thumb of his parents. That night George phoned him up. "I told him to look under the mat, that he'd find a little present there. See if he liked it and call me back."

Mr. T had been dealing dope since 1970, after he got out of the U.S. Navy, demobilized with some 500,000 other servicemen into a job market, on the Cape, at least, that was in a state of collapse. "I spent six months on unemployment," Mr. T recalls, "waiting for jobs in lines two blocks long in the snow and slush in Hyannis, freezing my fucking ass off. So I started dealing dope. I borrowed two hundred dollars from my mother and bought a pound of pot, and made four hundred dollars' profit and had two ounces to smoke myself. I said, 'Fuck *off*, Jack, this is *it*,' and that's how I began." As a general-assignment drug dealer, never knowing what might come along, Mr. T had all the paraphernalia—the scales, the plastic bags, and also a "hot box," which was used by the police and dealers alike for testing out the quality of cocaine, along with certain other drugs. By putting a small amount of the cocaine onto a two-inch-square hot plate, then gradually turning up the heat as measured by a thermometer attached to the top of the box, one can find out what the temperature is precisely at the moment the crystal substance on the hot plate begins to melt. Lab-pure cocaine hydrochloride, without a trace of imperfection—something almost impossible to achieve under the conditions in the processing plants in the Colombian jungle—melts at 195 degrees centigrade. The stuff it's cut with—mannite, quinine, lactose, or Methedrine—all melt at much lower temperatures, from 105 degrees for quinine, for instance, to 166 degrees for mannite. Street coke that's heavily cut, or stepped-on, in the parlance of the trade, might start melting at temperatures in the low 100s. The high-grade powder registers in the 160s and upper-170s.

Mr. T placed a smidgen of George's coke on his hot plate and began applying the heat. It got hotter and hotter, and hotter still as the mercury in the glass climbed past 165, past 170, past 175. Jesus! Past 180. Past 185. When the cocaine finally began to dribble off the hot plate and melt away, the thermometer had hit a temperature of 187 degrees.

George got the callback in about fifteen minutes. Mr. T seemed to have difficulty holding on to his cool. "His voice was higher than usual and he said: 'Holy shit, where'd you get this stuff?'"

"That was when I knew we really had something."

After Betsy and Winny returned with the rest of the coke, George started fronting his share of the kilos to Mr. T, a kilo at a time. Mr. T put on a little cut, not too much, since they both wanted to market a premium-grade product, then packaged it into one-ounce bags, which he sold to smaller dealers up and down the Cape. As Mr. T got paid, he paid George, at the rate of $47,000 a kilo, more than George had hoped for. George also unloaded a couple of kilos to a dealer in Cambridge named Louis, an Italian leather-goods importer he'd met at Danbury who had customers throughout the Northeast. One way or another, the five kilos vanished in a week, and George found himself in possession of $235,000 in cash.

While it was a pretty respectable return on a single run, the $235,000 rated as pin money compared to the proceeds that were heading his way in the not-distant future, when so much green would be pouring in that he had to store it in the hot-air ducts in Betsy's basement, cutting off the heat to parts of the house so as not to singe his liquid assets. Later on the cash would be lining the very walls of his house, dug into the floor of his basement, stuffed into hollowed-out air-conditioning units. Condensed into denominations of fifties and one hundreds, however, the quarter million dollars fit nicely into a compartment at the back of the top dresser drawer in Betsy's bedroom. It was easier for him to get at that way; he didn't have to keep people waiting for their money while he excused himself suddenly to go down to check out the boiler. This was also when he fell into a habit that lasted the rest of his cocaine days, of slipping ten grand into the left inside pocket of his jacket whenever he had to leave the house. To buy things, sure, but not only for that. George had found little else that had ever given him a greater sense of comfort or made the world seem more secure and welcoming than just feeling the presence of that packet of bills pressing up next to his heart.

A few days later Jemel and Cesar called from Boston to arrange for delivery of the other ten kilos. George met them for lunch at the Sheraton Hotel. He told them to tell Carlos to keep it coming. It looked as if he could move a lot of the product just on the Cape alone, without even tapping his man in L.A. yet. Then would come the real money storm. They told him Carlos would be in touch, gave him a key to the trunk of their car, and said good-bye. In the parking lot he took two suitcases containing the kilos out of his trunk, put it in theirs, and drove back to Weymouth.

Betsy and Winny received fifteen thousand dollars each for their work. He'd never discussed any money with Frank, but on his return to the States he offered him twenty-five thousand dollars for his part in the transaction. Frank wasn't very happy with that. Twenty-five seemed pretty mean, he said, considering the remuneration he could just imagine George was allowing himself. George insisted that it was good money for the limited work Frank had done, which amounted to not much more than transmitting a couple of messages, and having a good time in the bargain, all paid for. Frank grumbled more loudly and kept it up, until one day in the car, driving along with George, Winny, Betsy, and Betsy's Lhasa apso, Toby, Shea began whacking the little dog on the head when it got into a yapping fit. George suddenly blew up. He threatened to beat the shit out of Frank if he touched the goddamn dog once more, then stopped the car and told him to get the fuck out anyway, he was tired of all the bitching about the money. Frank glared at him before he got out and stormed off. The two never saw each other again, which was how George saved twenty-five thousand dollars. But with Frank out of the picture, he felt the urgent need to find a pilot, to stop this penny-ante suitcase stuff and start shifting the enterprise into a higher gear.

On July Fourth weekend, 1976, the U.S. Bicentennial celebrations were in full throttle, from atop Mars Hill in Maine, the point where the dawn's early light first graces the American coast, to the town of George, in Washington State, where the locals had baked a sixty-square-foot cherry pie. During the week-long celebration, New York and Boston each played host to the Tall Ships, the fleet of square-riggers that came from around the world to honor the occasion, among them the steel-hulled *Christian Radich* from Norway, with its figurehead of a woman in a full-length blue dress, and the *Sangres II* from Portugal, whose sails were emblazoned with the Maltese Cross. Traveling from port to port, the ships cut through the Cape Cod Canal rather than going around the tip at Provincetown, and to watch them sail by, so many yachts and powerboats had jammed into Buzzards Bay that you could have practically walked across the bay going from deck to deck.

One of these pleasure boats was a thirty-three-foot Egg Harbor sportfisherman belonging to a real estate developer who specialized in constructing inexpensive houses known as half-Capes (they had only a sleeping loft upstairs instead of the two bedrooms found in the traditional Cape). A partner of his, Teddy Fields, was also on board that day. So were George and Betsy. Teddy Fields had grown up across the street from George on the Circle in Weymouth. Teddy's family had money. The sons were sent off to private colleges, and it was in their garage that George first laid eyes on the Porsche. Fields was also one of the few boyhood friends George had kept up with after leaving Weymouth, and he had stayed at Teddy's house in Cotuit, a little west of Hyannis, on occasions when George was down on the Cape on marijuana business. Flush with proceeds from the recent suitcase trip, George had volunteered to bring along a dozen bottles of Dom Pérignon, some iced caviar, and lobsters. Besides helping to honor the country's birthday, George was there to ask his friend Teddy—since he knew everyone on the Cape—where he might locate a trustworthy pilot.

This was how George came to meet Barry Kane. Kane, a lawyer, was the Chatham town counsel. Prematurely gray, suave-looking, and smooth-mannered, he was sometimes referred to as the Silver Fox. He'd grown up in the Jamaica Plain section of Boston under modest circumstances and had had to borrow money to attend Boston College Law School, from which he graduated in 1958. When he arrived on the Cape three years later with his wife and their first baby, he was fourteen thousand dollars in debt and at night drove a cab in Boston to make ends meet. The next fifteen years saw him prosper from his law practice and from buying and selling real estate during a time of rapid growth in the area. Along with property in Hyannis, West Harwich, and South Yarmouth on the Cape, Kane owned a ski place in Mount Snow, Vermont, a condominium in Nassau in the Bahamas, a Porsche, a Cadillac, and a commodious sailboat. He lived in a rambling white-clapboard Victorian house, circa 1845, on Queen Anne Road, one of the oldest and most exclusive parts of Chatham. Chatham itself was one of the oldest and most exclusive towns on the Cape, its main street lined with sedate shops and outdoor cafés. The men of the town sported blue blazers and yellow trousers, the women wore pastel skirts, clutching tony straw baskets handcrafted on Nantucket at six hundred dollars a pop. Kane's wife, the daughter of William Moloney, M.D., a professor at the Harvard Medical School, died of an overdose of sleeping pills in 1972. Her death, which left Barry with five children to raise, was ruled as accidental by the coroner, but it created a bitter dispute in the family over who was ultimately to blame. At her funeral, according to a real estate developer friend at the time, the two sides of the family glared at each other over the coffin. Dr. Moloney blamed Barry. He said his daughter had died of a broken heart because of Kane's more or less constant philandering.

In the late 1960s Kane had taken up flying at the little Chatham airport, where he kept a twin-engine Cessna 310. In 1975 he'd upgraded his rating to commercial status, allowing him to carry passengers and cargo, and he regularly ferried his friends and girlfriends down to the Bahamas. The developer friend says Kane spent a lot of time in the Bahamas and would boast about the influential contacts he'd made in the islands. He also talked about the fortunes people there were making in the humming drug trade, whose operators used the islands as a stopping-off point for marijuana and cocaine headed for the United States. "Barry loved money," the friend says, "and I think he thought there was a lot of money to be made there, if only he could figure a way to break into it." Kane never told him in so many words that he wanted to run drugs, but there were certain things he'd say. "One time we were on our way down there, flying over Cape Hatteras off North Carolina. He was looking at the air charts, the radar vectors and all, and he said, 'You know, there's a gap between the radar rings right here. You could slip in between them, never be detected, and get into the country illegally.' The other thing, he asked me once was did I know that of all the drugs smuggled into the country and the drug runners operating that only 5 percent of them ever got arrested?"

Barry also appeared to be in a bit of trouble. The very month he met George he was due up before the Massachusetts Board of Bar Overseers, the group that watches over lawyers' ethics, on a complaint by one of his clients that Kane had fleeced him out of property he'd put up as collateral for a loan. A year later Kane would be publicly censored for the incident. But prior to that, in his testimony before the board in July of 1976, he said his real estate investments were in a precarious state and that his law business had actually lost money in the two preceding years. He could use a piece of change.

Two days after their discussion on the boat, Fields accompanied George to Barry Kane's law office, located in a shingled cottage on a quiet street on the outskirts of Chatham. "I admit I felt a little uptight about walking into a very prominent lawyer's office and asking if he wanted to smuggle cocaine," George says. After the introductions, however, George came directly to the point. "I told him there was an opportunity for him to make several million dollars tax-free. It would involve the use of his airplane. 'If you're not interested,' I said, 'I'll stop right here and walk out and not mention it again. We'll both forget this conversation ever took place.'"

"Don't leave, I'm interested," Barry said, hardly waiting for George to finish. "It's smuggling drugs we're talking about, right?"

"He then went on to tell me he had a place in the Bahamas, that he knew certain people down there, Nigel Bowe, a prominent lawyer who would be helpful, and we could do it like this and he had a plane. . . ."

Kane jumped on the deal so fast it took George aback. He felt compelled to give him some kind of warning. "I said, 'Look, you're a lawyer, this is against the law, all the penalties. If you say no, I'll walk out of here right now and forget the whole thing, we never met each other. It'll be over.' But he started quoting me the range between Medellín and the Bahamas as the crow flies, saying he'd have to get back to me on the precise mileage, 'But we can stop overnight at Nassau. I can use the Bahamas as a base, fly the stuff into the States from there.' He mentioned somewhere in the Carolinas. I was obviously talking to a guy who, if he hadn't actually done this before, had given it an awful lot of thought."

They agreed that Kane would do the runs. That summer he would have to work out a way to extend the range of his aircraft and check into getting some additional navigational aids. George busied himself with increasing his financial security with more small-scale trips, picking up the loads in Queens, New York, from Jemel, now a regular courier—not quite the mountain of money he was planning on, but averaging about fifty thousand dollars a month, enough for starters. To deliver the goods to Mr. T, he'd buy thirty-two-ounce jars of Coffee-mate, steam off the paper seal underneath the cap, and fill them up with cocaine, just a little short of a kilo, then glue the seal back on. He'd stick the jar into a bag of groceries, along with Wheaties, Dipsy Doodles, eggs, and a can of Dinty Moore's. A friend of Betsy's, Courtney, a welder by trade with a wife and several children who earned extra money from George doing drug errands, would meet George at a bar in Weymouth. George would hand over the bag of groceries, which Courtney took out and put in the trunk of a car in the parking lot that had been left there by Mr. T, who would come by later and drive it off. On one occasion, after a spate of car thefts, two plainclothes police officers were staking out the parking lot and saw this guy doing something funny with a bag of groceries, putting them in the trunk of one car, getting into another one and driving away. When they stopped him, Courtney stumbled a little at first, but recovered enough to say that this buddy of his couldn't get off work and had asked him to pick up some things at the market, put the stuff in his trunk. Here, see? Wheaties, eggs, Coffee-mate. Okay, the policemen said, have a good day. Drive carefully.

By now George felt he'd lived the monk's life long enough and could begin slowly unlimbering his talent for spending money. All for cash, since he didn't want any records kept, he bought a snow-white Porsche 924 to replace the one he'd had in California in his marijuana days. For the trips to New York he picked up a Ford Thunderbird, something more spacious. He liked the Thunderbirds because they were built on a Lincoln chassis, making for an easy ride, and had a powerful engine, which he fuel-injected by having blowers installed in the carburetor. He also bored and stroked the cylinders to boost the compression ratio. To catch George now, a police officer would have to push his usual wreck of a cruiser up to somewhere over 140 miles an hour.

From talking to Carlos, which he did now about once a week, George also saw that occasions were going soon to arise where he'd have to attend business meetings outside the country, and for these he'd need to equip himself with false ID. Trips would certainly have to be made to Medellín. Already a meeting had been planned for Toronto that fall to introduce Carlos to Barry Kane. Toronto was chosen because Carlos could fly there under his own name with no legal problems. Also, according to the wisdom passed on by jail-house lawyers at Danbury, talking with someone about drug smuggling in a foreign country made you arrest-proof on a conspiracy charge, since the meetings could not be used as evidence in an American court of law. This bit of wisdom was dangerously incorrect, as any criminal lawyer could have advised. As long as the conspiring was aimed at breaking laws in the United States, it could be carried on inside the dimly lit hut of a fakir on the banks of the Ganges and still be presented to an American jury. Talking in Canada, however, did lay a veneer of secrecy over their impending project, making it distinctly unlikely anyone would discover that the availability of high-grade powder on the East and West coasts was about to surge dramatically.

For his phony ID, George relied on the fact that local bureaus of vital statistics, the agencies that issue birth certificates, never in his experience bothered to note down alongside the name of some- one who was born whether that person had also died. To get a birth certificate, he simply filled out a form in the name of someone on the obit pages of the local paper, paid five dollars—no identification required—and walked out with the document within fifteen min- utes. From that, he could get everything else he needed—a voter registration card, a library card. He'd apply for a Social Security card, telling the lady he'd been working outside the country all these years and never had one. When he applied for a driver's license, he'd say he'd lived in London since he was a little boy and had always used public transportation. Given the number of times he'd taken it, he had the Massachusetts driving test fairly well mem- orized. George was careful in applying for a U.S. passport, since conceivably one could have been issued to his namesake before he'd passed away, and for all George knew, the normal waiting period of two weeks might entail a cross-check of the records, which would reveal that this guy seemed to have changed a lot—where'd he get all that hair? To cut down the risk, he'd purchase a round-trip air- plane ticket to London, the flight leaving two days hence. Then he'd go to the passport office with his driver's license and birth cer- tificate. He would explain that his best friend had announced he was getting married in two days and he had to get a passport quickly so he could make it to the ceremony. Seeing the evidence of the air- plane ticket, the agent invariably would rush it through by the next day, no problem.

In such a fashion, George raised from the dead Delbert Lapham, Brian Whittaker, and David Mahan. He'd garnish his offi- cial ID's with business cards, giving himself a variety of occupations. At one point, after Barry Kane had advised him to launder his money by buying gold and silver, he handed out cards announcing he was a precious-metals broker. He stayed in that line of work for quite some time, until, on a flight to Los Angeles one day, the man next to him said, gee, what a coincidence, he was in the precious-metals business, too. What did George think of the current market? That's when George's migraine problem suddenly returned and he begged off further conversation. After that, George decided to become an out-of-work movie actor.

That October, Kane landed his Cessna at the Norwood Airport near Weymouth to pick up George, and they headed up to Toronto, where they met Carlos at the Holiday Inn at the airport. Carlos seemed genuinely excited to see George again, in their first meeting since April of 1975, a year and a half before. They gave each other great hugs and did a lot of back thumping. Carlos's face had matured, and he was no longer the scrawny kid he was in prison. He still talked rapid-fire, brimming with enthusiasm. "Bouncing off the walls" was how George describes him. He was dressed in a dark suit and tie, still very businesslike in his ways. An attaché case had replaced the cardboard file he'd carried around at Danbury for organizing the notes he made, the brochures he collected on differ-ent airplanes and navigational equipment. He got on well with Kane, partly because both of them were detail men, absorbed by the facts and figures, whereas George stuck to the big picture. Carlos took elaborate notes as Barry gave him a tour of the plane and ticked off its vital statistics. Fuel capacity for the Cessna 310-R was just over two hundred gallons, including what was in the little tor-pedolike tip tanks attached to the ends of the wings. It could do 165 knots. Leaning out the fuel mixture to 65 percent, this meant it could cruise an hour on twenty-eight gallons, which gave it a range of just over thirteen hundred miles.

As Carlos had earlier explained, the cocaine would be packaged in kilo-size bricks, wrapped with cellophane and duct tape, and twenty-five of these would be packed into a rubberized sack the size of an army duffel bag. The Cessna had a cargo weight capacity of fourteen hundred pounds, but in cubic feet the space would be very tight. Kane thought if he removed the two passenger seats, leaving only those for the pilot and copilot, he could fit in as many as ten or twelve duffel bags, as much as 300 kilos' worth, or 660 pounds.

The planned airlift of 100 percent pure coke was a feat that would generate an astounding amount of money, even by today's standards. At the going retail price of $100 a gram, and figuring an average cut of just two to one, a single kilo of imported coke amounted to three thousand grams of retail product, which would bring in $300,000 in sales. This meant Barry's airplane trip would produce approximately $90 million in eventual revenue. And to George, this was just the maiden voyage. He was already badgering Carlos to get his compadres down there in the forests of Colombia organized, so by the time the machinery was humming in the States, with more planes, more pilots, and more places to land, they could average a trip like this once a month—why not?—and bring in more than $1 billion worth of cocaine a year.

As transporters rather than actual dealers, of course, George and Carlos and Barry would get to share in only a relatively small portion of these sales figures. This was perfectly okay with George. As he often repeated, it was better to let someone else take the risk, have the headaches selling the stuff; that's where you got caught. Of course, he himself was wholesaling then, with Mr. T, but that was just to generate the start-up cash. Once things developed, he wanted to cut that off. He would do the pilots and the planes, arrange the trips, see to it that the goods were flown safely out of Colombia and delivered inside the United States to whomever and wherever the Colombians designated. This service would pay well enough. For the first run, Carlos had already gotten his Colombian contacts to agree to pay $10,000 a kilo—$3 million. Barry said he wanted $1.8 million of this. Not only was he doing most of the work, and doing it with his own plane, but, as he was shortly to explain, there were expenses he'd incur, people to hire, officials to pay off. For their part, George and Carlos agreed to split the rest, which added up to $600,000 each, for essentially making some phone calls and organizing a few meetings. This was 1976, when that sum would buy sixty BMW's down at Trans-Atlantic Motors in Hyannis, when someone with a million dollars could say legitimately that he was independently wealthy. George saw his motor sailer gliding into view, the beaches and cafés of the Costa del Sol fast taking shape on his horizon.

To get the kilos, Carlos said, Kane would have to fly down to an airstrip located on a certain ranch owned by an acquaintance of his outside Medellín. The airstrip was five thousand feet long and had been built for the planes bringing in coca paste from Bolivia and Peru. Accommodations would be provided for spending the night, meaning Barry could fly in one day, load up and take off the next. Carlos would supply him with a Colombian national who knew where the field was and would fly down with him to help find it.

Regarding the flying part, Kane foresaw a number of interrelated problems here, none of which couldn't be solved with careful planning and money—mostly the latter. One way to go was simply to fly the cocaine straight from Medellín into somewhere in the United States on a straight shot. But the distance involved was too long, about fifteen hundred miles to the tip of Florida, and then there would be only a limited number of landing strips to choose from. Florida was also where the DEA expected drugs to come in. What you wanted to do was to land the plane at someplace in the interior of the country, where the authorities didn't know from drug flights. For this reason, he proposed using the Bahamas, where he had contacts, as a transshipment point. He'd fly down to Nassau from the Cape. Then, on a Friday night, the start of the weekend air-traffic jam, he'd file a flight plan with the tower saying he was heading for one of the other islands, but instead he would go directly to Medellín. He'd land, load up the plane, and return to Nassau on Saturday. Kane had a friend in Nassau named Nigel Bowe, a lawyer who knew everyone in the Bahamas, from Prime Minister Lynden Pindling and the defense minister to the head of state security and all the high police officials. (The file on Bowe's involvement in the drug trade would soon be filling up several drawers in the DEA office in Miami.) By knowing Bowe and paying some money, Kane could manage to park the plane on the runway in Nassau, leave it there overnight filled with cocaine, and fly out the next day. No one would bother it.

Only one hundred eighty miles separate Nassau from the United States. On Sunday afternoon Kane would take off amid the hordes of mom-and-pop flights headed back to Florida at the end of the weekend. Just as he neared the coast, he'd make an abrupt right-hand turn, drop down to the deck, 100 yards off the ocean, below radar range, and fly north toward Cape Hatteras, toward that open window he'd shown his developer pal on the radar maps. From there he'd fly inland to the Piedmont area of North Carolina, where he would have arranged to land at a private airfield. The duffel bags would be transferred from the plane to a vehicle of some kind and driven down to George and Carlos in Miami. They would then be responsible for delivering the goods to the recipient designated by the Colombians, and getting paid—especially getting paid.

The only problem seemed to be the range of Kane's airplane, which, as it stood now, couldn't quite make it. From Medellín to

Nassau was a little more than thirteen hundred miles as the crow flies—which meant flying straight over central Cuba, not a good idea unless you didn't mind getting shot out of the air. Allowing the plane to circumvent Cuba, taking it just to the east of the Guantá-namo naval base, would add over a hundred miles to the run. So Kane needed to expand his plane's fuel capacity. Drug pilots often installed "bladder" tanks—inflatable rubberized tanks fitted into the interior cargo area—to disguise how far their planes could really fly; "a little extra for the wife and kids," the expression ran. But bladder tanks, because they were undetectable from the outside, masking the plane's true range, were against the law. They violated the rules of the Federal Aviation Administration that set up strict limits on fuel capacity for the various types of aircraft, partly to inhibit smug-gling. To add legal range you had to get special permission, but then the narcs would know about it. But Barry didn't want bladder tanks anyway because they took up too much space when filled, meaning he would have to leave some of the cocaine behind. A better idea, he said, was to install saddle tanks, specially built into the fuselage of the aircraft. These were expensive. But not only would they disguise the plane's range should some DEA type be snooping around the airport at Nassau, they also would take up no additional cargo room.

Kane also said he wanted a marine loran. Developed by the mili-tary and regarded as a breakthrough in navigational aids, a loran was an instrument about the size of a modern lap-top computer that would allow him to punch in the coordinates of the landing strip outside Medellín, its latitude and longitude, and then keep him on course once he got in the air. Using radio beacons as a fix, the loran could put you down within fifteen feet of anywhere you wanted to go on the globe—"Find you a toilet seat in Bogotá," as one drug pilot put it. It could even help you land at night, with just a flash-light to show where the runway turned into jungle. But that's why the Colombian was coming along, Carlos reminded him—to show him how to get there. The Colombian was okay, Barry said, but he'd rely on himself, thanks.

With one thing and another, Kane figured he could get the plane ready for fifty thousand dollars, up front. No problem, Carlos told him, and promptly wrote out a check on Barclay's Bank, to cash. The meeting over, Barry declined the invitation to stay around to see the sights of Toronto, have some fun. Business and pleasure didn't mix with him, he said. Approximately three hours after he'd arrived, Kane had the plane back in the air and was winging his way home to Chatham.

Back living with Betsy in Weymouth—for parole needs, he still listed his parents' address as his own—George spent that fall feeling generally exuberant over his prospects, even trying in his own fashion to patch up some of the fences he'd smashed. He left an envelope at the Sad-Eyed Lady's with the ten thousand dollars he owed her for the fishing-boat fiasco; maybe she'd lighten up the curse she'd put on him. He also tried to get his father fixed up in a cushy political job. Ever since his stroke when George was a high school junior, Fred had been working half-days as groundskeeper at the Mount Hope Cemetery in Weymouth, never feeling great about it. One night at a bar George ran into a classmate of his from high school, a contractor who had gone into politics and got himself elected as a town selectman. During the conversation George learned that the job of commissioner of cemeteries for the town had come open, a political plum that paid pretty well for not a lot of work; there was some prestige in it, too. How much would it take to land that for his old man, George wanted to know. The selectman thought twenty thousand would just about do it. He'd have the cash ready tomorrow, George said. "This guy then called up my father and offered him the job. But Fred said he didn't want it. I think maybe he sensed something was wrong. Fred never took a nickel from anybody in his life without working for it."

Now that he didn't have to live with his mother, George even tried to smooth things over with Ermine. While his parents were away for a week visiting Marie and Otis in Indiana, he hired Courtney and his son to gut the family kitchen and replace all the cabinets and appliances. They installed walnut paneling, olive carpeting to match the new cabinets, a stainless-steel sink, a self-cleaning electric oven, and a frost-free refrigerator. When his mother returned, she told George she loved it, waxing very enthusiastic even over the color scheme. His father didn't say much directly, but George learned that he'd resented the intrusion. If Ermine really wanted one, it was his prerogative to provide her a new kitchen, which everyone knew he couldn't afford. All his father said to George was that the kitchen was nice, but he liked the old refrigerator better.

It was at about this time that Carlos's behavior started becoming somewhat aberrant; he started screwing up in annoying ways that threatened their impending enterprise. Although it was all George's contacts they were now exploiting in their common effort to transport the product into the States and to sell it, George couldn't help getting the feeling he was regarded ever so slightly as the junior partner in the arrangement. He still regarded Carlos as a "brother," but Carlos wasn't consulting him on every single matter these days, and he'd begun to lurch about a little recklessly. First, the $50,000 check he'd so blithely written out to Barry Kane bounced. Kane was someone they should avoid irritating at all costs. "Barry called me up and said, 'Your friend Carlos's credibility on a scale of one to ten just went down to minus one.'" George apologized and told him to meet him at the Hilltop Steakhouse in Braintree, where he gave him an envelope containing $25,000. Kane grudgingly accepted the lesser amount, since it just about covered the loran and the gas tanks. After that Carlos got himself arrested down in Colombia in a car-smuggling incident. This came in the middle of another suitcase trip they were running through Caracas, Venezuela, which had to be aborted, losing them $400,000 in potential sales and costing George another $20,000 or so in expenses. All over a car! George was really pissed at that one.

Then came the little episode with the police dogs, with Carlos running for his life through the snowbound woods of northern Vermont.

It began in February of 1977; Carlos had gotten out of jail on the car-smuggling charge and had called George to meet him at the Holiday Inn in Toronto—he had news that might cheer George up. There were fifty kilos waiting at a house in Miami. He wanted George to go down and pick it up and bring it up north. Carlos would slip over the border into the States and be waiting for him at the Hyatt Regency Hotel in Cambridge. They didn't discuss what exactly would happen next, but George assumed he'd be paid with at least five of the kilos to sell through Mr. T and Louis, the leather importer, and install an extra quarter-million in the heating ducts in Betsy's basement. The new money had a mollifying effect, and George and Carlos spent a couple of days in Toronto talking over plans. In George's presence, Carlos made several calls down to Colombia, conversing with someone in obviously deferential tones, the conversation always being a little one-sided. *"Sí, padrone. Sí, sí, padrone,"* Carlos would say. He never said who was on the line, but

George assumed it was the Big Man, the source of the voluminous amount of product they'd shortly begin winging in.

Life with Carlos proved to be not much fun. He'd come down from his hotel room to eat his meals, but he didn't drink and most of the time stayed up there poring obsessively over the piles of magazines and brochures he'd collect on airplanes and cars and trucks. Or he'd wander around the airport talking to airplane dealers, stop at Chevrolet lots to look over those infernal Chevy Blazers he couldn't get enough of. "Carlos began driving me nuts up there with the airplanes and Blazers, talking about the same thing over and over: 'It's got this range to it and this much cargo space and we can get this one here, and I've got all the statistics.' 'Look, Carlos,' I'd say. 'In America you do business and then you take time out, you live your life.' He had a real German mentality." At night George had to go out to the bars by himself, not that this posed a great hardship. "Canadian women seemed very loose to me. It was, you talked to them, you had money and dressed well, you got laid."

One night, about one or two in the morning, Carlos called George to his room. "He was sitting on the bed, and he said, 'I think I'm going to marry Jemel. What do you think about it?' I said I thought it was a wonderful idea. She was a beautiful young woman, a very nice girl. 'I think you would be a wonderful couple.'" Carlos meant right away. He immediately called Jemel in New York, she flew up the next day, and, after getting the blood tests and the papers signed, the three drove to the outskirts of Toronto to a justice of the peace, an elderly man who had a chapel rigged up in a paneled room in his basement. He put out the bouquet of flowers George had brought on the makeshift altar, cranked up Mendelssohn's "Wedding March" on a record player, and with George and the justice's wife witnessing the event, Carlos and Jemel tied the knot. Two hours later the happy couple drove to Montreal for their honeymoon, and George flew off to see about picking up the cocaine.

Always a little edgy about his phony passport—George, now briefly Brian Whittaker—took the precaution of flying home from Canada aboard Bar Harbor Airlines, clearing customs at Bangor, Maine, where travelers weren't burdened by too much scrutiny. "They had a little guy in a red-and-black checked hunting cap who'd come out and say, 'Everybody here American? Got anything to declare? No? Okay. Good-bye.'" For the trip to Florida, however, George thought it best to travel as a family man. Betsy would come along as his wife, her daughter, Lisa, as his little girl, and Betsy's friend, Kathy, a student at Northeastern, to provide additional domestic ambience. Actually, relations in George's little family had been slightly strained recently, it having come out that his suspicions about Betsy and Carlos's friend Cesar Toban had been correct—she *had* slept with him on that trip to Antigua. George hardly qualified as Mr. Constancy himself, of course, having slept with Betsy's friend, Kathy, as well as Lorraine, his courier on the aborted Caracas run, two other women friends he saw in Boston when business took him there, and, in a moment of real weakness, Courtney's fifteen-year-old daughter, who confided the matter to Betsy's daughter, who informed Betsy that George was a child molester. George had arrived home that day to find two large garbage bags lying out in the middle of the driveway; they contained all his clothes, cut up into thin strips. That was the same day Betsy chose to tell him about her liaison with Cesar, and George elected not to make a very big issue of it, considering. As it was he spent a few days at Teddy Fields's place before an uneasy peace descended on his household.

In Miami Beach he put everybody up at the Fontainebleau Hotel, and while the females hung out at the pool, George took a cab to a complex of garden apartments about fifteen minutes south of Miami, where Carlos had said a guy was waiting with the fifty kilos. He represented himself to the cabbie as a seashell collector from the Cape and told him the duffel bags he was about to collect were filled with rare shells from the Caribbean, very fragile. At the given address, George knocked at the door of a ground-floor apartment and told the man who answered that Carlos had sent him. It's about time, the guy said in a Spanish accent; he was very angry, George sensed. He'd been holding this stuff for three weeks now. Where the hell had Carlos been? They got the duffel bags from the bedroom, and as they lugged them outside the man asked where George's car was. He didn't have a car, he said, he'd come by the cab over there, at the curb. "He said, 'A cab? Are you fucking crazy?' But I figured it was in broad daylight, who'd think you were doing anything wrong? My philosophy was always if you did stuff in the open, right in front of people, and you looked like whoever you were supposed to be, you didn't have to worry about anything." The cabbie opened his trunk and helped George load in the bags carefully. They're very expensive, George told him, don't slam the lid.

George and his "family" decided to stay on a few days to catch more of the Florida sun before heading back to the snow and slush of Massachusetts in March. For the flight north, he transferred the kilos to four suitcases, which he stashed in Betsy's basement, unbeknownst to her, not bothering with drainage pipes this time since he'd be turning them over so quickly to Carlos. Four days later Carlos called from Canada. Jemel had gone back to New York, he said, and he wanted to come down to pick up the load. George said he would send up Courtney and his daughter in Betsy's Oldsmobile to drive Carlos from Montreal across the border. A teenage girl and her dad and her dad's friend—George thought they'd have no trouble with customs.

Then two days later, on the night of Saint Patrick's Day, Courtney's wife pounded at Betsy's door in a state close to hysteria. Courtney had just called. There was big trouble at the border. They'd searched the car and found Carlos's passport and his Colombian money. They were holding Courtney in custody. Carlos was gone. He'd run into the woods. Courtney said the police were chasing him with dogs.

Jesus, Carlos again! George first told her to calm down. Courtney would be all right, he assured her. They wouldn't find anything in the car. George promised to cover any legal expenses if there was trouble. "What I'm really thinking is the police now have Betsy's car with her address on the registration. They had the passport of a missing Colombian national who'd been kicked out of the country for drugs. They're starting to put two and two together, and here I am sitting with my thumb up my ass and fifty kilos of cocaine down in the basement." George told Betsy to take care of Courtney's wife, that he'd be in touch, that he had to go, don't ask where. Within five minutes he had the suitcases packed into the trunk of his Thunderbird, tore out of the driveway, and headed for the Southeast Expressway toward the Cape. Keeping the needle glued to the speed limit, he arrived at Teddy Fields's house in Cotuit, on Nantucket Sound, in less than an hour. He asked Teddy if he could stay a few days and store his suitcases in the attic. The only person he told where he was was his mother, in case Jo-Anne, the parole officer, chose this moment to spring a visit.

As it turned out, the customs people released Courtney later that very day. After calling his house constantly, George finally reached him to get a little more of the story. They'd driven down from Montreal, Courtney said, and had planned on crossing the border into Vermont, just to the east of Lake Champlain, north of St. Albans. Several hundred yards before the checkpoint, Carlos had suddenly panicked and changed the plan. He told Courtney to stop the car, he didn't feel confident of making it through customs. The roadway there ran through a dense patch of forest, and Carlos said he'd rather cut through the woods and meet Courtney on the highway about a mile on the other side of the border. But it was snowing out, and cold, Courtney said, all Carlos had on were street shoes. It wasn't all that far, Carlos said. Don't worry. Promising he'd see him in a bit, he walked off into the woods.

For reasons Courtney couldn't figure out, maybe just his nerves showing through, the inspectors on the U.S. side ordered them out of the car and proceeded to do a full-scale search. It didn't take long before they'd run across a number of discoveries striking them as exceedingly odd. Courtney's and his daughter's suitcases seemed in order, but there was this other suitcase, filled with a man's clothes. There was a Colombian passport in the name of a Carlos Lehder, and about twenty thousand dollars in Colombian currency. What the hell was this all about? Courtney answered that about ten miles back he'd picked up this hitchhiker, who just before they reached the border asked to be let out of the car and took off into the woods. Courtney didn't know who the guy was or what he was doing, didn't care to get involved, either. Maybe the guy just forgot his suitcase, or didn't want it, Courtney said. Didn't want his passport? Forgot his twenty thousand dollars? About now the teletype came through with the information that this Lehder character was a convicted felon and had been deported the previous year for a drug offense. Illegal alien? Drugs? This was when the customs agents put in a call for the dogs, Courtney said, and organized a search party to go into the woods. He and his daughter were released after about an hour, and he drove home. That's all he knew.

George waited a couple of days more at Teddy Fields's, checking in with Betsy to see if any message had come in from Carlos. When nothing happened, he sat down and did some serious thinking. Forget the running around in the woods like an asshole, Carlos also seemed to be in some kind of deep shit with this kilo deal. If that Colombian down in Florida was pissed off at having to hold the goods for three extra weeks while Carlos went tripping off on a honeymoon, there had to be other people now also waiting around even more pissed off, other Colombians in Boston or maybe New York, the people the kilos were being delivered to. Carlos was the transporter. These guys were the owners. Certainly they'd be just a tad anxious to know where over $2 million worth of cocaine, whole-sale price, had gone to.

"I suddenly saw how this could be great for me, really help me get my foot in the door," George says. "I mean, here I had more than $2 million worth of cocaine. I could have just disappeared with it, especially if Carlos was arrested, because right now he was the only one who knew I had it. Just take off and go to Australia, down to Mexico. How would they ever find me? But if I was honest about it when I didn't have to be honest, then the Colombians would start seeing me as trustworthy. So, I said, 'You're not just looking at $2 million here. What you're looking at is $200 million!'" Thus it happened that George resolved to unload the fifty kilos himself, collect the money, turn it over to the Colombians, and save the day.

Not only would he save the day, but he figured he'd end up making a lot more money on this deal than if Carlos were around. After all, he and Carlos had never discussed what would happen to the kilos once he handed them over. He'd get paid something for bringing them north, but he doubted it would be more than 10 percent, the five kilos' worth. As it stood now, he wasn't bound by any agreement. He could sell them for whatever he got, give the Colombians whatever he considered fair, set his own price structure. Carlos fucks up, George pulls it off, who's in a position to quibble?

The only person he knew who could possibly handle such a large load and do it fast, before people got really nervous, was Richard Barile out in Manhattan Beach. He had kept in touch with Richard, but vaguely, not really thinking about using him until they'd launched the Barry Kane trip. He now placed a call from Cotuit, and Richard told him things had picked up considerably since they'd last discussed the matter. "Things were happening very fast out there, he said. People really wanted it. He told me he was moving all he could get his hands on but he just didn't have enough supply. I said, 'Look, Richard, don't ask questions. I've got what you want, and I've got a lot of it. I'm on my way out. I want you to meet the plane, and I want you to be driving a car that has a big trunk.'"

When he landed at Los Angeles International Airport, it was

very early in the morning, still dark. Richard was there to meet him in a Cadillac Eldorado. He remembers that Bob Seger was singing "Night Moves" on the radio. They drove directly to Richard's house in Redondo Beach and took the suitcases into one of the bedrooms. "He had a hot box in there to test it out. But when I undid a package, he forgot about it. The coke was all shiny and flaky, like fresh snow with the moonlight on it. It doesn't have that gleam anymore if it's cut. All he had to do was take a little snort, and he said, 'Jesus Christ, this stuff is high-test! Where'd you get it?' Don't worry, this is only the beginning, I told him. There was a lot more of it. I was going to get him thousands of kilos. I was going to fill the goddamn Coliseum with the stuff."

It took Richard five days to unload the fifty kilos. He returned late every night with wads of fifties and one hundreds, which George counted methodically and stacked into piles of $10,000, each of which he wrapped with a rubber band. For security reasons, Richard didn't want George to leave the house. He'd get him his newspapers and some magazines, and George was free to soak in the hot tub out back, watch TV, look at the moon; Richard even offered to get him some women if he wanted, but he had to stay at the house. As long as he kept George's presence secret, Richard could maintain a lock on this veritable fountain of cocaine. Once the word got out, it would be hard to keep the vultures away. The days went by, the money came in. By the end of the week it lay all over the waterbed, all over the floor, piled up on the dresser, on the chairs, on the night stands, falling off the TV set—a total of $2.35 million. George had been literally sleeping and waking up with it for nearly a week now, but the sight of all that assembled cash still did something funny to his stomach.

Wasting no time, they packed it up as soon as the last hundred was counted, fitted it into a couple of aluminum camera cases, and headed for the airport. Richard came along on the plane to help with the bags, each of which contained more than a million dollars. During the X-ray session at the United Airlines check-in gate, the woman on the security detail took note of the baggage going by on her screen, told George only slightly under her breath: "Jeez, you guys have a *lot* of bread!"

"This about made Richard shit in his pants," George says. "I told her don't be too loud about it. We were couriers for a bank and this was a transfer of liquid funds."

Richard spent most of the six-hour return flight worrying about how many policemen would be waiting for them at Logan Airport. George gave that some thought himself, until he'd consumed about five little airplane bottles of Scotch, and the fear faded into the mist of alcohol. They met with no trouble back in Boston. Once the bags were packed into the Thunderbird, Richard shook George's hand, told him Don't be a stranger, now, and headed back to the West Coast. George drove down to Cotuit, to Teddy's house, where he went up the little ladder to the attic and put the camera cases in the same eaves where he'd kept the coke. When Teddy heard about the cases, he asked if he could go up and open one of them and take a look. *Look*, yes, George said.

There had been no word about Carlos. Two days later George's mother called. "She told me there was a nice young man and his very pretty wife who had come by the house to see me, said they were good friends of mine. Very polite, she said. It was, 'Yes, Mrs. Jung. Thank you, Mrs. Jung.'" Which was the first George heard that his partner had made it safely through the woods.

SEVEN

Miami

1977

I was the one who had the cocaine. There was no getting it except from me. If I didn't like you, then I'd stop supplying you and I'd give it to the guy you were selling it to. Pretty soon he'd be selling to you and your customers. So all of a sudden, instead of being King Shit, you're a piece of shit. At one time I could make you and break you.

—RICHARD BARILE, LOS ANGELES COCAINE DEALER

THE YEAR 1977 PROVED NOTABLE FOR SEVERAL REASONS in addition to George's arrival as a key player in the cocaine business. Elvis Presley, age forty-two, died of heart failure while sitting on the toilet at Graceland, his estate in Memphis, Tennessee. Gary Gilmore was executed in Salt Lake City, Utah, after urging the firing squad, "Let's do it." The police tracked down David Berkowitz, the "Son-of-Sam" killer, at his home in Yonkers, New York. "Well, you've got me," he told them. *Star Wars* and *Saturday Night Fever* rated as the big movies that year, with "Roots" breaking all viewing records on TV. And President Jimmy Carter, sworn into office in January, was urging Americans to cut down on their use of gasoline and pledged his administration to respond to the energy crisis with the "moral equivalent of war."

Talking to Carlos over the telephone, George detected a clear note of relief in his voice after he heard that the load had been sold and the money was safe and sound. George told him he'd decided the split would be $37,000 per kilo for Carlos and the Colombians, which came out to $1.85 million, with George taking $500,000 for himself, for all the worrying and schlepping he'd done. Carlos seemed more than agreeable, and they arranged to meet at the Hyatt Regency in Cambridge, where Carlos and Jemel were staying, to transfer the proceeds. By the time George arrived at the hotel, Carlos had regained his old cockiness. Far from apologizing for the jeopardy he'd put everyone in, he tossed it off as a splendid adventure.

He told Geroge that after leaving Courtney and the car, Carlos had skirted the customs checkpoint and was waiting in the trees just off the road about a half mile south of the border to be picked up. When Courtney failed to show, and then when the noise of baying hounds reached his ears, Carlos guessed what had happened and ran back into the forest, trying to make his way south while staying parallel with the road so as not to become lost. By now the short northern day had given way to night, and it grew much colder, the snow falling heavily, which was bad enough for Carlos but which also hampered the search party and reduced the dogs' ability to follow his scent. Pretty soon the barking receded and then died out, and he was alone in the forest. For hours, it seemed to him, Carlos stumbled blindly through the snow, falling into bogs, the tree branches tearing at his pants and overcoat. He could no longer detect any feeling in his feet. Lacking shelter or any means of lighting a fire, he began seriously to wonder whether he'd survive the night. Suddenly he saw a distant light glimmering through the trees, which turned out to be a house alongside the road. Knocking at the door, he encountered an elderly woman. He told her his car had broken down a mile or so back, and asked if he could use her phone to call a cab to take him to the nearest motel. A cab in northern Vermont? At this hour? Not likely, she said. Such a nice young man, why didn't he stay at her house for the night? She had an extra room. He could dry out his clothes, she'd give him something to eat, and he could sort out things in the morning. Exhausted from his ordeal, Carlos hardly needed persuading. So at about the same time Courtney was being released from custody at the border, phoning his wife to pass on to George the alarming details of what had occurred, Carlos was already tucked into a safe, warm bed, with a bowl of hot soup under his belt and his clothes drying on a radiator. The next day he caught a bus and made his way down to New York City, where he stayed a few days with Jemel and called around to find out what might have happened with George—and, more importantly, the kilos. When no one at Betsy's house knew where he'd gone, Carlos set out for Weymouth, knowing that he could be in some serious trouble here if he didn't recover the load.

For the number of kilos involved, for the rapid turnaround, and for the amount of money he brought back, George's trip to the West Coast had opened up eyes wide indeed down in Medellín. With one trip he'd found them probably the most important contact they'd had to date, delivered the goods without a hitch, and along with the riches, returned with the message that this was only the beginning, that this friend in L.A. was able to handle all they could ship. And George had also found them Barry Kane, who at that very moment was readying his plane for the task of flying in greater loads. "It was obvious from the way Carlos was acting that suddenly I was the prize," George says. "They had been dealing mostly with their own people, never with gringos before. They didn't know things like Hollywood even existed until I came along. Now they started treating me like the golden goose."

The Colombians urged George to move down to Miami immediately and wanted to supply him with as much cocaine as they could—by boat, by mules, however they could smuggle it in—and have him transport the loads to his contact on the West Coast on a regular basis. They planned to start shipping in May. George would be paid five to ten thousand dollars for every kilo, and they hoped to be moving between fifty and a hundred kilos every week. Then, by the end of the summer, Kane's operation would be ready to go.

Late that April Carlos brought his whole family up to the Cape for a visit—Jemel, his brother Guillermo, and his mother, Señora Rivas, who now needed a cane to get around with. George put them up at Dunfey's Hotel, the famous Hyannis hostelry, and squired them around for a week to all the sights. They ate at Baxter's at the steamship landing, where the ferries left for Nantucket and Martha's Vineyard, went out to the section of Hyannisport where you could peer over the fence and see some of the houses in the Kennedy compound. They drove to Provincetown, "P-town" to the locals, where George introduced them to the New England variety of lobster, with the claws, showing how to insert a fork into the tail and lever out the whole section in one deft movement. He took them out to Race

Point, to look out over the Atlantic Ocean from atop the three-hundred-foot-high bluff he and Malcolm MacGregor used to ride down the face of in an aluminum canoe when they were teenagers. On the trip back he stopped off at Chatham to show them where Barry Kane lived. The Colombians had been a little uneasy about Kane in the beginning, as they were where any gringos were concerned; and here they were trusting someone they'd never dealt with before to take off with ninety-odd million dollars' worth, retail, of their cocaine and not disappear with it into the wild blue. George had eased their minds on this score by asking Kane to bring him over to his house, show him family photos, snapshots of the people near and dear to him. As they would soon demonstrate to the world, the Colombians had little compunction when it came to dealing harshly with the immediate relatives of those who betrayed them, no matter what the age or sex. Kane's wife had died, George knew, but he did have his five children, whose pictures George demanded to see; he also made a point of learning the names of the prep schools they attended. "Three hundred kilos was an awful lot of cocaine to trust to a stranger," says George. "They wanted some kind of hook in him."

Predictably, about a week was all Carlos could take of the tourist bit, after which he sent his family back to New York, while he stayed around planning things with George and making more of those damn visits to local airports. After leaving the one in Hyannis, Carlos asked George to drive into Trans-Atlantic Motors, the BMW dealership nearby. He wanted to look over the cars. "We walked in and the sales manager came over thinking we were your typical people just browsing, and asked if he could help us. Carlos pointed to a black one, a 318i, and said he wanted that one, how much was it? They guy said something like eleven thousand, and Carlos pulled this brown paper bag out of his pocket. 'Here,' he said, and peeled off the money—he must have had fifty or sixty thousand in there—and put the rest back in his pocket. The guy's teeth almost fell out." As the manager fell all over himself trying to get the car ready by that afternoon, Carlos asked if there was also a Datsun dealer in town. Jemel needed a 280Z to drive. George seized him by the arm and took him aside, told him to cool it, for Christ's sake. Didn't he ever learn? "I told him, 'You're an illegal alien, they've got your passport sitting at the border. Don't you think that son of a bitch is going to remember this day the rest of his life? And remember you, too? I mean, even the Kennedys don't walk in and do something like that.'"

Managing to quash at least the Datsun purchase, George took Carlos the following day, their last on the Cape, to look at some summer property for his mother. They found nothing Carlos liked, and after supper they ended the day walking along the beach near the breakwater in Hyannisport, looking out into the blackness of Nantucket Sound. Carlos once again expressed his thanks to George for the way he'd handled the fifty kilos. It would have been his death warrant, for sure, if George had run off with the money, and he admitted now how worried he'd been. He said George had proven to be a true friend, someone Carlos felt he could always trust, and he hoped George felt the same way toward him. "I told him I'd given him my word and that I considered my handshake and my word as a sacred bond of honor," George recalls. "I said that we were brothers, and would always be brothers and that I would never betray that friendship."

After they'd pledged loyalty to each other, Carlos asked George, Oh, by the way, who *was* this friend in L.A., the one he delivered the coke to, the one they'd be dealing with now for a while? George looked at Carlos and told him no soap. He was sorry, but that was one piece of information, friendship aside, he intended to keep to himself. He hoped he understood. Carlos said yes, he did. He could respect that, he said. No problem.

Although the house at 523 North Lucia Street is only one story high, the people in Redondo Beach have always called it the Castle, because of the fact that it was constructed of stone instead of the usual stucco or wood, and because its peaks and arches make it look like something you'd be more likely to find in a Bavarian forest than in a beach town in Southern California. It was indeed built by a German in the late 1920s, a bootlegger, the story goes. He dug out a secret basement under half the house, accessible through a trap door located inside a closet, and used it for storing the illegal booze he ferried in from rumrunners anchored offshore. The house sits in what's known as the Tree section of town, a lush residential area on the lee side of the hill that overlooks the ocean. Richard Barile purchased the Castle in 1971 for fifty thousand dollars, putting three thousand down and financing the balance with a G.I. loan. Along with operating the Tonsorial Parlor in neighboring Manhattan Beach, Richard was half owner at the time of a popular restaurant just up the street called the Silo, notable for its interior paneling of old barn siding and its menu featuring expensive French food and wines.

Richard bought the Castle for the security it afforded him in his third, and most profitable, business, which was drug dealing. The backyard of the Castle, for instance, where George had sat in the hot tub waiting for his money on that first trip, was sealed from peering eyes by the thirty-foot wall of an adjacent apartment building. Across the front ran a wrought-iron fence, laden with blood-red bougainvillea, and at the gate there was a buzzer system. This prevented Detective Fred McKewen, the local narc who fruitlessly dogged Richard's trail for years, from walking right up to the front door and looking through the window to acquire probable cause to give the place a toss. Photoelectric sensors hidden in the shrubbery detected any movement on the lawn and announced it loudly, both in the house and out on the patio, with blinking lights and a screeching alarm. "No one had any reason to ever be in my yard, and if they were, I'd know about it right away," says Richard, who at one point augmented the system with a German shepherd attack dog trained to leap out snarling from behind the house every time someone buzzed at the gate. The animal grew so vicious that it attacked Richard once, and he got rid of it.

Regarding the quality and volume of the product and the way the business ran, Richard divides the history of the Los Angeles cocaine scene into before and after the arrival of George Jung. In the early-to-middle 1970s, as he moved from marijuana into cocaine, Richard had dealt mainly in ounces, not by preference but because of the scarcity of the product. He bought from mules, a little at a time, a pound here and there, adding a pound more of cut to earn a profit. By the time it reached him, the cocaine had already been stepped on, so with Richard's cut, and subsequent ones added further down the chain, "the stuff hitting the street was pretty beaten up," he says. It got so bad that on several occasions he recalls selling an ounce of "cocaine" that contained only a gram of pure coke, barely a trace. "In the beginning people out here didn't know good cocaine from bad anyway, so it wouldn't matter. They were doing it just as a social thing. Pure cocaine didn't come around until George and Carlos. And you could instantly tell the difference. This stuff came in a nice solid chunk, right from the factory, direct to you. It had an opalescent tinge to it. It glowed a little, like mother-of-pearl. That's when it really started to become big."

As Detective McKewen can readily testify, Richard ran a nearly seamless enterprise. Each facet, from receiving to storage to cutting to delivery, was intricately thought out, nothing was left vulnerable to chance discovery or detection by the police, even if they found some excuse to pry into his affairs. Richard knew all about Mc-Kewen's trick involving motor-vehicle violations, for instance, and was determined not to give him an edge where that went. "Richard drove a little brown Porsche around town and always made sure his record was clean," McKewen recalls. "I know that because I followed that car on a lot of nights. And for years and years, I can't tell you how many law-enforcement officers called me from other jurisdictions and from the feds, and said, 'What do you know about Richard Barile? We're working him.' 'Good luck,' I said."

Richard's success as a cocaine dealer came partly from the lessons he learned as point man in a U.S. Marine platoon stationed in the Philippines during the early 1960s. His job had been to help train infantrymen in jungle warfare before they went over to Vietnam to advise the South Vietnamese army. "In the Marine Corps there were two main things—you had to have your own shit together, and you had to be able to count on the other guy. Otherwise you could easily get killed." The two weeks at a shift he'd spend in the jungle trained him in the little things that could account for the difference between life and death—what all the different noises meant, the way shadows fell that could hide an enemy soldier. Much of his sensitivity to the environment came from watching a wizened old man in his late seventies, a former guerrilla with the HUK, who went out with the group to show them how to get sustenance off the jungle floor. He taught them how to locate snails and pop off the little trap door that hides the meat, how to find where the wild rice was growing and boil it up inside of bamboo shoots. "We'd be going along and suddenly the old man would hear something and stop in his tracks. He'd go, 'Peep, peeep, peeeeeeeep,' then walk a little bit and, 'Peeep, peeeeep,' then suddenly he'd start running like a son of a bitch and you'd hear a roaring of wings, and he'd grab that sucker with his bare hands—a wild hen—right before it took off."

In his own organization Barile became known as "the Little General" for the order he imposed and how quickly he banished people who couldn't operate up to standard. He regularly swept the cars and houses used by his dealers with electronic debugging devices to make sure their movements weren't being monitored. He conducted surprise inspection visits to wherever they were cutting the coke before moving it out. "This way you'd find that some guys were real sloppy. The scales would have coke caked on them, the spoons they used they never washed. They'd save the plastic bags, if there was a little bit of coke in there, so if they ran short they could scrape it out to complete an order. 'Either clean it up or dump it out, screw it,' I'd tell them. Cops come in and then you don't have time to wash the spoons or the scale. They find residue, they can make an ambient bust. It showed me that somebody wasn't being professional, and if they weren't professional, I wouldn't do business with them."

When it came to the police, there were three ways to get arrested in the drug business—by accident, by selling to or buying from an undercover cop, or by getting ratted on from the inside— and Richard went to great lengths to obviate all three possibilities.

First, he made sure no loose threads hung out for the police to pull on. If workers showed up high or drunk, they were gone. Not only would that screw up their judgment, but in those days a drunk-driving arrest gave the police wide latitude in searching your car and making other intrusions into your life. An expired driver's license could subject a worker to a visit from Detective McKewen. "If they had parking tickets," Barile explained, "I'd take them down to court and make sure they paid them." The same for an expired registration. "Headlights? Taillights? I would tell them that before anyone uses their car for anything, they had to make sure everything was working, everything was legal. I found that these were the things that made all the difference."

The real danger was getting caught red-handed, dealing unknowingly—buying or selling—with someone working for the police. On the buying part, he had no fear where George or Carlos were concerned, because if any bust came down on that end, it would most likely happen immediately, at the point the plane landed in the States from Colombia. As most large-scale dealers knew, the DEA maintained a strict bird-in-the-hand policy, one that proved a constant annoyance to the agents themselves. They could not allow a load of drugs, once it entered the country, from moving out on the street—by following a delivery, for instance, from Miami to Los Angeles to try to catch the West Coast members of the ring. The fear in the DEA was the agents could screw up along the way and lose track of the load. In that event, not only would the drugs be out in the population, but the agency would have lost the goods it needed to hang the case on, possibly jeopardizing the whole bust. So it was better to be safe than sorry. "When the cocaine reached L.A., I knew everything was secure up to that point, no cops following it," Richard says. "My worry was the other end. Busts usually come from the bottom up, not the top down, so you're not looking at the guy who's selling it to you. You're looking at your customers."

For this reason, Richard stayed as far away from the cocaine as he could. When it landed in L.A., he would have the load driven directly from the airport to one of several stash pads whose location he changed every three months. Except for recreational use, he never kept a serious amount of cocaine around the Castle, secret basement notwithstanding. "Most of your big dealers, if they had any brains, all had a stash pad and hired somebody to sit on it. When you're taking orders, coming in on a beeper, you meet the person to discuss it at a restaurant, then you'd tell a runner, someone else, to go pick it up here and drop it off there. You never go near it and you never touch it."

This still left the problem of his own people: How could he make sure, if there was a bust somewhere down the line, that no one he'd dealt with could be persuaded to turn him in to save their skin? One precaution Richard took was to cut the cocaine right away, when it arrived from Miami, rather than let it go out to any dealer as 100 percent pure. "In those days, because a lot of the street stuff was so bad, if you got caught with pure cocaine, the police would think you were close to Mr. Big, you must be getting it right from the main source. They'd put a lot more pressure on you to give him over. So if one of your dealers got caught with pure coke, this would be a heavy bust. The cop would say, 'Look, whoever you got this from you better give him up or we're going to lean pretty hard on you.' But if they busted them with coke that had already been cut, that comes back from the lab, say, only 30 or 50 percent pure, well, that meant whoever you got it from was pretty low down in the structure. Things went a lot easier for you. I had to pay a lot of legal bills, but none of my people ever turned me in."

In addition, he impressed upon his troops never to take chances that might expose them unnecessarily, and to get rid of the evidence fast, even if it meant losing a lot of Richard's coke. "I'd try to give them a lot of confidence. I'd tell them, 'Hey, look, here's three or four kilos, if you ever have a problem, flush it right down the toilet, you don't owe me a thing. Just don't get into trouble. You'll always make money with me. Just don't do anything stupid. You gotta be safe and cool.' I got that from the marine corps." For screw-ups, for people slow to pay, for those who committed infractions of the work rules, Richard didn't hesitate to use the power he held over their ability to succeed or fail in the coke business. "I was the one who had the cocaine. There was no getting it except from me. If I didn't like you, then I'd stop supplying you, and I'd give it to the guy you were selling it to. Pretty soon he'd be selling to you *and* your customers. So all of a sudden, instead of being King Shit, you're a piece of shit. At one time I could make you and break you."

Picking up kilos at the airport and distributing the tons of blow that disappeared up the collective nose of Hollywood, Beverly Hills, and points all over metropolitan Los Angeles, Richard stood well toward the top of a coke empire that reached into the farthest corner of the community—and where everyone connected with the trade made a heretofore inconceivable amount of money. As with any product, the money you made in the cocaine business depended on the quality of the goods you sold and how great the supply and demand were. Cocaine rarely went on the retail market in its pure form, since everyone's profits were linked arithmetically to how much the product had been cut. The kind of cuts varied according to their availability.

The cutting agents Richard liked best, because of their similarity to cocaine, were procaine or lidocaine. These are synthetic derivatives of the drug, commonly obtainable at chemical shops and used medically as local anesthetics. Procaine, for instance, is the same as Novocain—it has the numbing effect of cocaine but with only a tenth the power to generate a high. Other cuts were neutral white powders such as lactose, which is milk sugar, or mannite, a sweet substance taken from plants and used as a mild diuretic. Quinine was the least desirable cut, for the burning sensation it created in the nose, something dealers often tried to neutralize with a little dose of procaine to numb up the nasal passages. He'd usually cut the cocaine one to two, putting seventeen ounces of cut into a Pyrex baking dish together with a kilo, or thirty-five ounces, of pure cocaine, ending up with a sales product that was 67 percent pure. He'd sift the mixture through a flour sifter, ending up with a fine white powder. Unfortunately, to any reasonably sophisticated customer, the fine powder was the tip-off that the product had been cut and mixed up again. Pure cocaine arrives as a crystal, not a powder, and the crystals bind with one another to form little "rocks." The more rocks there are in evidence, the purer the product. So as a marketing ploy, after cutting the load, Richard had to "rock it back up," as the expression goes. "When they're buying cocaine, what they're looking for is what's solid," he says. "They see a lot of chips, or they see a solid brick, they're saying to themselves, 'Man, this stuff's pretty good.'"

To get the solid material back in, Richard would spray the mixture with a solvent—either acetone, which can be bought in any paint store, or ether, obtainable from a chemist's shop. The solvent would dissolve the cocaine crystals, making them bind. Then he'd bake the mixture in an oven. What emerged was a solid sheet, which when you crumbled it up and bagged it, contained a lot of rocks again and looked much more potent than the powder. As an alternative to the baking method, Richard used an iron press shaped like a hollowed-out brick, which he'd had fabricated at a local welding shop. After spraying a kilo with acetone, he'd double-wrap it into two plastic Baggies, lay it into the press, then fit an iron lid over it, which he could jack down on the Baggie, applying sixty thousand pounds of pressure to the inch. After forty-five minutes he opened the press, and what emerged was a crystalline brick, the real McCoy, as if straight from George.

As a big-time wholesaler, Richard had four dealers he supplied with up to five kilos each, sometimes unloading twenty kilos at a time. His mode of delivery varied, but one method was to buy grocery cans of various sizes from a supermarket supply house, put his cocaine inside, and seal them up with a canning machine he bought for $125. He'd then buy similar cans in the supermarket, for products like baby formula or powdered soft drinks, then steam off the labels and glue them on to his own cans of cocaine. Or he'd buy 2-pound cans of Maxwell House coffee, take off the top, insert a pound package of cocaine with the coffee, and seal it back up with his machine. The cans would be packed away at the stash house, and when orders came in, he'd have the runner deliver, say, three 16-ounce cans of Similac or raspberry Kool-Ade to wherever the dealer wanted. On some occasions the dealer might meet the runner inside the supermarket, throw a couple of cans of Richard's special blend of Maxwell House into his own shopping cart, and check them out through the cashier.

The price of the consumer product depended on many things, including the relationship between the buyer and seller, the quantity of goods involved, and, most important, the degree to which you exposed yourself to arrest. Ounce for ounce, on a unit-price basis, the richest rewards went to those lowest on the ladder, the street dealers, the guys most likely to sell a gram of coke mistakenly to the police. Considering the number of people involved and the fact that nothing ever got written down—not to mention that people routinely lied a lot—no one, the police included, has ever assembled the exact sales figures from any particular load, top to bottom. But using the fifty kilos George first delivered that March, and the prices generally obtaining during that period, it's possible at least to approach an appreciation of the kind of money that could be made.

George sold the 50 kilos of pure cocaine for $47,000 each and went back to the East Coast carrying $2.35 million. Richard's memory of that first deal has faded to a degree, but if he followed his standard procedure, he'd have cut the 50 kilos with 25 kilos of procaine or mannite, giving himself 75 kilos of product, which he would unload to his four dealers for $42,000 each. Net profit for him: $800,000. The dealers Richard sold to cut the load again by 50 percent, meaning that collectively, they now had 112.5 kilos of product to sell. These guys sold ounces, not kilos, to dealers lower down, and charged $1,200 each. So if they bought the 75 kilos in cut form from Richard for a total of $3.150 million, made it into 112.5 kilos or nearly 4,000 ounces, and retailed this for a total of $4.725 million, the profit split among the four of them came to $1.575 million.

Last came the gram dealers, the workhorses of the trade, who sold directly to the public. These guys were the most known on the street, the most caught, and the most likely to do time—and most of them had never heard of Richard Barile. Figuring that each of them bought an average of ten ounces at a time, this meant that it took some four hundred sales people to get rid of one load. The street dealers didn't cut the product any further because they didn't have to. They could make a profit with what they had, buying the ten ounces for $12,000 and gramming them out, 28 grams to the ounce, selling for $100 a gram, for a gross of $28,000 each. If all the gram dealers found customers for their goods, this meant that the fifty-kilo delivery, the one flown to California while Carlos was making his way down from the woods of northern Vermont, would have retailed for a total of $11.2 million. If each street customer bought just one gram each, about twenty lines' worth, went to a party and shared it with two friends—moderate users who would take a hit an hour and make it last through the night—this would mean that a total of 336,000 people in the greater Los Angeles area, a population group the size of Buffalo, Toledo, or Omaha, would have had their lives altered in some major or minor way, thanks to a single trip west by Boston George.

In early May 1977, when George flew down from the Cape to Florida to set up life with Carlos and Jemel, he discovered very quickly how far away this new scale of business would take him from his home turf. Demographically, in a city with a population that was 25 percent black and 56 percent Latino, the Anglos in Miami now qualified as the smallest minority. The first place they found to live in was a rundown motel Carlos knew about, located just off the Tamiami Trail in the heart of Little Havana, an area whose people, for all George comprehended of them, might just as well have come from Uranus. Not only had his meager facility in Spanish languished from lack of use since his Mexico days, but making sense of the world into which he'd been thrust, a volatile mix of Colombians and Cubans, was like picking one's way through an emotional minefield, comprised as it was of a tangle of subsurface alliances, long-smoldering feuds and resentments, and remembrances of love and fidelity betrayed, all of it overlaid by the politics of the cocaine business, which were about as honorable as a knife in the ribs. What's more, this motel Carlos had chosen for setting up the operation turned out to be a "regular shithole," in George's opinion. "Prostitutes were coming and going at all hours, you could see drug deals obviously going down in the rooms. I was the only gringo living with all these Latinos. And he was going to bring loads of cocaine in and out of this place? It was like going down on your knees and begging to be arrested." In short order, George demanded they get the hell out of Little Havana altogether, which was why the three of them, less than a week after he'd arrived, were tooling over the MacArthur Causeway in Carlos's little black BMW to check out places to stay in Miami Beach. If his whole business was dealing with the Colombians and the Cubans, he jolly well wasn't going to live with them, too.

You get no view of the beach in Miami Beach, at least not by driving down Collins Avenue, the main drag, since the sea is pretty thoroughly blocked off by high-rise hotels and apartment houses. The older resorts adhere to the Moroccan fantasy, constructed of stucco with Arabesque façades and painted in pinks and pale greens. The more modern ones—the Eden Roc, the Doral, the Castle, Las Villas in the Sky—are sheathed in glass, and a few are gussied up with fairly ridiculous-looking Victorian porches and balconies running thirty-odd stories up the front and back. Coming onto the Fountainebleau, still the Queen of the Beach, you're hit with a giant trompe l'oeil mural that introduces a view of the place through a Roman arch, decorated with a behemoth race of maidens balancing vases on their heads. In Miami, you don't get noticed by being subtle. I. Magnin, Saks Fifth Avenue, and Neiman Marcus rule the mercantile roost.

After investigating a few possibilities, they settled on the Ocean Pavilion at Fifty-sixth Street. Eighteen stories high, sporting an orange and blue motif, the hotel/condominium was owned by a man named Harvey Weinberg from Rockaway Beach in New York City, who had followed his father into the hotel trade and had been doing business in Miami Beach since the days of Benny Siegel—"They call him Bugsy now, but no one called him Bugsy then," he says. "At least we didn't." That was before Senator Estes Kefauver shut down Miami's wide-open gambling operations in the early 1950s and the mob changed its venue to Las Vegas, and the big resort hotels started going up on former oceanfront estates owned by the Firestones and other upper-class families. By the time George and Carlos arrived at the Beach, Miami's heyday as a resort capital had come and gone. Jet airplanes had opened up the Caribbean and Hawaii to fun-seekers. Those who used to come down just for a holiday were moving to Miami to live, and the hotels were hastening to convert themselves into condo apartments so as not to go bankrupt. Latin and Canadian money was helping to keep the place solvent. "Every resort has built in its own downfall, because sooner or later it becomes so popular it's no longer chic," says Weinberg, who sold off the Pavilion once but then had to take it back when its buyers couldn't make a go of it. "I mean, in Europe people don't go to St. Tropez anymore, or Nice or Cannes. They go to places like Rapallo, newer resorts. And that's what happened here."

For what George and Carlos wanted, the Pavilion was just about perfect. It had an underground parking garage, which would allow them to drive the goods right into the building without having to unload out front. There was a service elevator connected to the garage, so they could bring the load from the car straight up to the floor without walking through the lobby. Visitors could drop by without announcing the fact to the world. They rented one apartment for the three of them. It had a big central living room, two bedrooms at opposite ends, and a kitchen, so they could cook and live up there and not have to mingle much with the guests. This was more like it, George remembers thinking as he stood out on their tenth-floor balcony having a Scotch. The apartment faced west, out across Biscayne Bay, where toward evening the office towers of Miami were brought into glowing relief by the setting sun. The view also took in Indian Creek, the inland waterway that ran alongside Collins Avenue, servicing the Spanish-style villas on the strip between the creek and the bay. Powerboats sat tied up at backyard docks. Here and there a cigarette boat was suspended on a set of davits, kept nice and waxed so it would move faster over the water. One didn't see too many of those babies back on the more sedate Cape. The faster ones got up to seventy knots, with a roar coming out of the manifold like a 707 taking off ten feet over your head. George was going to look into getting one for himself, just as soon as things got organized.

George soon found life with the happy couple even more vexing than with Carlos himself. For one thing, although they had a well-equipped kitchen, Jemel had no clear idea how to cook, try as she did. Unloading the bags from her first shopping trip, for instance, she put the eggs in the freezer, because that's where she thought they belonged. To celebrate their arrival that night, she prepared a candlelight dinner featuring three prime sirloin steaks, which she had neglected to take out of the broiler until they looked like the soles of burnt-up fishing boots, smelling about the same. George took everyone out for dinner to keep the peace. The usual period of adjustment for newlyweds was taking more than its usual toll. On one occasion George returned from an errand to find the place a wreck—several chairs and the standing lamps were all smashed, the couch overturned. He found Carlos out on the balcony looking heavily displeased, while Jemel whimpered in the bedroom. What he finally got out of Jemel, because Carlos refused to talk, was that in an ill-advised moment of honesty she'd confessed to him once having had a brief love affair with another woman, competition from a quarter that Mr. Latin Machismo had found difficult to accommodate.

After that incident, Jemel would go out to eat with George to complain that Carlos was becoming boring, that all he wanted to talk about, even to her, was the airplane thing. Not like George, she said. He talked about interesting things. "I didn't like that either," says George, who was far from a natural in the role of marriage counselor. "The last thing I wanted was for her to come on to me, because with Carlos getting so crazy, that would have ended everything. I mean she was very pretty, very tempting. So I had to struggle pretty hard to keep up a wall between us."

At first George attributed Carlos's insistence that the three of them stay together to his paranoia, to the scare thrown into him when he lost track of those fifty kilos. Later on, though, he suspected it had more to do with the question Carlos had raised walking on the beach back on the Cape, about George's "friend in L.A." To his deepening annoyance, Carlos had raised the subject a couple of times since. If they were really partners, friends, brothers, whatever, he said, why couldn't he know who this guy was? Maybe he thought that by living with George he could get the name by osmosis, overhear a phone call or catch a number. But George was determined to play this one very close. Richard Barile was his lone ace in the hole, at least until he got well established with the Colombians. If they knew the contact he was selling to, why would they need him anymore? They'd sell it direct to Richard, save on the commission. As the loads increased, this could mean millions and millions. Why give this to George if they didn't have to?

And for that matter, George didn't trust Richard all that much either, which is why he'd given him Carlos's first name only. If Richard found out where George was getting the stuff, why wouldn't he deal direct, too? By cutting out the middleman, he could get the loads cheaper and make more money on his end. After all, this was no longer the marijuana business, with the God's herb and the brotherhood of the weed stuff. In the cocaine trade paranoia struck deep and permeated the atmosphere, all with good reason. So George made sure never to call Richard from the apartment, and he didn't tell Richard where he was getting the goods from, or even where he was living, other than south Florida somewhere. When he wanted to reach George, all Richard had was the phone number of an answering service in Miami. That was it. "Bob Dylan said, 'If you live outside the law, you have to be honest.' But I found that with the people you dealt with in the cocaine business, it didn't really pay."

To George's great relief, two weeks later the word came that the trips to L.A. were set to recommence. Carlos was told by his contacts that sufficient loads were being smuggled into Miami—on boats and aboard Avianca, the Colombian national airline—to support regular flights, and the first load, twenty-five kilos, would be ready to go the following day. It arrived right on schedule, and for the next several weeks the routine rarely changed. Twice a week a Ford Econoline van carrying three Colombians pulled into the parking garage underneath the Pavilion. They opened up the sliding doors, lifted out two shopping carts containing grocery bags, and two of them pushed the carts into the elevator. The third followed behind, holding on to something under his coat. At George's floor they wheeled the carts down to the room. The kilos in the grocery bags would be wrapped in duct tape and marked with symbols representing their various owners—either people back in Medellín who'd arranged transportation for their loads or people in Miami who'd bought the kilos back in Colombia and were reselling them in the States. Some were marked "Willie" or "Viejo," which meant "old man." Some had O's on them, with X's through the middle. Others, many of them, were marked with a P or an E.

In the bedroom George and Carlos wrapped the kilos again in double layers of shelving paper to reduce the chance that their scent could be picked up by drug dogs—not really a big worry then—and repacked them into four Samsonite suitcases, six or seven kilos in each. George, meanwhile, had called Lorraine, his courier on the Caracas trip, to come down to help, and the two of them carried the bags down to a cab out in front of the building, drove to the airport, and checked the bags on the 11:00 P.M. United flight for Los Angeles. Lorraine was outfitted usually in a conservative dress or business suit and George in a camel-hair blazer and white turtleneck; they made a nice-looking young couple.

Richard would be waiting in L.A. and drive George and the bags—Lorraine would get the return flight back—to another underground garage, this one under Richard's stash house, at the time an eleven-story condo at 531 Ocean Plaza, on the Esplanade in Redondo Beach, just a few blocks away from the Castle. George hung out in a top-floor suite, exchanging his view of Biscayne Bay for a sweeping panorama of the Pacific Ocean, the beach, the Redondo pier, and the Portofino marina. In two or three days Richard would get rid of the kilos, replacing them with $1,175,000 in cash, which George packed into a carry-on camera case, small enough to fit into the overhead compartment on the plane, and returned to Miami. For the first few trips George earned $10,000 a kilo for his service, meaning half a million for the two 25-kilo trips he averaged each week. The rest went to Carlos and he didn't know who else, whoever had owned the coke, George didn't know this in the beginning. As for his own money piling up, at first he had no time to do anything with it other than stick it up on the closet shelf in his room at the Pavilion, telling Carlos to keep an eye on it. After the first couple of weeks he managed to get Courtney to come down to Miami and take it back up north. Put it in a safe-deposit box, he asked him, or bury it in a hole, take some out for his wife and five kids, just do something with it. When he got a minute, he'd come up and sort it all out.

As word of the trips pervaded the Colombian community, more and more drug dealers began scurrying to queue up—contracting for loads in Medellín, arranging to have them smuggled into Miami, putting them into the pipeline that George—they called him Jorge—this gringo friend of Carlos's, had running to the West Coast. George was now spending twenty-five hours a week in airplanes or waiting in airports. Adding on the two-day turn-around time in Redondo, this meant that back in Miami he hardly had time to sleep before being sent on another run. "I didn't know where I was half the time," he says. "I'd fall asleep in the plane and wake up in my seat not knowing whether it was the money I had with me or the cocaine, or which airport I was landing at." He soon compounded his confusion with his efforts to stay on top of things, which involved vacuuming a lot of the product he was delivering to Richard up his own nose—giving Carlos something to grouse to George about. Carlos called cocaine "poison" and had never even sampled it. He didn't indulge in anything of a mind-altering nature, at most taking a glass of beer if everyone around him had succumbed to getting stoned or plastered. He especially disapproved of mixing it with business. How could George possibly do coke while he was working? he remonstrated. But out on the West Coast, with Richard still keeping the lid on the operation, not letting George go out and blow off steam with his old buddies in Manhattan Beach, there was nothing to do. Nothing, that is, except for the other way he knew how to recreate, which was to have sex. Which he did more or less constantly.

In L.A. the escort services all had listings in the telephone directory, and as soon as Richard would leave the condo to begin unloading the kilos, George was on the horn dialing in his order. Managers of the services were a good deal more motherly toward their women than is generally supposed in the prostitution field, and would check with the main desk after George had called to see whether he was a legitimate guest. And they'd call again after the woman arrived, to make sure she wasn't being chased around the room by Bluebeard or Dracula. The rates ranged from $150 to $250 an hour, starting with your common blow job and moving up to acts requiring artifice and physical endurance. "But when they got here," says George, "I'd have about $10,000 worth of coke piled high in a dish on the table, and once they saw all the blow, that was it. They'd call back the agency, tell them they were going off duty. I'd have them for as long as I wanted."

Coming right off the plane, he usually put in an order for two women at a time, one black and one white, to come over and do friendly things to him simultaneously, nothing that he had to respond to very strenuously. After that he'd put in for the special-order stuff, requiring equipment and some technical skill. There were women of various nationalities—Chinese, Japanese, Filipino, Vietnamese, Scandinavian, German, Mexican, Middle Eastern, East Indian. The "American" girls came in any of the fantasy styles current in the 1970s, from a Raquel Welch or Farah Fawcett down to a demure Audrey Hepburn. "Sometimes I'd say I'd want a girl who was into bondage and S and M. But nothing too heavy. I didn't want some maniac showing up. If you get handcuffed to the bed and you got a lunatic in your room, you're in for some trouble." He knew that Richard, for instance, had a number of friends who liked to patronize some of the more serious sex emporiums in L.A., where there were medieval dungeons complete with implements of torture. George saw pictures of the places and thought he'd pass. "I wasn't really into big-time pain."

About twenty minutes after he'd placed his order, the woman, in her late teens or early twenties, would appear at George's door, dressed in a skirt and top or blue jeans and a T-shirt, normal street clothes, carrying a large shoulder bag. She'd disappear into the bed-

room and in a few minutes call to George that she was ready. When
he peeked in, she'd be dressed in standard sex-shop sportif—stiletto
heels, three or four inches high, net stockings attached to a garter
belt suspended from a black leather corset. No top. Her breasts
would be bare, thrust up and out by the corset, a spiked leather collar would be fastened around her neck, and her face would be set in
a stern expression. George would take off his clothes and lie face-
down on the bed, where she'd manacle him to the headboard using
regulation police cuffs and secure his feet to the bottom of the bed
with pieces of rope. With George thus laid out, she'd give his rump
a good going over with her riding crop, or sometimes it was a cat-
o'-nine-tails or a bullwhip, whatever the agency had in the supply
closet. She'd give him a dozen or so good cracks with that, not
enough to raise any welts, but enough so he knew he'd been a bad
boy and had to be disciplined. He'd moan sometimes, to show her it
was all having some effect. After that she'd untie him, then fit him
out with a cock ring, which she would tighten up at the base with a
couple of plastic clips so he couldn't ejaculate, at least not easily.
Rigged out like that, maybe also a little fried on coke, George could
sometimes deploy himself up to two hours at a time. "I don't think I
can describe what it felt like," he says. "Different, is all I can think
of. One thing, though, is after all that I started looking at normal
sex as pretty boring."

Afterward he'd take the women out for dinner at the upper-deck
restaurant in the Portofino marina nearby, looking out over the
yachts and sportfishermen anchored in the slips. "Most of them
were pretty normal people, doing it to earn money so they could do
something else with their lives, like acting or going to college. Some
were housewives who were bored. They'd have to get up and leave
suddenly to pick up their kids at school." There was only one he still
remembers, a tall auburn-haired graduate student at UCLA whom
he'd ordered back a few times, who said she was working toward her
master's degree in abnormal psychology. "What she liked was to
spank," he says.

For all the cash he was funneling into their pockets back in
Miami, George became a regular local hero among the Colombians.
Everyone wanted Carlos to introduce them to this Jorge from
Boston, wanted him to do loads for them. One night Jemel took
George and Carlos to a party at the house of a cousin of hers,
Martha Hoyos. It was a scene that George soon came to appreciate

as typically Colombian. Martha's husband, Humberto, was formerly a bank president in Medellín, now involved in some way not immediately clear to George in the cocaine business. Handsome in the Gilbert Roland mold, he had standard Colombian features—pale white skin, a large supply of dark wavy hair, and a small mustache. He dressed immaculately, in a white guayabera shirt, black slacks, and one of a hundred pairs of soft Italian shoes he kept in his closet. He wore gold chains, a diamond ring on his little finger, and during parties, a wafer-thin Piaget watch, which he changed to a more masculine Rolex on workdays. Their house in Coral Gables was a large two-story Spanish job, stucco with a red tiled roof, formerly occupied by Esther Williams, the aquatic movie star. Out back, an Olympic-sized swimming pool served as the centerpiece of an elaborate patio. Ferraris, Lamborghinis, and Cadillac Eldorados were lined up out front. About a hundred guests were wandering about, including children, the little boys looking like nightclub emcees, dressed up in white jackets and black bow ties, their sisters in stiffly crinolined dresses. The wives fairly dripped with gold, emeralds, and diamonds, some almost bent low by their effort to dazzle. The men played poker at tables set out on the patio, or they competed in a gambling game that involved pitching quarters simultaneously into the swimming pool, two men playing at a time. The trick was to throw the coin so it hit flat and sank slowly in a sashaying fashion. The one whose quarter reached bottom first lost the game, meaning he had to turn over the keys to his car—his Maserati, Mercedes, whatever—to the winner. A lot of men were also snorting coke, discreetly, in a little anteroom off the dining room, but not their wives. As George would learn, that was one item on a long list of no-nos for Colombian women.

At one point Humberto, his brother, and some other Colombians got George alone in one of the bedrooms and started pumping him. They asked if he could help them line up airplanes for flights to Medellín. They asked if he could set them up with other outlets for cocaine besides the one in Los Angeles. "They were around me like flies—We can do this. We can do that. They all wanted to hook in. But I told them, Look, I was partners with Carlos, that he and I were together. They'd have to deal through him if they wanted to deal with me." Carlos soon got wind of the bedroom session and came in to get George away from these guys. But the more George got to know this cousin-in-law of Jemel's, the more he liked him. Unlike many of the Colombians, who crowed about how big they were in the business, claiming to know important people, Humberto exhibited no braggadocio. "It was the opposite with Humberto," George recalls. "He was a lot more than he ever appeared to be. He was a very smart man, so smart he didn't want anyone to really know how powerful and important he was. He would always send me other people who'd say the kilos belonged to them. 'Georgie, I'm turning you on to my friend. He's got something for you.' Then I'd find out eventually it was really Humberto's load." George didn't know it until later, but Humberto's kilos were the ones marked with the code names Willie and Viejo. Humberto had also arranged the import of other kilos on behalf of a good friend of his back in Medellín—the *P* and the *E* kilos. Carlos wasn't the only one who knew this Pablo Escobar.

In July, with the pressure mounting to sell more and more, the pace picked up, the loads doubled, and the stress level mounted. George was now transporting up to fifty kilos a trip, as many as one hundred kilos a week—too many suitcases to take aboard commercial flights, so he started chartering Learjets, for ten thousand dollars each way. Courtney had come down to help out Lorraine. The Lear landed them at the executive-airlines section of the small Santa Monica airport, where the pilot would phone ahead to have a limo waiting to take George and the load to Richard's condo. "I learned an important thing then, that when you fly around in a Learjet, nobody ever questions you. They don't know who you are, and they're afraid to ask. They just look in awe. You get out of the plane, you're wearing a cashmere jacket and an ascot, and there's a limo waiting for you—well, here's just one more multimillionaire. It's, 'Yes, sir,' and 'No, sir. Thank you, sir. Good-bye, sir.' You could be smuggling a nuclear warhead and they wouldn't dare stop you."

Riding in the jet was practically the only time George could sleep or have any peace and quiet. Once on the ground, he was subject to constant pressure to keep in motion, because only when George was on the move did people make any money. "It began to be an absolute nightmare—the money, the cocaine, everyone wanting more and more and more. The airports, the airplanes, all the sneaking around you had to do." He needed the cocaine to keep up the pace, but it made him so edgy and paranoid that when he transported the money from Richard's condo to the Santa Monica airport, he imagined that he was being followed by the police or by people out to steal his camera cases. He'd check in and out of two or three hotels on the way, entering through the front and leaving from the garage, to satisfy himself he'd lost the phantoms he thought were on his trail.

The money itself, the staggering amount of it, also got everyone just a little unhinged. On each trip back he was now transporting more than $2 million, almost $5 million in a week. It had to be counted, recounted, stacked, wrapped, packaged, taken to Miami, unwrapped, recounted, packed up again. In the Redondo Beach condo George generally waited until the cash had all accumulated before doing the big count. He put it off for as long as he could, because it was serious work that went on for hours. He'd stack the hundreds and fifties into piles of $10,000 each, two to four inches high, writing the amount on the top bill with a yellow magic marker. The twenties he put in stacks of five thousand dollars so they'd fit into the camera cases. In the beginning he did it all meticulously, counting each stack once, then getting someone else to do it again. Richard would come over to the condo with his retinue to help. "He always had all these young girls around him, 'little surfer hoodsies,' I'd call them. They'd be running around the condo half-naked in their bikini bottoms, drinking champagne, doing coke. When I brought out the coke, it was sex city, and the money counting got a little, what you would call casual. It reached a point where we'd count and count and then snort some coke and count some more, until finally I'd say, 'Fuck it, that's enough! That's about right. Let's go.' I'd get in the Learjet with the suitcases and deliver the money to the Colombians who would come by the Ocean Pavilion. Sometimes it was, 'Here. Here's two and a half million dollars, and maybe it's fifty thousand off the number, I don't know.' And nobody would care. It was just, 'When can you leave and bring back some more?'"

George's personal assets were now accruing into such a large wad as to present a serious storage problem. When the deliveries hit one hundred kilos a week, the Colombians cut his commission back to $5,000 a kilo—they didn't want him making more than they did—but this still added up to half a million a week, which by the beginning of August gave him a total of nearly $6 million, in cash. Forget spending it, or washing it, he could barely figure out where to put it. For one thing, it was heavy. As people in the cocaine business soon discovered, $1 million dollars in hundreds weighs exactly

20.4 pounds, double that if it's in fifties. George's stash, half in fifties, half in hundreds, tipped the scales at about 180 pounds, which meant that George's liquid capital now outweighed him by 5 pounds, and he was tending a little to pork these days. And it had a lot of bulk to it. In fresh, crisp hundred-dollar bills, $6 million in a single stack runs 21.5 feet high, about as tall as a two-story house; in fifties it's over 43 feet high. In other words, it's not something that you shove under the mattress when you hear a knock at the door.

What George needed to hide his growing mound of money in was a house, and it had to be back on the Cape, away from the Colombians and the frazzling life in Miami. Betsy's house was no longer available, their romance having fallen victim to George's newfound reliance on the escort services. He'd dropped by to break it off with her during a trip north in early July. Finding her out, he'd left a note on the kitchen table along with twenty thousand dollars in cash and the keys to his Thunderbird, packed his clothes and left. As a location for his own stash house, he looked in the town of Wellfleet, toward the end of the Cape and not as crowded as Hyannis. He told the real estate lady he wanted something on the water, with hot-air heat, if possible; it helped his sinuses.

The place she found was a large three-story cottage with weathered shingles and a big screened-in porch overlooking Cape Cod Bay. He hired his man Courtney, the welder by trade, regularly to courier the cash up from Miami and to construct additional heating ducts to nowhere in the basement at Wellfleet as a repository for the cash. George came up once or twice to check on things and transfer some of his pile to the Rockland Trust Company in Weymouth, where he got his father to cosign for a couple of safe-deposit boxes—the big ones, with the large drawers. By now, Fred had decided not to ask any questions about his son's financial success.

With his money safe, at least temporarily, George threw himself back into the plane trips and the preparations for Barry Kane's first run. So preoccupied was he in these matters that when a letter arrived from Jo-Anne Carr, forwarded to him by his mother, it came as a small shock for him to realize that he was still, despite it all, on parole. In recent months, his obligation to report on his activities had been reduced to sending in a monthly form attesting to the fact that he still resided at Abigail Adams Circle and was still employed in the fishing business, earning an income George put down as three hundred dollars a week. No foreign travel, no associating with people who had criminal backgrounds, no taking drugs. In her letter, Jo-Anne praised him for his successful effort at staying out of trouble and his commendable progress toward rehabilitating himself, in consideration of which she had therefore recommended releasing him from his parole obligations ahead of schedule. All the best, she said, for a happy and prosperous future.

Somewhere around this time George suffered a serious lapse in judgment and decided to introduce Carlos to Richard after all. Carlos's insistence that the meeting take place had eventually worn George down. Carlos had argued that since he had introduced George to everyone *he* knew, he now had a right to meet this guy. And if George refused to tell him Richard's name, this must mean he didn't trust him, and if that was the case, how could Carlos continue to trust George? George liked to say they were brothers, didn't he? Was this acting brotherly? He badgered George constantly. In addition, George's coke intake had escalated to the point where it was seriously clouding his judgment. He was up to four and five grams a day during the trips to and from L.A., whereas the pharmacology textbooks commonly put the toxicity level for normal people at 1.4 grams. Finally, there was the money: There was just so much of it lying around, what possible difference could it make whether he introduced them or not? In two years, George figured, he'd have $50 million dollars and get out of the business for good, convert some of his fantasies into reality. "Even if it wasn't $50 million, if it was only $20 million cash, you can do anything you want the rest of your life, put it into securities, make 12 or 15 percent interest. When you've got that kind of cash, they'll give you that kind of interest. At that time Mexico was giving in bonds something like 18 percent. Or the Mediterranean. This was not a vague plan of mine. I was going to do this thing with Carlos for a year or two, and I was getting out, because I didn't want to go back to jail, because I knew if you played this game, there were only two results—jail or death. So it was the motor sailer and be happy and drink the best wines and eat cheese and gamble in Monte Carlo, go to Hong Kong. Not in my wildest dreams did I think he would stab me in the back."

The occasion for the introduction was a party in late July in the upper-middle-class community of Palos Verdes, at a sprawling house rented by Nick Hunter, an electronics-store owner and one of Richard's major dealers. There was a pool out back. Guests included the usual mix of rock artists and movie people, a lot of Hunter's high-end customers. About a pound of cocaine was piled up on a mirror sitting on a coffee table in the living room, there for the taking. Topless women were serving the drinks and bands were spelling each other so no one would have to endure more than a minute or so free of rock and roll. George was staying at the Castle with Richard that weekend, and he had invited Carlos to fly out for the party. After all the build-up, the meeting itself proved anticlimactic. George went with Richard to pick Carlos up at the airport. The two shook hands, and that was about it. Indeed, they seemed a little awkward with each other. Richard offered Carlos a snort, and to George's surprise Carlos took it. But whereas it usually brought people out of themselves, the coke only made Carlos seem quieter and more withdrawn. At the party, George noticed that Carlos talked mostly to the host, Nick Hunter, while sipping his mineral water. A crowd gathered around this exotic foreigner, but Carlos seemed pained by the attention. A couple of hours later he went back to his hotel and the next day returned to Miami.

EIGHT

Norman Cay

1978

I said, "Carlos, I hope you never betray me." He said
he never would. And he almost started to cry.
                                                        —GEORGE JUNG

IN THE CRUISING GUIDE TO THE BAHAMAS, YACHTSMEN desirous of
putting into Norman Cay for the night are warned that during certain months of the year, if you anchor in the large protected lagoon
at the northern end of the island, it's not a great idea to dive in for a
swim before lunch because you might get seriously eaten by a ham-
merhead shark. The sharks are born in the lagoon and return there
every year to fulfill their instinct to copulate and perpetuate the
species. Whether drawn by a fondly recalled feature of the place or
reacting to a compass in their brains that homes in on some magnetic force in the bedrock underneath the island, as scientists more
commonly believe, they leave the lagoon as small fry and reappear
when they're ten feet long and in such numbers as to blacken the
waters with their presence. Hammerheads aside, in all the other categories Norman Cay rates as being as close to paradise as any of the
other seven hundred islands that make up the Bahamas. Shaped in
the form of a giant fishhook, with the barbed end curving around
the shark lagoon and the shank consisting of a blindingly white
beach a little over four miles long, the island lies at the head of the

Exuma chain, an easy day's sail southeast of Nassau. Sparsely populated, Norman Cay possesses a harbor famous throughout the
Bahamas for providing a haven from sudden tropical storms. A virgin coral reef eleven miles long and filled with tropical fish and
wondrous underwater vegetation is situated just offshore. Out
beyond the reef is the Exuma Sound, a thousand-foot-deep trench
in the ocean that produces some of the best big-game fishing in the
Caribbean.

In the 1960s, hoping to exploit its commercial potential, a land
developer from Ohio constructed a modest twelve-unit hotel and
restaurant there, along with a three-thousand-foot airstrip and a
marina with an L-shaped dock. The venture languished after the
Bahamas gained its independence from Great Britain and investors
became jittery over what sort of business climate would be fostered
by the new, all-black government. The island was then sold to a
group of New York and Canadian businessmen, who by the late
1970s were still looking for someone to sink big money into the
place.

In addition to sharks, Norman Cay has provided a refuge over
the years for marine denizens of another variety, namely smugglers
and sea pirates. It was named for a minor English pirate, and in the
seventeenth century, it served Blackbeard and Henry Morgan as a
launching point for their plundering. In the 1920s it was used as a
way station for bootleggers running rum from the West Indies to
the Florida coast, which lies 210 miles away, barely an hour's trip by
airplane. There's no customs post on the island, or police presence
of any kind. At night and in bad weather, airplanes can find the
landing strip at Norman by locking on to the powerful radio beacon
at Nassau International Airport, just twenty minutes away. And during the period in question there was the powerful advantage of what
was referred to euphemistically as "the Bahamian way of life."
Loosely translated, this meant that under the government of Prime
Minister Lynden O. Pindling just about anything you might conceivably want in the Bahamas was up for sale, be it the courtesy of
ample warning should the national police, for form's sake, decide to
conduct a raid on your premises, or protection from any interference in your privately constituted affairs by any representative of a
foreign power, especially including agents of the United States
Drug Enforcement Administration.

The hospitality of the Bahamian government in regard to the

drug business had been widely known among smugglers since the late 1960s, which was why during the summer of 1977, while George was doing the red-eye runs to the West Coast, Carlos Lehder had gone out scouting the region to find the kind of island empire he'd dreamed about ever since Danbury. On Norman Cay he immediately began negotiations with its corporate owners to buy a large amount of acreage on the southern end, which included the hotel, the airstrip, and the marina, with the stated object of developing the property. Carlos told them how he'd like to extend the airstrip a thousand feet or so, dredge the harbor, and expand the hotel, maybe also build a gambling casino. All this appealed to the owners, since they intended to retain a few building lots, which couldn't help but appreciate should Norman become a resort.

What Carlos neglected to tell them, of course, was that attracting tourists wasn't what he had in mind. As he related to George, the deeper docking facilities could be used for landing freighters—vessels with real carrying capacity, their holds fairly bursting with duffel bags of cocaine. From the dock he'd move the coke to airplane hangars he intended to construct along the runway, and fly it out on cargo planes, up to the DC-3s he could bring in once the airstrip had been extended. The hotel would be outfitted to house the kind of staff you'd need to keep a place like this humming—people to unload the ships, load up the planes, and keep everyone fed, entertained, and stimulated.

In the eyes of people back in Medellín, Carlos had by now proved his worth. Thanks largely to George's series of runs to the West Coast, the processors had convinced themselves Carlos was the man with the right ideas and the right contacts, the one who could put the cocaine business on the track toward achieving its ultimate market potential. This was no piddling 100- or 200-kilo operation he envisioned anymore. Carlos was talking jumbo loads: 500 kilos at a time, 750 kilos, 1,000 kilos at a time now—more than a ton of 100 percent pure product going in and out on each trip, with a trip a week or more. He was planning to have a veritable blizzard of blow—billions and billions of dollars' worth—headed toward the United States. Look, he told George, they'd always talked about cranking this thing up, right? Well, now he was ready to launch their little operation into stellar orbit.

"He was totally obsessed with this island thing and owning it and having an empire," says George. "It was all he could talk about, he wouldn't listen to anything else. And we started to have big fights about it. I basically thought it was ridiculous to do this. Even if he could buy off officials in the Bahamas, to entrench himself and fight the governments of the world, saying 'Here I am, I've got my own little island. Fuck everybody, this is my drug-transport business, come and get me.' I told him, 'Are you shittin' me? If the United States government finds out who you are and where you are and you're breaking the law, I mean, we took down Japan, Germany, and Italy. You don't think they can't take down Carlos Lehder on Norman Cay?'"

George tried to bring Carlos back to the original plan they'd talked about back at Danbury: bringing the loads across the border through different access points, some through Mexico into California, others into Louisiana, Florida, and other southern states. "The islands were fine, but my plan was to keep moving, keep changing, be secretive, be light on our feet. Nobody knows what you're doing or where you are or who you are, and as long as they don't know who you are, they can't get you." In conversations about their business, George and Carlos had already begun referring to themselves as "the company," which they thought of as also including Humberto, this Pablo Escobar down in Medellín, whom George hadn't met yet, Barry Kane, and a few others. "It wasn't called the 'Cartel' then, it was *la compañía*," says George. "My job was to get the pilots and the planes and arrange the landings and be like the vice-president of the American end of things. Carlos would handle the liaison in Colombia, arrange for the shipments. That was the original concept."

Trying to rein in Carlos after he settled on Norman Cay, though, was like trying to keep a horse in check with a piece of string. In conversations with George, he was soon beyond Norman and into more expansive schemes, much grander designs of what he could do with the cocaine profits. "'Money is power,' he said, and he was going to have an unlimited amount of money," George recalls. "He wanted to use it to liberate the people of Colombia. He said that something like 87 percent of all the arable land was owned by 12 percent of the people. You had women sitting on church steps purposely crippling their own children to make them sympathetic beggars. He wanted to take over the country and give the people back their land. I asked him if he'd ever seen the movie *The Adventurers*, based on the Harold Robbins novel. Ernest Borgnine was in it. It's about a country in South America where this guy forms a revolution in the hills and finally he comes down and takes over the palace and he's holding a gun to the head of *el presidente*, who's a corrupt son of a bitch but tells him, 'Go ahead, shoot me and take this chair, because you will become what I am.' I told Carlos that power corrupted people and he would eventually become the man he hated."

But George had never stood up terribly well to an assault of Carlos's revolutionary rhetoric, and as he'd done back at Danbury, he simply gave up protesting after a while and let the little Colombian keep the floor. "When a twenty-eight-year-old kid tells you he's going to take over a country, what do you say to him? And I mean, what did I really care, anyway? I wanted one thing. I wanted the cocaine and I wanted the money. That's all. Carlos's scheme was forever, he was in for the whole show. I figured I wasn't going to stay around long enough to see the last act."

It wasn't long after these conversations that George began getting the message, indistinct at first, that there were about to be some management shifts in the corporate structure of *la compañía*. It was nothing as dramatic as losing the corner office or executive dining-room privileges, yet he felt in all the transactions now going on between Miami and L.A. that in some way he was being left out of the loop. For one thing, by the end of the summer Carlos's attention was clearly shifting from Miami to the islands. He still had to be in Miami occasionally, if only to deal with his own cash supply (a problem he solved by secreting the money inside the body panels of Chevy Blazers and shipped them down to his contacts in Medellín). But his main time these days was taken up with plans and negotiations in the Bahamas that seemed to require almost no consultation with George. For another, the coke George now took West was turning out to be second-class stuff, cut with quinine, the clumsiest of adulterating agents. Richard could no longer move the loads for top dollar, which meant he greeted George less enthusiastically, and sent him back with less take-home pay. When confronted about the deteriorating quality of the product, Carlos would tell George to wait for the next batch. But then that wouldn't be much better. What was going on here? "I'd go out to L.A. with twenty-five or fifty kilos, and Richard would say it was cut and he didn't have to take this shit, and I'd have to almost beg him. Then he'd say, 'All right, I'll take it,' but like it was a big favor. And here we had been the best of friends. It didn't take any genius to start thinking that he was getting stuff from some other source and that I'd better make a move here or I was done dealing."

George's worries were put on hold for a few weeks when Barry Kane suddenly called to say he was finally ready to make the two runs, transporting 250 kilos each, back to back. He drove over to the Pavilion and picked up George and Carlos in his rangy four-door convertible Lincoln Continental, a vintage model from the early 1960s that had the doors opening out as on a cabinet and became a hit among oil sheikhs and Latin dictators. Carlos the car buff seemed very impressed. To discuss final plans, Barry drove them to the Castaways Motel in south Miami Beach, whose bar was constructed underneath a swimming pool to give an underwater view of all the women in their bikinis cavorting in the water like a school of guppies.

The delivery they were embarking on was a little more problematical than any they'd tried; before, George simply took the kilos out to someone he knew and handed the money over to the Colombians on his return. There was more cash involved here: The transportation fee for the two trips came to $5 million—$3 million for Kane and $1 million each for George and Carlos. More to the point, this was the first time they'd be dealing with Colombians they didn't know personally, and also the first time the money and the cocaine would be brought together in the same place, a notoriously precarious situation in the drug business. When the money came in close proximity to the kilos, it seemed to raise the greed level of the Colombians to such irresistible heights—here was a chance to put their hands on the coke *and* all the money, double the profit—that the guns would come out from underneath the jackets, a lot of bodies left around for the police to sort out. In this particular instance, the likelihood of such a thing happening seemed pretty remote. After all, the coke belonged to people in Medellín who were using George's group to fly it in to their own people in the States. The only thing they could recoup in a rip-off was the $5-million transportation cost. Since they needed Kane to keep flying, it was definitely not in their interest to take a short-term profit and lose the long-term asset. Still, you never knew. Some Colombian with a wild hair up his ass, a not-terribly-future-oriented guy, maybe hyped up on coke, might decide to make a play for the jackpot, just go ahead and grab it all, blow the people away and face the consequences later. Miami was still three years away from hitting its peak in the category of drug killings, which by 1980 were increasing at a fairly astounding rate. But there had been enough headlines in the newspaper to make George announce that he intended to bring along a gun, and he advised Kane to do the same.

George possessed a nickel-plated Smith & Wesson .357 Magnum revolver with walnut grips, which he kept in a holster clipped on to his belt on his right hip so he could reach across and whip it out with his left hand should the fateful moment arrive. He'd bought it from his friend Mr. T, the drug dealer up in Hyannis who moonlighted as an armorer and gunsmith. Whatever the requirement, Mr. T could thread a muzzle so as to fit on a silencer, file off serial numbers, convert a semiautomatic into a burp gun, and make other alterations required in the drug business, down to sawing off the barrels of a 12-gauge shotgun if what you needed was a room cleaner. The .357 was loaded with 158-grain super-high-velocity hollow points that achieved 1,500-foot seconds at the muzzle and slammed into the target with 700-foot pounds of energy, compared to a puny 179 pounds for the standard-issue .38 revolver carried at the time by most police departments. Many of the Colombians preferred one or another of the 9-millimeter machine pistols, the American-made Mach 10 or the Israeli Uzi, the latter having fewer working parts and regarded as more reliable. These could be concealed under one's coat, the clips were easy to get in and out, and they kicked off a lot of rounds in a hurry, 600 to 800 a minute. But what George prized about the .357 was that it was a regular canon, the force of the thing capable of driving a slug through an engine block and knocking a 200-pound man off his feet on the other side. He'd never actually shot it at anyone so far, and he'd been shot at himself only once, in that raid on the marijuana field above Mazatlán by the Federales, who banged away uselessly at Manuel and George as they scooted down through the jungle. To confirm just what the .357 could do, George drove out into the Everglades one afternoon and set up some watermelons in the woods, and with a single shot each he vaporized them, one after the other, into a mist of pink and green. That seemed about enough to handle the job.

Several days later Kane flew down as planned to the designated ranch outside Medellín. With him was a Colombian gofer supplied by Carlos to help him find the right place. Kane liked to keep the details of his flights to himself, so all George knew was that everything went as planned and Kane flew back from Colombia through the Bahamas, then to his secret landing place somewhere in North Carolina. There he put half the load, 125 kilos, into the trunks of two used cars he'd bought off a lot with phony papers and had them driven to the parking lot outside a little bachelor's-pad condominium he owned off Route 1 just north of Fort Lauderdale, a forty-five-minute drive north of Miami. At the appointed time, four Colombians showed up at Barry's apartment and he gave them the keys to one of the cars. The deal was that the Colombians would drive off with half the load one day and pay nothing. They would return the next day with full payment in order to get the other half. This way, if for some reason they took off with 125 of kilos, the remaining 125 would more than compensate for the loss.

When the four returned the next day, they carried two large suitcases, each containing $1.25 million. It took about an hour to count the whole amount. The Colombians sat around and drank beer and watched. Three of them wore guayabera shirts, and George could see bulges at their waistbands. A fourth had on a suit jacket, concealing something with more firepower, George assumed. George and Barry counted the money twice, riffing through the bundles of $10,000, all new bills. Everything being deemed in order, Kane took out the keys to the second car, and with George and Carlos very alert now, taking in every little move by the Colombians—right here was when it would happen—one of the Colombians took the keys in his hand, the four backed slowly out of the room, the door closed, was locked, and the deal was done.

"The whole thing was pretty heavy," says George, "but when it was over, I walked out of there with a little click in my heels, a bright smile on my face." The second such exchange occurred in the same manner one week later, George having done another run to L.A. in the interim. And Courtney came down to relieve him of the accumulated proceeds, advising George that with all this damn money he needed to fit in a couple more ducts back in the house at Wellfleet, where there was now upward of $10 million.

Not long after the Kane run, Carlos urged George to come down to the Bahamas and see for himself what the excitement was about at Norman Cay. George flew to Nassau, where Carlos picked him up at the airport, and the two chartered a sportfisherman and headed for the island. The boat run took less than two hours; it was a typically gorgeous Bahamas day, the sun penetrating the turquoise waters so one could see down to the coral reefs and the bright sandy bottom. As they approached the island, they could make out the hotel up by the airstrip, and also the little yacht club overlooking the marina. Standing on dock to greet them was a stocky man in his fifties, about George's height. He wore cut-offs and dark sunglasses and had a large belly, black bushy hair, and a beard. Suspended from his neck was a pair of binoculars, which he kept trained on the horizon of the surrounding ocean. They landed and tied up, and Carlos introduced George to Robert Vesco—"Call me Bobby," he told George—the arch-swindler who had fled the United States during the Nixon years after defrauding investors of some $224 million (and also illegally donating $200,000 to the president's re-election campaign).

Vesco owned his own island, Cistern Cay, about ten miles south of Norman. Carlos had run into him while looking for an island to buy, and after they'd talked a bit, Vesco had said straight out that he wanted to invest in the cocaine business and help bankroll Carlos's plans for Norman. He said he knew just about everyone in the Bahamas who could help you or hurt you, depending on whether they were sufficiently paid off. "Carlos was really enthralled with the guy, how he'd stolen all this money and gotten away with it," George says. "The thing he liked best was that the United States government couldn't touch him. He'd fucked the U.S.A. and gotten away with it." The three repaired to the bar in the little yacht club, a rounded structure with glass façade resembling an airport lounge, and ordered Bloody Marys. They were the only ones in the place. Vesco grilled George a little, asking how he'd operated in the marijuana business, what the demand for coke was like on the West Coast. He expressed interest in hearing about prison life at Danbury and the inmates there, especially the bank embezzler from Wakefield, Massachusetts, and the Medicaid doctor who'd fled to Belize. "At one point Vesco went into the men's room, and Carlos leaned over and sort of whispered, 'This guy is getting us the prime minister of the Bahamas.'"

The island has but one road, which runs from the airport down the shank of the fishhook and around to the tip of its barb, alongside the lagoon filled with sharks. The rest of the day they drove around the island in a jeep, Vesco still looking all over through his glasses. Carlos showed George a house known as the Volcano for its cone-shaped roof. He was negotiating to buy it from a man named Beckwith, a part owner of Ocean World in Fort Lauderdale. There were just three of four other private houses constructed in little copses of pine trees to preserve their privacy. "He talked about buying up all the houses and getting rid of the people. 'If they don't want to leave, they'll be sorry they didn't,' he'd say. 'We'll get rid of them one way or another, maybe permanently if necessary.' Here was this passive little guy in Danbury who could get pushed around at the weight rack, and all of a sudden he's talking about exterminating people. He suddenly seemed to have all this newfound power, believing he could pay off the prime minister and do any goddamn thing he wanted. I said okay, not knowing what to say. It was obvious to me I was dealing with a very changed man."

After about four hours, the two said good-bye to Vesco—he'd come over in his own eighty-foot cruiser—and ran on back to Nassau. That night at the Holiday Inn lounge, sitting in peacock chairs having drinks amid the bamboo, George described to Carlos how Richard had been getting pretty cocky lately, acting very much as if he was getting his supply of cocaine from someone else, as much as telling George he could go fuck himself with his kilos. Don't worry about Richard, Carlos said. The runs to the West Coast were going to be penny-ante stuff anyway pretty soon. Norman Cay was the future, he said, and don't worry about that either. George was going to be in the command structure here; he could count on it. But Carlos had to leave Miami for a while now, he said. He needed to be out here to get things organized, make some trips back to Medellín. Until then, George should deal as best as he could with Humberto, get the kilos from him, and see what Richard would be willing to take. It may be a little dry for a while, but big things lay ahead. George recalls there being a silence in the conversation after that. And then, "I said, 'Carlos, I hope you never betray me.' He said he never would. And he almost started to cry. He said he would never do that. 'I hope you never do that, because we're brothers. I don't believe you would ever hurt me.' And he said he never would. But I knew at the time that it was over. He couldn't lie to me, and that's why he nearly cried. I think he was hurt, too, because I think he did love me."

Her name was Mirtha Calderón. She was Cuban, twenty-four years old in the summer of 1977, with penetrating brown eyes, black hair, and a soft, seductive voice, until she got angry, and then it could shatter a display case filled with crystal, the case included. She had fair skin, an inheritance from her Castilian ancestors. Her mother, Clara Luz (Clear Light), had been married several times; her father had served as an officer in the army of General Fulgencio Batista. After Castro came to power, Clara Luz brought her two daughters, Mirtha and Martha, to the United States, to Chicago, where she met an Italian named DiNicola who had been connected to the mob and could regale his family with tales of Al Capone. In 1968, when Mirtha was fifteen, she married a soldier returning from Vietnam, and she had a child named Clarie. A divorce soon followed, and Mirtha moved to New York City, where she found office work in the firm of a jewelry broker and resided in a modest basement apartment. She liked to shop for trendy clothes, and at night she hit the Manhattan discos then catching on, where she danced to Donna Summer records and the soundtrack for *Saturday Night Fever.* Her office salary provided her basic needs, but she didn't have to worry much about money because her family possessed important connections. The previous spring a cousin on her mother's side, Jemel Nacel, had married Carlos Lehder. Her sister, Martha, was married to Humberto Hoyos, a close associate of Pablo Escobar. Mirtha herself was also engaged to remarry, very advantageously, to an acquaintance of Carlos Lehder named Cesar Toban, the scion of a wealthy Colombian coffee family, the same Cesar Toban of the suitcase trips to Antigua. Mirtha's stepfather, the former mobster, had expressed great enthusiasm over the alliance, and a big wedding was being planned, but he never got to see it. He died in May of 1977, and shortly thereafter the engagement was called off when Mirtha fell in love with another man.

Humberto and Martha maintained a large apartment off Central Park West in Manhattan, right next to the Dakota, where John Lennon would be assassinated in 1980. Along with moving kilos to the West Coast, Humberto controlled a certain portion of the lucrative market for the product on the Upper East Side. One day that summer of 1977 he was expecting a certain visitor from Miami, who was going to drop off a small amount of money, about $100,000, for three kilos Humberto had sent out on consignment to L.A. The man was on his way to Cape Cod with some kilos of his own to unload and needed to be picked up at the Airway Motor Lodge at La Guardia Airport and brought to the West Side apartment. Humberto couldn't make it and asked Martha to go instead, and she asked her sister to come along for company.

"You had heard rumors about this man they referred to as 'the Gringo' or 'the Americano,'" she recalls. "At that time all the Latins were very tight and nobody else was allowed in, he was the only one. My sister said they knew this man from Miami. So we went up to the hotel room and he was there with another woman, named Lorraine, who was carrying stuff for him. She opened the door. He was standing back in the living room, and he just had this look. He had on a tan suit, with these hazel eyes, shaggy blond hair. Very good-looking. Very well dressed. He could do this thing with his eyes. All of a sudden they were like stars—this twinkle there, this spark. I still remember that look. 'What is this?' I said to myself. 'What *is* this?'"

What George recalls of the meeting was giving Mirtha his patented once-over and being impressed. "I was talking to Martha during the ride to the apartment but looking at Mirtha," he says. "She had a good body, her breasts weren't too big, but she was wearing a mini-skirt and you could see she had good legs. Legs were what I liked." At the Hoyoses' apartment they had drinks and dinner, talked a lot, and George asked Lorraine if she wouldn't mind taking the kilos the rest of the way on her own and dropping them off at Mr. T.'s. He wanted to stay in New York and get better acquainted.

Mirtha and George talked all night. During the 1960s she had painted flowers on her face, demonstrated in Chicago against the war and in support of the Chicago Seven. George detailed his experiences with LSD, his trips to Jefferson Airplane concerts at the Fillmore. She particularly wanted to hear what it was like the decade before in Haight-Ashbury. He also ran down some of his own political philosophy, threw in his Bob Dylan set piece, although he was a little rusty on that since switching into the cocaine business—Mr. Tambourine Man didn't figure too highly in the Colombians' view of things. "We talked until late and everyone had gone to bed," he recalls. "She wanted to take me to show me her apartment. On the way we ran out of gas. We finally got gas, but it was late and I was tired so I said, 'Let's check into this hotel. I'm not going to sleep with you, we'll get two beds, you sleep in one and I'll sleep in the other.' So we did that, and I'm lying there for about fifteen minutes trying to sleep, when she said, 'Well, would you like to come over here?' 'No, I'm tired,' I said. That kind of freaked her out. I always thought reverse psychology worked the best in these situations."

Humberto was furious at first. What business did she have going out with this American, given her engagement to Cesar? He was yelling at her in the bedroom and George thought he heard a slap. "Humberto could throw pretty good temper tantrums. They were over pretty quickly, but he'd break up some furniture first, but, shit, they all did, the whole family, and all the women—Martha, Mirtha, and their mother—they drove him truly nuts. When Martha got angry, whoooh, you didn't want to be anywhere near the place. One day she got mad at him and faked that she'd drowned herself in the East River. She left a suicide note and Humberto was hysterical, crying, he had all these people looking for her, even called the police out. All the time she was hiding out. She'd just wanted to torture him. He used to tell me, 'Georgie, don't ever get married, you'll never stop regretting it. They're all witch-bitches, believe me. You don't know it now, but you'll find out.'"

The flap about Mirtha's night out blew over quickly enough, but she canceled her marriage to Cesar shortly afterward, a payback that provided secret satisfaction for George, considering Betsy's fling with the guy in Antigua. And the new romance blossomed apace. "What I liked most was that George had class, the way he walked and talked, reading Shakespeare and all those books. He knew about van Gogh and Picasso, he gave me a book about Dali. And just the way he conducted himself, you could see it. He was very elegant in his manners—your all-American gringo. The Latin women loved American men, because they're not with the machismo. They're very mellow. They help the wives do the dishes, take care of the kids. The Latin men, all they think about is, okay, they have a wife, but she's a slave. Not George."

By the end of the summer Mirtha had been up to Weymouth to meet George's parents, gotten the tour of his old room, been told how he'd crawl out the window at night when he was a little boy. She peered into the cubbyhole under the eaves, heard what he felt like when Agent Trout came to catch him. In Miami Beach they put up at the Castaways. He was relieved for an excuse to get away from Carlos and Jemel, and at night they'd have romantic dinners brought up to the room, served under candlelight. "He taught me how to drink the best wines, like Château Rothschild, Dom Pérignon champagne, eat lobster," she says. "When we were alone, he'd tell me about the other women he'd loved, but he would say, 'I love *you* now.' And then he would stand up in front of me and start singing, 'You Make Me Feel Like Dancing,' and do it, I mean start dancing. And singing. He was very romantic. He made me feel so young."

And George liked Mirtha, too, at least well enough. To be sure, her limited education and her narrow upbringing in Chicago had produced gaps in her knowledge about the world that occasionally proved fairly stunning. When later that year they rented a beach house on the Cape, for instance, George announced over lunch one day that he was going to perform a little trick involving the ocean. He was going to command it to move back from the beach. Later that day, he told her, by the time Mirtha had come back from a shopping trip to Hyannis, the water level would be thirty feet short of where it was now. He went down and stuck a stick in the sand so she could see the difference. Mirtha just laughed—another of George's jokes. But when she returned five hours later and checked where the stick was, just to make sure, she saw that, My God, he'd done it! No, no, George explained, it's the tide. It went out while you were gone.

The tide? said Mirtha.

He did, however, enjoy her companionship in the evenings and the fact that she loved and admired him. She also provided an audience to whom he could unburden himself, a human refuge at the end of a day or a trip. Besides all that, Mirtha brought a distinct asset to the relationship, one that appreciated considerably in George's mind the more he saw himself being isolated by Carlos from the enterprise now picking up speed in the Bahamas. It was one thing for George to make runs to the West Coast and bring back a lot of money and make the Colombians rich. For this they appreciated and trusted him. But he was still a gringo, still not one of them, not someone they would bring into their inner circle and let him listen to the important discussions. George could never change his country or ethnic background. The only thing that could alter George in the perception of the Colombians was his becoming a member of the family, especially a family that had important connections down in Medellín. So here it was, staring him right in the face. Carlos or no Carlos, Humberto Hoyos in his own right was a powerful player in the cocaine game. George and Humberto got along fine and liked each other well, which was good for George and got him a lot of kilos to sell. Clara Luz, Mirtha's mother, was also stuck on George, liked to tell him about the family history in Cuba and Chicago and to tip him off to things she heard were going on in the business. Still, friendship was one thing; it would be so much better to have firm family ties, to be a son-in-law, a brother-in-law. Clearly, the right thing to do here where Mirtha was concerned was to make her an honest woman. He was going to marry the girl.

Well, not marry, exactly. As his various girlfriends knew too well, from junior high school days on up, George suffered from a constitutional incapacity to maintain a monogamous relationship. Put plainly, he was a hopelessly compulsive fornicator, to the degree that occasionally even he had to stand aside from himself and stare back in wonder. As for actual marriage, to tie himself *legally* to a person for the rest of his life flew directly in the face of all his dreams, of the Costa del Sol, of the cafés in Ibiza, of the women—especially the latter, the countless, unending supply of women. Actual marriage seemed too much to ask of himself, even under these opportune circumstances. But, despite his reservations, when Mirtha raised the subject, he told her he just might entertain the possibility. Someday, maybe. "I really can't remember exactly what I told her," George says. "I promised her I'd think about it, or I said we'd get married eventually. I was doing a lot of cocaine in that period, and sometimes I'd say things that didn't stay with me very long. But I knew the Colombians were definitely big into families, into respecting the family, even though the guys screwed around a lot. They were also big into the Catholic church and christening children. So being married meant I would be solidified within the family. As far as I was concerned, it was a very advantageous thing to do."

George eventually told Mirtha that if she really wanted to get married, they could act the part; they could pretend. So that fall he chartered a Learjet and took her on a vacation to Quebec City, where he got them a room in the venerable Château Frontenac, on the bluff overlooking the St. Lawrence River. And on their return Mirtha announced to her friends and family in New York and Miami that, yes, she and George had just done a wild, crazy thing. They'd eloped and gotten married up in Canada. He'd given her a ring, a coral-and-turquoise job she'd picked out herself. And she'd bought George one, too, a ruby set in gold, a stone the Colombians called *sangre de pichón*, or "blood of the pigeon." For whatever difference it made, in Mirtha's social life and George's business, they henceforth presented themselves as Mr. and Mrs. Jung, husband and wife.

At first the liaison with the Hoyoses and the everyday demands of the cocaine business took George's mind off worrying about his prospects for the future. Through Humberto, he was given a new wholesaler to supply in Manhattan. Richard was still there on the West Coast, not as big as before and still getting uppity, but still willing to move kilos. George also had a good contact in Ann Arbor, Michigan, from his marijuana days, and he resurrected his relationship with Earl the Pearl, now a prime cocaine wholesaler throughout Marin County, a solid market area with good growth potential. And, of course, there was Mr. T back on the Cape, as well as his dealer in Cambridge.

George also had to begin giving some attention to all the millions in cash clogging the heating system in Wellfleet. At one point Barry Kane had talked to him about putting his money into gold certificates in Switzerland. Not only could this be done quietly, but gold was going crazy during that period, at one point getting up over six hundred dollars an ounce. The idea was to transport the money to the Bahamas, deposit it in one of the offshore banks, such as the Nassau branch of the Bank of Nova Scotia—an institution that had come a long way since its founding as a repository for the hard-earned savings of Scotch-Irish fishermen—and purchase the certificates through the bank by wire. Or wire the money from the Bahamas into a numbered account in Switzerland, or the Bank of Nova Scotia branch in Panama City. But Kane these days seemed to be drifting into Carlos's circles, and George felt a little uneasy about carting all his money down to Nassau.

What's more, with his "marriage" to Mirtha he seemed to have included a family that was developing considerable financial needs. There was Clarie, her daughter from her first marriage, and her stepbrother, Armando, who repaired cars in his backyard in Miami and seemed more adept at spending money—George's mostly—than making it. His mother-in-law, Clara Luz, lost no time in declaring dependent status for herself, exchanging her residence in the Hoyoses' apartment for one with George and Mirtha, in a house she got George to rent for them all near Barry Kane's condo north of Fort Lauderdale. And Mirtha herself was proving no slouch when it came to contributing to the profits of the shopping malls. All in all, George thought, he'd better hold off transferring the cash out of the country just yet. It looked like he'd find sufficient use for it close to home.

After a few months, though, it was obvious that his unhappiness over Carlos wasn't going to disappear. Getting his kilos from Humberto meant George had to work in the capacity of a dealer, selling them to small-timers around the country, somthing he disliked intensely. He now had to load up the door panels of a Jeep Cherokee with ten or fifteen kilos and schlep them out to his contact in Ann Arbor, a guy who sold hot tubs by day and at night attended the business school at the University of Michigan. Another customer was a would-be writer living in a shack lit by kerosene lamps in the woods near Buffalo, New York, who peddled kilos to finance his novel. There was also a black record-store owner in New York City, the only person of his race George ever encountered in the drug trade, who made George bring the goods to a drop-off point in an industrial area of Livingston, New Jersey. "To me, it was all degrading, like going from being Lee Iacocca to being a used-car salesman. I hated it," says George. Not only was he making less than a tenth of his former income—barely a hundred thousand dollars a month—but the work put him at considerable risk. "It was a lot of exposure for not much money. You'd never know if the guy you were dealing with had gotten arrested and they'd let him out on bail so he could set you up."

Transportation—that was George's baby, and the best way to stay clear of the law. But Carlos seemed to have a lock on that end right now. Carlos! He'd hear things from Humberto about what was happening on Norman Cay, and he didn't like any of it. In the last conversation he'd had with Carlos, the deal was that George would be called down when things got cooking. Well, they were obviously cooking up a storm, and George's phone hadn't rung at all. Carlos did indeed buy the house, the Volcano, paid $190,000 cash for it, the story being that he'd given the owner a suitcase full of money counted so casually that there was $8,000 too much. He'd also, as planned, picked up a 165-acre parcel, including the airstrip, hotel, and marina, from the investing company in New York, again for cash, $875,000, George later heard. A couple of dozen employees were now working on Norman Cay, building the hangars and some kennels near the runway for guard dogs. There were rumors that Carlos had hired a couple of high-tech bodyguards trained at a special security school in Stuttgart, Germany. He'd heard that Kane had made some more flights down to Medellín that George certainly hadn't been consulted on, even though he regarded Kane as his own recruit. He'd heard that even Frank Shea, his former boyhood pal, the one he'd gotten to help Carlos bring in the early loads, and his girlfriend Winny, were working on Norman Cay. And according to Humberto, the loads were certainly starting to come in and go out with considerably frequency. Carlos now had a fleet of three large boats, a fifty-one-foot powerboat, a cruiser ninety feet long, as well as all manner of airplanes.

In the middle of this, Richard Barile finally just shut George down, said he was getting about as much as he could handle from Carlos, with whom he now had a regular relationship, and that George would have to take his kilos elsewhere. "I blew up at him and said, 'Listen, I set you up in this business, and then you fucked me over and went behind my back.' He said, 'Well, that's business. George, I can't help it.' And I said, 'Well, I'm telling you now that eventually some form of revenge is going to take place. I'm not going to stand for this.' 'It's not my problem,' he said. 'It's Carlos's problem. It's between you and Carlos.'"

George was now going to parties with the Colombians, where he'd be the only gringo, and the subject of Carlos invariably came up. The men would talk about it in their groups, the women in theirs—how well Carlos was doing, how big he was getting, how George had been screwed over, how he'd been responsible for Carlos's success, and now look at the way he was getting treated. "Then Mirtha would start talking about it around the house, so I couldn't get away from it. They wouldn't stop talking about it or let me forget it. I mean, I had this dream here, and Carlos had stolen my dream. Now no one would let me get on with my life." This went on until early in 1978, at which point George called up Carlos at the Holiday Inn in Nassau, where he stayed when not on his island, and said he was coming down to settle the situation.

After landing at the airport and taking a cab to the hotel, George called Carlos in his room, and Carlos told him he'd meet him in the lounge. Carlos showed up in about five minutes, ordered a beer, and this time there was no obfuscating. George was out, as far as the Norman Cay operation went. "He said there was room for only one person to run the operation and that was going to be him. He said, 'It's my world, my empire, and I have to run it.' He said it wasn't the end of the world for me, that I wasn't going to go broke with Humberto." While Carlos was talking, George noticed two fairly large individuals enter the lounge and seat themselves at the next table. One was blond, wearing a polo shirt and khaki shorts, the other had dark hair and a bushy beard. Both were over six feet tall with thick necks and ballooning biceps; they looked like professional athletes in a sport with a lot of body contact. They sat there keeping George and Carlos under surveillance, until George started getting loud, causing some heads to turn in the bar, at which point they rose to their feet.

"Instead of being humble," George recalls, "and humiliating myself like the last time, hoping he would come back to me, I suddenly realized that he was never coming back, and I just crossed over the line and had no fear, no insecurity. My anger just seemed to encompass my whole life. 'So I'm fucked, is that it?' I told him. I said, 'Well I'm fucking tired of getting fucked around like this. I'm in with some pretty heavy-weight people in Boston that you're going to find out about. You're going to pay for this, you and Barile and everyone.'" In the middle of his speech, George suddenly became aware that the two big guys were looming over the table, and Carlos interrupted him to say he wanted George to meet a couple of his employees, come all the way from Germany. This was Heinrich, he said, gesturing toward the one with the beard. The blonde was named Manfred. Why didn't George just lower his voice a little bit, not attract so much attention. This was a public place. They could talk about this like gentlemen. "By this time I was too pissed to talk about anything anymore and got up and said, 'You're not going to get away with this. There are going to be reprisals for this. This is not the end of it.' And I walked out, got a cab to the airport, and flew home."

It was right after this confrontation that George received the present. They were all having dinner at Humberto's apartment in Manhattan, and George was describing his meeting with Carlos, the German bodyguards, the threats he'd made. At this point, an elderly woman whom George understood to be an aunt of Humberto's, reached into her purse and took out something folded in a piece of linen cloth, which she placed on the table in front of everyone. Here, take this, she told George. When he unwrapped it, he saw it was an ice pick. "She told me, 'My late husband said to always carry this for protection. The hole is so small a person doesn't bleed. If you don't get him now, everyone will look down on you.' I took the ice pick and said I'd think about what she said, and I put it in my briefcase. I didn't tell her, but I knew I wasn't going to kill anyone with a fucking ice pick. If I was going to get someone, I was going to shoot him."

NINE

Eastham

1978–1980

We are finally alone this morning. He's having coffee on the deck and looking out at the bay. I love his blond hair. When he looks into my eyes I feel his love. He tells me he loves me and that he is happy for the first time in his life.
—FROM MIRTHA'S DIARY, SUNDAY, APRIL 24, 1978

SINCE GEORGE WAS AWAY ON BUSINESS, TEDDY FIELDS offered to take Mirtha around to the real estate dealers to look for a house they could live in on the Cape. She rented the place in Eastham on a gray day late in the fall of 1977. Built to a modern design, with sharp angles, an open deck, and weathered shingles and trim, it sat on a seventy-five-foot-high bluff offering a spectacular view out over Cape Cod Bay. A set of rickety stairs led down to a stretch of sand, which was known as First Encounter Beach. The encounter had occurred in 1620 after a party of Pilgrims stole a cache of corn from the Indians up in Truro and had to fight off a band of pissed-off Wampanoags who attacked them when the *Mayflower* put in to take on water. Eastham lies between the ocean and the bay just beyond the bend in the Cape, where it turns sharply north and heads up toward Provincetown. Besides its beach, the town is known to historians for its wind-driven grist mill, built in 1793 and still turning strong, and also for the three original *Mayflower* passengers buried in its cemetery. From George's house on the bluff you could make out the lighthouse on Race Point at the tip of the Cape. But the best show came from due west across the bay late in the day, when the sinking sun spread the entire horizon with a ruddy orange glow.

George wasn't much of a local-history buff, but he liked the view and listening to the gentle lapping of the waves. The house itself seemed perfectly designed and located for his line of business. Its shingle-covered chimney, built to disguise the flue for the basement oil burner, provided an ideal stash for the three hundred or so kilos he often needed to hide temporarily while the load was still in transit. The approach to the house was difficult to find, located several miles from Route 6, the main highway on the Cape, on a twisting series of back roads. A loft area over the kitchen, normally reserved for little Clarie's playroom, had a vertical dormer that gave George a commanding view over all the access roads. At his back was the sea. All in all, it was in a strong defensive position, not an easy place to approach without being seen. The situation of the place proved its value not many months hence when three Colombians with whom George had had a grave misunderstanding called down from Logan Airport and wanted him to come up and meet them—to discuss the problem, they said—at what he knew was a deserted stretch of waterfront just south of Boston. If they were that hot to see him, George suggested they drive down to Eastham. He'd set up a little reception committee in the window in Clarie's playroom, her dollhouse and the stuffed animals shoved over to one side so he could sit there in comfort while he leveled on the approaches to the house with a civilian version of the army M-16 that Mr. T had fixed up for him, its breech mechanism altered so as to fire on full automatic. Come on down, he told them. No one showed.

Mirtha knew he planned to stay for a while when, a week or so after settling in, he rented a jackhammer and cut a three-foot-square hole in the concrete floor under the 250-gallon oil-storage tank in the basement. George wanted it to be large enough to store $3 million in cash. He put a steel plate over the hole, then replaced the oil tank on top of the plate. To get at the money, he'd raise the tank off the plate with a come-along winch suspended from a pipe attached to the overhead beams. "Otherwise," he says, "you looked in there you'd never dream you were staring at more money than most people earn in three or four lifetimes."

The house had a lot of space—three bedrooms, plus a maid's quarters downstairs next to the garage, along with two sleeping lofts. But George's family had already begun to grow. Along with Mirtha's relatives, there was now Uncle Jack O'Neill, from Baton Rouge, Louisiana, his mother's only sibling, who decided in his early seventies to give up the music stores he owned in Louisiana, divorce his wife of forty years, and come up north and join his nephew in the cocaine business. An old-fashioned Irish dandy, who in his younger years trimmed his mustache pencil-thin, wore a diamond pinky ring, and manicured his nails, Jack came from the musical side of the family. He'd studied at the New England Conservatory of Music and played piano in concerts and in nightclubs, at one point for Gordon and Sheila MacRae. A cousin, Don O'Neill, had a radio program out of Chicago. His mother, Ethel O'Neill, George's grandmother, was the one who had sung in music halls in Boston. George remembered visiting Uncle Jack's house in Baton Rouge as a boy. "I always loved him," George says. "He was a big gambler, played cards and billiards, also a golfer. He'd bring me along out on the golf course, and when they reached the green they'd putt for a thousand dollars a shot. He'd say to me, 'Georgie, this guy loves to lose money. Watch this.' And when the other guy was ready to shoot, Jack would unloosen his false teeth and have them fall out right on the green. The guy lost all his concentration."

Jack was soon helping George regain his big-time status by coming up with new smuggling schemes. The two of them flew down to Bay Saint Louis on the Gulf of Mexico, just over the Mississippi line from New Orleans, where Jack knew the manager of a country club/condo complex, a whole community on the water, complete with its own stores, golf course—and landing strip. When Jack came north, he brought along some old friends, a newly retired couple in their late sixties. Wilmer had operated a rental-car agency in Baton Rouge, and he and his wife were looking for something to occupy their declining years. "'Wilmer, he'll do anything,' Jack told me. So I soon had him and his wife running suitcase trips down to Caracas, staying in good hotels, flying first-class. They brought in two loads worth about one and a half million. They said they'd never had so much excitement in their life. Wilmer asked me if I knew anyone else they could do trips for."

As Mirtha remembers them, the early days in Eastham provided her and George happy times, almost all the way through 1978. She spent a lot of money on a decorator to fix the place to her liking. She chose an orange shag carpet for the living room and orange drapes for the windows and across the sliding glass doors in front, a combination that made the place seem to burst into flame when exposed to the sunsets. She couldn't find any furniture to her taste on the Cape, so she ordered the living room and bedroom sets, a bamboo and rattan motif, from a store in Baton Rouge when they were down on a visit. "I was used to living in a house with all French provincial, like a museum, with chandeliers and marble tables, and silver. But it wasn't me. I was very down-to-earth."

Life settled in. "In the evenings we'd sit out on the deck, looking out onto the bay. He would read and was relaxed. He felt good because he had accomplished what he'd wanted to do. He was doing what he knew best and was truly happy, especially after he found some new pilots. He'd always wear white, white and beige. A jacket with this little silk scarf. I'd buy him light blue shirts that looked so good with his hazel eyes. He'd have his cognac, the Rémy Martin. We talked about how we'd stay on the Cape, and I was going to play music, and he was going to write his book, about his life. This was the dream we were going to live."

They also shared a few secrets in the safe house in Wellfleet. That place also looked out over the bay, had a wide, screened-in porch in front, and a large attic room on the third floor that George and Mirtha made over into their special fantasy place. Other than Courtney, who had brought the money there from Florida, no one knew about the Wellfleet house, not Mr. T or Teddy Fields, and not the Colombians. Even his brother-in-law Humberto had only the telephone number of Wellfleet, not the address. On the days he couldn't reach George in Eastham he'd try this other number, always getting Mirtha on the phone, who'd invariably tell him that George wasn't available just then; he was tied up. Not always tied up, actually. And some days he wasn't even George. He would transform himself into "Georgette," someone Humberto would probably not have recognized very readily because of the makeup—lipstick, eye shadow, the blond wig, and because of the brassiere he wore, and the woman's panties. "I would more or less pick out what I thought would look good on him," says Mirtha, who got the stuff at a department store in Hyannis. "It was very hard, because basically he was so *big*, I mean huge shoulders. He was a very hard person to shop for."

Georgette's main assignment was to do the housework, per-
forming the chores dressed in a scanty hostess apron and her econ-
omy-size ladies' underwear. Her lipstick was a neon pink, royal blue
rimmed her eyes, and her wig was cut in a Dutch-boy style that
hung down toward her shoulders. Georgette would run the vacuum
cleaner busily around the room, bending over to jab it under the
sofa, making sure not to miss those corners—surprising, how much
sand gets into the hard-to-reach places with a house at the shore.
She'd give the books a once-over with her dust cloth, climbing onto
a stool and reaching up on her tippy toes to get the top of the china
cabinet. The cleaning done, she'd set out places for dinner, forks on
the left, knives on the right—had to get it right or "Mistress Mirth,"
the stern one who ran the household, would get upset and do something to Georgette that might smart. Goodness knows, Mistress was
hard to please. In short order Georgette would find herself told to
go upstairs to the big bed in the attic, where she was made to lie
down on her back with her hands and feet tied. Mistress Mirth got
the hang of it as she went along. "At first I would tie him up with
ropes, but he would say, 'Look,' and I would walk back into the
room thinking he was all tied up, and he'd be loose, standing there,
saying, 'I told you you didn't tie me right.' So then I began to get
serious." On a trip to visit her sister in New York City, Mirtha
stopped in at the Pleasure Chest, a sex shop in Greenwich Village,
and bought a variety of equipment—chains and handcuffs, leather
straps, dog collars and leashes, a selection of whips. Back on the
Cape she created a little outfit of her own, fashioned from a picture
she'd cut out of a skin magazine and taken to a tailor in Provincetown she'd heard felt comfortable with such requests.

The Provincetown tailor made several versions for her, one
white, one red, and one black, all consisting of a leather corset
extending from her breasts to her crotch, held together by strings
that laced up the front. She also ordered up leather bikinis to go
with each set. Back in the attic, she'd put on her stuff and firmly
affix Georgette to the bed, make her into the slave of Mistress
Mirth. If Georgette wanted a snort of coke, she'd have to beg for it.
The same for when she wanted a meal, and sometimes, if Georgette
hadn't done a good job downstairs or had said something naughty,
she might go a whole day without food, be left up there for hours
and hours while Mistress Mirth stayed downstairs entering the day's
events into her Kahlil Gibran diary, in which each week was head-

lined with some piece of wisdom from *The Prophet*.

"George always wanted me to do more, saying I wasn't mean enough, so I'd constantly have to be thinking up things." She kept Georgette fairly well shaved in the lower regions, lathering the Gillette Foamy all over the place, and using the occasion to carve her initials just above the pubic area with a razor blade. She'd allow him to come downstairs where she'd have a fire going in the fireplace and handcuff him to a rocking chair. Or she'd fasten on his dog collar and a leash and lead him around the house on all fours, once threatening to take him out on the street like that if he didn't behave. She also thought of putting clothespins on his nipples, making him endure that for four or five days. On one occasion when Mirtha returned to Eastham and he stayed on at Wellfleet, he called her up to leave a breathy message on the answering machine: "This is your slave Georgette calling to tell you I'm taking the clothespins off. They're painful. Perhaps when we meet again you can extend the time period. Good-bye."

Early in 1978 the activities at Wellfleet had to be suspended shortly after Mr. and Mrs. Jung discovered they were going to have to accommodate a new member of the household, due to arrive the first week in August. Mirtha heard the news first from her doctor, and she rushed home to tell George. "I didn't want another child, really. I had Clarie. But he wanted one of his own. Oh, he definitely did. But I didn't know if he could handle it. When I told him, he hugged me and kissed me and said that's wonderful, he was really excited, and Jack was excited, too. They started to take care of me. 'Sit down.' And, 'You've got to eat this and that.' I remember how pleased he was. It was like a fresh start."

Actually, before this moment George couldn't have given less thought to children, and especially to whether he might want one of his own. "The kind of life I'd led, raising a family, that stuff, the subject had never come up," he says. "The way I thought, adventurers don't have time for children and dogs and cats. None of my girlfriends were interested in any of that. And the people I'd known in California, they might have had a dog, but that was it. I'd always assumed Mirtha was on the pill. But then I found out she wasn't." Nevertheless, now that the event was at hand, he decided that maybe it wouldn't be so bad. The baby would be a boy—there was never a question in his mind about that—and he'd name him after his own father, Christian Frederick Jung. As the date got closer, he helped Mirtha shop for baby things and get the little room ready. "He'd go to the store with me, and everything we picked out was blue. Blue blankets, T-shirts with little blue borders on them. A little blue rattle. He bought the first stuffed toy the baby had. It was a teddy bear, really cute, with a little T-shirt that said 'Hug me.'"

From Mirtha's diary entry for Thursday, May 4, 1978:

> George has found another pilot and we're getting ready to leave for Norfolk in a few days. George buys me ice cream, our craving. We both eat it in the middle of the night. He likes coffee. I love chocolate. We were sharing this craving together. They say that men don't become pregnant. They do. I want this baby and he wants this baby, too. He placed his hands and felt the baby move today. He was in a trance after that. It's funny to see this mafioso man when it comes to expecting. We had a good day.

Whatever his feelings toward the blessed event, George's best day that spring was the one when he once again found a pilot and was back in the transportation business for the first time since the Kane flights nine months earlier. The source was a publication called *Trade-a-Plane*, a periodical that serious smugglers rarely missed. He'd answered an ad for a de Havilland Dove, the British version of the DC-3, which was for sale by a pilot named Hank, who operated out of the airport in Norfolk, Virginia. "I called the guy and said I was in the real estate development business and his plane sounded like what I wanted. He said to come on down, his wife would pick me up and bring me out to his hangar. I flew down and she showed up in a station wagon, three or four kids in the back. We drive over there, and here's this guy Hank, swigging from a bottle of tequila and sitting in the middle of all these airplanes. When we're alone he says, 'Who're you shittin'? No real estate developer wants a goddamn plane this big. You're a smuggler.'

"'You're goddamn right I am,' I said, 'And so are you, you motherfucker.' And that's how we got started."

For years Hank had augmented his salary as a Pan Am pilot by flying pot out of Colombia and Mexico, and at about the time George happened along he'd been considering moving into a more profitable product line. In the years between 1978 and 1980 things began cooking over a high flame in the cocaine business. Coca paste was flooding into the processing plants in Medellín and Cali, flown in from the three thousand-odd landing strips in the Alto Beni growing region of Bolivia, trucked up the Pan American Highway from Peru and Ecuador, landed from coastal freighters putting in at the Colombian port of Buenaventura and little coastal villages all along the Pacific, most of them reachable only by donkey trails. When Hank started making flights for George, he reported back that the airstrips he was directed to outside of Medellín and up near Barranquilla in the north were like miniature O'Hares in Chicago, with so many aircraft coming and going that the planes had to circle around for a while until they found a moment clear for a landing. At night the fields would be outlined by piles of burning automobile tires, which lit up the forest region like dozens of primitive encampments. Pilots would sometimes get confused and land at the wrong strip, then have to take off again and hopscotch to the next set of signal fires. In these go-go years of the trade, efforts to interdict the flights by federal and local police agencies in the United States were haphazard at best. Total seizures of cocaine by the DEA in 1980 amounted to only 2,590 pounds, equivalent to less than five of Barry Kane's planeloads. And it was not until 1982 that the Reagan administration declared its much vaunted war on drugs, with Vice President George Bush the general in charge.

Meanwhile, with the word out about the huge profits being made in the American market, Colombians were pouring into the States with the avidity of miners on the scent of a gold strike. The processors from Medellín controlled sales in Florida and most other areas of the country, which accounted for about 70 percent of the business; the balance, which went largely to New York City, was given over to traffickers from the Cali region, in the south. The cocaine lords weren't widely known as the "Medellín cartel" until around 1985, the year they made the covers of *Time* and *Newsweek*; but by the turn of the decade they had already formed the manufacturing end into a smooth-running industrial enterprise.

On the board of directors, as it were, was Pablo Escobar, who ranked as first among equals and had charge over most of the production facilities. With him sat the Ochoa clan from up north in Barranquilla. Unlike most of the others in the trade, who came from uncertain backgrounds—Pablo was part Lebanese, for instance—the Ochoas were an old family, proud of their roots in northern Spain. The patriarch, Don Fabio Ochoa, was an obese man with courtly manners who often dressed completely in white, from shoes to hat, invested in Picasso paintings, and devoted much of his time to the family's bullfighting interests and raising walking horses. Don Fabio had three sons, all active in the business, foremost of whom was Jorge Luis Ochoa Vasquez, or El Gordo, "the Fat Man." Short and stocky, clean-shaven with a pudding face, Jorge worked in the sales end of the company, coordinating much of the distribution in the southern United States. In his spare time he collected classic Harley-Davidsons and helped run the family's Hacienda Veracruz, a vast holding outside Barranquilla that, like Pablo's place outside Medellín, contained a private zoo with animals brought over from Africa. Also on the board was José Gonzalo Rodríguez Gacha, known as "the Mexican," who owned large tracts of forestland and oversaw the transport of the coca paste from the farms to the factories, now and then helping Pablo on the enforcing end. And then Carlos, of course, figured in overseas transportation. Carlos had begun building his own hacienda, complete with zoo, down in Armenia, to the south of Medellín.

Hundreds of others worked at high levels of the trade, buying kilos in Colombia, combining them with other loads for shipment to the States, or arranging for transportation on their own, if they had the bulk to make it pay. Whatever arrangement they worked out in their native land, they had a frantic need these days for airplanes and pilots, and for people they could trust who could put the trips together. In this part of the enterprise the Colombians clothed every piece of the deal in a cloak of secrecy; they had nothing to learn from the Byzantines when it came to the arts of deception. Most of the Colombians who sought out George and his airplanes came through Humberto—or George thought they did. But he never knew if Humberto was sending the Colombians as a service to them, for which Humberto got paid, or if the kilos these people wanted George to fly into the country really belonged to them or to Humberto, who might have been masking the fact for some reason. Or was Humberto possibly agenting the whole operation on behalf of his friend Pablo Escobar, and this was Pablo's personal cocaine? George suspected all of the above held true at one time or another, but he didn't know which it was, and he didn't much care, as long as the Colombians came.

"Humberto was now calling up constantly," George recalls, "saying he's got this guy and that guy, they want to move three hundred kilos, five hundred kilos. He'd call and say, 'Can you get me two planes by tomorrow? This guy has a thousand kilos.' I'd say, 'Hey, slow down here, will you?' But I'd get them. Because by then it was snowballing. Everyone had started to do it. I was meeting ten different Colombians a week. They all had kilos to bring in. They all needed airplanes."

It soon became clear that George couldn't run the business out of Eastham, and so he had Clara Luz rent another house for the family on the inland waterway in Pompano Beach, just north of Fort Lauderdale. He liked Fort Lauderdale because it had two airports, a lot of good restaurants, the Bahia Mar Yacht Basin, the lushly decorated Pier Sixty Six Resort and Marina. Living there also distanced him from the Colombian stomping ground in Miami, giving him a little peace and quiet when he wanted it. Yet getting to a business meeting in Coconut Grove or Little Havana or Coral Gables involved just a short hop down I-95.

Hank did six trips for George in rapid succession, carrying three hundred kilos each time, for a total of nearly two tons. George charged the Colombians the usual $10,000 a kilo, split it down the middle with Hank, and in about four months they were each better off by some $9 million. The operation won no prizes for sophistication. Figuring that the police in Norfolk, Virginia, weren't exactly turning over every rock looking for cocaine smugglers, they simply flew the loads in at night, straight from Colombia to the Norfolk airport. Once on the ground, the plane would taxi to a dark end of the runway and pause there so the kilos could be thrown out to George's guys waiting in the bushes, then taxi over to check in at the U.S. Customs shed. The kilos would be trucked down to a stash apartment in Miami and negotiations would be initiated with the Colombians for transferring the goods in return for payment for the trip.

When George sent word that the load had arrived, he'd be provided with the address of a house in Miami where the cocaine should be delivered. Usually it was located in a quiet middle-class area of Little Havana and occupied by Colombians trying to blend in with the socioeconomic mien of the neighborhood. At one point a trafficker even went so far as to print up a set of instructions for how these operators should act, a sort of Emily Post guide for the cocaine trade. According to one of the pamphlets confiscated during a DEA bust in the 1980s, the house should have an attached two-car garage and the people living there be a couple, thirty-something, with children. The man should leave in the morning carrying an attaché case, dressed for going to the office. "Try to imitate an American in all his habits," it said, "like mow the lawn, wash the car, etc." The couples were warned "not to have any extravagant social events at the house, but [they] may have an occasional barbecue, inviting trusted relatives. It is recommended that every occupant have a well-maintained dog. Preferably a Great Dane."

George would drop off half the load at the house, wait until it was in turn unloaded to wholesalers, then demand his fee for the plane trip before delivering the rest—again, holding on to the second half as collateral against their disappearing without paying the freight. When the Colombians showed up with the money and George showed up with the coke, George would bring along a bodyguard. George employed several over the years, but easily the most formidable was Richard Starkland, alias "Bird," from Natick, Massachusetts. A former air-force ground crewman who saw service in Vietnam, Bird was built like a piece of earth-moving equipment—six feet six inches tall, 260 pounds, with a broad, slightly pitted face and a big bushy beard. A fisherman by trade, Bird got his name several years earlier when he and a confederate were surprised by the game warden while tonging for clams in illegal waters. His pal was caught, but Starkland took off by land and succeeded in outrunning the marshal, even with three bushels of clams slung over his back. "Tell that big bird running over the marshes that he hasn't seen the last of me," the marshal told Starkland's accomplice, and the name stuck. George met Bird in jail in Massachusetts following his early pot bust, and the two became pals. Bird had been arrested down near Yuma, Arizona, in connection with a purchase he'd made of thirty-five hundred pounds of marijuana from the mayor of San Luis, Mexico, right across the border. He carried the whole load on his back, two hundred pounds a trip, through the Colorado River to a location on the U.S. side in the Yuma Desert. He then returned east and paid two gofers from Framingham to go down in a jeep, pick up the pot, and bring it back. "I told them right where it was, that there were only two trees in the state of Arizona, and this was next to one of them, but they still couldn't find it." Bird went down and found it himself, unfortunately at the same time as did agents from the U.S. Border Patrol, and so the Bird was in the bag.

For his bodyguard duty he charged George $5,000 an appearance, plus the cost of his hardware, which consisted of a short-barreled .357 Magnum Smith & Wesson State Trooper, and also a Colt .45 automatic—not the erratic army model, but one of the Gold Cup competition series, capable of putting five slugs into a circle the size of a quarter at twenty paces. He'd arm the clip with mercury loads, which were hollow-point bullets bored out and filled with mercury and sealed over with wax. One hit anywhere in the upper body with this mother and half a man's back would be oozing down the wallpaper. When the Colombians arrived, Bird would monitor their entrance into the apartment and then, while the coke was being inspected and the money counted, stand next to the door, his back to the wall, not say anything, and stare. "They'd feel you out with their eyes, so you'd never want to look down and you'd never want to blink," he says. Bird made about eight appearances for George, supervising the orderly transference of somewhere in the vicinity of three tons of cocaine and $10 million to $15 million in cash—no problem.

After his last trip for George, Hank and his Dove hired out on another job and disappeared altogether. He gave no warning to George, left his wife and children, just vanished. George figured he either crashed his plane or made cocaine connections on his own and set up another life. With his string of Colombians to satisfy, however, George now needed another pilot, another plane, and another piece of luck. He had a chance meeting with the man who owned the house in Eastham, an Italian contractor named Dino Viprini. Dino dropped by one day because Mirtha had complained that their refrigerator, a brand-new Hotpoint, wasn't getting cold enough. Dino had never met George before this, but he'd heard stories. "I started talking to this Italian guy," recalls George. "And he says, 'Ya know, I know what you're doin'.'

"'What are you talking about, What I'm doin'?'

"'Come on,' he says, 'Come on. Guy comes in here, throws money and cash around, pays the rent in cash. You know, I got an airplane. I know some people in Florida, too.'

"I said, 'Is that right, Dino?'

"And he says, 'Yeah, that's right,' and I said, 'Let's talk some more.'"

It turned out that, like Hank, Dino had also been a pot smuggler, bringing tons of it in by boat from Jamaica to the Cordage Pier in Plymouth Harbor, just a few hundred yards from the crowds of tourists who stand around staring at what's left of Plymouth Rock.

Dino told George he knew a wealthy developer in Palm Beach and also a pilot who'd been flying pot into Texas and guns back into South America. Both of these guys were named Ralph—Big Ralph and Little Ralph. Dino said that Big Ralph, the developer, was looking to make a large investment of money and time and effort in the cocaine business. One thing led to another, and soon George was going down to Palm Beach for a visit. "At the time, he was married to a wealthy woman and living in this $5 million estate on the water," George says. "I'd call his house and his wife would say, 'Let me see, the Lamborghini's here, so's the Ferrari. Let me check with the maid whether he's at the polo club'—he was a member of the Palm Beach Polo Club—or he'd be hanging out by his stables on the estate."

Rather than chartering planes, Big Ralph suggested they go in together to buy one of their own and just hire the pilots. They chose a $1.2 million Cessna Conquest, a nine-passenger twin-engine turboprop. By taking out the seats they could fill the cargo area with just over a ton of cocaine. The Conquest had a speed of nearly 400 miles an hour and a range of 2,300 miles, meaning you could fly back from Colombia and go deep into the States without refueling. Because its turbo engines needed less oxygen than those on a straight prop job, the Conquest could fly in thinner atmosphere, up around 30,000 feet, almost beyond the view of groundlings, and its steep climb ratio enabled it to land and take off on the proverbial dime. The plane also had the advantage over a full jet in that its props allowed it to operate in heavy atmosphere as well as thin, so it could get right down on the deck, sneak underneath any radar surveillance, and come nipping into U.S. airspace fifty feet above the wave tops.

In the import company they formed, George was vice president in charge of sales, arranging the trips, ensuring the planes had a load to bring back, collecting payment for the job. The two Ralphs ran the operation itself, hired the pilots, made sure the flights got off the ground on schedule, came back in good order. Operating in such perfect symbiosis, they began flying regularly out of Fort Lauderdale Executive Airfield, and returning to tiny strips in the Everglades, North Florida, Alabama, and the Carolinas. From there they would truck the product back to Miami, where George turned it over to the Colombians. "All of a sudden I didn't give a shit about Carlos Lehder anymore," he says. "I was married to the Colombians, and I had the two Ralphs, with all the equipment and wherewithal. I was running with all these people, the flights going in and out. Barry Kane and his little shitbox of an airplane! Doing little piss-ant trips! I wouldn't even talk about less than 1 million, 2 million, 3 million a run anymore. This was the dream I had had, right here. And it was all happening. What did I care about Carlos now? I was becoming as big a cocaine king as he was."

George was acting pretty royally in the consumption category as well, with Mirtha keeping him company most of the way. He'd been using cocaine more or less regularly since late 1976, after the suitcase runs to Antigua, but these days his intake moved toward a level that, had the category existed, might have qualified him for a place in the *Guinness Book of World Records*. When it comes to snorting coke, of course, establishing any level of use as "average" seems a fairly fruitless enterprise, considering how the drug tends to encourage the pursuit of extremes. Nevertheless, as calibrated in several academic studies of the subject, the standard hit for someone characterized as a regular but moderate user is usually figured at a couple of lines, one to a nostril, each line about an eighth of an inch wide by an inch long, containing fifty to a hundred milligrams of cocaine, done two or three times during an evening, maybe once or twice a week. This cocaine would most likely have been cut, so it's far from pure, not like the stuff to which George had access. Although snorting is the most socially acceptable form of intake, the nasal membranes offer one of the slower routes to the brain, since the coke must travel all through the secondary circulatory system to get there, arriving badly diluted in the bargain.

Much faster is what Sigmund Freud, Sherlock Holmes, and John Belushi enjoyed doing, which was to dissolve the cocaine in water and shoot up intravenously (Belushi's fatal shot had a dash of heroin in it, making it what's known as a speedball). "In my last severe depression I took coca again," Freud wrote back in 1884, "and a small dose lifted me to the heights in a wonderful fashion. I am just busy collecting the literature for a song of praise to this magical substance." Shot directly into a vein, the coke takes just two minutes to impress itself on the brain cells, and maintains its effect for ten or fifteen minutes. In solution form, the coke contains more wallop than when snorted, and can create sensations that, as Freud observed when he stayed up one night monitoring the habit of a friend, proved to be more than mildly disconcerting. The friend, whose name was von Fleischl, had been trying to cure his morphine habit with cocaine. One night he suffered a paranoid reaction and, with Freud at his side, began hallucinating that monsters were trying to get at him and insects were gnawing at his skin. More or less promptly after that, Freud decided he'd better knock it off.

The fastest route to a high, one that didn't make its appearance in the United States until around 1986, and then mostly in cities on the East Coast, is to cook up the cocaine into crack and smoke it in a little pipe. The kernel of crack doesn't stay lit very well, so you have to keep firing it up with a butane lighter, hence the telltale burn scar on the outer edge of a crack addict's thumb. After a hit on the crack pipe, the rush comes on in only ten seconds and envelops the mind with the intensity of a fierce squall at sea. Three or four minutes later, it tails off, vanishing as rapidly as it appeared, to be replaced by a sharp psychological crash and an agonizing hunger for more.

When snorted, the only way George did it, coke takes a little longer to produce an effect, four to five minutes from nose to neuron. But the euphoria lasts longer, from fifteen minutes to half an hour, at which point the good feelings inevitably start turning sour and the high takes a downhill slide, reaching its half-life—the point when the half drug has been eliminated from the body—in forty-five minutes to an hour after the hit. That's when you want to check into the coatroom or the john to do it again; and this goes on maybe five times a night, so that you can knock off a fifth of a gram, half a gram if you're a fairly heavy user, or a whole gram if you're near to going over the edge. When the crash would come for George, the feelings he missed most were the sense of possessing total control over his environment, of having a heightened sensitivity to things— "when you're having a conversation with someone and you know what they're going to say before they say it"—feeling magnificently superior to the other people in the room, of being a superman, a person whom no one can touch and no one can bring down.

By his own account, between 1978 and 1980, his years of heaviest use, George averaged about five grams a day, between 100 and 150 lines, five thousand milligrams. This was his maintenance dose. Some days he'd be up to ten, even twelve or fifteen grams, and he recalls on at least one occasion making a whole ounce—twenty-eight grams—disappear in a period of eighteen hours. "I just seemed to have this tremendous capacity for coke," he says. "I never met anyone who could snort more coke at a sitting than I could. You put ten grams in front of me, and I could go through that stuff in ten minutes. One of the Colombians, Victor, would come up to Eastham and we'd do two or three grams and he'd have his head in the toilet. I'd do it with Mr. T, and after nine or ten lines he wouldn't know where he was."

After a while, snorting lines or doing little coke spoons got in the way of George's travel schedule—he was always on airplanes or in cars, going or coming—so he took to filling up a Tylenol bottle with a few ounces, which he would pop into his shirt pocket. When he wanted a hit, he'd uncap it and insert a straw, not even taking the bottle out of his pocket, and a constant flow of coke would be vacuumed into his nose. Mirtha recalls that at parties in Miami with the Colombians, "the coke would be out on the table on a silver platter and the men would be doing these little lines, maybe taking just a hit with their spoons. George would measure out a line twelve inches long, run up the whole thing with his nose, and in one hit it would all be gone, like that." The Colombians would say that George didn't do your normal lines, he did boulevards. "Mr. I-95," they called him, in reference to the endless string of white lines that mark the lanes on the interstate.

Averaging 5 grams a day, throwing in a few extra for the binges, this added up to somewhere around 6,000 grams, or 13.2 pounds of 100 percent pure cocaine that he visited on his brain cells from 1978 to the end of 1980. Cut and sold on the street, the amount would have cost close to $2 million. But the financial consequences of his habit paled alongside what it did to his personality and the general pace of his life.

The effect cocaine has on the brain is essentially to make the billions of neurons "talk" to each other, and in turn send out messages to the various parts of the body telling them how to act and feel. A brain cell, cell 1, say, normally communicates in an orderly fashion by firing off a neurotransmitter containing its message into the space between cell 1 and cell 2, known as the synapse. There the message from cell 1 is picked up by cell 2 through its receptor, whereupon cell 1 terminates the transmission by cleaning the remains of the neurotransmitter out of the synaptic space and getting off the line, as it were. It does this by employing a mechanism known as "reuptake." The conversation having stopped, cell 2 can react to the message without getting confused by any static residue. One of the most important effects of cocaine is to cause the neurons to fire off their neurotransmitters into the synaptic space, willy-nilly, shooting out one impulse after the other and creating a lot of general chatter in the head. Another thing it does is to block the reuptake mechanism, which prevents cell 1 from clearing its former message out of the synaptic space before issuing a new one. This means that for the duration cocaine is present in the brain the cells never stop talking, the general effect of which is like a party telephone line with billions of customers, all blabbing at once, and no one will shut up, and you have to do what everyone says, and do it now.

Among the messages that come across loud and clear is the one that gears up the body to cope with an emergency—adrenaline shoots into the system, the pupils dilate, and the heart rate accelerates, pumping blood to the muscles. The senses go on high alert, the need for sleep and food gets suppressed, the energy level soars. For the same reason the Indians in the Andes could run twice as far when they chewed coca leaves, George Jung could stay up for four and five days at a time with no sleep, talking incessantly, making deals, doing business, fast-forwarding his life in general until it resembled the action in single-reel film from the 1920s. This was especially evident to anyone having the misfortune of being present when he was behind the wheel of a car. Once, when he was driving a Colombian visitor from the house at Eastham to the airport in Hyannis, George informed his alarmed passenger that he'd drop him off at the rotary by the air terminal, but that he was in too big a hurry to stop the car. "I told him, 'Look, I'm really rushed, I haven't got the time to stop, but I'll slow down a little. You'll just have to jump.' It took two times going around that rotary, but he did it." As a driver, George had been a public menace ever since his teenage days, but on coke he gave "speed demon" a new dimension of meaning. After midnight one night, trying to get to the Cape to supervise a money delivery, he drove his Thunderbird from the center of Boston to the Sagamore Bridge, fifty-four miles, in the space of twenty-five minutes, and this included negotiating two cloverleafs.

Coke also intruded into most aspects of George's home life at Eastham, where Mirtha would try to keep up with George, at least part of the way; Clarie would sometimes wake up wondering why her mother was running the vacuum cleaner around at three or four in the morning. George liked to take Clarie off to her fourth-grade class at the Eastham elementary school, and on more than one occasion he ended up in some confrontation with a teacher or the principal, on whom George would unload the brunt of his own teaching philosophy from the pimp classes at Danbury. "Going to school in the car, I'd be having a little pick-me-up out of the Tylenol bottle, and Clarie would ask what I was doing. 'It's my medicine, Clarie. The doctors say I have to have this all the time.'" Arriving at the school at 8:00 A.M., he'd storm in with his sunglasses on, a silk scarf, leather jacket, his Porsche burbling to itself outside in a no-parking spot, whereupon he would discharge himself of some opinions to anyone in sight, then tear off. "I remember Clarie looking at me once and saying, 'Why can't you just be like the rest of the dads?' I knew she was mortified a lot, but I couldn't stop."

That summer, however, he decided abruptly that maybe he'd been doing too much coke after all and resolved to tail off some on the grammage. The occasion came six days before his thirty-sixth birthday, on the same day his child was born, when George suffered a heart attack. He'd already experienced some physical consequences from the drug, one of them a subspecies of cocaine psychosis that had to do with what the medical books call "tactile hallucinations"—thinking things are crawling on your skin. This comes about because the same neurotransmitters that fool you into believing you're physically invincible, sexually irresistible, and intellectually formidable, not to mention the life of the party, can also cause you to lose touch with reality in negative ways as well. You begin to suffer symptoms of paranoid schizophrenia, thinking people are after you, that there's stuff on you that shouldn't be there. What George felt was an unbearable burning sensation in his feet. He thought his soles were peeling off, that he'd been walking on a bed of coals, like some Indian fakir, only not because he wanted to. A doctor he saw couldn't figure it out, probably because George neglected to tell him about his coke habit. Walking being too painful, George stayed in bed, and he also stopped snorting coke, since getting high while lying on your back isn't much fun. Abstinence, it turned out, was the cure, and eventually the sensation went away.

Late in July, with the baby's arrival drawing nigh, Clara Luz had the family move to the Pompano Beach house so Mirtha could give birth in Cedars of Lebanon hospital in Miami, where they had good Cuban doctors. Mirtha's water broke early in the morning a few days after they arrived, and George found himself barreling down I-95, his wife beside him growing steadily more panicked, telling him to hurry or she'd have it by the roadside. George had thought to get a little blasted on coke before they left in order to speed passage of the birthing experience—and in Miami he became disoriented and couldn't find the hospital. Finally he flagged down a cabbie and gave him two hundred dollars to lead the way. The cab promptly pulled a U-turn over the median strip, and George followed suit in the big Thunderbird, which took the divider by leaping about a foot into the air, causing Mirtha's head to smash into the roof, not doing wonders for her emotional state. They reached the hospital with plenty of time, it turned out, since the baby didn't arrive until that evening—a girl. She was named Kristina Sunshine Jung, the first name because it resembled Christian, George's father's name, the second to honor the fact that she'd been born in the Sunshine State. The initial glimpse George and Clara Luz got of her was through the little window in the nursery, and at first George wasn't too impressed. "You look at them and to me they all looked the same, like wizened little midgets. But Clara Luz was going, 'Oh, she's beautiful, she's so wonderful.' 'Okay,' I said. 'Now, let's go home.'"

He felt the pain right after he got in the car and was putting it into drive. It hit him in the chest, with the force of a sledgehammer. More pain began shooting up and down both arms, and he started sweating profusely and growing faint. Clara Luz took his pulse, which was racing wildly, and quickly got him into the emergency room, where the doctor informed him he'd had a violent heart attack. He laid George out on a gurney, plugged him into an EKG monitor, and gave him a shot to calm the heart muscle. "You just about blew up the machine. You've got to tell me what you've been doing," George recalls him saying. "I said that I'd probably done an ounce of cocaine in the last fifteen hours. He looked at me as if I was fucking insane." Cocaine heart attacks arrive compliments of another neurotransmitter—norepinephrine—which pumps stimulating signals into the heart muscle. These cause the muscle not only to work extra hard but to go into overtime, so that it fails to take the usual rest periods, during which it normally gets replenished with blood and oxygen, enabling it to continue to work. The sledgehammer blow George felt to his chest was, in effect, his heart muscle crying out for more oxygen. After the shot slowed down his heart, and after lying there for a couple of hours, George felt considerably better, and during a moment when the doctor was otherwise engaged, he walked out of the emergency room, got into his car, and drove home.

As it turned out, the heart attack wasn't the half of it. Something much worse, in terms of family relations, happened the following day, when George found himself so hung over from the cocaine binge that he couldn't get out of bed to make the little champagne pour the hospital gave for the new daddies coming in to see their wives and babies. "I never heard the end of that one," he says. "Mirtha got hysterical about it, crying, shouting, going on about how I was the only father who wasn't there. She'd bring it up later over and over, when we'd argue—'You rotten son of a bitch, you couldn't even get to the hospital when your daughter was born.' You know how women can throw in your face what you did ten years ago. They'll go back twenty if it's good enough. They've got everything categorized in their minds, all the dates and times, every fuckup you ever made. Mirtha was so pissed she didn't even want to hear about the heart attack."

For a while, after the baby came home, George actually managed to cut back a little on his habit, and happy times resumed in the Jung household. George would get up in the middle of the night to feed Kristina her bottle or change her diaper. He'd sit by her high chair spooning in the baby food, play with her down on the beach, or take her on a walk with him in the stroller when he went to the convenience store a couple of miles away on Route 6 to use its pay phone to call down to Colombia. He was so attentive that, when Kristina started to talk, it was George she'd ask for if she woke up at night. "*La leche, poppi. La leche,*" she'd say. "It was all new for George, and I think that was one of the times he was very happy," Mirtha says. "I would go to sleep and he would stay up and watch the baby, hour after hour. The baby was so fragile he didn't want Clarie to carry her, he thought that she'd drop her. Everybody was excited. And it was a good time, a happy time. It was really a happy time."

With the money pouring in like a veritable deluge, George had to give serious thought these days to what to do with it all. He certainly couldn't start blowing millions of dollars, buying yachts and houses, without drawing attention from the IRS or any number of police agencies who would want to know where it had come from. Now that he was a full-fledged family man, with a wife, two children, and a mother-in-law, not to mention Mirtha's brother and Uncle Jack, along with a live-in nanny to take care of the children and two houses to keep up, it didn't seem quite the right moment to take off for the Great Barrier Reef or find a permanent seat at that café in Ibiza. There was now somewhere around $30 million stashed at Wellfleet, with a few more sitting underneath the oil burner at Eastham. He kept the presence of most of it a secret, even from Mirtha, or rather, especially from Mirtha, since everything that reached Mirtha's ears went directly to Martha, and pretty soon every Colombian in the business would be expressing interest in those heating ducts. For walking-around money, he maintained a general fund in a bureau drawer in the bedroom, replenishing it regularly. "Everybody could have money anytime they wanted, like a candy store," he says. "Jack and his friend Wilmer, all they had to do was go to the bureau drawer, or Mirtha, when she wanted to go to the mall, just take out a handful."

When Mirtha would be down in Florida, he'd also secrete money throughout the structure of the house. He had a carpenter come in to refit the medicine cabinet in the bathroom so it could be pulled out easily, if you knew the trick, and behind it mounds of cash could be stuffed in between the studs in the wall. He unfastened part of the living room paneling and put money in there, fitting the pieces back together with a hidden metal clamp. Over the clamp he hung up a framed print he'd always liked, Andrew Wyeth's *Christina's World*. And every month now he began hiring a Learjet to take several million from Wellfleet down to Big Ralph in Palm Beach, who was transporting cash to various accounts in banks with discreet branches in the Cayman Islands and Panama City. In return for their discretion when it came to accommodating people bringing in suitcases of cash, the offshore banks began exacting a 1 percent "counting fee" from the drug traffickers, which provided a good piece of change in addition to the usual profits from lending the money out at interest. Once it was in the offshore bank, the cash could then be transferred secretly by wire to anywhere in the world, even back into the United States, a factor that was contributing in no small way to the construction boom in Miami and elsewhere in Florida.

George thought vaguely about eventually moving his share to Switzerland, but right now he was content to let Big Ralph handle things. He seemed to have the right contacts, and George had little time to make any complicated decisions himself. After each trip Ralph simply gave him a receipt from the bank confirming the deposit, with a seven-digit number on it representing his growing account. He stored the receipts in the safe under the oil burner at Eastham. At night he liked to sit out on the deck, watching the moon reflecting off the water, drinking his Rémy Martin and thinking about his life and what he'd done and where he'd been, about his nest egg, all safe, sound, and secret. When he took it all out someday, wouldn't *that* be a kick?

Of course, George was blowing a lot of the money too, the hell with the IRS. He bought the Eastham house outright, paying Dino Viprini $185,000 in cash and closing the deal with a handshake, not bothering with any legal folderol such as getting a deed. Clara Luz wanted to go on a nice long trip to Europe, so George sent her. Were the commercial flights to Florida too much of a hassle for Mirtha? He would send her down on a Learjet. There were the cars, always three or four up at Eastham, plus a couple parked in Florida. George had a Porsche 924, now a burnt umber one, as well as his turbo-charged Carrera, the stand-by Thunderbirds, '75s and '76s, BMW's, a couple of Mercedes Benzes, and a Ferrari. He had to trade in the Ferrari after the Japanese came out with a lookalike model. "I didn't want to go around and have people think I was driving a fucking Datsun," he says. For her casual trips around the Cape, when she didn't feel like ordering a limo, Mirtha had a bright silver Oldsmobile Toronado, which she'd tear off in up the dirt road in back of the house, leaving sand and rocks flying in her wake. "The Silver Bullet's on the move," the neighbors would say. George also tried once more to give his parents a present, arriving at their house one day with a brand new Ford Country Squire station wagon. They never used it. After it sat in their garage for six months, he went up to Weymouth and took it back.

The normal household expenses ran about sixty thousand dollars a week, what with keeping the bureau drawer up to the mark and feeding Mirtha's addiction to the malls. Out in Provincetown, the general business confidence along the main drag rose appreciably whenever Mirtha and her girlfriends from New York and Miami hove into sight. George was never exactly a clotheshorse, but he did his part, buying dozens of expensive leather jackets, five-hundred-dollar silk shirts, and his favorite Bruno Magli loafers, now up to twelve hundred dollars a pair. "I didn't really like to shop for things, so I'd do it all at once," he says. "I'd go into Neiman Marcus in Miami and tell them I wanted that and I wanted that and that, and I'd take off my clothes and say, 'Here, throw these away,' and put on the new stuff and tell them to deliver all the rest and walk out." On one occasion he had a tailor in Fort Lauderdale line his blue jeans with silk because they felt so good that way. And he ordered a half dozen pairs of cashmere pants. Cashmere pants, sir? "The guy said he'd never heard of anyone wearing cashmere pants, but when I started peeling off the hundreds, he started seeing what a good idea it was after all."

George also gave money away, just dropped it on people. He would send people like Courtney on simple errands and pay them five or ten thousand dollars for a day's work. He invariably picked up checks for elaborate meals, spent fifteen hundred or two thousand dollars on a bottle of wine—Château Lafite-Rothschild—and put visitors up at resort hotels on the Cape. And he'd throw parties, usually down on the beach at Eastham, having grown less secretive these days about where he lived. He'd have parties in honor of the Colombians sometimes, and sometimes for his new batch of acquaintances in Boston—Mayor Kevin White and his wife Kathryn would show up, along with a lot of expensive lawyers. He ordered caterers to set up tents on the sand, and brought in four-piece combos to play Cole Porter, or rock bands for Mirtha. He'd have whole canoes sitting out on the beach filled with shrimp and lobster tails and Beluga caviar. There'd be twenty cases or so of Dom Pérignon champagne, limousines and expensive cars clogging the roads to the house. At one party, a noted mob lawyer from Boston pulled George aside and told him: "You know what all this is, George? It's a goddamn accident waiting to happen. You're the king in his castle here, with all the little serfs watching you and wondering who the fuck *is* this guy and what is he doing? Why don't you just put out a big neon sign, make it easier for cops? Because, sure as hell, you're gonna get busted in this house. Why don't you stay down in Fort Lauderdale, where you blend in better?"

That fall of 1978 was particularly memorable in George's life for two important events, one of them being a trip he took with his mother and father on a Sunday afternoon up to Wakefield, to pay a last visit to his ailing grandmother, Nana Jung, before she died. Uncle George was going to be there, too; it would be the first time George would see him since graduating from high school and getting offered the sweeper's job down at the Boston Edison plant in Quincy. George stopped off in Weymouth to pick up his parents and drove them up in a brand new Lincoln Continental he'd rented for the occasion. He was dressed in a sharp-looking blue blazer with brass buttons and his special cashmere pants, and had on a Rolex watch with clusters of diamonds in it, worth about eleven grand, which Humberto had given him as a birthday present. Also a Gucci tie, which Aunt Myrna commented on right away when she opened the door. Aunt Jenny and Uncle Ray Silva, the parents of George's cousin Bobby, the bank president, were there. Also Auntie Gertrude, who ran the beauty parlor in Filene's. And of course Uncle George, who strode across the carpet to give Ermine a kiss, shake Fred's hand, and notice that George was puffing on a little Dutch cigar, one of the Schimmelpfennigs that came in the tin.

"The first thing he said to me was, 'There will be no smoking in this house.' And I said, 'Oh, yeah? Is that right!' and I kept right on smoking. Aunt Myrna came rushing over and said, 'Oh, Georgie, don't mind him, he's a senile old fool. I want you to sit down and tell me *all* about Danbury.'" So George got on the couch and told them stories about G. Gordon Liddy and the Wakefield bank president. Aunt Myrna asked him what he was doing with himself these days. And before George could come up with something—the precious-metals business or investment counseling, bring out one of his phony business cards—his mother piped up and told everyone that, Oh, George was doing very well. He was in real estate development now. Obviously miffed at the attention being awarded his good-for-nothing nephew, Uncle George grabbed Fred's arm. "'Come on, Fred,' he said. 'You and I'll go in and watch the game.' He never said another word the rest of the afternoon. That's how I could tell that I got him that day."

The other thing that happened that fall was that George decided to check in at the home office, to fly down to Medellín and pay his respects to the man whom the Colombians, in their penchant for emulating the Italian Mafia, had begun referring to as El Padrino, or "the Godfather"—Señor Pablo Escobar Gaviria.

That first time, George went alone to see Pablo. Mirtha had the new baby to take care of, of course, but besides that, the Colombians weren't too keen on having women around when business got discussed. There were a lot of things they didn't like the women doing with them. "At the parties you'd never see the men talking to the women, if there were any other men there," says Mirtha. "Except for George, of course. He'd talk with the men, but he liked talking to the women, too. The women would stay over by themselves and talk about the things their men had bought them, their cars and jewelry. They'd talk about their men, their personalities and the things they did to them when they were mean." With the Colombians, at least those in the cocaine culture, it was a common practice for many of the men to go off on weekends to see their mistresses and girlfriends, returning to their wives and children on Sunday, in time for mass, which they rarely missed. Humberto, much more the homebody, was particularly religious and would ask George and Mirtha to accompany him and his family to church sometimes. George would sit next to him, hearing him praying out loud for the success of the impending trip, beseeching God to let nothing go wrong with bringing in the next load.

"But even though the men were often gone, they'd hire guys to spy on us," says Mirtha. "They'd watch the homes, watch their apartments. They'd report back to him everything she did that day, who she saw or who she was seen with in public. The women got very crazy—paranoid—especially the ones who were fooling around, because the men could be very cruel." At the parties featuring coke, which could go on for days, the men snorted out in the open, but the women were expected to do it on the sly, slipping into the powder room for a couple of lines. And when the business discussions began, the women automatically left the room. "The women would be around, but they weren't actually allowed in on the planning of things, because the Colombians never really trusted women. They felt vulnerable. They always felt the women are the ones who are going to go squealing on them. And they resented me, because I would make sure to be there. I thought George and I were one, and I would stay and be quiet and listen to what was going on. George knew Spanish well enough to say what he wanted, but he didn't really know the language. He couldn't tell how they'd say things that meant something else because of the tone of voice they used. I wanted to protect him. There was no way I was going to allow them to, excuse my vocabulary, fuck him over. No way."

As arranged by Humberto, the plan was for George to spend the night at the Intercontinental Hotel and be taken by Carlos's brother, Guillermo, out to Escobar's ranch the following day. Along with cementing his relationship with Pablo, George also had a political agenda in mind. "Escobar knew I'd been feuding with Carlos, after all, and there'd been threats. Now here I was coming down alone to Medellín, into his own backyard. I wanted to show that I wasn't afraid of Carlos. I felt like it was taking a hell of a chance, but that it would solidify my status. And I guess I wanted to get back my respect, too."

George found flying into Medellín an interesting experience, since the plane had to circle round and round in order to descend low enough into the bowl formed by the surrounding mountains so it could land. Located on a hill about fifteen minutes out of town, the Intercontinental is the most exclusive hotel in Medellín, with a lavish bar by the pool, tennis courts, and its own riding stable. The next morning Guillermo picked George up in—what else?—a Chevy Blazer, and off they went on the ninety-minute drive to Escobar's seven-thousand-acre Hacienda los Nápoles. The car drove through the soon-to-be famous gate at the ranch, topped with its Piper Cub airplane—one of the planes Pablo had used in the early days to fly in coca paste from Bolivia—over the arch. The car was stopped by bodyguards with side arms, some carrying M-16s, and escorted down a long dirt driveway to the house, which was a sprawling one-story affair, about fifteen rooms, with a tiled roof. George was told to wait in the living room, which was floored in a red mosaic tile and filled with Spanish-looking furniture, mostly oak upholstered in cowhide. There was no glass in the windows, since it never got very cold in this part of the Andes. Several pictures of Pelé, the soccer hero, adorned the walls, reminding visitors that Escobar supported several soccer teams in Antioquía Province. Soon George was ushered down a hallway and into Pablo's office. Escobar stood up in back of his large oak desk when George entered the room. He was about George's height, tall for a Colombian, with dark wavy hair and a slightly cheeky face, and when he came out from behind the desk to shake hands, George saw he wore snakeskin cowboy boots fitted with solid gold tips.

Pablo's English was about as good as George's Spanish, and so the two stumbled through the conversation in both languages. "He told me it was a pleasure to meet me and that he'd heard a lot about me. 'And now you are here,' he said. 'We can do a lot together. You have the planes and the pilots and I will take you and show you where they will land and where they will stay. I will personally supervise it and make them feel very comfortable.' He said that I would stay the night in his own house. And he asked me if I would like some *perico*, which means 'the bird that talks a lot.' And I said yes, I would very much, and he reaches into a drawer and takes out this big fucking rock of cocaine and slams it down on the table. I'd never seen anything like it, it was as big as a softball, and he took a machete and hacked it in half. It was pure cocaine, even better than the stuff we had handled, tinged blue, like the inside of a cave lined with ice. He chopped some up into a little pile and he handed it to me and I sniffed it and said, *'Muy bueno, sí, amigo.'* We each had a couple of large hits from his spoon. I got the feeling he was trying to see if I became insecure after doing the drug. *'Tu quieres más?'* he said—'Did I want more?' And I said I *'quiero mucho más,'* and he laughed, *'Muy bien. Ha ha ha.'* He said he liked me and that I was a 'good *gringo.'* He said he knew of the feud with Carlos and said it was *'un problema,'* and that he felt Carlos had wronged me, but that he couldn't take sides. He said he respected me for coming down here."

Pablo then took George around in a jeep to see the spread. The tour included the stables where he kept Arabian horses, a miniature bull ring, about fifty yards across, with seats for two to three hundred spectators. He had a helicopter pad, with a Huey 500 parked to one side. The landing strip was paved, about a hundred yards wide and nearly a mile long. Sheds were built in under the trees as temporary storage for some of the cocaine. Fifty-gallon drums of 80- to 100-octane aviation fuel, or avgas, were stacked everywhere, along with electric fuel pumps and generators. He also had a powerful radio transmitter, capable of reaching all the way into the United States. Everywhere were men with guns. "He said everything was protected here, the police were taken care of, that they wouldn't dare come near the place. They really didn't have a choice. They earned almost nothing for pay, and here they were asked, 'Do you want to make $250,000 and have a ranch for your family?' And if they didn't want that, it was, 'Do you want to be dead?'"

Staying over at the ranch proved fairly uneventful. After a lot of Glenlivet Scotch and a supper of rice and beans and a Colombian stew called *san cocho*, made of beef and carrots and potatoes, George and Pablo and a half dozen others adjourned to one of the bedrooms, where Pablo put on a Betamax cassette of the movie *Patton*, starring George C. Scott, in English. George had already seen it, but it was Pablo's favorite movie, a taste he shared with the former gringo *presidente*, Richard Nixon, and he watched it at least once a week. After the first run-through, he asked George if he wanted to see it again. George begged off, said it had been a long day and that he'd just as soon get some sleep.

The next day, before Guillermo arrived to drive him back, George and Pablo were walking over by the landing pad with some Colombians, including an interpreter assigned to George, when they heard the thwacking noise of a helicopter. Soon a small Bell model appeared over the jungle canopy and settled into a landing. In the cab beside the pilot were two other Colombians, one of them in handcuffs and not appearing terribly happy to be there. The interpreter told George the man was a police informer and to stand back a little. Pablo barked an order and the man was brought over to him, hanging his head. Pablo then yelled a lot of things at him, of which George caught only a few, all of them negative. "I heard *rata*, which I knew was 'rat,' and he called him a *maletón*, which was a 'bad' something, maybe just a general son of a bitch, and also *cabrón*, and that means someone who allows another man to make love to his wife but doesn't do anything about it. It also means 'faggot.'" It grew quiet all of a sudden, and in a move that seemed prearranged, someone handed Pablo a large automatic pistol that looked to George like a U.S. Army Colt .45. With no further ado, standing about five feet away from the informer, Pablo casually raised the pistol and shot him square in the chest. The force of the impact hurled him backward to the ground, where he quivered a little and then lay still. This was the first person George had observed being shot to death, and he recalls spending the moment trying to compose his facial expression into some kind of appropriate response. "I mean, in their eyes I was supposed to be this big fucking American gangster, and they were all these really macho guys, acting casual about it, so I was trying to be casual, too. Inside, I'm thinking, 'Holy shit! I'm glad he doesn't think I'm a *maletón*.'"

The interpreter explained to George that the dead man, although a stool pigeon, had actually acted very courageously. It had been his choice to come out there to the ranch instead of fleeing Medellín, or seeking the protection of the police. Had he run, he knew they would almost certainly have come after his wife and children. Such a serious offense against Pablo could not be allowed to go unpunished. So in what must have been a stark moment, the man had chosen to sacrifice his own life for those of his family.

While the body was being dragged away, Pablo came over to shake George's hand and tell him good-bye. He made no reference to the killing and instead said that right around the corner from the Intercontinental Hotel was the best steak house in all of Medellín. "He said you could get châteaubriand there that you could cut with a fork, and that I shouldn't fly back to the States without tasting what a Colombian steak could really be like."

It was after returning from Medellín that George had his first run-in with one of the Miami Colombians, a situation that threatened to erupt into serious hostilities. The issue arose with a protégé of Humberto's named Victor, who wanted to contract with him for a load to be flown in and also to front a number of kilos for George to sell directly on his behalf. Now that he was back in transportation, George didn't like playing the role of dealer anymore, but he performed the service now and then, moving the kilos through Mr. T or his contact in Ann Arbor, strictly as a favor, to maintain good PR with the clientele. He got Barry Kane to do the flight. Kane had also fallen out with Carlos in the past year and was available now for other missions. The load was 250 kilos, for which George charged Victor $3,000 instead of $10,000, the balance going to Kane, who had his own plane and did nearly all the work. Victor also handed George 25 kilos to sell, which would net him another $250,000 in commissions, meaning the whole transaction added up to an even million, his customary minimum. He stayed up in Eastham during the actual flight and got the call up there that the "marriage" had been performed with the "children"—Colombian code for reporting a successful trip—after which Kane drove the kilos to Florida to exchange them for the transportation fee. It was there that things got off the track.

Kane received payment from Victor for his own work, but instead of holding on to part of the shipment until he got George's money as well, he accepted the promise that Victor would take care of that part himself. It was a big mistake. When George called down the next day to inquire as to the whereabouts of his $750,000, Victor told him that, well, he didn't have it yet and that George would have to wait until the kilos were moved on the street. Fine, said George, only in the interim he'd just hold on to Victor's twenty-five kilos as collateral, and if his payment didn't arrive very soon, he planned to sell them and keep all the money for himself. And, quite frankly, now that he'd given it a second's thought, he was going to do that anyway, since Victor was being such an asshole, not playing according to the rules. "We then had a little conversation in which Victor said I couldn't do that, and I said, 'Fuck you, Victor, I already have. You're really a stupid son of a bitch to pull this when I've got all your stuff. I'll see ya later.' And I hung up. In a little while Humberto called to tell me that Victor was very angry and said he was going to kill me. I told him, 'Good. Come ahead. My gun's right here.' And that's when the war started."

It was getting on toward December—which was when some of Victor's friends flew up to Logan Airport that time and called down to Eastham for George—and Clara Luz, who never liked being north in the winter, wanted everyone to go down to the house in Pompano Beach for Christmas. George agreed to change the family's venue, but since this would take him pretty far off his turf, he resolved to hire a little assistance in this matter with Victor. "It wasn't just going to be Victor who was coming after me, by himself. It would be maybe half a dozen of them with machine guns. People were getting shot in broad daylight all over Florida, in restaurants, in parking lots. We'd go to the Colombians' houses and the conversation was constantly about, 'Well, so-and-so got it yesterday,' and 'They just shot so-and-so.' It was getting to be open warfare down there." George put in a call to a well-known mob lawyer he knew in Boston. The man had made quite a bit on the side investing in a few of George's trips, providing cash up front for planes and other expenses. Like any good investment broker, George never liked to sink his own money into a deal when he could use someone else's; he could make just about as much that way, with no loss involved if it fell through. "I told him, 'I'm in a little trouble and I need some help.' The lawyer suggested a guy he knew named Hubert, a black man in his late thirties. Normally he was a pimp, but he hired out for jobs like this. He told me I could trust him and that he'd do what I needed. Hubert would also bring along his two sons, in their teens or early twenties. 'If the shit hits the fan, this guy is a very serious player,' he said."

Despite the protection it would afford him, George's plan for taking on some backup didn't go over very well in the household. For one thing, the security detail was likely to draw more than casual attention in their exclusive neighborhood of Pompano Beach, where Mirtha was still trying to make friends with the neighbors and the only visible black people were the ones doing lawn work or wheeling around other people's children. "I still loved George, but it was starting not to be the way I thought it was going to happen," she says. "What we had talked about was he would retire and we were going to buy his sailboat and live on the Cape and write his book. Now, I mean, come on! Here we're living in Pompano Beach in a very nice area, and he's bringing like three black people down, running around with machine guns in our house. I mean what kind of a Christmas is that? And why do they have machine guns? Because we were good people? No. Because someone was threatening to blow us up! What kind of enjoyment was that?"

For her part, Clara Luz was also upset, not so much because of the enforcers—after all, she had always urged George to kick ass a little harder than he was inclined to. It was their skin color; Clara Luz just wasn't a big fan of black people. She hadn't even liked the black maids they'd been getting to take care of Kristina and Clarie and to clean the house. Mirtha went through dozens of them. They'd always ended up quitting because of some run-in with her mother, George remembers. "I mean, they would be hired originally to watch the kids, but she'd have them in the back of the house working in some room moving boxes and furniture around, like moving men, no air-conditioning, sweat pouring off them, and Clara Luz would never be happy about what they did. She'd always complain about them. Mirtha also played a role in this because she kept hiring new ones and they'd always be black, and so Clara Luz was constantly going crazy."

Hubert and his sons showed up in a cab from the airport on Christmas Eve day, looking not as George had expected. Hubert was a slender guy, a little darker than café au lait, with a close-cropped Afro and dressed in a conservative dark suit, more Brooks Brothers than pimp attire. He spoke in soft tones, and his two boys, younger copies of their dad, leaped to respond to his slightest command. In view of the firepower they brought along—two handguns each, a revolver and an automatic, three Mach-10 machine pistols, and a couple of M-16s, fully automatic—Hubert had chartered a plane for the flight down. They were put up in one of the guest rooms, and when on duty one of the sons sat in a car out front with a Mach-10, the other in the back patio with the M-16. The day after Christmas, however, Hubert determined that the house just wasn't safe—it was too open in the back, people could just come through the hedges and blast away—and so George packed up everything, along with the Christmas tree and all the decorations, the presents, including a huge four-foot-high lion he'd bought for Kristina, and they moved the whole troop down to two suites at the Pier Sixty Six on the inland waterway in Fort Lauderdale proper. The move was a little expensive—five hundred dollars each for the two suites, on top of Hubert's five-thousand-a-day fee, but it provided much more security and was also good in regard to Clara Luz's color-consciousness, since Hubert and the sons could stay in the adjoining room and call up room service for their meals; they all didn't have to live with one another. With his new privacy, Hubert felt it was okay to bring down a girlfriend from Boston, who turned out to be a white woman. Clara Luz was scandalized all over again.

That New Year's Eve George was determined to emerge from his room and take his family down to the hotel's Crystal Ballroom to celebrate. His current difficulties aside, it had been a banner year in the cocaine business, and he felt confident that a lot more good fortune lay ahead. A twenty-piece orchestra had been brought on for the occasion, and an elaborate champagne breakfast was planned for sometime after midnight. Mirtha and Clara Luz got dressed up in special gowns for the occasion, and George invited Hubert and his girlfriend to join the party. They all went down at about ten o'clock, just as the festivities were heating up. The band played mostly Latin jazz rhythms, George doing his turn out on the floor with Mirtha, trying bravely to keep up with Hubert's moves. The champagne flowed, and shortly after midnight, when the band had slowed the tempo a little and was playing "Moon River" or something like that, Hubert stood up from his chair, walked around the table, and asked Clara Luz if he might have this dance. "I thought she would shit her pants, the expression on her face," George says. "But she did it. Clara Luz danced with Hubert." And a few days later Humberto called, and the storm with Victor blew out to sea.

Humberto said he wanted to meet with George at the house in Pompano Beach, alone; he asked him to leave Hubert and his boys back at the hotel. He had something to tell him. "I got there first, and Humberto arrived with Martha, in his Cadillac—he had a yellow Eldorado with a sunroof. Martha hugged me, and she came into the house with us to be an interpreter, since Humberto's English wasn't that great. I gave him a drink, and pretty soon he said,

'Georgie, I have to tell you this. Those kilos you took from Victor. They weren't Victor's kilos. They were my kilos. But keep them, Georgie. It's all over. My kilos, not Victor's. But it's all right.'" It was then that George understood why Victor had felt safe grabbing the $750,000 he owed for the airplane trip: The twenty-five kilos George was holding weren't Victor's to lose. And tricky Humberto, trying to conceal the fact that they really belonged to him, had finally outsmarted himself here. "So I laughed, and Humberto laughed. 'Ha ha ha, ha ha ha.' We had a couple more drinks, and then we never talked about it again. Except that six months later Humberto told me Victor had got himself shot. 'Victor, no more,' he said. He'd apparently tried to pull the same kind of shit with someone else that he'd tried with me, only this time he was dead."

Nineteen-seventy-nine was the year that Margaret Thatcher first became the prime minister of the United Kingdom, that the Sandinistas deposed General Anastasio Somoza Debayle and took over in Nicaragua, and that the adherents of Ayatollah Ruholla Khomeini, ten months after the shah of Iran announced he was leaving on a "vacation," made hostages of the United States Embassy staff in Teheran. On the home front, Hollywood came out with *Apocalypse Now*, and Americans had their first encounter with the possibility of nuclear disaster when a leak developed in the electrical generating plant at Three Mile Island in Pennsylvania. The year also marked the last time Senator Edward M. Kennedy of Massachusetts would attempt to capture the Democratic nomination for president of the United States.

For George, the hurt, anger, and humiliation left over from his last encounter with Carlos in the Holiday Inn lounge in Nassau had still refused to go away. Clara Luz had been right. Forget the loads he was bringing in and the money he was making, the "Carlos thing," as it became known among George's friends and associates, had become psychological baggage he couldn't seem to jettison. He and Mirtha had moved into an even nicer house in Pompano Beach, this one on the Intracoastal Waterway. It had a little dock out back, and George bought himself a cigarette boat, which he'd bomb off in with Mirtha to eat dinner at one of the canalside restaurants along the waterway. But at the parties with the Colombians he still couldn't escape hearing what a success Carlos was and how indispensable his transportation business had become to Pablo Escobar and the Ochoas. George would remind them that he'd just been down to Medellín himself to see Pablo; that showed he wasn't afraid of Carlos. But after several go-rounds, the trip lost its power to impress. "Carlos was on my mind every day. Even if I wanted to get him off, everywhere we went, I'd still be introduced as the guy who started him out. It began to drive me out of my mind, everyone talking about how much money he was making at Norman Cay."

By now the word had gotten out to the yachting community in the Bahamas that something nefarious was going on at the cay and to give it a lot of sea room. As George heard about it at the parties, Carlos had turned the place into something out of Ian Fleming, like the sinister island hideout of Dr. No. A boat had been found drifting off its shore with blood splattered all over the cabin but no one on board. Yachtsmen would tell of being swooped down upon by a helicopter as they neared the island, and having someone yell at them over its loudspeaker to clear out fast. Carlos had bought a thirty-seven-foot red racing Scarab capable of doing upward of sixty knots, which his German bodyguards would take out on patrol, waving their guns at sportfishermen that came in too close. A houseboat had been hauled up atop the highest knoll on the island so lookouts could search the horizon for intruders. In one notable incident, the CBS anchorman Walter Cronkite, an accomplished blue-water sailor, put into the little harbor at Norman Cay to top off his water tanks and was told unceremoniously to beat it. Although he'd failed to buy up every house on the island, Carlos had made good his boast to George and frightened the few private homeowners left into staying away from the place, putting their plans for vacations in the Bahamas on hold for a while. Flights were landing and taking off almost around the clock, and the airstrip was guarded by some twenty Dobermans, which were kept in pens along its fringe, the bodyguards regularly patrolling up and down the lone road in their jeeps. George also heard stories about wild sex parties going on in Carlos's house, the Volcano. Hookers were imported from Nassau and Freeport to entertain the resident staff, running naked all over, Carlos himself having taken recently to smoking *basuco*, getting stoned a lot, zoning out on John Lennon's "Imagine" and "Helter Skelter" by the Beatles. A lot of automatic weapon fire was reported at night, the result of an undisciplined guard force shooting at shadows in the trees.

Carlos's success had unhinged George to the degree that he now imagined people were talking about it even if they weren't, thinking they, too, were about to stab him in the back. So at the parties he'd raise the subject himself; blitzed on coke, he'd grab hold of people to rail on about his old buddy, routinely threatening to kill him, to put out a hit on him and blow the fucker away, the ungrateful little cocksucker. People would try to edge out of the room when he'd get going on this. Among the gatherings ruined by his tirades was a dinner party Mirtha threw in Pompano Beach for their little circle of friends. Martha and Humberto came. The Mejias were there, Arturo and his girlfriend, also a woman in the trade, powerful in her own right, known as the Woman of the Alhajas, or Jewels, for the way she dripped with emeralds and diamonds and gold. And there was Hernando, nicknamed the Old Man, for his seniority in the business. Hernando lived in Hialeah and was known for stashing guns in every room in his house. They'd be stuffed under cushions on the couch, hidden behind the curtains. In his sauna out back he kept a gun in the pocket of his bathrobe, hanging on a hook. The sauna was famous in the Colombian community for the fact that, like roaches in a Roach Motel, certain people had checked into the place but never checked out. "When somebody did anything to Hernando, all he did was invite them over to go into the sauna, and that would be the end of it," recalls Mirtha. "Give them some coke, turn on the dry heat, and, 'Boom.' They'd be done."

For her dinner party, Mirtha had her mother get up a big shrimp dish, put fresh roses and white snowballs on the piano. George brought out the Chivas Regal and the Rémy Martin, and Frank Sinatra alternated with Colombian music on the stereo. "We were having cocktails and entertaining like normal human beings, when George says, 'I think what this party needs is a little livening up. I'm going to bring out the coke.'" Soon the dinner was sitting cold and forgotten on the table, arguments were bursting out. Martha began weeping. Humberto, who couldn't do much coke without it making him sick, threw up in the Florida room. It was now after midnight, and the men were wondering how they could ditch their wives and go out on the town. "George is now completely out of his mind and starts getting nasty, telling everybody off. 'When you people want something, it's Mr. Georgie this, and Mr. Georgie that. You're all sons of bitches, you know that? You've all taken from me,' and on and on. Pretty soon everyone left, and George left with them. And that was the party."

Whether it came from George's threats getting back to Carlos or from something else he'd done, pretty soon it was obvious that someone wanted to shut George up permanently. First there was the business with the nursemaid Mirtha had hired to stay up in Eastham with the children. One day when he was down in Pompano Beach George got a phone call from the woman saying three Latin-looking guys had shown up at the house looking for him, and she saw they all had guns. He'd have to get a new nursemaid; she quit. After that, there was the warning from Humberto, who said he'd heard that Carlos had become sick of all the mouthing off and that there was talk of a hit having been put out. Maybe it was true, maybe it wasn't, but George should watch himself. Which proved to be good advice about a week later, on a day George had driven down to see Humberto in a condo he had in Kendall, south of Miami, and parked his car against a curb outside. When he came out, he found he'd been hemmed in on three sides. At first he thought this was possibly a ploy, to keep him standing there long enough to furnish someone with an easy target. A little VW blocked him in the rear, which he resolved to just push out of the way and get the hell out of there. He got in his car and started the motor, then changed his mind. On second thought, he'd just better run for it. "I don't know why it was, but this feeling came over me and something said, '*Get out of this fucking car!*' I leaped out and ran as fast as I could, and about fifty feet away the goddamn thing exploded. I looked back and it was all on fire. People were running over to see what happened." After he got back to Pompano Beach and collected himself, George figured the device must have been tripped by a timer set to go off a certain number of seconds after he'd opened the door and gotten into the front seat. But however it worked, the explosion finally did it for George. No more talk. Now he definitely had to do something about Carlos.

Because it would enhance his rep with the Colombians, George determined to do the hit right on Norman Cay. "I wanted to get him where he lived," he says. "That was the only way to do it, because it would show everybody that, well, Carlos had his bodyguards and everything, but I went right there and took him out in his own backyard." One day that spring he flew out to the Bahamas to do some research. He learned from contacts in Nassau that the Germans were in the habit of flying in often in the evening to gamble and partake of the nightlife, leaving Carlos out on the island alone, with just a few Colombians to maintain security. Then he chartered a sportfisherman and went out to Norman Cay himself, anchoring about a half mile off the island pretending to fish, watching the routine of the place for a day and into the night. From what he'd seen, George thought the best way was to approach the island in a Zodiac pontoon boat with an outboard motor, land it on the rocky shore near the Volcano, and do it.

Not alone, of course. As he'd threatened Carlos in their last meeting, George knew there were people in Boston who could help with this kind of operation. To find some, he put in a call to his old pal from Danbury, Fat Harry of the Winter Hill Gang. Harry said he'd bring him up to the auto-body shop in Somerville that served as the gang's headquarters and introduce him around, let George explain his needs.

"They had an office in the back of the shop, and I brought along a chart of the island, all the information," says George. "They told me they'd make the arrangements, that it wouldn't really be a problem. There were some ex-Vietnam guys, two were Rangers, that'd been in the mob and came back to Boston after the war." But it wouldn't be cheap, getting down to the island and all, and also because some of the materiél they needed was expensive. They'd like, for instance, to find some percussion grenades, to throw a little confusion into the island population. It would be handy also if they could get their hands on a bazooka, what with the guards running around in the jeep. The price would be $250,000, with $125,000 up front, nonreturnable no matter what happened, and the rest afterward, plus expenses, which might run another $50,000 or $100,000. Fine, George said, and a couple of days later he delivered the down payment. "I also said that if this worked, I'd cut them in on some of the transportation stuff. They seemed to like this. They said they had control of the Norwood airport, and we could land loads there, no problem. Big things could happen. Actually, I wasn't really going to cut them in on that because I knew they were all fucking cutthroats and I didn't want to be around them, always watching your back. This mob lawyer friend of mine had told me, 'George, you're playing with some really sick, dangerous people here. You can't trust these kinds of people, ever.'"

As it turned out, the affair cost him heavily, in other ways as well as financially. Somehow Humberto got wind of the plans for the hit, and George soon received a fairly frantic call to come to his New

York apartment to talk. More like listen, really, while Humberto got hysterical. "Everyone was there, including Martha, Mirtha, and Clara Luz, and it went on for hours," George says. "'You can't do this, Georgie. You can't do this.' He was pacing up and down the living room, throwing his hands in the air. 'It's going to cause big wars in the families. Please don't! You can have anything you want, all the kilos. I'll get more people for you.'" Others disagreed. "'Kill him!'" he recalls one of the women shouting. "'If you don't kill him now, it will be too late, and you will be *nothing.*'

"And she was right. I knew inside that if I gave in, I was fucked. He'd fucked me over, this Latin kid, and I didn't do anything about it, like somebody in the school yard who hits you in the face or takes your lunch money and you don't do anything about it. What are you considered to be? If one guy can do it to you and get away with it, they'll all do it to you. Then you're done in crime. So why didn't I do it? Because Humberto begged me not to. He said they'd all be killed—him, Martha, Mirtha. There'd be great retribution. His family would be wiped out down in Colombia, we'd all get it up here. There would be endless war, and they'd all blame me for being responsible. They didn't care how I felt. They cared about that Carlos was making money for all of them, and this would fuck up everything big-time.

"So what could I do? I said, Okay. Fuck it. I've got more money than I know what to do with anyway. Why do I need all this? Why put everyone through it? But personally, I felt it would never be the same again."

In late summer of 1980, nearly a year and a half after he aborted the hit on Carlos—and just as his lawyer friend from Boston had warned him concerning those big parties and his high style of living—George finally succeeded in attracting the attention of the police. Ironically, the situation arose after he'd turned over a new leaf in regard to the spending, toned things down an octave or two. For instance, Mirtha had found another house she liked—a $500,000 modernistic place with an elaborate Japanese garden, also overlooking the water—but George had said no, it was too ostentatious. He cut out the shopping sprees, closed down the candy store in the bureau drawer in the bedroom. The money coming in from the trips he was sending right down to his numbered bank account in Panama, leaving just enough around the house to keep them afloat. "I started making out that I was almost broke, on the edge all the time, so no one would know how much I really had," he says.

He also began securing money for the runs, the up-front cash needed for the cars and trucks and manpower, by hitting up outside investors on the Cape and in Boston, rather than raiding his own stash. Many of these individuals were high-living criminal defense attorneys who fed their big spending habits by bankrolling their clients. They'd often cover themselves by drawing up legitimate loan agreements, spelling out how they were lending this money to a client with the understanding it would be used for starting up a wholesale fish business or investing in a Dunkin' Donuts franchise. How could they possibly know the funds would be spent on smuggling a controlled substance over the border? In addition to putting their own money into cocaine runs, the lawyers would serve as brokers for a deal, pooling together smaller sums from their friends and colleagues—the orthodontist who lived next door, say, who had fifty thousand dollars he could afford to drop on a high-risk venture in hopes of doubling his money overnight. And not just once. Often, George says, the lawyers would insist on bankrolling a series of trips so as to ensure themselves a long-term relationship. "They'd say, 'I'll loan you the money, but I want to be in on three trips, do it three times with you. You need me now, but if you're successful, you won't need me after the first time. So if I get you this money, I want to be in on two more.' This was good for me, because having an investor was like insurance money. If something happens and the trip goes down, he knows he's not going to get anything, because that's the deal. If it's successful, I don't make quite so much, but if it gets busted, I don't lose anything either."

It was a local who got on to George, an Eastham cop named Wynn Deschamps. His father did yard work for Miss Toomey, George's old high school teacher, who had a summer place there. Deschamps had heard all the talk, starting back in 1979, about the big bashes and the fancy cars that clogged Bayberry Lane, the little dirt road that ran in back of George's house. It made him wonder how George earned his living. And George himself, through his driving habits, had done little to mask his presence from the police all up and down the Cape—for the number of speeding tickets he'd gotten, the drift turns and the 180s he'd practice in the Porsche out there on Route 6. As with most small police departments, however, the Eastham force had little resources of its own for following up on

Deschamps's suspicions. What they customarily did in these instances was to call for assistance from the Massachusetts State Police, which was why on August 2, 1980, Trooper William G. McGreal latched on to the case of George Jung.

At the time, the state police had just fifteen officers concentrating on narcotics, only five of whom, like Billy McGreal, worked as undercover specialists. Considering that his normally neat appearance—close-cropped hair, conservative clothes—made him look about two days out of the police academy, he'd taken pains to dress down for the job. He'd grown a scraggly beard, let his hair sprout into a minor Afro, had an ear pierced. He drove around in an old-model Lincoln Continental, maintained in cherry condition—not exactly your run-of-the-mill surveillance vehicle. To further cloud his image, he kept company with a large disheveled German shepherd named Paco. He'd inherited Paco from another undercover cop whose assignment had ended but who couldn't bring the creature home with him because it struck terror into the heart of his wife's Chihuahua.

McGreal had planned to spend that weekend relaxing down on the Cape, at a summer cottage in West Dennis he shared with other guys on the state police force, when he got the call from his boss saying there was an Eastham cop who'd requested a little specialized help, and Billy was the one he wanted to send. His boss said he didn't expect much to come of it, but he'd appreciate Billy doing this favor because it would help out relations with the locals. Normally the job would have gone to a senior undercover cop named Paul Gregory. But Gregory knew George Jung. He'd played football with him back at Central Junior High School in Weymouth, and he couldn't be sure that George hadn't heard he'd gone on to become a trooper. So he passed the case on to Billy. "The boss said Eastham had a guy they wanted us to take a peek at that they thought was up to no good, supposed to be a big drug smuggler from the West Coast," Billy recalls. "He said, 'You're not going to actually meet the guy, just get a six-pack of beer and a newspaper and hang around his beach. Let the locals meet you, jerk them around for a couple of hours, then say until we get an informant on the guy there's nothing we can do. It's easy overtime.'"

After checking in with Deschamps, McGreal drove over to Bayberry Lane, took a cooler of beer out of the car, and made his way down to the beach, stretched out on a blanket to catch a few rays. It was about one in the afternoon. Two hours passed, during which he'd struck up a conversation with an attractive young woman who had come down to the beach from the house next to the Jungs. "She didn't know much about this guy, but she was kind of cute, and I'm single, so I'm thinking if I don't meet this big dope dealer, I'll at least get a date out of it. While I'm thinking this, suddenly he comes out on his deck at the top of the stairs. I only had a description of him from Eastham. Blond hair, looks like a leftover hippie from California. And I hear this voice, 'Hey, you! You down there!' I figure he's going to chase me off his beach. 'Hey, do me a favor, will you? Would you pull in my catamaran there? The tide's coming in, I don't want it to drift away.' 'Hey, sure,' I said. 'No problem.'"

McGreal stayed through a couple more beers, then made his way up the stairs to George's house to ask if he could use the bathroom. Be my guest, George told him. "He says his name is George Jung, and I say I'm Bill Sullivan. 'What're you doing around here?' he asks. Now, I never expected even to meet him, so now I've got to think quick. I'd been undercover for two years, and I knew I had to come up with something logical, some reason why a young guy would want to come down to a private beach and sit by himself. 'I just have to be alone,' I told him. And he asks me what happened, and I said, 'You don't want to hear this, but my wife just got killed in a car accident.' And I started breaking down. 'God! Bill, this is awful. Mirtha! Come quick!' He tells me to sit down and he goes to get me a drink. 'Mirtha, this is our new friend, Bill Sullivan. His wife just got killed in a car accident.' And she asked me if I wanted to stay for dinner. I'm saying to myself, No, this is going much too quick. I mean, why would I want to stay for dinner at some stranger's house? Normally you'd wait a few days so as not to look like you're latching on to him too fast. So, I said, 'Thanks, but, no, I've gotta go.' But I ask them if it would be okay if I parked my car out front tomorrow and came back to use their beach. 'Anything you want,' they said."

When McGreal returned the next day, George told him his car was being fixed; would Billy mind driving him up to the convenience store to get some groceries? On the way, McGreal told George he was staying down in West Dennis, that he'd moved in with some guys for the time being. "You try to keep your story as close to real as possible. Use your real first name, where you really live. If I tell him I live in Harwich, and after a few drinks I switch it to West Dennis, they're going to say, 'Wait a minute.' After the errand, we're sitting out talking on the deck when suddenly George says to me, 'You son of a bitch, I know what you're up to!' And of course I'm thinking he's on to me. Holy shit, here I am in a bathing suit, no gun, all alone. There's no backup. But then he's, 'You're a fucking dope dealer, aren't you! And you know what? So am I!' I say, 'No, no. I'm not a dope dealer. I mean, I do some credit cards, some small stuff, larceny, but, hey, no.' He told me, 'Bullshit,' and then went on about how he'd gone through five or ten million dollars in the last year or so and how he'd snorted about a half million dollars' worth of cocaine himself. He told me he could make me a very wealthy man, and he goes on bragging about it all, and before I know it, I'm his goddamn aide-de-camp."

Gofer was more like it. But if McGreal felt momentarily like turning cartwheels over his good fortune, bringing this bust in to home base was going to involve a considerable amount of work, and of a nature he hadn't figured on. George had Billy driving him all over the Cape, doing errands here and there, taking him ten times a day up to make calls to Miami and Colombia at the pay phone on the corner, running into the store to get him change. He chauffeured Mirtha to the malls, took her and the children to appointments, did chores around the house. Occasionally he would have to deal with the residue from one or another of George's escapades. On one excursion to a pharmacy in Orleans, George and Billy were standing by the car while Mirtha went in to get a prescription, when out of nowhere a couple of guys approach George and the one holding the baseball bat starts yelling curses at him and swinging away in what Billy interpreted as an unprovoked attack. As it turned out, during one of his cocaine and alcohol episodes a few days earlier, George had encountered the bat wielder and his wife at the counter of a local grocery store and elbowed them both aside so he could pay for his cigarettes and get on his way, threatening to beat the shit out of the guy and telling his wife she could go fuck herself, which she probably had to since she looked like a pig. The guy had gone out and gotten a friend and the two of them had been looking for George ever since. As Billy wrote it up later in his report:

> This officer attempted to disarm the subject who was swinging the bat wildly. When this failed, this officer utilized the motor vehicle and chased the subject into a shop. Mirtha came out of the pharmacy at this time and the three of us left the area. A short time later while traveling

on Route 6 in Eastham this officer was stopped by two officers of the Eastham P.D. Subsequently two officers from Orleans P.D. arrived. We explained the situation to them and this officer was arrested for assault by means of a deadly weapon, i.e. the car. This officer was transported to Orleans where he was printed, mugged, made use of the phone and placed in a cell. About fifteen minutes after being placed in a cell, the bondsman arrived and this officer was released on $5 personal recognizance. Upon release from custody I rejoined George and Mirtha in the parking lot.

Billy says George told him not to worry about it, that he'd get him one of the mob lawyers from Boston who'd continue the case into the next millennium, until it died of everyone's indifference.

As close as he got to George, however, McGreal still had nothing he could use as the basis for a bust. There was no sign of any cocaine in the house. Plenty of plans got discussed, for cocaine trips, for marijuana trips—including one being developed by a boat captain Billy was introduced to who planned to bring in twenty tons of pot aboard a scalloper and off-load it into a ten-wheel dump truck filled with gravel as a cover. But the only actual illegality he'd witnessed was the assault with the car, for which he himself had been arrested.

Then on August 12 George and Mirtha left for Miami, expecting to continue on for an extended visit to Colombia, to see this fellow George knew who had a big ranch. They told Billy to take care of the house while they were gone and gave him a written list of two dozen or so chores—be sure to water and prune the plants, let in the carpenter to fix the screens, rent a pair of Winnebagos for a transportation job George had in mind, call up Mirtha's mother in Pompano Beach every day to check on how the children were doing, get a hold of four handguns George had promised someone. They left a number in Medellín to call if he had to get in touch. "Ask whoever answers for 'Mr. Georgie.'" He also should call up *AERO* magazine, a publication for flying enthusiasts, and get the details about this piece of property they were advertising: "Country escape, private mountain lake, 21 miles from Hancock, N.Y. Immaculate 2-story lodge, tastefully furnished, 200-foot lake front, 3 boats, 2600 ft. airstrip." George wanted him to find out if the airstrip was dirt or paved.

They were gone for two months, and when Billy met them at Logan Airport in mid-October, they had some people with them he'd never seen before. There was a cousin of Mirtha's, along with her boyfriend. There was also a short guy with a receding hairline and a beard, whom George introduced as his "ex-partner from Los Angeles," name of Richard Barile. George said Richard had flown up in a private plane after seeing his father in Connecticut and would fly on down to the Cape, while Billy drove everyone in the car. They'd collect Richard at the Hyannis airport and continue out to Eastham for a celebration that night. The trip to Colombia had been very successful, and George told Billy he'd brought along a little blow for the party—not much, about two-thirds of a pound. Hearing this, Billy felt his eyes widen and joy leap into his heart. "In this area, the biggest amount of cocaine we'd been seeing had been maybe a pound here and a pound there. There had recently been a massacre in Boston, people shot, over just a pound and a half of coke and thirty-five thousand dollars in cash. So this was no small amount."

As for how to proceed from here, the state police, like most police agencies, had a strict policy of "buy-or-bust." This meant that if you came upon someone in possession of drugs, the only way you could overlook the offense was to try to use the person to worm further into the organization, and to buy up the load right then, with money from the department budget. If you couldn't do that, then you had to make an arrest on the spot—it was one or the other. "We had to do something," Billy says. "The amount of cocaine here, we're talking then about twenty-two thousand dollars on the street, and there's no way we had that kind of money. Even the DEA wasn't coming up with that much at the time. So it was obvious the bust had to go down that night."

After excusing himself to visit the bathroom—to call his department and alert them to get things ready—Billy drove George, Mirtha, and her cousin down to the Cape, stopping off at the Hyannis airport to pick up Barile. Billy went into the lounge to get him, and when they greeted each other again, Richard shook his hand, and somehow his arm brushed against the gun Billy had stuck in his pants underneath his shirt. Richard stiffened at the discovery but said nothing. Out at the car, however, Billy saw him whispering frantically to George. And he heard George tell him: "Of course he's got a gun! He's my bodyguard."

By now, Billy was no longer alone. He'd been accompanied on the drive to the Cape by at least ten state troopers driving in unmarked cars ahead of and behind them. They picked up another ten or so cops in Eastham, which meant that when the party got into full swing out on Bayberry Lane, upward of twenty police officers were crouching in the bushes, hunkered down by the beach, or plastered up against the walls of neighboring houses, their pistols and shotguns drawn and ready, waiting for Billy to give the word to charge in. "But I hadn't actually seen the cocaine yet, and we couldn't do anything until I knew exactly where it was." Billy had brought along two bottles of champagne to contribute to the party, which he'd put in the trunk of the car. The signal for the bust to commence was when Billy went out to get the bottles, hoisted one over each shoulder, and headed back into the house. From that moment, the guys would wait five minutes, to give McGreal time to locate all the people inside and prevent anyone from slipping out unnoticed, and then they'd pile in. The only thing that made Billy nervous was Barile. George's assurance aside, Richard had seemed jumpy ever since discovering that Billy had a gun. And on the drive out to Eastham, Richard had mentioned pointedly to Billy that he'd handle whatever security problems there were himself, with this machine gun he'd brought along in his suitcase.

At last George produced the coke. It had been in a package in his flight bag, and he set the whole amount, eleven ounces, right out on the table. After huffing up a huge sample for himself, he invited everyone to jump in. "When I saw that, I said, 'Well, George, I've got a surprise for you, too,' and I went out to get the champagne from the trunk." By the time he returned with the bottles, people were already getting pretty speedy, but for Billy the next five minutes seemed fairly to crawl. Finally, the time was up. But no guys. Then seven minutes, eight minutes went by. "George and the others are all coked out, Barile is getting more and more fidgety. He starts saying, 'I'm getting my machine gun out and spray the beach out there. I don't like the sound of things.' And he was right. I could hear the guys rustling around myself. What the *fuck* were they waiting for?" Finally, McGreal could stand it no longer, and at what he later noted down as precisely 2:10 A.M. on October 14, the trooper pulled out his gun and pointed it at Barile. "I yelled, *'Freeze, state police. Don't anybody move. You're all under arrest.'* But nothing happened! Mirtha comes over to me and pushes the gun away and says, 'Oh, come on, Billy, cut the shit.' They didn't believe me! George is just snorting away, having a great old time, not paying any attention at all. Just then, thank God, 'Wild Bill' Shaughnessy, I think it was, comes crashing right through the screen, guys are suddenly running up from the basement, people charging in from the deck, everyone's shouting and yelling, pointing their guns, putting people down on their faces. That basically cemented in their minds who we were."

George, too, remembers that night in some detail, but not quite as distinctly as McGreal. "I was pretty fried at the time, and it took a while for it to dawn on me what was happening. I was thinking it was such a little bit of coke, how could you possibly get arrested for that? They didn't know it, but there was fifty kilos in the chimney and three hundred thousand in cash behind the medicine cabinet. Except then I saw the cops lifting Kristina out of the crib. That's when it finally got to me, when I started to get upset. I mean, at two years old. The baby's first bust."

TEN

Fort Lauderdale

1985

Whether you're the bad guys or the good guys, you both have the same goal in any cocaine deal, and that is to get through it alive.
—Detective Sergeant Greg Kridos, Organized Crime Division,
Narcotics Intelligence, Fort Lauderdale Police Department

HAD THE AMOUNT OF COCAINE THEY CAUGHT HIM WITH in Eastham weighed just four ounces less, George might have been right in thinking nothing terribly serious would happen to him. Unfortunately, it exceeded the eight ounces specified in a strict new minimum-sentencing statute signed into law only months earlier by Governor Michael Dukakis, and suddenly George was staring straight at a mandatory prison sentence of ten years, with no possibility of parole. Once he was apprised of the situation, very little doubt remained in George's mind as to his next move. As soon as a lawyer from Boston bailed him, Mirtha, and the baby out of the Barnstable County House of Corrections, George signed an affidavit assuming the entire blame for bringing in the coke that night, which effectively exonerated everyone else caught in the raid. He said the others didn't know about the coke. This gesture extended even to Richard Barile, whom George had befriended again several months earlier. Barile, too, had been aced out by Carlos, who had gone behind his back as well as George's to sell loads directly to

Richard's main dealer, Nick Hunter, the one who had given the party for Carlos on his first trip to L.A. The second thing George did was to have Clara Luz clear out the Pompano Beach house and come up and take baby Kristina back down with her and little Clarie to a rented house in Miami.

Lastly, he made a cash withdrawal from all the hidey-holes in the Eastham house. He winched up the oil burner in the basement, cleaned out the wall behind the Andrew Wyeth and the studs in back of the trick bathroom medicine cabinet. Other than a small travel bag for the money, they didn't pack any clothes or other things for fear of alerting anyone who might be monitoring the house, and on the morning he was scheduled to be re-arraigned before superior court on his indictment, George and Mirtha drove up to Weymouth in his Thunderbird to tell his parents he'd be going away for a little while.

For Fred and Ermine, who were now in their mid-to-late sixties, the recent events in George's life had given them a wearying sense of déjà vu, intruding in their own lives in a way that was difficult to endure. Once again it had been all over the TV; friends and neighbors had watched their son being led off to court in handcuffs. Stories on the bust had run in the papers, telling how the police had stormed this "posh North Eastham beach house" that had turned out to be a drug den. There was no mention of Billy's role in any of this, but Wynn Deschamps was being extensively quoted, making sure the world knew the bust "was the result of an investigation started by Eastham police."

The visit to Abigail Adams Circle didn't last long. George told his parents he wasn't going to show up for his hearing that day; he feared that the court, knowing about his skipping out in Chicago, might refuse him bail altogether, and then he'd be seriously stuck. The only choice that lay open to him, he said, was to run away again. "Fred looked at me, and he said, 'I'm sorry, but this is the end. Your mother and I just don't want you to come back. We just can't take it anymore. We're too old. We love you. Good luck, and good-bye.' There was really nothing left to say. What could I say? And so I just said, 'Okay then. Good-bye.' And we left." George never saw his parents again.

The last time George had lived as a wanted man, he'd been young, free of ties, highly mobile—not approaching forty and encumbered by a wife and two children, one of whom had to be put in school. And as she shortly brought home to him, Mirtha didn't take very naturally to life on the lam. The first thing they did upon arriving in Miami was to alter their looks and identity. Mirtha dyed her jet-black hair deep red and told the people she met that her name was Francesca. George took scissors to his own shaggy hair and dyed it black. He took on the name of David Mahan, giving new life to a long-dead guy whose name he'd gotten out of the obit files up in Hingham. Clarie was put into a school near Clara Luz's house, under her mother's maiden name. Through contacts among the Colombians they found a safe apartment to rent in a mostly Haitian neighborhood, not a great location to Mirtha's way of thinking, considering that the ghetto neighborhood of Liberty City, which lay just a few blocks to the west, had exploded in a deadly antiwhite riot just six months earlier, its commercial strips still largely burned out. "The place was a real dump, and we were totally isolated," she recalls. "We could see my mother because the police didn't know where she lived. But it was horrible—the fact that you're not even able to use your own name, knowing you couldn't talk to a lot of people because you're hot. When you're hot, no one wants to deal with you. Nobody wants anything to do with you, because they think you'll bring the heat down on them. We had to leave absolutely everything behind—my bamboo living room set, my bedroom set, my plants. I'd loved my plants, and the fish tank, my tropical fish, the Black Lace angels, the Angelicas. Eastham was our home. I loved it there."

Mirtha tried to ease her distress by seeking out the counsel of a priest practiced in the healing arts of *Santería*, the mystical religion prevalent among several immigrant groups from the Caribbean. "He said the reason all this had happened to us is we'd neglected the saints; that was why there were these, like, repercussions with the law," she says. "So he was going to work some kind of a ritual, the way he said it, 'to put the man to the side.'" Despite his considerable misgivings about it all, George went along with Mirtha for the first session, more or less to humor her. "We arrived at this guy's house. He's dressed in a flowing white robe, and he has these pigeons in a cage. He takes out three of them and circles them one at a time around our heads. He said it was supposed to collect all the bad shit that had been happening to us and fly out the door with it. Well, he let loose the first one, and it took right off into the sky. The same thing happened with the second one. But the third one dive-bombed right into the side of my car and knocked itself out. We all kind of looked at each other and I'm thinking, Uh-oh."

After that one Mirtha tried something with a pumpkin, but it didn't work out much better. It was late one afternoon while George was out taking Kristina for a walk and after Mirtha had gotten a long way into a bottle of Jamaican rum, from which she was seeking comfort pretty regularly these days. "We had the top floor of this apartment along a hallway on the outside of the building with a little table out there, and that's where the priest told me to set it up," she recalls. The pumpkin was about twelve inches in diameter. Following the priest's instructions, she'd scraped out all the seeds and stuff from inside and filled it with about a pound of honey mixed with water and different types of oil she'd gotten at a neighborhood *botánica*, where they sold curative herbs and sex potions. "I wasn't really into this kind of thing, but I knew that the forces were against us and that I wasn't in tune with my spiritual being during this period we're talking about here. And also I was pretty drunk."

As she'd been instructed, Mirtha put on a white gown and set up a candle on the table, and then she knelt down and prayed to the pumpkin. "I said a lot of different prayers, for helping us, for protecting us, hoping this situation would be solved, to guard us against the evil forces of the law. But that night I got really mad at the pumpkin. We went out to a Latin nightclub called Harlow's and George got into a big fight with some people, there was shooting outside, I don't remember any of it too well, but it was a mess. I was really outraged after the prayers and things, so afterwards when I got home and there's the pumpkin sitting there looking at me, I take it and just smash it down the stairs, all in pieces. But later I felt that that was a mistake. I feel now it did something to hurt the spell, because things started getting worse."

That Christmas they moved down to a rented house in Homestead, bought Kristina a Husky puppy for a present, and tried to restore some order to their lives—an entirely fruitless endeavor, as it turned out. Tortured by the pain that snorting coke was causing his feet, George had some success these days in once again reducing his consumption. But whatever that might have done to bring peace and quiet to the household was overshadowed by Mirtha's increasing alcohol binges, and also a new habit she'd acquired from her Latin girlfriends: smoking crack. "It was a different rush, much faster, so much you almost think you're going to have a heart attack," Mirtha recalls. "It only lasted a few minutes, which is why you'd smoke so much of it. But a lot of people got into it because they didn't want to wreck their noses." Smoking crack and drinking rum didn't much improve Mirtha's capacity for running a tight ship. One night she fell asleep with a candle flickering next to her. It set the curtains on fire, and George woke up in a room filled with smoke and flames and barely got everyone out of the house alive. They lost their house and all their clothes in the fire, along with whatever other possessions they'd accumulated since abandoning Eastham.

What also went up in flames was that little box in which George had kept the receipts for his numbered bank account down in Panama City. Did he need to actually produce the receipts to withdraw his money? His experience had been that banks just wanted to know you were really who you said you were, and they'd give you a new bank book. Big Ralph had been handling all his bank business; he'd have to get a hold of him now to set his mind at rest that there wasn't going to be an unhappy ending. But alas, Big Ralph was busy at the moment, having gotten busted during a foul-up with one of the runs, in which the Cessna Conquest was confiscated by the federal government.

To tide himself over during this dry period, George found himself another plane and a pilot, and Humberto set him up to transport five hundred of Pablo's kilos from a mountain landing strip lying between Medellín and coastal Barranquilla. With a passport made out to the erstwhile David Mahan, George flew down on a commercial flight to inspect the landing field and was driven into the mountains by two of Pablo's Colombians, along with an interpreter for George and a young woman whom everyone was apparently supposed to share to ease the rigors of traveling on the mountain road. Whether it was because George, now middle-aged, had simply grown too old for this stuff or because he was just grumpy over the uncertainty of his present situation, that trip turned out to be more than a little unnerving. "We're eight thousand feet up in the mountains on some goddamn dirt road six feet wide and they're all smoking *basuco* and drinking rum, speeding down these roads that were twisting all over the place, and I'm looking down into these gorges. There were no guardrails. They're passing the pipe around and pawing at the girl, grabbing her tits and kissing her and laughing, the car's weaving all over. I'm thinking pretty soon I'm a dead man here. When we got to Barranquilla, I jumped out of the car at a stoplight and ran into the first bar I saw. 'Please, Mr. Georgie, come with us,' and I'm telling them, 'You motherfuckers get away from me, I'm staying right here and having a few drinks before we go any farther.'"

The ride to Barranquilla was quickly outclassed by what transpired next, another sample of how Pablo Escobar imposed order over his empire. "The interpreter who'd come with us from Medellín, he was paid by Pablo just to make the trip, but he took me aside and said he wanted me to meet some people who had some dope too. We went to this apartment building in Barranquilla, and there were these guys who said they also had kilos. 'We want you to move them for us, too. Nothing is to be said to anybody about this, and we can make some real money.' I just listened and didn't say anything, but I was thinking to myself, 'I'm not going for any of this bullshit. I'm not crossing Pablo or any other motherfucker down here.' I told them I'd think about it, but I had to get back to the hotel. The interpreter said to go ahead and that he'd be along shortly.

"When I got back to the hotel room, there were four of Pablo's people there, and I told them exactly what was going down, that I was just down here to do my job and didn't want to get mixed up in anything. They said, 'Don't worry about it, Mr. Georgie, we'll take care of it.'" A few minutes later George sauntered out on the balcony, which was ten floors up and had a sweeping view of the city and out to the sea beyond. By happenstance he saw the interpreter down below park his car in the lot and saunter into the lobby. A few moments later he knocked at the door. "They opened the door and let him in, two guys on each side of him, and it happened so fast he didn't know what hit him. They grabbed him by the arms and ran him across the room without saying a word—I don't think his feet even touched the carpet—and they ushered him right off the fucking balcony. He was gone! The whole thing took about two seconds. He landed in the parking lot not far from his car. I looked over and a little crowd was gathering. I mean, I thought they might do something to him, but do it later, for Christ's sake, up in the mountains, not kill him right in the fucking hotel, while I'm right there doing a job, in broad daylight, in the middle of Barranquilla, a big beach resort town, just throw the fucker right off the balcony! I said, 'Uh, well, I think I have to be getting back to the States now. I've got something really important I have to do. I'll get back to you fucking guys later.'"

And he would have, too, to complete the run, if an event hadn't interceded that abruptly changed George's plans for a long time to come. The event was a fight with Mirtha, one of a series of battles between them that during their days of being wanted in Miami evened out into continuous warfare. They had "horrendous fights," George recalls. "We were arguing all the time, and because the houses next door in Homestead were only thirty feet away, the neighbors would always end up calling the police. We'd argue over money, over her smoking crack. She'd go on about why we had to leave the Cape, the beautiful house we'd lost. I mean, suddenly she loved the Cape. When she was there, it was too lonely, she always wanted to be in Miami or New York. And when Mirtha got drunk, she got hard to control, even for me. She threw things a lot, at me, or smashed them against the wall—ashtrays, vases, pitchers, anything, so long as it would break."

One night after the fire—by now they'd moved to another house, in North Miami—they were driving home from a party at the house of some Colombians down in Kendall, south of Coral Gables. "Mirtha thought I was trying to get it on with this guy's girlfriend. She thought we were making eyes at each other, and she was probably right. But anyway, she suddenly flips out and grabs my hair and starts yanking on it and screaming at me. It's a little after midnight on Saturday, on I-95 going north through the center of Miami, which is like rush hour, only everyone's going eighty miles an hour, and I'm right in the center lane, with cars on both sides. My hair's long again now, and she's got it in both hands, yanking my head back and forth. I'm trying to hold on to the wheel, the car's weaving all over, I'm yelling at her that she's gonna fucking get us killed. The only thing I could do, I let her have it with my right hand, and I broke her nose."

Blood now streaming down over her mouth and chin, Mirtha let go of George's hair to attend to her own problem, and the incident might have ended in a hospital emergency room had not the car right behind them contained two members of the Dade County Public Safety Department, now known as the Metro Police. "They'd seen us fighting and me hitting her, the car's going all over the road. When they pull us over, Mirtha's so pissed off she begins yelling, 'He's a fucking cocaine smuggler! He's wanted by the police up in Massachusetts! Take that motherfucker away to jail!' So they put the cuffs on me, drive me down to the police station, and that was it. Two days later they came and asked if I'd waive my rights and sign the extradition papers. I said, sure. I had had it. I knew I was in trouble big-time here, what with running away and also the drug charge. But one thing about going to jail: I knew Mirtha wouldn't be in there with me."

From the bust onward, that October of 1981, life took George on a fairly bumpy trip for a while. After being escorted back to Massachusetts, he languished for thirteen months in the Barnstable jail while his lawyer tried to work out some deal with the prosecutor. Mirtha had managed to remain free for a few weeks because the Miami police hadn't thought to check her record when they locked up George. But she, too, was arrested shortly afterward on a fugitive warrant and also sent back to Massachusetts, to the women's facility in Framingham. By early in 1983, George's lawyer, a criminal attorney from Quincy named Elliot R. Levine, a former teaching fellow at the Harvard Law School, had convinced the district attorney that the state's mandatory sentencing law was so constitutionally vague that, in exchange for Levine's not challenging the statute in the appellate courts, the prosecutor agreed to let George and Mirtha plead guilty and receive only the time they'd already served.

A few days after they got out George collected his family, and they all headed down to Florida. There he ran into Hank, the pilot from Norfolk, Virginia, who had suddenly disappeared a couple of years before. He was now living with a Colombian woman in Palm Beach, and he and George began flying in more loads. In the fall of 1983, however, as a favor to a down-and-out pilot in Massachusetts, who had begged George to get him some cocaine to sell so he could get back on his feet, George delivered a kilo to the man at a Howard Johnson's Motel outside of Plymouth, only to discover that the guy was working for the state police. Busted again!

For Mirtha, this was the last straw. Shortly afterward, she gathered the children and moved out to San Francisco to start anew, continuing the program she'd begun in prison to get off alcohol and drugs. Where the raising of five-year-old Kristina was concerned, Mirtha resolved to make the life she had shared with George Jung disappear altogether. "I told her that Daddy had gotten into a very bad boat accident, and that he was in the hospital and was being taken care of very well, but that he was paralyzed from the neck down. This was what my counselor and I agreed on, to tell her this, because it was better than telling a five-year-old, 'You know, your daddy is a drug smuggler, and do you know how many keys he brought in with Carlos Lehder?' So, he was in a hospital back East and he couldn't move his arms and legs."

By now the Massachusetts state legislature had repaired the defects in the mandatory sentencing law, which meant that George, having been busted with a whole kilo, was facing serious time. On top of the state charge, they'd also found a 9-millimeter pistol in the trunk of his car, so the feds had him for interstate transportation of a weapon in connection with the commission of a felony, that is, the sale of the kilo of cocaine. As dark as things appeared, however, George had always experienced considerable luck where the criminal justice system was concerned, and the gods didn't choose this moment to cast him adrift. Somehow the kilo of cocaine he'd been caught with miraculously disappeared from the locker at the Middleboro state police barracks, where it was being stored as evidence. All the state had left was the sample that had been sent to the police lab for testing. In negotiating with the prosecutor for a deal, George's lawyer threatened to call to the witness stand every trooper in the barracks to get to the bottom of what had happened. Figuring this would not only tie up the case endlessly but also bring down more embarrassment on the state cops, the prosecutor agreed to a compromise. George would serve forty months on the drug charge, instead of the twenty years he faced had they pressed the matter. As an added bonus, he could do two years of that in the minimum-security forestry camp in Plymouth, where inmates worked at the not-particularly onerous task of tidying up the grounds of Miles Standish State Park for the tourists. And so as not to inconvenience him terribly on the federal gun charge, they would let the eighteen additional months for that one run concurrently. Once he heard about that minimum-security forestry camp, George listened to all the other details with only half an ear. Because he'd already made up his mind that right after he'd done his federal time, he would pull off an escape.

One motive for the escape was simply that George was George. "I didn't have that much more time to do, really, but my mind didn't work like other people's," he says. "Ninety-five percent of them would have stayed. But I would just go. Leave. I always ran away, every chance I got." More important, though, something he was careful not to share with anyone, was the worry that had begun to seep into his mind about the money in Panama, the stash he'd been mounting up all these years, which the last time he'd added up his bank receipts had totaled just short of $68 million. Because of Mirtha and her goddamn crack habit, all the receipts were gone now. He'd memorized the account number, of course. But he'd completely lost touch with Big Ralph, who was out of prison by now but didn't stay in close touch with George. One thing George could do was send a lawyer down to Panama to look into it, to see if things were okay. But George had seen too much of lawyers in the cocaine trade to regard that as a smart idea. In his experience, the lawyers were like wolves stalking a herd of caribou—ravenously hungry but biding their time, watching for a weakened animal, then moving in to devour their prey. No, he really had to go himself. But the trip would require a lot of cash, and with his bad luck in the last year and a half, he was just about tapped out, especially when it came to the funds he would need to pull this off. His name might be on all kinds of international watch lists, and he could just imagine what sort of reception a paroled ex-convict cocaine smuggler would get asking the vice president of the bank to please give him his $68 million, or wire it to Switzerland, whatever. He'd need a lot of grease here, maybe have to pay people off, maybe get help from Pablo Escobar, who by now had become friendly with the man who ran Panama, Colonel Manuel Noriega. Whatever he devised, it would take money to get it done—to make that big withdrawal and retire finally from the smuggling business. Retire to the motor sailer, the Great Barrier Reef. Maybe he could even get back with Mirtha, give her 68 million reasons to remember the good old days. He could see the children. For all these reasons, George was determined to get out of captivity as soon as he fucking well could, get his ass down to Florida, and set himself up to do just one more run.

To rate being sent to the forestry camp at Plymouth required his first spending a year in the prison system, during which he filtered down through the upper security levels, like a piece of food moving along the alimentary canal. First there was time in a maximum-security joint, the Massachusetts Correctional Institution at Walpole; then there was "close" security, which meant the MCIs at Norfolk and Concord. He passed much of the time reading, and sending off literature samples to Mirtha: "The changing seasons are but a four-act play, leaving us to obey the applause and filling us with curtain calls and laughter, for you and I are the center of the universe," went one epistle. "There's a book called the *I Ching*. It is a book of wisdom written by holy men. One sentence is enough to busy one's mind and penetrate deep into you. I wanted to teach you of the book but our life was filled with such turmoil that as you well know I lost touch with the inner truth. . . . P.S. If you send peanuts they must be in pressure sealed cans. Cheese and meats can be wrapped in original cellophane wrapper. Also discuss with attorney that I want to be moved to Plymouth MCI. Take picture with Polaroid with red background similar to passport photo. Will explain later."

He also wrote to Kristina—his arms and legs might be paralyzed, but there was still life in his fingers.

Dear Sunshine,
I wish you a very happy birthday. You are the Sunshine of my life. I love you. Be happy always. Try to give joy and happiness to those around you. Be kind to others. Love and love life. Love is a precious sacred gift which I give to you.

Love,
Daddy

Underneath his signature George drew in a large smiling face of the sun.

Actually, "escape" doesn't seem quite the appropriate word for what George did about six months after he'd reached Plymouth, on the night of February 13, 1985, to be exact. "Walking away" describes it more accurately, since the place has no real fence around it, and the inmates were pretty loosely watched. For a payment of two thousand dollars, he'd arranged to have a confederate bring him a change of clothes and drive along a road close by the prison, slow down near a copse of trees where George would be waiting for him at precisely nine-thirty at night. George had chosen that time because it would be dark then, and also because the last count was done at 9:00 P.M., by a guard who wandered around the place with a clipboard. An hour later, at ten, everyone had to be in their rooms, and the place was locked up. Shortly afterward, around ten-thirty, a guard would check again, to see that all the beds were occupied. George figured this gave him an hour's head start, from

9:30 to 10:30, before his absence would be noticed. So right after the count George sauntered over toward the outside of the floodlit area, and when the guard with the clipboard disappeared into the building, he slipped into the darkness. The car appeared on schedule, and less than an hour later he'd changed into a sports jacket and slacks and was ensconced in a chair at a revolving bar at the top of the Hyatt Regency in Cambridge, sipping his Scotch and looking out over the city lights. Just for the style of it, he'd left a note on his bed for the prison administration to ponder. "Freedom is a realm of illusion," it read. "And I am a master of illusion."

While in prison, George had found the intellectual level of the Massachusetts inmates to be a good deal lower than that at Danbury. Nevertheless, he did manage to make several useful acquaintances, one of whom he was thinking about now as he sat slowly revolving above Cambridge. Dale Habel was a forty-five-year-old prisoner who had been serving time for helping to smuggle several tons of pot into the old whaling port of New Bedford. Having to do his time in the North imposed a special hardship on Dale, since he normally lived in Florida and had never managed to acclimate himself to the cold. Dale and George had in common the fact that they'd both lived in the Fort Lauderdale area; Dale had lived west of the city, in the farming community of Davie. In prison, he and George had talked a lot about smuggling. If George ever needed help getting planes or finding landing fields, Dale had told him, he had a good buddy down there who could be of service. He was a farmer, an old guy, but still a tough son of a bitch and reliable, who ran a farm labor camp, renting out migrant pickers during harvest time. The farmer had been a marijuana smuggler, had rigged it so the bales were dropped out of an airplane into a cornfield out near his place where he also raised horses, out near Davie in a town called Sunrise. But this old farmer would be just as interested, Dale thought, in working on the importation of some other product. And so it was that when George got back down to Florida, a fugitive now for the third and weariest time in his life, he did just as Dale had suggested and hooked himself up with Leon Harbuck.

George had missed a year and a half of action while being a guest of the Commonwealth of Massachusetts, and when 1985 rolled around, a few new faces had come on to the scene. Madonna and Prince had caught on in the music business. In sports that year,

Boris Becker, age seventeen, became the youngest player ever to win the tournament at Wimbledon. On the international scene, the Soviet premiers had been dying right and left, and now there was a new Russian name to learn, that of Mikhail Gorbachev, fifty-four, the youngest leader to take over since Stalin. In the cocaine business, too, circumstances had changed dramatically. With the sharp decrease in wholesale prices, George had to bargain hard now to get less than half his accustomed payment for transportation, down to between three and four thousand dollars a kilo these days.

Right after leaving Plymouth, George put in a call to Humberto down in Medellín to line up some kilos for their last trip, then he flew out to his old stomping grounds in Manhattan Beach, California, to see about acquiring a plane and a pilot. The news back from Colombia proved encouraging. His brother-in-law said that three to four hundred kilos, maybe more, would be ready to ship in early April. This time around, Humberto would appreciate George making some use of his stepson, and George's nephew-in-law, Joseph Ahmed. Joseph, who was Martha's son from a previous marriage, was twenty-five years old, and Humberto thought it was high time for him to earn his spurs in the business, to show the powers that be, Pablo and the others, that he was old enough now to be trusted with his own loads. The news from California turned out to be less welcoming. In Manhattan Beach George had looked up some of the marijuana pilots, including Here-We-Go Bob, whom he found through his motorcycle, a custom-built chrome job with high-rise handlebars and a stretch fork in the front, parked just off the beach, as if Bob hadn't budged an inch in fifteen years. Although he and the others seemed glad enough to see George again, they reacted with suspicion when he broached the subject of flying in cocaine. "They knew I'd been arrested, but they didn't know whether I'd really escaped or was working for Uncle Sam," he says. "After all, how'd I keep escaping and getting away? You begin to wonder after a while. Either you're working for the government or you're a certified lunatic. 'You're saying you just walked out of prison? No, this is too much, George, I don't want any part of it.'"

So it was early in March when he arrived in Florida, still looking for a means of transportation. Dale, his newfound friend from Massachusetts, had also been released from prison by now, and the two of them went out to see this guy Leon Harbuck at a trailer he lived in with his young wife in the middle of a horse pasture out in the boonies west of Fort Lauderdale. Harbuck turned out to be a leather-tough Florida cowboy, with jug ears, a bulbous nose, a lot of missing teeth, and thinning hair that stuck up in wispy tufts. He talked with a brittle cracker twang, and his face was set in a more or less permanent glare, not a guy well endowed with a sense of humor. During a break in the discussion over how to get an airplane, Harbuck asked George if he'd ever ridden a horse. Sure, George said, thinking of the well-broken beasts the beach boys had gotten him down in Puerto Vallarta. "I got up on the back of this horse, and all of a sudden the son of a bitch takes off like a rocket, nothing I could do to stop it. He's heading right for this fence, and I'm thinking either he's going to jump over it or stop short and throw *me* over it. Either way I had to get off, so the only thing I could think of was to hurl myself off backward, and I landed on the ground with a crash, flat on my back, thought I'd broken every goddamn bone in my body. This guy Harbuck comes running up to me yelling, 'Holy shit! That was the greatest dismount I've seen in my life!'"

Within a couple of weeks, Harbuck called George to say he'd put out the word and had found a couple of guys in the transportation business. Their names were Tom and Greg, and they seemed to have what was needed—pilots, planes, manpower, anything George wanted. George said it sounded good, but that he'd agree to meet them only if they brought along their pilot. He was the crucial factor here, and George didn't want to spin his wheels on a deal that wasn't going to pan out. The meeting was set for the night of March 27 in George's room at the Days Inn, off I-95.

George doesn't recall much about Tom and Greg during that first meeting, because his attention was almost completely devoted to the guy they brought with them to fly in the load. Here staring at him, hardly changed since he'd last seen him, was his old pal and buddy from Mexico days, the FLYBOY himself, Cliff Guttersrud. During that first encounter, George kept the recognition to himself, as did Cliff, but seeing his old pilot here renewed his confidence. "I hadn't seen Cliff since Mexico, in ten or fifteen years, but I recognized him right away," recalls George. "I mean, he had been with Ramón and Frank, and Annette, and the two Wendys. He'd stayed with all of us at the beach house in Puerto Vallarta. We'd done a whole bunch of things together, and he was a damn good pilot. Harbuck I wasn't terribly thrilled dealing with, and I didn't really know much about Tom and Greg. But seeing Cliff eased my mind a lot. It gave me a really good feeling about the trip."

By about the same time, March of 1985, the police in Florida—and just about everywhere else in the country—had been in steady retreat when it came to waging President Reagan's war on drugs. For all the manpower, intelligence capability, and equipment provided by the much vaunted South Florida Task Force—and the big seizures it flaunted now and then before the TV cameras—the aggressive battle was by now proving itself a sad exercise in futility. At the time of its formation under the leadership of Vice President George Bush in January of 1982, the task force had been given an unprecedented amount of resources to interdict cocaine smugglers and track down money launderers. The DEA's Florida office was provided with 60 new agents, 10 supervisors, and 3 intelligence analysts; 43 agents were added to the FBI in Florida, 145 to the Customs Service, 45 to the Bureau of Alcohol, Tobacco and Firearms, 20 to the Federal Law Enforcement Training Center of the Treasury Department, 11 to the U.S. Marshals Service, and an unspecified number of accountants to the Internal Revenue Service. The U.S. Attorney's Office was bolstered with prosecutors. Chief Justice Warren Burger of the U.S. Supreme Court promised to provide more federal judges to try the cases. The Coast Guard got additional cutters with which to blockade the coast. Navy warships were authorized to stop suspected vessels on the high seas. The U.S. Army contributed Cobra helicopter gunships, famous for their fire support during the Vietnam War, which would now chase after suspected drug planes. The Cobras would get help from the navy's sophisticated EC-2 surveillance planes, capable of tracking drug flights emanating from the Bahamas and the Caribbean by radar. As commander-in-chief of the operation, the vice president came to Florida in February of 1982 and told a gathering of the Miami Citizens Against Crime: "To those who commit crime, who engage in violence, we say, the American people have great patience, but that patience has been sapped."

If the object of it all was to reduce the supply of cocaine available to those who wanted it in the forty-eight contiguous American states plus Alaska, the task force in its first three years of operation had been a dismal failure. At the time of its inception, federal estimates put the amount of cocaine arriving in the United States at somewhere between 60 and 80 tons a year; the wholesale price for a kilo of 100 percent pure coke was fifty to sixty thousand dollars; and the police were finding the strength of the average gram they seized on the street to be 12.5 percent cocaine. By 1985, despite record seizures by agencies cooperating in the task-force effort, it was estimated that between 100 and 125 tons were being imported each year, the price of a kilo of pure cocaine had dropped to twenty thousand dollars—and would keep going down for another two years—and the strength of a street gram was moving on up toward 30 percent cocaine. There was more coke around than ever, it was better than ever, and it cost a lot less; in fact, it was becoming affordable for just about everyone. Poor and working-class Americans, black and white, could now get themselves a taste of what the privileged minority had been shouting about. And no one knew it yet, but the devastating crack epidemic lay just around the corner.

As a police problem, not only were the drug smugglers too numerous and absolutely relentless in their pursuit of the American market bonanza, but on balance they had proved much more clever than the cops. "It took us a while to learn how far ahead of us they were in terms of technology and sophistication," says Michael McManus, a special agent for the Drug Enforcement Administration in Fort Lauderdale. No matter what hardware the feds added to their arsenal, the smugglers always seemed to go them one better. In the bust of one smuggling operation, McManus says, the DEA confiscated an elaborate code book, which consisted of forty legal-size, typewritten pages of radio frequencies that had enabled the smugglers to pinpoint not only the location of interceptor boats operated by the police, but also the whereabouts of the Coast Guard, the army, the navy, even the Secret Service. They also had plenty of money to overwhelm the police with surveillance. At Port Everglades, for instance, the main entrance from the sea into the Intracoastal Waterway in Fort Lauderdale, they'd have spies sitting on the jetties, monitoring the marine traffic, watching the U.S. Customs and local police boats move in and out of the port. "There are no more predictable people in the world than cops," says McManus. "From 8:00 to 9:00 A.M. they'd stop and have their coffee. At 12:00 noon they'd cruise over to the Coast Guard station to get a cheap lunch. So the boats loaded with drugs would just wait offshore until the guy watching the traffic radioed out to them, 'Come on down. Bring the fish in to market.'"

What seizures they did manage to make were weighted heavily toward the marijuana end of the business, the blizzard of incoming cocaine being nearly invisible as far as the police were concerned. Up until March of 1985, the biggest cocaine seizure by the Fort Lauderdale Police Department was a four-kilo bust back in 1983, and that occasioned a big party in the squad room. Yet that bust came a full six years after Barry Kane alone smuggled over half a ton of cocaine into the city, when the business was still in its infancy, smugglers not yet getting up to speed.

That was the situation in the spring of 1985, when two detectives for the Fort Lauderdale police department had the good fortune to stumble into a mother lode of a cocaine deal. The case would prove remarkable in many respects, but the first thing that struck everybody involved was how such an important tip could come in off the street from such a small-time hood. Billy Fitzgerald, forty-one, was a scraggly alcoholic, one rung above wino status, who hung out at redneck dives in the featureless and desolate farming country west of Fort Lauderdale. As a low-level dope pusher, he dealt just enough coke or marijuana to pay for his own needs, and earned a little extra as a snitch, selling information to the police. "We took him out to dinner, he's got spaghetti all over his face, picking up food with his hands, it was hard to watch while you were eating," says Tom Tiderington, who worked at the time as an undercover narcotics detective for the department's Organized Crime Division. He and his partner, Greg Kridos, had been together for about two years, doing mostly buy-and-bust stings, a kilo here, a kilo there. "One of the officers who knew this guy said he had something interesting to tell us. We didn't expect much, but we figured, what the hell. Then suddenly he's going on about how he can introduce us to members of the Medellín cartel!" Billy told Tom and Greg that there was this old farmer who lived out toward the Everglades, bred and raised horses on a small spread. "He told us this old man had an important connection down in Colombia and was looking for someone to bring in a big load of cocaine. We're thinking, 'In his seventies? Doing a cocaine run?'"

Billy said he'd gotten the information from another man named McWilliams, who was working on the deal directly with the farmer, looking to find someone who could help them out. Billy said if they wanted him to, he could set up a meeting with this guy. Tom and Greg told him okay. The story they wanted him to tell McWilliams was that he knew a couple of guys this farmer might be interested in meeting. Tell him these two guys are in the transportation business. Tell him they have access to boats and airplanes, and, from what you've heard about their operation, they've got the knowledge and the wherewithal to handle heavy loads.

This was the last time Tom and Greg saw Billy alive. A couple of months later they heard he'd stolen some drugs from a group of black cocaine dealers in the northwest part of Fort Lauderdale, an ill-advised move they assumed had some connection with the fact that shortly afterward a couple of police officers investigating a nasty smell in the neighborhood found that it came from Billy having been shot to death and stuffed into the trunk of a car. But although his story about the farmer had sounded a little implausible, even the vague prospect of pulling off a victory on the cocaine front provided incentive enough to follow up any lead they had.

Several days after talking to Billy, Tom and Greg met with the go-between, McWilliams, at a cowboy bar out in Davie. McWilliams drove semis for a living, and he repeated Billy's story that this farmer was looking for transportation, adding that the amount he wanted flown in was five hundred kilos, a startling quantity considering the stir their little four-kilo bust had caused. The next day McWilliams introduced them to the principal himself, at another redneck bar out toward the Everglades. The man's name was Leon Harbuck. Checking afterward on the registration for the long-bed pick-up he'd driven to the bar, they found out that Harbuck was sixty-one years old, not seventy, and he had a police record, but not for drugs. Besides a speeding ticket the previous year, he'd been arrested back in 1981 for "reckless display of a weapon," that is, waving a shotgun at somebody in a menacing fashion, and had been given six months on probation.

"He didn't feel comfortable with us right away," says Greg Kridos, a former state trooper in New Hampshire who joined the Fort Lauderdale force in 1980 after growing weary of doing nothing but writing speeding tickets. "They wanted to know a lot about what we had as an operation. We were pretty vague at first. You never want to be too specific about what you have because you don't really have all those resources at the time that you're purporting to have them.

Being too specific can mess you up in the end if you have to change plans or can't come up with something. So we told them just generally that we'd been doing this awhile, we had a good safe house, good transportation, solid planes that could go to Colombia and pick up what you needed. Our pilots were excellent, they'd flown down there before."

Harbuck took it all in. He told them he was thinking about something like an airdrop, rather than actually landing a plane. He had a trailer he was living in in the middle of a horse pasture out in Sunrise, two miles north of Lauderdale and twelve to fourteen miles west. Right nearby was a cornfield. His idea was to have a plane fly in low, make two or three passes close off the ground, and kick the duffel bags out the cargo door so they fell into a field of six-foot-high cornstalks. He'd have four or five guys go through the field like a human chain, pick up the bags and hide them in the neighboring woods, then exit the area in a couple of pick-ups, riding empty. That way, if they were stopped on the way out by any police who might have been alerted by the low-flying aircraft, they'd be free and clear, and could go back later and get the dope. Harbuck told them he'd done a dry run on the idea, sending some guys into the woods with bales of hay, and he thought the whole operation would take only a few minutes.

By the time they left the bar, having told Harbuck they needed to check on a few things and would get back to him on the details, Tom and Greg knew they'd need a good deal of help. Not for the human-relations part; after working together for two years now, they were confident enough of handling that end pretty smoothly. A graduate of Saint Anselm College in New Hampshire, Greg played the low-key partner, never getting very excited, handling matter-of-factly all the numerous problems that arose in any drug deal. His olive complexion also gave him a distinct advantage. Although derived from Greek ancestors, it created the impression in people's minds that he had roots somewhere south of the border, an assumption he gladly let stand. Tom Tiderington came from up in Michigan, and looked it—fresh-faced with clean features, his expression frozen in a state of eagerness. Perhaps because he appeared less like a smuggler than Kridos did, he played the more aggressive half of the team, the one more prone to push people, quick to get irritated if things didn't go right. The object was to distract people with his hard-nosed personality so they'd forget he didn't look right for the part. His cover story was that his father was a wealthy businessman from Detroit, and when not smuggling cocaine, Tom worked as a charter fishing-boat captain.

It was the resource end of the thing that posed the problem. The Fort Lauderdale Police Department had a few accoutrements—flashy cars such as Mercedes Benzes and BMW's that had been confiscated in drug busts. They'd also acquired a couple of marine vessels, a fifty-eight-foot Hatteras sportfisherman and a sixty-three-foot trawler, which could double as drug runners. But as for the flying part—the planes and the pilots, being able to demonstrate the kind of know-how expected of veteran cocaine transporters—they possessed nothing in this area whatsoever. "This was the first importation case we'd worked on at that level, so our expertise only went to a certain point," Greg recalls. "We didn't know what type of plane we'd need, for instance. He was talking of flying in at a low altitude to air-drop the cocaine. Well, you can't drop it too high or it'll burst all over. You have to fly in maybe at 150 feet. You needed a particular plane that, first, would fly low enough to do that, and, second, that you could get the coke out of easily, with the right kind of cargo doors. They were talking five hundred kilos here."

This was why, right after the first meeting with Harbuck, they put in a call to the local office of the DEA, to Mike McManus, to tell him what they seemed to have glommed onto. McManus, a short, compact Audie Murphy lookalike, a graduate of Florida State University, had grown up in the nearby town of Plantation and had worked undercover for that police department before joining the DEA. He got so good at posing as a drug dealer that more than once he sat in a bar in Plantation buying tabs of LSD and ounces of grass from dealers who felt compelled to warn him that "there's an undercover cop around here named Mike that you've really got to watch out for." The father of three girls, McManus took a fifteen-thousand-dollar pay cut to join the DEA and harbors something of a messianic attitude toward the job of catching smugglers. "I realized after getting in that I'm not going to change the world," he says. "I'm a firm believer in education, and until you make it not a socially acceptable thing to do, you're not going to solve the drug problem. But I do believe that I can make a difference. The role of the DEA is to locate, identify, successfully penetrate, and arrest, and, I would add, *destroy* the major smuggling networks. If I just take a load, I can hurt them, but if I take down the whole organization, I've destroyed them." So there's that, he says, but he also went into undercover work "because I love the excitement. I can't stand sitting behind a desk. I look at it as a game. I've got a set of rules, and the bad guys have no rules. But I beat them at their own game and in their own ballpark. They don't play by the rules, and I do, and I still beat them."

The three of them, Mike, Tom, and Greg, had worked together before, on much smaller cases. If Harbuck wasn't living in Fantasy Land here, they were staring at an unprecedented opportunity, ideal for the tactic McManus terms the "controlled delivery"—posing as smugglers, Tom and Greg would organize the airlift, and the dope would be flown in on their own airplane and by their own contract pilot. Once it landed back in Fort Lauderdale, it would be trucked by Tom and Greg to a safe house that would be guarded by police officers hiding in the bushes. Doing it this way, they would not only confiscate the dope and arrest people involved in its delivery, but they'd score an intelligence coup as well. By negotiating with the people who owned the cocaine back in Colombia, they'd see to some extent how that end of the operation worked. By flying to the landing strip outside Medellín, they'd get information on the actual operations of the cartel. And by holding the dope in the States and dealing with the Colombians in Miami for its delivery, they'd have a chance to penetrate that part of the network as well. "If you do it right, with a controlled delivery you can identify who's in the organization that owns the stuff and the organization that distributes the stuff back in the States, because you've got something both groups want and you're negotiating on both ends of the deal." As a DEA agent, McManus had access to a lot of resources, most important of which were airplanes and pilots. Many of the latter were former drug pilots who either were doing penance for a bust or had done their prison time and were now earning a living working on stings. McManus told them he had a line on a special pilot who'd done work for the DEA on other deals just like this. The pilot's name was Cliff Guttersrud.

For the next meeting, Tom and Greg told Harbuck to meet them on the *Land's End*, the department's trawler anchored in the New River near Port Everglades, which Tom now passed off as one of the boats he chartered out on as a fishing captain. The whole place was wired for sound and video, so McManus could get a good view of things in absentia. The news they had to tell Harbuck was that the plane they'd be using was a twin-engine Beechcraft Queen Air, which had plenty of range to make it to Colombia, as well as cargo doors so they could easily jettison the bags into his cornfield. The pilot who'd be bringing in the load was named Cliff. He'd made the trip to Colombia several times before and would be flying the plane in shortly from the West Coast so Harbuck could meet him and inspect the aircraft. For his part, Harbuck also had a little news for them. He could now divulge that he wasn't really the one in charge here. His task had been simply to find someone who could do the transportation. The man running the show was an American and was coming to Fort Lauderdale in two days, and he'd like to meet them, and he also wanted to meet the pilot. They asked where the meeting was going to be held. Harbuck said he couldn't tell them. He'd take them there at the appointed time.

That was Monday. At about seven-thirty Wednesday night Harbuck came by to collect Tom, Greg, and Cliff. With him was another man named Steve, his son-in-law. "It was something you'd expect to see on TV," says Greg. "He was very secretive, he wouldn't tell us where we were going. He took us two miles north to a Days Inn off Route 84 at I-95 and brought us up to this guy's room. It was dark in there, and the guy we were supposed to meet was standing at the extreme end of the room. He had the TV on, and he stood behind it with closed curtains at his back. The TV illuminated us, but we couldn't really see him." As recorded in one of the "dailies," the detailed accounts of their activities the two detectives wrote up at the end of each shift, the stranger introduced himself as George, and during the meeting he asked most of the questions and did most of the talking.

> After these detectives were let into the room by Leon Harbuck and they were introduced to the subject identified as George, he asked who the pilot was. After stating that the subject with these detectives was the pilot, George began to ask these detectives and the pilot questions. The subject then told these detectives that he had married into a Colombian family, that his wife is Colombian. . . . George further stated that the Colombian who was the connection for the cocaine, and whose family George was now a part of, was presently in Colombia getting the coordinates for the landing strip. George stated that he had sent his nephew who is Colombian down with maps showing the flight pattern from South Florida to

Colombia and that he was coming back with the coordinates. . . . George asked these detectives and the pilot, "If everything goes smooth the first time, are you willing to make several trips?" George stated he was out of circulation for a while but now he was back in it.

The meeting lasted an hour and twenty minutes, after which Harbuck and his son-in-law headed out westbound in separate cars; Tom, Greg, and Cliff drove back toward the city, leaving George alone in the hotel. So far the detectives had been able to identify everyone involved in the operation, either because they gave their names voluntarily or through the license plates on their cars. But George had no car. He hadn't given his last name. And the room was registered to a Delbert Lapham, a name they assumed, correctly, was an alias.

But when they were alone together driving off in the car, Cliff told the detectives, Jesus, he *knew* that guy. From the late 1960s, in Manhattan Beach. He'd flown loads for him, kilos of marijuana out of Mexico, into the dry lake beds of Southern California. The last he heard he'd gotten busted bringing three hundred kilos of marijuana into the Playboy Club in Chicago back in 1972. That guy is Boston George! Cliff said. That guy is George Jung!

In undercover work something new happens every day, and there was plenty of action. These were two reasons why Detective Kridos considers the five years he worked as a narcotics detective for the Fort Lauderdale Police Department as "the best years I'd spent as a police officer. The standard TV image you have of what police work is like is what we were actually doing—dealing with people who were dangerous, thousands of pounds of drugs. In undercover work, the most important thing was to establish your believability. You've got to blend your personality with what you know to be the narcotics traffickers' personality." He learned early on to avoid the flashy attire associated with drug dealers in the movies. "I'd wear a watch, a single gold chain, and a wedding band, and that was it. Dopers get nervous when you wear a lot of jewelry because you're too high-profile. I mean, I'm standing to make a million dollars here. Why would I draw attention to myself? I'd want to look just like everybody else."

Then there's "walking the walk and talking the talk"—knowing the price structures, falling in with the lingo. "If you're not very comfortable with the vernacular, a guy may throw something at you that you should know and don't. Like in a marijuana deal, 'How much am I getting on the wrappings?' Which means, how much is he going to take off the price of a bale of marijuana so I'm paying for net-weight marijuana, not for two and a half pounds of plastic wrap? You could be stuck and not know what he's talking about, and they're immediately going to think something's funny. You also don't jump through hoops for them. Only cops jump through hoops for people. You call a guy and he says meet him at three o'clock at the Rainbow Restaurant in Lauderdale, you show up, wait fifteen minutes, and he doesn't show, you leave. He calls up and says something came up, he's down in Miami, why don't you meet him down there? You say, 'Screw you! You want to do this deal, meet me here, or meet me halfway.' If you jump to get the deal done, they're going to suspect something, so you make it a little hard for them."

One of the most crucial things Greg had to learn was the art of the "flash," the money flash or the drug flash, usually employed to get a deal that's become bogged down in a Mexican stand-off moving again. "Say you're selling the cocaine. They might want to see the dope before they bring out the money. But that goes against your principles. You tell them, 'No, you show me the money. You can't get arrested for just showing money. But if I show you the fifty keys, first I'm heating up where the keys are. I've gotta have somebody go to the stash house, bring them out on the street.' But if it's 'No, I'm still not showing the money until I see the coke,' then you've got to do a flash. You make a phone call and have someone drive in and flash some stuff. And when you're flashing it, particularly if you're the buyer and you're flashing money, the first and foremost, the cardinal rule is when you show it, you show it when this guy has no clue he's going to see it. You may say, 'Hey, take a ride with me.' He hasn't any idea where he's going or why, and you show him the money, like, fast. You open up the bag or the suitcase, let him riffle it but not count it, then you leave right away. You can't give him time to set something up, have some of his people around to get a countersurveillance going."

Whether he was playing the seller, the buyer, or the transporter—the three standard roles in a drug sting—the most nerve-racking part for Greg was always the moment the deal went down, when the goods and the money actually changed hands. "Whether you're the bad guys or the good guys, you both have the same goal in any cocaine deal, and that is to get through it alive. And here the most crucial thing is that you're never going to put the money and the dope together. You're going to keep them separate. If you put them together, the potential for being ripped off and shot and killed goes up immensely. The various ways the exchange happens are, 'Give me the dope, I'll sell it and bring you the money back'—that's probably the worst way. Another is, 'Give me half the dope, I'll pay for half and sell it and come back and get the rest later.' Third is, 'Give me half and I'll pay you after I sell it, but you hold the other half as collateral.' The way the transfer works is each side sends a representative to a neutral place, and they sit down and work out how it's going to happen. It's usually, 'I'll send two of my guys with the money to meet two of your guys. I'll send two other guys to another location to meet two other of your guys who have the dope. So then I talk to my guys on the phone who are looking at the dope, and you talk to your guys who are looking at the money. We exchange everything and we walk away.' Of course, even doing it this way you can get ripped off, and if you're going to get ripped off, remember, they don't know you're cops, they just think you're drug dealers, so you're probably going to get killed. They don't want any witnesses, and they don't want anyone coming after them."

From the beginning Tom and Greg could hardly believe the bonanza they'd stumbled upon—a three- to four-hundred-kilo cocaine deal involving a large network of traffickers. George's nephew, Joseph Ahmed, had appeared on the scene, so counting noses, they had six conspirators so far—McWilliams, their initial contact with Harbuck; Harbuck and his son-in-law, Steven Fuller; another gofer who popped up named Walsh; and George. And this was just on the American side. If they could use the cocaine they'd be flying in to pry into the Colombian organization in Miami, there was no telling how many they'd land. They were also going to discover, though they would not be the first ones, that in dealing with George they had a tiger by the tail.

The first surprise came when they ran George's name through the FBI's computer and found out that here was someone who'd just escaped from a state prison. So right away came a major problem. The Fort Lauderdale police had no proscriptions against dealing with fugitives. But Mike McManus of the DEA was operating under a strict policy that said anytime he ran across someone wanted by another jurisdiction he couldn't fool around, he had to arrest him right away—unless he could get the jurisdiction to sign off on keeping the fugitive for the duration of the trip. McManus found the state police in Massachusetts were willing to go along with the operation, but the Department of Corrections up there wasn't too keen on letting this guy, the "master of illusion" smart-ass, stay free any longer. "We were pleading with them that we were into a really big thing here," says McManus, who handled all the back-up work. "This was the Medellín cartel! George was a documented heavy player, and all the names we're coming up with are major, major players in the cartel. We had such a good handle on this guy. He was eating out of our hand." Still, Corrections wasn't satisfied. Hey, come on, putting George up at a hotel? He could walk away from the operation any minute. To get Corrections to cooperate, Fort Lauderdale at least had to put him on a tighter leash.

That was when they thought of housing George and his nephew on the boat, along with Cliff, who could help keep tabs on them. It was this fifty-eight-foot Hatteras, which the Fort Lauderdale PD had confiscated from a dirty cop who, under everyone's noses, had been running a huge marijuana-smuggling ring, with mother ships offshore and go-fast boats ferrying the goods in at night. The Hatteras was a $750,000 lushly appointed yacht moored at a slip in the New River alongside other luxury craft. It had plenty of room below deck for five or six people. It was wired for sound, with microphones all over the boat, under the carpet. There was a video camera in one of the stereo speakers. The story they told George was that it belonged to Tom's father in Detroit and was just sitting there unused, so they might as well stay there. "George loved the idea, he thought it was great," says Greg. "The big yacht owner. It fit the profile he had of himself to a tee."

As plans moved along, it became apparent that the delivery wasn't going to happen as quickly as everyone had assumed. It was the rainy season down in Colombia, so difficulties arose with transporting the bales through the jungle. And the gravel airstrips weren't in good shape. The longer the delay, the higher expenses mounted. Until they moved to the boat, George, Cliff, and Joseph Ahmed had been put up at hotels, and even afterward there were meals to pay for; covering George and Cliff's bar bills alone was enough to support a family of four over quite a stretch. Joseph had to be flown down to Colombia to check on how things were going.

Colombians would come up to Fort Lauderdale to look things over, check on Cliff's plane. On that occasion, Tom and Greg took them out to eat at the Marriott Hotel, and although the Marriott boasted the most expensive restaurant in town, they still had difficulty explaining to the stingy accountants at the police department how they managed to spend five hundred dollars on lunch. Thus Tom and Greg were encouraged by the department to get as much money back as possible from the Colombians. Ideally they would make them pay for their own bust.

So they started putting pressure on George and Joseph to get the people in Medellín to produce forty thousand dollars up front. They said they needed it to pay Cliff, to purchase equipment for the airplane, get vehicles ready for the trucking end of it. Cliff had to hire a copilot to help him, a friend named B. D. Good, from Arizona. But they also started demanding money because it made them believable. "We were supposed to be transporters," says Greg, "and that's the way the typical transportation deal was done: You give us money up front. If we had agreed to go down and get it before getting paid, we wouldn't be legitimate. So with George it was always, 'Hey, where's the money? You said you can do this, you say you're part of a large organization. We're not seeing squat here. You guys for real, or are we wasting our time here, spinning our wheels? You stroking us? We're seeing nothing here.'"

As George busied himself getting the cash, solving other problems, Tom and Greg had the opportunity to get a peek into the organization to see how things worked. When Joseph was getting cash from the Colombians, for instance, Tom and Greg would drive him down to Miami, note all the people he talked to, the addresses, the car registrations. They'd furnish George or Joseph cellular phones for the calls down to Medellín, then reclaim them quickly and press the redial button to find out what number they'd called.

At one point the Colombians in Medellín wanted to meet the pilot George had found to make sure he wasn't working for the police, that he hadn't flown previous missions resulting inexplicably in a bust. Cliff didn't want to fly down, because he'd done other flights for the DEA, and so B.D. went in his place. Unlike Cliff, B.D. was a regular commercial pilot, had never flown drugs or been to Medellín, so sending him down seemed safe enough— except from B.D.'s point of view. For him, the experience proved fairly unnerving. "He said he was taken to a room on the top floor of the Intercontinental Hotel in Medellín," Greg recalls, "and he's waiting in there when the door opens and these twelve Colombians come in. Nothing is said to him. Each one comes over and looks him up and down and then leaves. At that point he said he was thinking it could go either way. 'You're thinking the worst thoughts at that point. They think I'm someone, but I'm really not.' He held his breath through the whole thing, until they all had left and he got the nod. If not, no two ways about it, he would have been killed right away. Afterward he said he went into the bathroom and threw up."

It was hardly surprising, operating as they were in the midst of a ring of individuals whose business was breaking the law, that Tom, Greg, and Mike occasionally found themselves cutting a few corners of their own. Aside from harboring an escaped fugitive, not to mention feeding him a steady diet of steaks, lobsters, and Glenlivet Scotch, they had to contend with Joseph Ahmed's lack of control where women were concerned. One night, before everyone was moved to the boat, George called up Tom frantic from their hotel saying that Joseph had just attacked some young girl. "I mean, I'm a police officer, and he's telling me Joseph had just assaulted a girl, and wants me to come over and get them out of the hotel before the police come and they get arrested." As it turned out, the girl had some of her clothes torn, but she suffered no physical harm and was persuaded eventually not to file a complaint.

Then came the kidnapping. Essentially, it came about because Leon Harbuck had gotten his feelings hurt when the two Colombians who'd come up to look at the plane also went out to inspect his field and immediately nixed the idea of throwing out their cocaine into a bunch of cornstalks. It might burst open, they felt; Harbuck's guys might not find it all right away. The idea seemed just too flaky. Harbuck told them he'd plow the corn under and they could put the plane down on the ground. As for that big drainage ditch that ran right through the middle of the field, he'd bridge it over with plywood. The Colombians looked at each other, and then at George, as if to say, Where'd you'd get this guy?

Instead, it was decided to fly the load into a regular landing strip, a reasonably out-of-the-way field they had found up in Vero Beach, about a hundred miles north of Fort Lauderdale. This decision to abandon the cornfield, however, made Harbuck and his son-in-law unhappy, because it seemed as if they were getting nudged out of the deal. "Harbuck had always wanted to be the controller of the operation, right under George," says Tom. "But once George started living on the boat, his loyalty changed from Harbuck to us. Leon thought he was going to get cut out completely. He'd also given us fifteen thousand dollars for expenses, and now he wanted at least to get his money back." While Harbuck was contemplating the best way to accomplish this, there were a couple of developments involving the boat that almost blew up the whole deal. While luxurious, the quarters aboard were also tight, which meant that tempers could easily flare up. At one point George and Ahmed, who was snorting coke pretty consistently—another infraction Tom and Greg regularly had to overlook—got into such a violent fight with each other that people on the neighboring yachts called the Fort Lauderdale police. The cops showed up, not knowing they'd barged in on an undercover operation, and a lot of diplomacy had to be used to settle the dispute without having George and Joseph hauled down to the police station, where it would have been discovered that, my God, here was an escapee from a state prison.

Then, in a piece of coincidence worthy of Charles Dickens, Cliff Guttersrud one night met at a singles bar the ex-wife of the dirty cop whose boat they were living on. Cliff brought her back to the yacht, whereupon in the presence of George she remarked on the fact that this vessel looked very familiar. In fact, this was her husband's boat! "I remember I was on my honeymoon in Napa Valley, California," says Tom, "when I got this call from George. He said, 'Hey, I found out that the boat we're staying on is a cop's boat.' But he didn't think, 'Hey, you guys must be cops.' It was, 'What are we going to do? She told us we were being set up. The police seized it. She could show us the newspaper articles.'" Tom told George to relax. It was his father's boat, all right. He'd bought it at the auction where the police sell all the stuff they've confiscated. Hadn't he told him that before?

Nevertheless, they felt they'd already pressed their luck too far with the boat, so they moved George and Joseph back into a hotel, to a Holiday Inn out in Davie, thinking they'd cause less trouble farther from civilization. And that worked okay for a few days, until May 12, when George opened his door to a knock and found Harbuck standing there with his son-in-law, Steve Fuller, and Fuller was pointing at George with a .38-caliber revolver. Harbuck announced that he had nothing particularly against George, but he'd decided the only way to get back the money he'd invested was to commit a kidnapping, and George and Joseph were going to be his victims. George asked Harbuck who the fuck he thought he was kidding. And if he wanted to shoot him, go ahead. Where would that get him? Joseph, however, took the situation a little more to heart, especially as he saw Fuller pick up one of the pillows on the couch to use, supposedly, to muffle a gunshot, and he raced past them out the door screaming down the hallway that they were being kidnapped and somebody call the police. "Now we're all in trouble," recalls George. "So I tell Harbuck, 'Look, Leon, we better get the fuck out of here before the cops come, because I'm a goddamn fugitive, and we'll all get arrested, you stupid son of a bitch.' So in effect, you could say I facilitated my own kidnapping." The next day Harbuck called up Tom and Greg to tell them what he'd done and what he wanted. And after George got on the phone to say he was okay, they drove out to meet Harbuck, gave him back his money, and secured the return of George.

By now the operation was into its third month, and patience on all sides was wearing thin. "We had been at these guys' beck and call seven days a week, twenty-four hours a day," says Greg. "Drive us here, drive us there, get us this, get us that, take them to Miami, take them out to the airplane. It was getting pretty tiring." Greg pulled an eight-hour wait at the Miami passport office getting Joseph his papers so he could fly down to Medellín. Just about the last straw came the day when George said that, despite everything they'd done for him, he needed to find out more about them. After all, the only thing he knew was what they'd told him. "He told us, 'I've got to know where at least one of you lives,'" says Greg. "And he was adamant about it. 'We just can't do this deal unless you show me. If anything goes wrong, it shows your good faith.'

"Well, we had a real estate friend who was selling a house about forty-five minutes north of Lauderdale. It was a nice place, going for $400,000, the furnishings were still there, even a little dog, a miniature poodle, running around. We decided to show him that house and tell him it belonged to Tom." Before they took him out there, Tom stuck some family snaps up on the wall to personalize the place. "When we arrived with George, I told him my wife was out at the store, but to look around, take his time. The poodle was yapping at us the whole time we were there. I told him, 'Don't mind the dog, George, it does that to everyone.' And anyway, he bought it."

Finally, after some three and a half months of on-again, off-again preparation, the plane was set to go down early on the morning of Saturday, May 25, and return sometime after midnight, right in the middle of Memorial Day weekend. George had brought down two gofers he knew from Massachusetts to act as a security detail, to help watch out for the police. Joseph had gone down to Medellín earlier to get the coordinates of the field they'd be using. The way George set it up with Humberto, Joseph would fly down in the Queen Air with Cliff and B.D. to supervise the actual loading. Coming back, they'd stop off in the Cayman Islands to take on fuel. Cliff had said the plane would be too heavy to make it to the States in one jump. In Florida, they'd land up in Vero Beach. The three hundred kilos, packed in duffel bags, would be off-loaded into a truck and a station wagon and driven down to this safe house that Tom and Greg had rented in Lauderdale. On the drive down, the two guys from Massachusetts would follow behind in another car, and if they saw any police on their tail, their job was to take off down the highway, to draw the cops away from the load.

Once it was safely in the stash house, negotiations would begin to transfer the coke to the Colombians in Miami. George had negotiated with Humberto to be paid $4,000 a kilo for the trip, a good price, considering the drop in the wholesale rates. This meant a total of $1.2 million. Of this, $300,000 was going to Tom and Greg for their part, and another $300,000 to Harbuck and his people. George was keeping $600,000 for himself, enough to get him to Panama, where he would check out things with the bank. With a little left over if he needed it.

Tom, Greg, and Mike McManus had a plan of their own for Memorial Day weekend. And if the one George was counting on didn't work out in exactly the way he'd hoped, neither quite did theirs. Adding in the two new guys from Massachusetts, and also two Colombians who had surfaced in Miami as representatives of the people for whom the shipment was intended, they now had ten cocaine conspirators they could lay their hands on, and hoped to haul in more. To make sure things went off without a hitch, they had prepared for the plane trip down and back with military precision. The stop in the Caymans on the way back wasn't really so Cliff could refuel. It was so he could make contact with a DEA agent at the airport there, to tell him exactly how much dope was on board and also whether anyone else besides Joseph had come along for the ride from Colombia. Tom and Greg didn't want any surprises popping out of the cockpit when the plane landed. In the Caymans a DEA chase plane would also pick them up and follow the Queen Air into Florida to keep the ground people advised on the progress of the flight.

On Saturday morning, May 25, the flight took off from the Fort Lauderdale Executive Airfield. On board were Cliff, B.D., and Joseph, and right away came plan deviation number one. Cliff hadn't confessed this to McManus, but he'd been harboring a lot of fear over the possibility of being recognized as a DEA pilot by someone down at the airstrip. So he had never really intended to fly to Medellín in the first place. He was loath to tell this to the DEA, however, because if he didn't make the trip, he wouldn't get paid, which meant he'd lose out on twenty-five thousand dollars. The solution he thought of was to have the plane stop off in the Caymans, not only on the way back, but on the way down as well. Which is what indeed occurred, and in the Caymans Cliff got off and had B.D. fly down to Colombia by himself; he would pick Cliff up on the return trip.

In Fort Lauderdale that day it was mostly sit and wait. George and his security detail from Massachusetts, Dennis and Ray, stayed with Tom at a place called the Berkeley Inn, while Greg supposedly went up to check the field in Vero Beach. Greg called in at about 6:30 P.M. to say it had rained a lot up there and the strip was too muddy; they'd have to bring the load directly into Fort Lauderdale Executive Airfield. The truth was that Greg never went up to Vero Beach, and they had always planned on bringing it into Fort Lauderdale, because the load would be easier to keep under surveillance that way. They knew, however, that George would object to the airport as too risky, and would only agree to it if it was broached as an emergency. A little over three hours later, at 9:50 P.M., the call came in from the agent in the Caymans that the plane had landed. It was carrying 300 kilos, or 660 pounds, packed in thirteen duffel bags. Cliff, B.D., and Joseph were the only ones on board. It would take off shortly, and the ETA in Fort Lauderdale would be between 1:30 and 2:30 A.M. Sunday. Oh, by the way, the agent asked. How come Cliff had gotten off there and hadn't gone down to Colombia?

Because they were using the airport in town, George's two security guys wouldn't be needed right away. Tom suggested they go over to the Holiday Inn, rent a couple of rooms, and stay there until he or George called them. They'd be needed tomorrow to help with the load. Tom, Greg, and George then drove out to the airport to wait for the plane. They had a camper truck and a station wagon, with plenty of room for the thirteen bags. George told Greg he was nervous about using such an open landing site. Greg said he agreed, but there was nothing they could do about the weather. He and George were waiting outside the hangar. Tom was inside talking to the plane on a radio set. At 12:30 A.M., an hour early, Tom banged on the hangar door to have Greg open it, and he said the plane was just about to touch down. Pretty soon they could see its landing lights approaching in the distance, and then the roar of the Queen Air as it taxied on by them into the hangar, with Cliff waving triumphantly from the cockpit. He offed its lights as soon as it pulled to a stop. The cargo door swung open, and out stepped Joseph Ahmed. He was dirty and greasy from loading the cocaine in Colombia and helping with the refueling, but he wore a big smile. "Let's go," he said, and started lowering the bags to the three of them, who transferred them quickly to the waiting vehicles.

As Cliff and B.D. drove off in their own car, George got into the truck with Tom, and Joseph and Greg took the wagon. They headed to the stash house in the southwest part of Fort Lauderdale. Joseph couldn't contain his excitement. He clapped his hands several times and wrung Greg's in congratulations. He said his stepfather had wanted them to bring up fifty more kilos, but they couldn't fit them on the plane. There was also another load all ready to go, and Humberto wanted them to come back in three or four days and pick up three to five hundred more keys. Joseph was jigging around in the seat, babbling on about how they were all going to be rich. From what he'd seen at the landing strip, the amount of cocaine being shipped out just this weekend was fairly staggering. He was told their plane had been the fifth to land that morning, each plane taking off with what he thought were between two and five hundred kilos. In an underground shed next to the strip, he saw forty more duffel bags waiting to be picked up by planes coming in after them. All in all, counting the coke they'd brought in on this flight, the coke they'd get in a few days, as well as what he saw down there, it came to more than seven thousand pounds, or three and a half tons! Greg made a mental note to get hold of McManus as soon as he was clear of Joseph to have him alert the DEA down there, to see if they couldn't get the Colombian police to pull off a quick raid.

Several minutes later the two vehicles pulled up at the stash house, a low, sprawling Florida ranch located on a dead-end street off Riverland Road in the ritzy Riverland Isles section of Fort Lauderdale. The houses in this neighborhood—some of them with million-dollar price tags—were built along fingerlike canals that led into the south fork of the New River. Residents could hop aboard their boats in the backyard and follow the river right down to Port Everglades and out to sea. It was dark, so George couldn't see that the stash house stood out in the neighborhood for the way it had been neglected. Whereas the other lawns on the street had hardly a blade of grass out of place, the lawn here was badly overgrown, the bushes untrimmed. In the swimming pool out back the water was coated over with a scum of algae. The house actually belonged to the state of Florida, another piece of property confiscated from the rogue marijuana policeman at the same time they took his boat. After driving the vehicles into the two-car garage and closing the door, they all went into the house to begin dealing with the transfer to the Colombians.

What Tom, Greg, and Mike had hoped was not only to seize the three hundred kilos, but also get their hands on the $1.2 million the Colombians in Miami were forking over for the transportation. That would pay for quite a few sting operations in the future. They also wanted to reach further into the distribution network and take off a few more people. While Tom and Joseph went off to begin negotiations over a pay phone at a convenience store nearby called the Majik Market, Greg stayed in the house with George, who sought to elevate his already high level of ecstasy by snorting some coke. "He was so elated," recalls Greg. "All this cocaine was sitting in the garage, and he knew the money he was going to make from it. Plus, when Joseph said there was another five hundred kilos sitting down there that Humberto wanted brought up, and forty more duffel bags, this put him in seventh heaven. This was what he'd spent time in prison for. He talked about doing future deals. We had a great relationship, he said. He said this deal had been hard because it was the first time we'd all been together, but from now on they'd go a lot easier."

The more George snorted, however, the more his elation gave way to paranoia, and at about 3:00 A.M. he started telling Greg he thought he heard something rustling around out on the lawn. This was one of the few coke deals where he hadn't been armed with his favorite .357 Magnum, and he was growing anxious over the security of the load. He'd asked Tom and Greg numerous times to find him a gun, and they'd debated over whether to supply him one that had a defective firing pin. In the end they promised to get one from a guy they knew but kept putting it off, and at the last moment they said the guy never showed up. So now George was looking around for a stick, anything. Finally he found a two-by-four piece of lumber. Brandishing that as a weapon, he sallied forth to check the grounds. George had been right in thinking there were people out there—nearly fifty of them, in fact, members of a special strike force put together by the DEA and the Fort Lauderdale PD. They were armed with pistols, rifles, shotguns, and submachine guns, all waiting for Greg or Tom to call it down, so they could rush in and bring this baby home. But everyone was hiding a good way back from the house, crouching down behind cover of one kind or another and not making any noise. What George had heard was coming out of his own head. After a couple of circuits around the yard he came back indoors, lay down on the floor, and using his sports jacket as a blanket, fell fast asleep.

Meanwhile, the negotiations Tom and Joseph were having with the Colombians in Miami weren't going too well. The Colombians told them they'd been sending all their cash down to Medellín, which meant they were cocaine-rich but money-poor. There was no way they could come up with the whole $1.2 million without first getting some of the kilos to sell. During these conversations, Tom found out that most of the load had been contracted for by a woman, but he didn't get a name. At one point, the Colombians proposed that he put a hundred kilos in the trunk of a car and drive it down to a parking lot in Kendall, south of Miami, where it would be picked up by agents for this woman. Twenty-four hours later the Colombians would deliver the $1.2 million, in return for the two hundred remaining kilos. Tom and Greg wanted to go for this, maybe set up surveillance around the parking lot and follow the Colombians as they tried to unload the coke. Mike McManus, however, said his superiors at the DEA were afraid to take the chance of losing the trail and allowing the cocaine to disappear onto the street.

Tom and Greg next proposed that they stonewall the Colombians, force them to come up to Lauderdale with the money or they just wouldn't get the coke. The DEA nixed this too. "Everybody thinks the DEA is very conservative, but the only time they got conservative on us was at the very end," says Greg. "We wanted them to be a little more liberal. The way we wanted to do it—and Mike and I and Tom felt we had a feel for it—was push the Colombians to the point where, 'You don't get your cocaine, or at least half of it, until you come up with some good-faith money. We did our part. We took our chances. We flew our people down to Colombia. We landed at Executive Airport. We're stashing the cocaine. Now you're telling us you're not giving us any money?'" But the DEA didn't want to take the chance of making the Colombians angry enough so that they'd try to come and take their coke by force. After all, the Colombians didn't know it was a police trap. "We felt, Hey, we had forty, fifty guys in the bushes, we could have at least tried it," says Greg. "That was the frustrating point for me."

So, the decision was made at 9:00 Sunday morning to go in and collect what they had. "There are just two of us in the house now, because they took Joseph off by the phone booth," says Greg. "George had fallen dead asleep. Everybody came through the front door without making any noise. They were extremely quiet. They came over and pointed their guns at George and woke him up, and said, 'George, you're under arrest.' He was very groggy, his mouth was gaping open. Wide eyes. He was flabbergasted. Devastated. He was in utter shock. He had been so ecstatic just before, and now it was all over."

George doesn't remember the bust being quite so gentle. "I woke up and I see all these guys pointing at me with guns, there's about twenty of them coming in from all sides of the house, and they're looking like they can hardly control themselves. One thing I've noticed about the police is they get very hyper at times like these. Some of them were shaking like a leaf, they were so excited. 'Don't you move, you cocksucker, dirtbag, you piece of shit, I've got kids you're selling drugs to, motherfucker.' One of them starts yelling, 'Watch out! He could have a gun under that sports coat! You move, you rotten son of a bitch, and I'll blow your brains out!'"

Seeing George there on the floor surrounded by the cops jabbing at him with their shotguns and pistols, then watching him being hauled out through a cluster of gawking neighbors, arms handcuffed behind his back, Greg couldn't help experience just a twinge, a vague discomfort that tempered, albeit ever so slightly, the elation he derived from bringing off what to this day ranks as the biggest cocaine seizure in the department's history. "I don't care who you are, if you're an undercover officer, there are times you can become involved with the people you work with. You figure you're with him three and a half months, and George is a personable guy. A funny guy. A nice guy. I've seen where he could get mean, but I never saw him become violent. You don't feel bad he's going to jail because he deserves to go to jail. You don't have regrets, obviously, but you think to yourself, 'You know, it's too bad. Under a different situation, you might develop a friendly relationship. Under normal conditions he probably would have been a good guy to know.'"

ELEVEN

Jacksonville

1987

Dylan said, "Ain't no use in calling out my name, babe, I'm on the dark side of the road." Well, I'm there! And it's rock bottom, believe me
—LETTER TO MIRTHA FROM GEORGE JUNG AT THE UNITED
STATES PENITENTIARY, LEWISBURG, PENNSYLVANIA

AS DISCONCERTING AS THE BUST WAS TO GEORGE, THE conduct of the arresting officers also caused no small uproar among the well-to-do residents of Fort Lauderdale's Riverland Isles neighborhood. And their complaints received more than passing attention in a story bannered across the top of the front page in Monday morning's *News and Sun-Sentinel*, overshadowing even the story about the arrest. "Those cars—sixteen to twenty of them—came roaring in here at 50 mph. Machine guns. Regular guns. Cops with hats that read 'Miami Vice.' It was like a war zone. They couldn't even put anything like that in the *movies*," said one woman, whom the reporter described as "visibly shaken" by the event. "You want the bad guys caught, but you don't want to put yourself and your family in jeopardy," another homeowner was quoted as saying. "This type of thing really puts the neighborhood in danger."

For George, of course, the arrest procedures and their aftermath had become a depressingly familiar scenario in recent years. After prying him away from their hyperventilating colleagues, Tom,

Greg, and Mike inveighed upon George to make a couple of phone calls to the Colombians in Miami; if they couldn't nab the principals involved in the deal, they'd at least bag the two guys who'd been acting as the go-betweens. George readily agreed to help out, thinking that playing the hard-ass was hardly going to do his case any good. He was then taken to be booked and transported to the North Dade Detention Center, a county facility that rented out cell space for housing federal prisoners.

Along the way, someone had logged in his personal effects the police had found back in his room at the Holiday Inn, which comprised pretty much all he owned these days, besides the clothes on his back—and not to mention the $68 million he hoped was down in Panama. Going through his bag, they found George had already supplied himself with the documents he'd need for traveling to a foreign clime—birth certificates for two deceased males born in the early 1940s in Dedham and Melrose, Massachusetts, along with a couple of applications for U.S. passports. There was a *Time* magazine appointment book for the year 1983, with the telephone number of his parents scrawled in the back along with that of Leon Harbuck. There were picture postcards Mirtha had sent him from trips to Big Sur, of the cliffs overlooking the beach up at Mendocino. "The coast is beautiful," she wrote on one of them, and expressed the wish that they could see it together someday. The police also found a three-inch-square snapshot of Kristina taken on her sixth birthday the year before. She's smiling into the camera, her paper hat affixed to her head with a rubber band, a Coke in one hand and an ice-cream cone in the other.

Sitting in jail, George had plenty of time to think ruefully, self-disgustedly, over how he could possibly have fallen for all the deception and the games played on him during the past three and a half months. His pain at having been so thoroughly fooled reached its zenith one night about a month after he got there, when a segment of ABC-TV's "World News Tonight," came on the tube, scoring high in the jailhouse Nielsens for the fact that it featured an interview with a former drug smuggler who earned his living working as a confidential informant helping the DEA conduct stings on old associates. The son of a bitch was dressed up for the camera in a phony beard and had on dark glasses and a watch cap pulled down over his forehead. But to anyone who'd known him as long as George had, no amount of disguise could hide the fact that staring out at him from the TV monitor was his old pal and good buddy, Cliff Guttersrud.

The next ritual in the process consisted of visits by the lawyers. Following up on the large play George's arrest had gotten in the Fort Lauderdale press, a half dozen or so attorneys specializing in drug cases made appointments to see him at North Dade to try to get his business. "They came in, one after the other," he recalls. "'We can do this,' and 'We can do that.' 'Help you make some kind of a deal.' I'd been through it fifty times before. 'George, if they taped you on the telephone, did they have proper warrants from the judge? Did they go through proper procedures? Protect your constitutional rights? Otherwise we can get it thrown out.' I mean, you're caught red-handed, and they try actually to make you believe you have a chance to fight it. In my mind, you're already stupid enough to get arrested, but if you're stupid enough to believe that bullshit, which a lot of people are, then you deserve to spend the rest of your life in jail. After they get done with their spiel, they talk about the money they think you've got stashed away. 'We can work any kind of a deal you want on the money. If you've got money hidden, I can send someone, or if you've got gold buried, or diamonds, whatever you have, tell us where it is, whatever country it's in, and we'll go get it and protect you.' They're like barracudas. The people they really take are the Colombians—usually some poor bastard they've got dead to rights, and the lawyers will take a quarter of a million dollars from him, and then after they lose the case, they tell him, 'Give me another quarter of a million, and we'll win an appeal.' They aren't going to win any appeal! The conviction rate in federal courts is something like 96 percent. The federal government has unlimited resources, and when they come after your ass, they're fucking ready."

The lawyer he eventually chose was a British transplant to Florida named Maurice Graham, who'd followed a younger brother to the States for better employment opportunities after college and had first hung out his shingle in Lauderdale in the 1970s. "You start off with whoever comes in the door, shoplifters, home closings," Graham says. Gradually, he began specializing in marijuana defendants and had a couple of airplane cases that got some attention in the media, spreading the word that even if your case looked hopeless, here was a fellow who could get you off. One of them involved a plane loaded up with marijuana that lost its way in bad weather and made an emergency landing on the shores of Lake Okeechobee, on the grounds of an Indian reservation. The tribal police chief impounded the plane, the county sheriff arrived, and a squabble ensued about who had jurisdiction. With the issue somewhat up in the air, Graham was able to negotiate with the prosecutor a deal where the pilot would get five years' probation and a fine of ten thousand dollars. "Then I looked the fellow right in the eye, I'm ashamed to admit, and I told him, 'Look, there's no way this guy can raise ten thousand dollars in that time. Why not give him a twenty-thousand-dollar fine and indefinite probation until he comes up with the money?' The prosecutor is thinking that this way he'll have the poor guy on probation, have a hold on him for the rest of his natural life. And so he agreed. The very next day, the pilot walked into his office with a paper bag containing twenty thousand dollars, paid his fine, and flew off into the sunset, having been on probation for twenty-four hours. We got quite a lot of cases after that."

Since then, Graham had graduated to representing cocaine defendants, whose business was considerably more lucrative; but by the time George came around he was losing his stomach for it, especially when it meant going into federal court. For one thing, there was a new ruling that allowed prosecutors to go after a defense lawyer's fee if he could show it was paid from illegally gotten gains. Considering the money involved, this was offering an increasingly tempting gambit where cocaine cases were concerned. Federal judges in the Reagan years also seemed to be growing more conservative, allowing prosecutors wider latitude, from Graham's point of view, on the admissibility of evidence. And unlike the state judiciaries, the federal courts had guidelines preventing the use of before-trial depositions taken from the police to impeach their testimony or cause them confusion when they appeared on the stand. If he could depose the officers first, then grill them during the trial, Graham could often come up with significant inconsistencies. "It's not easy for people to tell the exact same story about a situation if they have to tell it twice," he says.

In talking to George, Graham gave some of the same spiel as the others did, about how the case might actually be won. Entrapment wasn't much of a defense here, because with George's smuggling history it would be difficult to show he harbored no predisposition to commit the crime. Nevertheless, he said, the authorities had behaved disgracefully during the sting, having made several significant gaffes that could prove useful in muddying up the prosecution case before a jury. "In the first place, the guys George had fallen in with here were hopelessly inept smugglers who couldn't possibly have committed the crime without the help of the police." The police provided George a place to stay, on their own boat and then at hotels. They gave him money for meals and also for booze. They'd gotten him the airplane. They'd found him the pilot, a place to land. "Here's a guy who's just gotten out of prison, with nothing but the clothes on his back. He knew people in South America who had cocaine, but he could never have pulled it off by himself." Then there was the fact that the police, together with those who worked for them, that is, Cliff Guttersrud, had come very close to committing some serious crimes themselves. One instance Graham planned to bring up was their involvement in the Harbuck kidnapping caper—which amounted to tolerating the commission of a major felony in order to keep the sting alive. According to George, Cliff had also lent him his 9-millimeter Mauser pistol to carry around for protection while they were both living on the boat. He'd gotten George some pot to smoke, helped him meet girls. The way Graham would have put it, the police had supplied guns and drugs and women to a known escaped fugitive from a state prison. Where do you draw the line? "In view of the tremendous sentence George was faced with," Graham recounts, "I felt we had to try it. Either that, or use it to the extent we could to convince the prosecutor that it was going to be a long and expensive case to win." Not to mention hugely embarrassing.

This latter strategy struck George as the smart way to go in this instance, especially since Graham assured him he had good relations with Lurana Snow, the assistant United States attorney who would be prosecuting the case. "What I liked about Graham is he didn't give me any of the bullshit about going before a jury," says George. "He said Lurana Snow was a friend of his and that he could make a deal. That's what I listened to." Which is eventually what happened. It took the better part of a year, but in the end, considering his record, George got better than he had any right to expect. In the indictment he had been accused on four counts, two of importing and possession of cocaine with the intention to distribute and two more of conspiring with others to import and distribute. Coming up, as he would be, before Judge Norman Roettger, the hangingest federal judge in the whole Southeast, each count could have brought him a sentence of fifteen years in prison, a total of sixty years, with George walking out a free man at around age 104. But Graham's presentation to the prosecutor, emphasizing George's willingness to help with the other busts, the arguably questionable police conduct during the sting, and the expense and trouble involved in taking the case to trial, succeeded in getting the charges reduced to a single count. George would do fifteen years.

"He knew I was fucked," George says. "And I knew I was fucked. This was the best way out of it. Fifteen years is no walk in the park, but it's better than sixty. And there was the money sitting in Panama. So I was prepared to do it." At least up until he got wind of a couple of FBI agents named Richie Garcia and Bobby Levinson, and heard what they were shopping around for.

As much as George's circumstances had altered in the past eight years, so had those of his old *compadre* in crime, Carlos Lehder. Norman Cay had received so much notoriety in the press, including being featured in an outraged documentary by NBC News, that the Bahamian parliament was embarrassed into funding an investigation by a royal commission into bribery and drug-running throughout the islands. Where payoffs were concerned, the commission found out readily enough that Prime Minister Lynden Pindling's expenditures had far exceeded his income, but it couldn't prove that the overage came from drug smugglers. In any event, Norman Cay was becoming too hot for Carlos in the early 1980s, and by 1983 he'd returned to Colombia, where he bought a cattle ranch and began spending his millions to further his dreams of achieving national power. About 125 miles south of Medellín, on the outskirts of his native Armenia, he built a sprawling alpine resort named Posada Alemana, to rival the Hacienda Veracruz owned by the Ochoas and also Pablo Escobar's Hacienda los Nápoles, where George had seen the police informer shot several years earlier. Built at a cost of $3 million, the complex contained a restaurant of gourmet pretensions, a good-sized zoo and wired-in aviary, swimming pools, and thirty separate guest villas, two stories tall and covered in thatch. Carlos also built a discotheque at the place, naming it after his musical muse, John Lennon, whose utopian reverie "Imagine" had been Carlos's all-time favorite song. He hired the noted Colombian architect, Rodrigo Arenas Betancourt, to design a life-size statue of the late Beatle and installed it at the entrance to the *posada*. The statue shows Lennon standing naked, his right hand holding on to a guitar, his left displaying the letters *PAZ* for "peace," and the assassin's bullet wound visible in his back.

On the political side, Carlos organized the Movimento Latino Nacional, a party that used Colombian nationalism as a guise for railing against extraditing drug traffickers to the United States. He assigned to himself the title of "maximum chief" and installed a twelve-foot-high poster of himself at the party's headquarters in downtown Armenia. In speeches to the faithful he would rant on like a junior-varsity Hitler, saying that the rabbis collected taxes for Israel and laying blame for all the terrorism and oppression in Latin America at the feet of "international Zionism." A bunch of youthful thugs called Woodchoppers maintained decorum at party rallies, marching around in khaki uniforms and hard hats and brandishing four-foot truncheons. In a weekly newspaper published by the party, *Quindio Libre*, the editor regularly praised Carlos as "a man of a new era, captain of the seas and the skies."

It all didn't last very long. Unbeknownst to Carlos, in the late 1970s and 1980, the United States attorney for the Middle District of Florida, based in Jacksonville, had been gathering evidence about Carlos's activities in the States, as well as the drug operation on Norman Cay. In January of 1981 he'd succeeded in getting a federal grand jury to indict Carlos and thirteen of his American confederates and pilots on thirty-nine counts of cocaine smuggling and income-tax evasion. The prosecutor, a 245-pound former running back at Notre Dame named Robert W. Merkle, had flown the indictments down to Colombia himself and presented them to the supreme court in Bogotá for a ruling on their constitutionality. On September 2, 1983, the court decided in favor of the United States. Immediately afterward, the justice minister, Rodrigo Lara Bonilla, signed the papers, sent them on to President Belisario Betancur for his signature, and promptly issued a warrant for Carlos's arrest. Almost overnight the maximum chief had become a fugitive from justice and took himself off into hiding. His political party collapsed, his zoo animals were taken away to save them from starving, the *posada* fell into ruins, and a year later it was all but destroyed by an unexplained fire.

George wasn't the only one who'd experienced a comedown.

In 1986 agents Garcia and Levinson were stationed in the Miami office of the FBI as part of something called the Joint Drug

Intelligence Group, working with their counterparts at the DEA to develop knowledge about the Medellín cartel and other South American drug operations. Normally the two agencies get along about as nicely as Israelis and Arabs, but here the object was to develop intelligence jointly, then take it back to their respective organizations for use in whatever way seemed appropriate, so there was little opportunity for rivalry. "Part of the assignment involved debriefing people in prison in an attempt to get together all the pieces of the puzzle so we could see the big picture," says Garcia, the senior partner on the team, whose darkish complexion, brush-cut mustache, and stern eyes make him resemble Burt Reynolds. Garcia had earned a B.S. in law enforcement from Southwest Texas State University, an M.S. in management and human relations from Abilene Christian University, and he came to the Bureau after five years on the Dallas Police Department. Both his wife and his brother are FBI agents. He wears white shirts and conservative dark suits and speaks fluent Spanish.

"We were getting every little bit of information we could, every little scribble and piece," he says. "As one person put it, we debrief people by putting a vacuum to their head and in two or three days sucking out every bit of knowledge they have." At this point the FBI was treating drug traffickers like agents of a foreign power, and when they found one who agreed to talk, they grilled him as they would have a Communist defector. "'What is your part in the organization? Who did you report to? Who did that person report to? What forms of communications do you use? How do you recruit people?' We'd get all the names, full descriptions, who they were related to, addresses, phone numbers. 'What numbers did they know you had?' Step by step by step, until we got to the point where they start to say, 'I think,' or, 'It could be.' And we put that part over on the fuzzy side."

To mask the identity of those they talked to, Garcia and Levinson would arrange for federal marshals to take the people out of the two major lockups in the region, North Dade and the Miami Metropolitan Correctional Center, and escort them to the federal courthouse, supposedly for a hearing on their cases, then they would whisk them down another corridor, where the two agents would be waiting in a borrowed office. George showed up one day as a surprise. He came in with another North Dade inmate they'd been talking to named Danny McGinniss. Danny had been arrested as part of what to law-enforcement people was a famous marijuana sting conducted by the DEA called Operation Grouper, named for the way the bales of pot dropped into water by drug planes had resembled fish of that name. For his involvement, Danny had been convicted of being part of a continuing criminal enterprise, or CCE, and sentenced to sixty years in prison. He'd been talking to the FBI for a while now in a fruitless attempt to shave some years off the sentence, when one day at North Dade he met this celebrity prisoner who was related to high-ups in the cartel and had been picked up in a big cocaine bust up in Fort Lauderdale.

"Danny's problem," says George, "was he waited too long to play the game. By the time he was ready to talk, they knew everything he knew, and anyway, it was only marijuana, whereas I had the fucking cartel in my pocket. He was a streetwise Irishman from Connecticut, I think it was, and he thought by getting me involved he could help himself out. So he came over one day and asked me if I'd be interested in talking to some friends of his. And I said, sure."

"My first impression of George was that he'd been 'rode hard,' he'd been through the mill," recalls Garcia. "He looked a lot older than he was, and I think he was getting at his wit's end. So when he showed up with McGinniss, he didn't know *why* he was here, but he knew he wanted to *be* here. He knew he had got arrested with three hundred kilos and he knew he had to do something to try to get out of that." The agents were certainly right that George had a goal, but not so right in thinking he didn't have any idea about how to reach it. He did. And not long after he began talking to Garcia and Levinson, he made it clearly known to them in only two words: Carlos Lehder.

They knew in a vague way that George had once done some work with Carlos, but they were ignorant of the Danbury connection and the closeness the two of them once shared. And they knew nothing about the depth of George's fury at being thrown over back in 1977, a humiliation now nearly nine years old, but which George had never managed to overcome. The FBI certainly didn't know about the hit he'd almost attempted, and George wasn't going to tell them. He'd give them just enough now to dwell on the falling-out they'd had, give himself a plausible reason to be sitting there in the first place, willing to tell them what they wanted to know. "I get the sense he didn't know how far to take this with us," Garcia recalls. "He didn't know what was in it for him, deal-wise. We said we couldn't promise anything, of course. The three hundred kilos was between him and the DEA. 'But any information you give us we will make known to the judge, and you go from there.'"

Garcia and Levinson knew that here in their grasp was one of the best information sources they'd ever turned up on the cartel; it was difficult to fathom how the DEA had passed this one up. "Here we had a source, not like someone who'd worked as just a pilot at one point in time. This was a different caliber of individual we had. He wasn't a runner. He was actually one of the founders of this thing. And we had no reason to doubt what he was saying. We were checking the details he'd tell us as we went along, and it was all coming back right."

So they took out Danny and George on a daily basis now, Danny more or less so he wouldn't feel left out of the deal and spread the word on what was going on around the lockup. They had the marshals switch the delivery site from the courthouse to a plush suite at the Omni Hotel in downtown Miami, where the agents supplied them little nips of Scotch from the bar, ordered up steak and lobster for lunch and dinner. And where they'd talk. And talk. Ten or fifteen days of solid grilling went by, during which George told them more than even he realized he knew about Carlos, how the cocaine business worked, what he'd seen on his trips down to Medellín. It went on like that until the day arrived when he told them he'd just about depleted all his knowledge on the subject, but now he had another idea.

Instead of just *talking* about Carlos Lehder, why not try to catch him? Wasn't that the object here—to actually lay their hands on the guy? It was a day Garcia remembers very well, when the purpose of these little sessions at the Omni switched from gathering intelligence on the cartel to discussing how to launch an actual operation against it. "Levinson said, 'Well, I don't know.' And I asked George, 'Okay, but will Carlos Lehder leave Colombia?' And George says, 'Yeah, he'll leave Colombia, if he has a reason to leave.' So, like what? we're thinking. Women? Money? No, it has to be something real big. 'Well,' I said, 'what about if we had a way to offer him Stinger missiles? He's that type of military guy, be into that kind of thing.'

"George's eyes light up. 'Yeah! But how do we do it?' 'No problem. For instance, we get you out, and we get you down to Colombia. You make friends with Carlos again, and you tell him you've got a contact for Stinger missiles. This guy has these Stinger missiles. And you meet him out at sea. You call him up to the Bahamas, you'd be on a sailboat, in international waters, with Stinger missiles. And we get Carlos on the boat. Maybe we even have a Stinger he can hold on to, give him a dummy that you can't fire. After we get him on the boat and verify him, the Coast Guard, navy, whatever, a Seal team, come by and we take him. We got him!'"

It took several more sessions for them to figure out how exactly it might work. There was no doubt, once they'd been mentioned, that the Stingers were the proper draw. "You had all these revolutionary groups down there, FARC and M-19, having a constant war and such," says Garcia. "Stinger missiles would go over pretty big. They had good press from the Afghan war at the time. That's where I really thought of the idea from. It's portable. Carlos would be like the new kid on the block with a better weapon. We knew from sources that Carlos Lehder was in the jungle at the time. Sources we were talking to said he really wanted to battle it out with the government. We had a source who said one time Lehder showed up at a meeting the Ochoas and Escobar were at with crossed *bandoleras* and hand grenades hanging off his belt, yelling and screaming, 'We ought to kill these people! Go in fighting!' We figure George goes down there saying he's got a guy with a load of Stingers, Carlos would light up and come right out and get them, especially since he's being chased by the Colombian military and their helicopters. They'd figure now they could shoot them down."

Garcia thought of luring him on to a sailboat rather than a big powerboat, he says, because powerboats got heavy attention from law-enforcement types in the area. Sailboats fitted right in with the tourist traffic. He had in mind a Morgan 45 sloop, which he'd sailed himself when stationed in the Bureau's Puerto Rico office. "You didn't want something that would flag attention to us. The Morgan 45 is a beautiful boat, teak deck, teak finish, nice stereo system. It could hold five or ten missiles. But it's not something out of James Bond. It was less likely to be boarded by the Coast Guard or the DEA." But wouldn't the DEA be let in on the deal, help the FBI bring off the sting? he was asked. Garcia's expression went a little stony at this suggestion. "The DEA?"

The mechanics would need to be finely tuned. They'd have to decide whether to stage an actual break at an armory, for instance, or just feed a phony story to the press, to convince them down in

Colombia that the missiles were on the street. The plan would have to be pushed up through channels, first at FBI headquarters in Washington, and, if approved there, at the Department of Justice. Something this big would need the express approval of Attorney General Edwin Meese. Then they had to devise a way to bolster George's credibility. The Colombians would have to feel good enough about him to take him to Carlos. After all, George had hated Carlos for so long, and here he's just been busted for three hundred kilos. The first thing anyone's going to think is that he's turned into a fink to save his skin, which, of course, he had.

That's when they arrived at the escape. It would happen in Miami, while Garcia and Levinson were transporting George and Danny McGinniss from jail to one of their supposed court hearings. And it must be totally believable, even inside the Bureau. "It would have to be done where myself and Mr. Levinson would be the persons actually called on the carpet for losing a prisoner. In order to make it so believable the agents themselves that we worked with would have to believe that we screwed up. We'd have to go through the whole nine yards, of an investigation by the Office of Professional Responsibility, which is the internal-affairs unit. We'd probably get time on the bricks, time off without pay. Censored, for whatever negligence there was."

But they didn't want to go overboard. There were limits, after all, to their willingness to become the Bureau's laughing stock. "We were going to try to work it so it wasn't really our fault; it was circumstances that caused it to happen. The way I was thinking, we'd have Dan and George out the way we'd normally been doing, transporting them to the place. We would stage an automobile accident, crack a car up against a pole, not right on Main Street but in a neighborhood somewhere a little out of the way. Crack up the car and stage an unconsciousness, to the extent where George would escape, but not Dan. One of us would be out cold, and the other would be semi-out cold, and he's the one who grabs McGinniss. Dan didn't like that part of the idea too much. But I told him flat out, 'Dan, you've got a sixty-year sentence. There is no way I'm going to let you go. Forget about that pipe dream.'

"But publicity-wise, it would be in the papers, one guy out cold, everybody injured. The concept of George escaping would be credibility in itself for why he would show up in Colombia. There'd be stories all over the news. Maybe shots fired, we hadn't worked that out yet. But George would be in the right front seat, the driver knocked out, the door pops open, and George, who's handcuffed behind his back, gets out. The guy in the back is cushioned in the crash by the seats, so he grabs McGinniss, but George is going off and we can't catch him. He gets away. Of course he wouldn't really escape. He'd be running into a net of people who'd know it was a staged deal, and would get him away from the area to another place and hide him out and smuggle him back into Colombia. We had to get him out of the area, because whoever wasn't unconscious would grab on to the radio and be calling it in, 'We've had an accident, we've got a prisoner on the ground, da dah, da dah, da dah.' So you really don't want George running around, because we don't want him caught by the team coming out to investigate."

The car hits a pole? A staged unconsciousness? A phony break-in at an armory? Stinger missiles? Where'd he get this idea? "I don't know," he says. "I might have seen it in the movies."

George contributed a few suggestions of his own during the discussions, touches here and there to move the operation into the realm of high-concept, so it wouldn't look like it was run by a bunch of pikers. "He wanted us to provide him with a nice yacht of his own for him to sail down to Colombia on from his escape, something about a hundred feet long. We'd give him all this money, and he'd have all these women on board, have access to an airplane when he got there, one he could call up when he wanted. He wanted to be set up like some millionaire. Sail down there, have access to villas at places in the Bahamas along the way, pick up Carlos himself in his boat. And his idea was it was going to be a long trip, take him a couple of months to make it down there." The others looked on in silence as George laid out how it should really happen, if they wanted to do the thing properly. "I remember I didn't say a word. I was just staring at George. And he finally stopped and said, 'Ah, come on, Richard. What's the matter?'"

In the end, to everyone's dismay if not surprise, the Bureau chickened out. Garcia and Levinson had written up a brief description of their proposal, even came up with a code name, Cap-Tel, for "Capture Cartel"—and fired it on up the chain of command. In its rough outline the idea reached as far as an assistant section chief at headquarters in Washington, who told Garcia he was vetoing it on the grounds that he just couldn't picture the Justice Department signing off on something requiring such audacity. "We knew it would be a hard sell," says Garcia. "But conservatism was taking place, where the reaction was, 'Let's not try this right now.' The Bureau was just at the point of coming out with a national drug strategy as far as how to approach investigations. Headquarters was still growing as far as how they're going to be doing things. In Miami, you learn quickly about how far you can go. What's feasible for us in Miami is really off the wall for them in Washington, because they had not been exposed to what we'd been exposed to. With all the debriefing we'd been doing, Levinson and I thought we had a pretty good idea of what would fly and what wouldn't fly. But this was not the sort of institutional knowledge that they had in Washington."

As it worked out, Garcia never had to inform George that their grand scheme had been nixed. For on February 4, 1987, while he was watching TV in the day room at North Dade, the same set on which he spotted Cliff Guttersrud more than a year and a half before, George caught a news story out of Bogotá, Colombia. The screen showed a bunch of DEA agents on some military installation hustling a short, tousle-haired figure in handcuffs into the body of an Aerocommander turboprop jet, which was warming up to take off for Tampa, Florida. The guy they were loading into the plane, without a single scrap of help from George, was Carlos Lehder.

Most people in a position to know believe that Carlos had made himself into such a loudmouthed nuisance as far as the reigning cartel members were concerned that they were the ones who turned him in. The story given out to the press was that the caretaker of a mountainside chalet in a pine forest outside Medellín had been grousing to a friend about a large party of men who had rented the house, complaining about the loud partying they were doing and the way they were messing up the place in general. The friend passed on the complaint to a local constable, and the constable called a major in the national police named William Lemus, who just happened to be in the Medellín area looking around for Carlos. Major Lemus went up to nose around and hid in the bushes until he saw a man walking the grounds who looked like Lehder. The next morning he returned with a force of men, and after a brief firefight, Lemus himself nabbed Carlos, leveling on him with his pistol. "Little chief, don't shoot me," Carlos is supposed to have begged. That was on February 4, 1987. By 1:15 A.M. the following morning, the DEA landed with him at the airport in Tampa.

Whether the tip on where Carlos was hiding arrived via the caretaker, the caretaker's friend, or the constable, there seems little doubt that the ultimate dime on Carlos was dropped by Escobar and the Ochoas. "From my understanding, talking to sources, the cartel members were saying to each other that Lehder was off the wall," says Garcia. "They were under a lot of pressure. There were these extraditions involved. They'd be in danger of losing a lot of support they might have for sovereignty in Colombia, to get rid of the extradition law, if this guy keeps doing what he's doing. My personal belief is the cartel set up Lehder. The government wants someone to extradite? They want to take a token person? Let them take Carlos. He's a whacko. He should be out of here anyway. And he's gone!"

Gone from Colombia, and now in the possession of the United States government, but the task of convicting Carlos in a court of law still lay ahead. Like George, Agent Garcia had also heard the news about the capture from TV, during a trip he had to make to Boston. "My first thought was, 'Oh, boy, I bet old Dan and George, their hearts are down in their stomachs right now.' I called George from Boston and asked him what about testifying? I told him, 'I think you should do it. It's the right thing to do. And all the revenge you felt? You wanted to be in on his capture. Well, he's already captured. Now your best thing to do is to sit right there in the courtroom and look him straight in the eye and tell them what he did.'" George said no, he didn't think he'd do that. He told Garcia that the code he'd followed ever since he first became involved in the marijuana business mandated that you don't give people up. It was one thing to pull off a slick operation like the one they'd been planning, to go down on a boat and nab Carlos himself; it was something else to come slithering into the courtroom and open up on him from the witness chair like a rat, like a *rata*. "He didn't seem ready to change his mind," says Garcia. "So I said, 'Fine, George.' And that's the way we left it."

George did testify in the end. In fact, he opened the proceedings as the leadoff witness, playing one of the two starring roles in the whole trial, along with another convicted smuggler named Ed Ward, who had worked directly for Carlos on Norman Cay. The turnaround in George's attitude had come in the spring of 1987, after a number of things happened to alter his perspective on life in general. One of them was a peek he got inside a heavy-duty federal prison, which convinced him that the existence there promised to be significantly less jovial than what he'd experienced at Danbury. In a bureaucratic mix-up, before his plea bargain had become official, he was sent off to the United States Penitentiary in Lewisburg, Pennsylvania, one of six maximum-security institutions on the federal roster, along with ones in Atlanta, Georgia; Leavenworth, Kansas; Lompoc, California; Terre Haute, Indiana; and Marion, Illinois. For some unexplained reason, he was thrown immediately on arrival into an administrative segregation cell, the hole, that is, along with a wiry, hyperactive Mexican-American murderer from Texas with tear-gas burns all over his body from where the guards had had to subdue him whenever he went berserk in his cell. "He's got skulls tattooed all over his arms and chest with knives sticking through the eyes, a huge Virgin Mary on his back," recalls George. "He's jabbering to himself all the time, washing himself constantly in the toilet bowl. I said to myself, 'Jesus, you've really done it this time.' Even once I got out of the hole, the atmosphere in that place you could cut it with a knife, nobody smiled or laughed. There weren't a lot of guys you'd want to hang around with. I had my little talk with the caseworker, and he wasn't anything like the guy at Danbury, who tried to help you. It was, 'What I've got to say to you is, Here, you stay with your own group, you mind your own business, and you keep your back to the wall at all times. Fuck up at Lewisburg, you go to Marion, and that's the last stop on the bus.'"

It took six weeks before George convinced the authorities of their mistake and got himself transferred back to North Dade. That was when he decided finally to send one of the lawyers who'd been paying him court down to check on his money in Panama. If he was going to do the time, he wanted to be sure there was something pleasant to think about as it went by, to know there'd be a happy ending to his life story, at least on the material side of things. He found a lawyer who'd been recommended by Maurice Graham; he was a big man with a bushy beard who smoked a Meerschaum pipe. Even though back at Danbury Fat Harry had told him one of the things he'd learned long ago was never to trust anyone who smoked a pipe, no matter what kind it was, George gave the lawyer the account number and sent him to Panama City. The lawyer was gone for about ten days. When he got back, he told George he'd found the account all right, still active. And it had had an awful lot of money in it during the time George was shipping cash down in the late 1970s and early 1980s. But checking the bank's calculations, setting off the money that went in against the money that got withdrawn at various points, he came up with the same result the bank did, which was a balance of zero. There was nothing there, George. Just a big double aught. The motor sailer, the beaches on Ibiza, just a life without having to go to work and slave for a dollar—he could pack all that away, put it into the category of a dream he'd had during the night and woken up from early in the morning and found that it was all gone and that, indeed, it never was.

So there he had it, the empty bank account to ponder. He'd heard of this happening to other guys who'd sent money down to Noriega-land, but knowing he had company in his expanding sense of misery gave him precious small comfort now. Then he found out about the letter. He saw it in a story in the *Miami Herald* one morning. It was written to Vice President George Bush from Carlos, sitting in the Atlanta penitentiary, where a whole tier had been emptied of prisoners so he could have the thing entirely to himself. Carlos told the head of the war on drugs that he wanted to make a deal. In return for immunity from prosecution, he'd tell everything he knew about the drug business. He'd turn in all the operatives he'd relied on in his network, the hundreds of Colombians and Americans he'd dealt with from Miami to Los Angeles. He'd tell the police anything they wanted to know about Escobar and the other cartel figures. He'd say anything they wanted him to say in court, against anyone they wanted to put up. Just let him get out of jail free, let him leave the country, and he'd promise never to smuggle drugs again.

The Reagan administration making a deal on the eve of an election year with the biggest cartel figure they'd ever caught, a man they'd billed as evil incarnate, seemed about as likely a prospect as Carlos had of levitating the walls around Atlanta and crawling out from underneath. But to George, the letter itself, just the brashness of it, came as the final insult. Given even the remotest possibility that at any time in the future Carlos might be walking the streets somewhere as a free man, while George was rotting in a place like Lewisburg, making conversation with people covered with skulls and daggers, moved his hand as if it had a will of its own toward the pay phone in the dayroom at North Dade to begin the negotiations on a deal. The first person he called was Mirtha, out on the West Coast. He told her to call down to Humberto in Medellín, and to have Humberto call Pablo Escobar and tell him the circumstances, and ask if it would be okay with him if George took the stand against Carlos. In two days the word came back from Pablo, through the same network in reverse. It was actually two words: "Fuck him."

Thus it was that George next placed a phone call to Agent Richard Garcia at the FBI. He'd had some time now to think over what Garcia had said to him right after Carlos's capture, and he'd concluded that Richie was right, that testifying against Carlos was the right thing to do. He told Garcia to tell Merkle, the U.S. attorney in Jacksonville who would be prosecuting the case, that George Jung was on the team. "Maybe I might have testified eventually anyway, but I don't think so, not without that letter," says George. "It was too much. I mean, looking back, the first person Carlos put in the box, the 'fuck-you box,' was me. Then he put Richard Barile in the fuck-you box. Then he put Nick Hunter in the fuck-you box. Then he put Barry Kane in the fuck-you box. Then he put Ed Ward and all the people on Norman Cay in the fuck-you box. And pretty soon the box was filled up with 150 people, looking like a bunch of broken rag dolls in a toy chest with their stuffing all coming out. Then one day it was as if they all got out of the box at once, and now Carlos was in the box, and they all came to his trial and said, *fuck you*.'"

The trial itself, in the U.S. courthouse in Jacksonville, rated easily as one of the most exciting events in the city's history. Parking was banned on all the adjacent streets. Snipers patrolled the rooftop, alert for an attack by narcoterrorists. Dogs with the ability to sniff out bombs patrolled the corridors inside the building. Metal detectors at the entrances were cranked down so low you had to take off your shoes so the metal eyelets and the nails in the soles wouldn't set off the alarm.

In his three-hour opening statement to the jury of nine women and three men, Merkle charged that "Carlos Lehder was to cocaine transportation as Henry Ford was to automobiles." As George's contribution toward proving that contention, he sat in the witness box for three days and gave testimony about Carlos that filled up 564 pages of transcript. He told all about their meeting at Danbury and the dream they shared of cornering the transportation market. He told about hooking up with Carlos after prison. He told about the first suitcase trip from Antigua. He told about introducing Carlos to Barry Kane. To show how close George had been to Carlos, Merkle introduced into evidence Carlos's marriage license from Canada, when George had stood up as his best man. "And does your signature appear on that document, sir?" Merkle asked with some theatricality.

"Yes, it does," George answered. "Approximately an inch above the date."

Merkle led him through Carlos's tramp through the Vermont woods, even produced one of the customs people to bolster the story. George told the jury all about the red-eye flights to Los Angeles, the hundreds of kilos they unloaded through Barile, the heavy amount of money that was beginning to roll in. That BMW Carlos had bought for cash in Hyannis? Just as George had warned, it returned to haunt him when Merkle produced the manager of the dealership so he could point the guy out to the jury who'd given him eleven thousand dollars in a paper bag. George told them about his trip to Norman Cay, their falling-out, about going to see Fat Harry when George wanted to set up a hit. In all, Merkle paraded 115 witnesses past the jury, along with providing them stacks and stacks of documents, so they could see the aircraft and boats that Carlos owned, the dummy corporations he'd set up. Merkle even put Walter Cronkite, the former CBS anchorman, on the stand, to describe how abruptly he'd been run off of Norman Cay. At the close of this piece of testimony, Merkle lowered his voice an octave or two, gearing it down to broadcast level, and asked, "Was that the way it was, Mr. Cronkite?"

"Yes," Cronkite answered. "That's the way it was."

For a fee reputed to be somewhere between $1.5 and $2 million, Carlos had hired two Miami defense lawyers who were already well known in the society of moneyed cocaine defendants, Edward Shohat and José Quiñón. "This is the type of case that represents to us the highest mountain, and we're going after it," Quiñón was quoted as saying, "This is our Everest." Throughout the trial they referred to their client as "Joe" Lehder, an early alias of Carlos's, in an apparent effort to de-Colombianize him for the jury. Their basic argument turned out to be that Joe was a much maligned and misunderstood businessman, whose activities on Norman Cay had nothing to do with cocaine whatsoever. Lengthening the airstrip, building the hangars and such, that was all part of a plan to make the island into a tourist resort. All this testimony to the contrary, they said, that was just part of "Pick-on-Joe-Lehder Month." Carlos himself never took the stand during his trial, and his lawyers presented not a single witness in his defense. Instead, they concentrated their guns on the cross-examination, grilling the prosecution witnesses, twenty-nine of whom had been convicted of one drug offense or another, in an effort to show the jury that these people were all lying about Carlos in order to get a reduction in their sentences or get out of jail altogether. One of the worst of these, they said in their opening statement, was George Jung. Yet when his turn came to be cross-examined, on the fourth day of the trial, George not only managed to keep his story well intact, but in the fencing battle with Quiñón, he gave just about as good as he got.

Q: Knowing you to have used people before when it fits your interest, would you be using Mr. Lehder in this case in order to lower your prison sentence maybe?

A: Do you really believe that?

Q: I'm asking the questions.

A: Then, no. . . .

Q: And when you wrote down that you had been to Pablo Escobar's farm numerous times weren't you trying to sort of puff up your importance in this case, to see if you can get a better deal, better letter from the government, to see if they will reduce your parole and your sentence? Were you trying to do that, knowing Pablo Escobar to be somebody who has been publicized?

A: No. I didn't have to expand my role. I was married into a Colombian family that is tied in to people down there. That was well known. I didn't have to exaggerate my role. I mean, I was arrested in 1985 with 660 pounds of cocaine, and, in essence, they suddenly confiscated more on the airstrip, close to 3,000 pounds of cocaine. I don't believe that I had to exaggerate my role with 3,000 pounds of cocaine.

Regarding the matter of George's aborted hit against Carlos, Quiñón tried to suggest that he'd invented Carlos's whole betrayal of him as a way to support the fact that he'd had any meaningful relationship with Carlos in the first place.

Q: How long had you known Fat Harry?

A: In effect, I met him while in Danbury.

Q: Okay. And did you go as far as to discuss the amount of money that it would take to do a hit?

A: He was looking more to that, once Lehder was eliminated, a partnership effect, taking over where Lehder left off.

Q: And these discussions took place with Fat Harry?

A: That's correct.

Q: All right. Was anybody else present in addition to Fat Harry?

A: No. You usually don't have too many people present when you're discussing to the effect that you'd like to kill somebody.

The trial opened the week before Thanksgiving of 1987 and ended more than seven months later, in mid-May of 1988, when the jury finally received its instructions from U.S. district judge Howell W. Melton and retired to ponder the evidence. It took them seven days to reach a verdict, betraying a degree of uncertainty that surprised most of the observers, considering the overwhelming nature of Merkle's case. Part of the problem, one juror later told a reporter for the *Tampa Tribune*, was that they took to heart the complaint of Shohat and Quiñón that much of the evidence against their client came from "bought testimony" and would have preferred the government to have found some way of convicting Carlos other than turning loose half the prison population. "The more you listened to, the more you heard, you knew you could not find him innocent," one juror was quoted as saying. Nevertheless, he said, "I sat there and ground my teeth at what the government had given them. I actually busted a crown on my tooth, I got so mad." Of all the witnesses, he was asked, who had been the most compelling? Walter Cronkite, he said. "It surprised me when he testified. He looked like he did on the news. He was probably one of the first people you could turn around and say, 'I haven't got a convict here.'"

The verdict came down on May 19—guilty on all eleven counts

on which he'd been tried, involving the smuggling of 3.3 tons of cocaine into the United States. And two months later Carlos was brought in for sentencing. For nearly half an hour he lectured the judge on the fact that he was a political prisoner, that he'd been kidnapped out of his own country. "I feel like an Indian in a white man's court," he said. Judge Melton listened to the speech, then sentenced him to life in prison without the possibility of parole, plus an additional 135 years. "This sentence is a signal," the judge said, "that our country will do everything in its power and within the laws to battle the drug problem that threatens the very fabric of our society."

Around Christmastime, about a month after George had testified, a pair of federal marshals came to where he was being held in the county jail in Jacksonville. They said that Merkle's office had just received a call from Mirtha. She had heard from George's sister, Marie, that George's father was dying. He had contracted cancer of the colon and was currently in the hospital undergoing an operation. No one was holding out hope that he would live for more than a short time after he returned home. George hadn't seen his father or mother in more than seven years, not since the arrest in Eastham. Shortly after that, Fred and Ermine had moved out to Indiana to be near their daughter and son-in-law in Greenwood, outside of Indianapolis. Marie and Otis lived in a five-bedroom, split-level house on a street named Serenity Way with ample room for them and their three children, a barbecue and a pool out back, a two-car garage, and a good-sized yard. Rather than have her parents live with them, Marie thought it more practical to put them up in a community of pre-fabs nearby. They'd have their privacy, yet they'd still be close if they needed anything.

When George heard the news, the first thing he did was to telephone Merkle and ask if he could somehow get permission to leave the jail and fly up to Greenwood and see his father for what would be the last time. Merkle said he'd not only give him permission, but he personally would take George there, drive him up to the house himself. And he promptly called Marie and Otis to see to the arrangements. No, Marie told him. She was really sorry, but she did not think it was a good idea for George to come at this time. He had already caused his father enough heartache, not to mention the pain and humiliation he'd visited on everyone else in the family. Now, at his father's deathbed, it would be much too unsettling suddenly for her brother to make an appearance. "They told Merkle they just didn't want me there," says George. "So he got me a tape recorder and told me if I wanted to say good-bye to my father, I could do it on tape. The two marshals brought me into a little room at the jail. There was a chair and table set up, and we put the tape recorder on the table, and I talked into it."

"Hello, Fred," the tape begins.

You know, I remember a lifetime ago I was about three and a half feet tall weighing all of sixty pounds with a determined look on my face. Some Saturday mornings you'd wake me up. It was still dark outside. The earth was covered with snow, and together we'd climb up into your big yellow truck. You know, I used to think that truck was the biggest truck in the world and how important the job was we had to do. If it weren't for us, people would run out of oil and freeze to death. We'd stop after driving it seemed forever in a world that was entirely alien to me, a place called South Boston, with huge brick buildings and strange-looking black people everywhere. I was in awe of these strange-looking people and somewhat afraid, but felt safe with you. Together, we'd get out of that big yellow truck and you'd let me pull the hose down the alleyway to the oil spout. I would struggle desperately through the snow, but the oil spout seemed forever away. I'd never make it more than halfway, and then you'd grab the whole of the hose, taking it the rest of the way with ease. I thought you were the strongest guy in the world, and the toughest. Everywhere we went it seemed you knew everyone. I remained under that impression for quite some time.

Remember when you bought the boat for me and the outboard motor? Christ, I couldn't even swim. Are you sure it wasn't a plot to get rid of me? You must have lived in fear, wondering what crazy idea I was about to conceive of next. I believe getting my driver's license was probably the most traumatic experience of your life. It was most definitely the point when you had to give up going to sleep on weekends until the blue-and-white Mercury was safe in the garage.

Football. Now that's an interesting subject. You were my most loyal fan, never missing a game. Remember when Jack Fisher turned against me? And I was going to quit the team? You stuck by me and talked me out of quitting. Every kid on the block loved you, Fred. Remember how they all would hang out at our house? They came to see you, not me. You were unique, and everyone and anybody was always welcome at our house. You were certainly the Pied Piper sitting there with cigar in hand and giving orders and free advice. You always managed to get the guys into some job, cutting the lawn, painting the house, putting up a fence.

They never said, No, Fred. They all loved you. In essence, you had a dozen sons, not just one, making you the richest man in the world. What you had was priceless. In between all this activity, you kept me busy digging up the yard. For the longest time I lived under the impression you were in the septic-tank business. Even Marie would pick up a shovel before Otis would arrive for the Saturday-night date.

Track meets. Remember the old track meets? You were always there to watch me throw the discus. Remember the day I broke the record? Little League baseball. Remember how you encouraged me to become a pitcher? And the day I pitched the first no-hit game for the Federal League? I guess we were both proud of each other that day. We did have some crowning achievements, didn't we? Do you think we became legends in our own time, Fred? Well, maybe in Weymouth, anyway.

Then I kind of grew up, well, almost grew up, and went away to college. Two or three colleges, to be exact. Remember Waino, the Tuna? They broke the mold when they made Tuna. How about the day Tuna and I left for California, in that little black sports car. I often wonder what went through your mind that day as you watched Tuna and I drive away in that sports car, to travel three thousand miles to where we'd never been, California. After a few years in California, I returned home with the FBI chasing me. Of course, everyone comes home with the FBI chasing him, right? The day they caught me in the living room, remember, Fred? I was standing in there, handcuffed, and that FBI agent, Trout, the crazy one that was after me for two years, had to get on his knees to put my boots on. You looked down at him and said, 'That's where you belong, putting on his boots.' That was one of your best lines, Fred. That was right out of a John Wayne movie. You even came to visit me in Danbury, remember that? How about the day you picked me up from Danbury, and the car broke down in Connecticut? We made it though, didn't we, buddy? What a team, able to overcome any obstacle.

Well, eventually I did reach the pinnacle of success, and I became a big-time smuggler. Money, Learjets, fast cars, wild women, houses with maids. Remember how you would say for me to give you half the money to save, otherwise I'd end up broke someday? You were right again, Fred. Well, old man, I'm forty-five years old right now, and I've finally learned what you tried to tell me all those years. As the gambler says, "You got to know when to hold, know when to fold, and know when to walk away when the dealing's done." At least I've learned that much. I'm going to be all right, buddy. You know, I've written a book about all my adventures called *Grazing in the Grass Until the Snow Came*. And the book is dedicated to my father. "With love, from your son."

"May the wind always be at your back and the sun upon your face, and the winds of destiny carry you aloft to dance with the stars." Dutchmen never give up, do they, Fred? The book comes out in the fall. And I know you're going to be around to read it. I love you. George.

When Fred died three months later, on April 26, 1988, George got the news right away. What he didn't hear about until long afterward, when Auntie Gertrude finally told him, was that after the tape arrived in Greenwood, Fred would take it out to his car where he could be alone, away from everyone, and he'd sit there in the front seat with a little battery-operated tape recorder and play the tape over and over again, listening to his son try to tell his father good-bye.

Epilogue

OF THE OLD CROWD FROM WEYMOUTH, BARRY DAMON, the "White Rabbit," who played center for the Weymouth Maroons and waited for George to pick him up in the Mercury for their Saturday night dates, earned an associate degree in engineering and became a supervisor in the documents department of the nuclear generating plant at Plymouth. Mike Grable, team quarterback who handed off to George for his first touchdown run, married a junior high school girlfriend of George's, with whom he has three children, and works as a general manager for an electrical contractor in Boston. John Hollander, the end who smashed George during the scrimmage just before the Brockton game, married Gerry Lee, George's high school sweetheart; they have two children and live in an eighteenth-century white colonial house just below the Circle. Waino Tuominen—Tuna—lives in western Massachusetts, where he works as an assistant herdsman on a large dairy farm and is active in local environmental politics for the Green Party. Malcolm Mac-Gregor, George's best boyhood friend, graduated from Worcester Polytechnic Institute, earned a doctorate in theoretical chemistry at the University of Connecticut, and teaches physics at the Massachusetts Maritime Academy; he's married, with three sons. Clem Horrigan, the Weymouth High School English teacher who read to George and his friends from the pages of Jack London, died in the fall of 1986.

Otis and Marie Godfrey still live in Greenwood, Indiana, where

Otis is a senior research scientist at Eli Lilly & Co. in Indianapolis. One of their sons graduated from West Point, another from law school, and a daughter became an engineer via Purdue University. Ermine continues to live in the pre-fab not far away. Uncle George died in 1991, five years after Aunt Myrna. Auntie Gertrude, who moved into their house in Wakefield, gave George his uncle's clothes, including a sterling silver belt buckle, inscribed with the initials G J J. Considering that they shared the same name, George might get some use out of it.

Most of the policemen who arrested George over the years have since moved up a notch professionally. Special Agent J. J. Trout advanced from the FBI's warrant squad to pursuing bank robbers, still working out of Boston. His first inkling of what happened to the young man he arrested in his bedroom that day back in 1973 came fifteen years later when he saw George on TV during the Lehder trial in Jacksonville, in an interview with Ron Gollobin, star crime reporter for Boston's Channel 5. "A guy like him, from a middle class family, I thought he would do a couple of years and get out and get on with his life," says Trout. "It blows my mind that he went all the way to the top."

Trooper Billy McGreal made sergeant and won the "Trooper of the Year" award after the Eastham bust and is working in the highway patrol division out of the barracks in Foxboro, Massachusetts. Detectives Greg Kridos and Tom Tiderington of the Fort Lauderdale PD were also promoted to sergeant and captain, respectively; Kridos began attending law school at night, hoping to open up a practice after he retires from the force. Tiderington uses George's bust as the basis for his drug lecture at Broward County Police Academy. Agent Mike McManus was moved up several grades in the Drug Enforcement Administration and relocated with his family to the Bahamas office. Special Agent Richard Garcia, the Stinger missile man, won the Attorney General's Distinguished Service Award in 1988 for an undercover operation and was promoted to a supervisory position in Washington, where he used to think "conservatism was taking place."

All the major drug smugglers with whom George associated have been arrested or, as in the case of his brother-in-law, Humberto, fled the country and went back to Colombia. The Yaqui Indian, Ramón, spent four years in prison in Chihuahua, Mexico, in the late 1980s, a year more than he had to for the fact that he retaliated against a bullying inmate by stabbing the fellow in the stomach. The man survived, "but now he can only eat mushy thing," says Ramón, who's back in Puerto Vallarta with his wife, Emily, and their two sons. Barry Kane, in what was dubbed the "Son of Lehder trial," was convicted in 1988 of the two drug flights he made for George and Carlos back in 1977 and sentenced to twelve years in prison and fined $500,000. Richard Barile pleaded guilty in 1989 to cocaine distribution charges stemming from his own activities with George and Carlos. He ended up serving only two and a half years, and is now living in Cuernavaca, Mexico.

Carlos won a reprieve of sorts in 1992, after he provided key testimony helping to convict Manuel Antonio Noriega, the former Panamanian dictator, as a drug trafficker. In payment, he was moved out of his basement cell in the U.S. penitentiary in Marion, Illinois, placed in the Witness Protection Program and relocated to cheerier prison quarters elsewhere in the country. The *Miami Herald* ranked him eighty-fourth out of the One Hundred Most Influential People in South Florida History. Pablo Escobar turned himself in to the Colombian government in June of 1991 in exhange for the promise that he would not be extradited to the United States and would do his time in comfortable prison quarters in his native province of Antioquía. A year later Pablo escaped after getting word that he was being moved to a harsher prison setting elsewhere. He avoided capture until December of 1993, when about 500 members of the government's elite Strike Bloc surrounded his safe house in Medellín and shot him dead as he tried to flee over the rooftop. American officials said Pablo's death would have a "negligible" effect on the drug trade. "If Lee Iacocca left, would Chrysler stop making automobiles?" said Tom Cash, former head of the DEA office in Miami.

Mirtha is still living on the West Coast. Frederica is now twenty-two years old and discovered finally that her father wasn't lying paralyzed in a hospital bed. Lucia is married and has a daughter of her own.

And George. In exchange for his testimony at the Lehder trial, he was free to walk out of prison in July of 1989, no parole, his debt to society marked PAID IN FULL. In all his life, he had never had a checking account, never had a Social Security card, never paid income taxes. He calculates he made around $100 million through his association with the Medellín cartel, but, penniless, he returned to the Cape after prison to a job delivering fish to seafood restaurants for Bird, his former bodyguard. Shortly, he reentered the drug business with his Yacqui Indian friend Ramón, and in 1994 was caught importing several hundred pounds of marijuana from Mexico and sentenced to twenty-two years in prison. Now fifty-eight years old, he works as head gardener at the Federal Correctional Institution in Otisville, New York, where he brightens the prison walkways with marigolds and chrysanthemums. Occasionally, overhead he can see the crows wheeling about and hear their cries, but otherwise the woods surrounding the place is empty and quiet. So life is for George, the motor sailer, all the dreams having receded so far into the distance as to no longer be in view.

Acknowledgments

First of all, thanks to George, for the hundreds of hours he spent and the thousands of miles he traveled in the effort to bring his past into focus, not always a pleasant journey, from California to Cape Cod, from Mexico to Miami, from the Valley of the Moon and the Dry Lake Beds to Norman Cay and the mostly vanished haunts of his teenage days in Weymouth.

This book was also made possible by the willingness of many people to share their memories of George and of Carlos and to describe their experiences in connection with the cocaine and marijuana trades, on both sides of the law, and thanks to them is hereby given. Their names appear throughout the chapters and the nature of their help is self-evident. In this regard, I wish particularly to note the assistance of Mirtha Jung and her mother, Clara Luz; of Ramón Moreno, Arthur Davey, Richard Barile, and Mr. T.; and of Agents James J. Trout and Richard Garcia of the FBI, Agent Michael McManus of the DEA, Sergeants Greg Kridos and Tom Tiderington of the Fort Lauderdale Police Department, Sergeant William McGreal of the Massachusetts State Police, and Sergeant Fred McKewen of the Manhattan Beach Police Department, now retired.

Others contributed in ways not made apparent in the book, and I would like to use this space to express my gratitude. Among the many I talked to in Weymouth, I'd like especially to thank Benny Ells, retired member of the Weymouth Fire Department and devoted statistician to the Weymouth High School Maroons since 1946; Donald Cormack, lecturer at the Weymouth Historical Museum; and Eddie Beck, guidance counselor at Braintree High School, who encountered George as his football coach at Central Junior High School in Weymouth.

In Manhattan Beach, there was Jan Dennis, its former mayor and also author of a lively history of the town, *A Walk Beside the Sea;* in Puerto Vallarta, Ramón's wife, Emily, an earthy cook and tour guide and hostess to wandering journalists; in Mazatlán, Mauro Delgado Millan, a/k/a "Morris the Jewish Joker," who passed along lore of the marijuana days, and in Durango, Alfonso Trevino, warden of the Durango penitentiary, who allowed a free-ranging tour of his facility. In Miami, thanks to Mark Teitelbaum, Dr. James Lipton, and criminologist Cloud Miller, Ph.D., for their views of George under lock and key. In Fort Lauderdale, to Eileen O'Connor, assistant United States Attorney, for her explications on matters of plea bargaining, and to Dick Kelly, a veteran flyboy with expertise relating to drug aircraft. In Jacksonville, thanks to Agent Sheila Smith of the Drug Enforcement Administration, for her assistance in obtaining documents. In Washington, thanks to Special Agent Frank Scafidi of the FBI, who inveighed upon the Bureau to permit its agents to tell their stories, and in Danbury, to Lisa Austin, management analyst at the Federal Correctional Institution, for her guidance through the prison labyrinth.

Among the numerous people who gave aid and comfort out on the Cape, thanks to Tim White, managing editor of the *Cape Cod Times;* to Johnny Scott and Bird, pliers of the fisher's trade; to Jeanne Flamburis; to Steven and Cathy Faucher, George's good neighbors in times of need, and, for her graciousness and her acts of kindness, to Marilyn Anderson, who cared for George over the course of two and a half years, until her tragic death on February 10, 1992.

For their assistance in other ways, my special thanks to Nell Porter Brown, reporter for the *Troy Record,* who provided valuable research help; to her husband, Andrew Brown, M.D., for patiently explaining the physiological effects of cocaine use; to Alexandra Porter and to Adelaide Porter, for their critical reading of the manuscript; and to Schellie Hagan, fact checker; John Mabie, of the legal department of HarperCollins; Rick Turner, in Sales at HarperCollins; Margaret Wimberger, the book's copyeditor; and Keonaona Peterson, its production editor.

The book would have been difficult to write had not other journalists and scholars gone down the cocaine road before and illuminated the way. Of particular help in understanding the broad reach of the Medellín cartel were the encyclopedic work done by Guy

Gugliotta and Jeff Leen in *Kings of Cocaine*, and by Paul Eddy, Hugo Sabogal, and Sara Walden in *The Cocaine Wars*. Among other useful works were *Deep Cover* by DEA Special Agent Michael Levine, *Turning the Tide* by Sidney Kirkpatrick and Peter Abrahams, *Desperadoes* by Elaine Shannon, *The Fruit Palace* by Charles Nicholl, *Snowblind* by Robert Sabbag, and *Drugs and Human Behavior* by Tibor Palfai and Henry Jankiewicz of Syracuse University.

I owe a lasting debt to my agent, Sarah Lazin, for engendering the project and for being wise in many ways, start to finish, and to my editor, Wendy Wolf, who numerous times over saved me from falling prey to embarrassing sins of commission and omission alike.

And, of course, to my wife, Sara Jane, but for whom nothing anywhere would ever seem possible.

FINISHED MAR 28/01
2:25 P.M. WEDSDAY

P1

ABOUT THE AUTHOR

Bruce Porter, a former newspaper reporter and editor of *Newsweek,* teaches at the Columbia University Graduate School of Journalism. He has also written for *The New York Times Magazine, The Washington Post, Rolling Stone, Playboy,* and *Connoisseur,* among other publications.